Children's Encyclopedia of
Earth, Stars and Planets

Compiled and edited by Kenneth Bailey

Collins

Glasgow and London

Contents

Written by Anthony Harvey, Barry Cork, Maurice Allward

Designed by Max Ansell, David Nash

Illustrated by Max Ansell, M. J. Atkinson, Thelma Bissex,
Gordon Davies, Ronald Embleton, Gwen Green
Harry Green, Richard Hook, Angus McBride,
David Nash, Christine Robins, Gwen Simpson,
John Smith, Charlotte Snook, Bill Stallion

First published 1976
Published by William Collins Sons and Company Limited, Glasgow and London
© 1976 William Collins Sons and Company Limited

Printed in Great Britain

ISBN 0 00 106165 8

The Science of the Earth

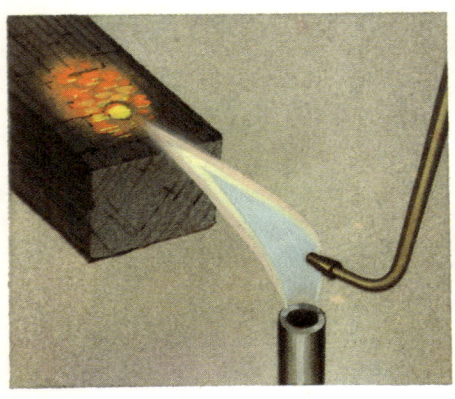

Oxidising flame heats ore on charcoal block.

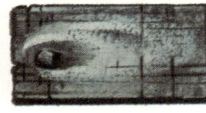

Zinc   Antimony

Bismuth   Copper

Blowpipe tests to ascertain the metallic element in mineral specimens produce varying colours from the four different minerals seen in the drawings above.

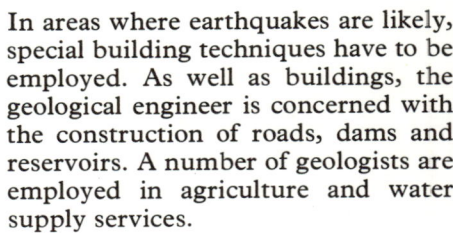

Since earliest times man has used the Earth to keep him alive and well. At first his interest was limited to locating suitable food and shelter. As he developed the ability to make tools, so came the need to locate suitable materials. Many different rocks were used in the manufacture of his tools, including flint, basalt, granite and obsidian (a black, glassy volcanic rock). This use of stone has given the name to one of the earliest stages in man's development, the Stone Age. The first tools he made were simple and rough but gradually over thousands of years he became more skilled and the tools themselves more finely worked.

Flint was originally obtained from the surface of the Earth or from natural cuttings, but by Neolithic times it was mined. Such mines, which go back over 5,000 years, have been discovered in Belgium, England, France, Portugal and Sweden. Even before this man had located suitable clays for making pottery, for the earliest fragment is estimated to be 12,000 years old.

While undertaking these activities man gradually gained a knowledge of the rocks of the Earth. The coming of agriculture and the tilling of the soils increased this knowledge and soon the relationships between rocks and soil were discovered. On the beaches many different kinds of stones and pebbles attracted attention.

The Age of Metal

The Stone Age was followed by the age of metal. First came the Bronze Age. Bronze is made from copper and tin. Then came the Iron Age, when man again had to learn more about the rocks if he was to survive. Later, when stone was used for building, it became important to recognise its different properties so that it could be carved and yet be strong enough to withstand the action of the weather.

Today our way of life is threatened because the resources of the Earth are rapidly being used up. New deposits of coal and oil are urgently sought to provide for man's increasing energy needs. For years, the Earth's resources have been removed without thought that one day they might be exhausted. To replenish them naturally would take the Earth hundreds of millions of years, and man is unable to wait that long. During the nineteenth century there was a massive rise in the use of coal in industry, on the railways and in the home. There has been a similar rise in the use of oil in the twentieth century. But with dwindling supplies of both these materials—especially oil—man is forced to look for other sources of energy. The steam of geysers and hot springs has been utilised to provide heating and generate electricity in several countries. There is now a growing world interest in using the heat of the Earth itself, known as geothermal power. Man has harnessed rivers and tides to turn his turbines and produce electricity. He is even looking to the waves which crash on the shore as a possible energy source. The age of nuclear power is already with us and will develop greatly over the next few years.

In the search for new sources of energy and materials useful to man, geological information is always needed. But the geologist is not only concerned with location of energy sources. He also has to know about the soils and underlying deposits on which the engineer wishes to build. With increasing pressure on the use of land, man is sometimes forced to build in less hospitable regions. These may be subject to frequent earthquakes or the effects of volcanic eruption, and there is a need to be able to predict such events. Large sums of money are being spent on research to discover if an early warning system can be devised.

In areas where earthquakes are likely, special building techniques have to be employed. As well as buildings, the geological engineer is concerned with the construction of roads, dams and reservoirs. A number of geologists are employed in agriculture and water supply services.

Economic Resources

Geology also plays an important part in military decisions and in politics. Because of the exploration of continental shelves and deep oceans and the extraction of their mineral and oil resources, geological advice is vital to government agencies. Most countries of the world have established a geological survey. Each survey is concerned with the study of all the many aspects of geology within its area and particularly with the location of economic deposits of minerals, metals and oil. The geological aspects of water resources and conservation also form part of the work of the survey. The most important job is the preparation of geological maps. These are maps which show the distribution of the various outcrops of rocks. Such maps will also indicate the incline of the rocks and where they are fractured. Other maps will concentrate on the various types of soils and land forms, and the distribution of minerals and metals.

The maps are prepared from the work which geologists undertake in the field. They also make use of borings and the records of rocks that are passed through when wells are sunk. The geologists' observations are recorded on large-scale maps and by means of notes. There have been many experiments in the use of a special sheet for recording information so that a computer can be programmed to produce maps. This method, which has had some success, is much quicker than others at present used.

Small section of a geological map which records structural features of the Earth.

Palaeontology is concerned with the study of fossils.

Glaciologist prepares a sample of ice for study.

The fact that geologists have become involved in so many different areas of work is itself an indication of the very wide nature of geology. Geology means the science of the Earth. It is concerned with all aspects of our planet since its formation to the present time: its rocks and minerals, the forces acting on and below the surface and the evolution of life. The term 'Earth sciences' is often used to widen this scope to include the study of the oceans (oceanography), climate (climatology) and weather (meteorology).

Geological Sciences

A number of different areas of investigation go to make up the main part of the geological sciences. Geomorphology is concerned with the features on the surface of the Earth and their origin and development. Stratigraphy has different meanings. In Europe it is used to describe the study of the conditions of the Earth during past geological time, including past climates and the distribution of land and sea. In North America this study is called historical geology. A much narrower meaning of stratigraphy is the study of strata.

Most of the areas of geology are connected with the other sciences. Palaeontology is concerned with the study of fossils and has links with both stratigraphy and biology. Mineralogy is the science of the study of minerals, while the study of rocks is called petrology. These both have links with physics, mathematics and chemistry.

Other subjects are more recent in origin and have contributed to the better use of the world's resources. Hydrology, the study of water, has developed as an important subject from geomorphology. Geophysics is concerned with the physics of the

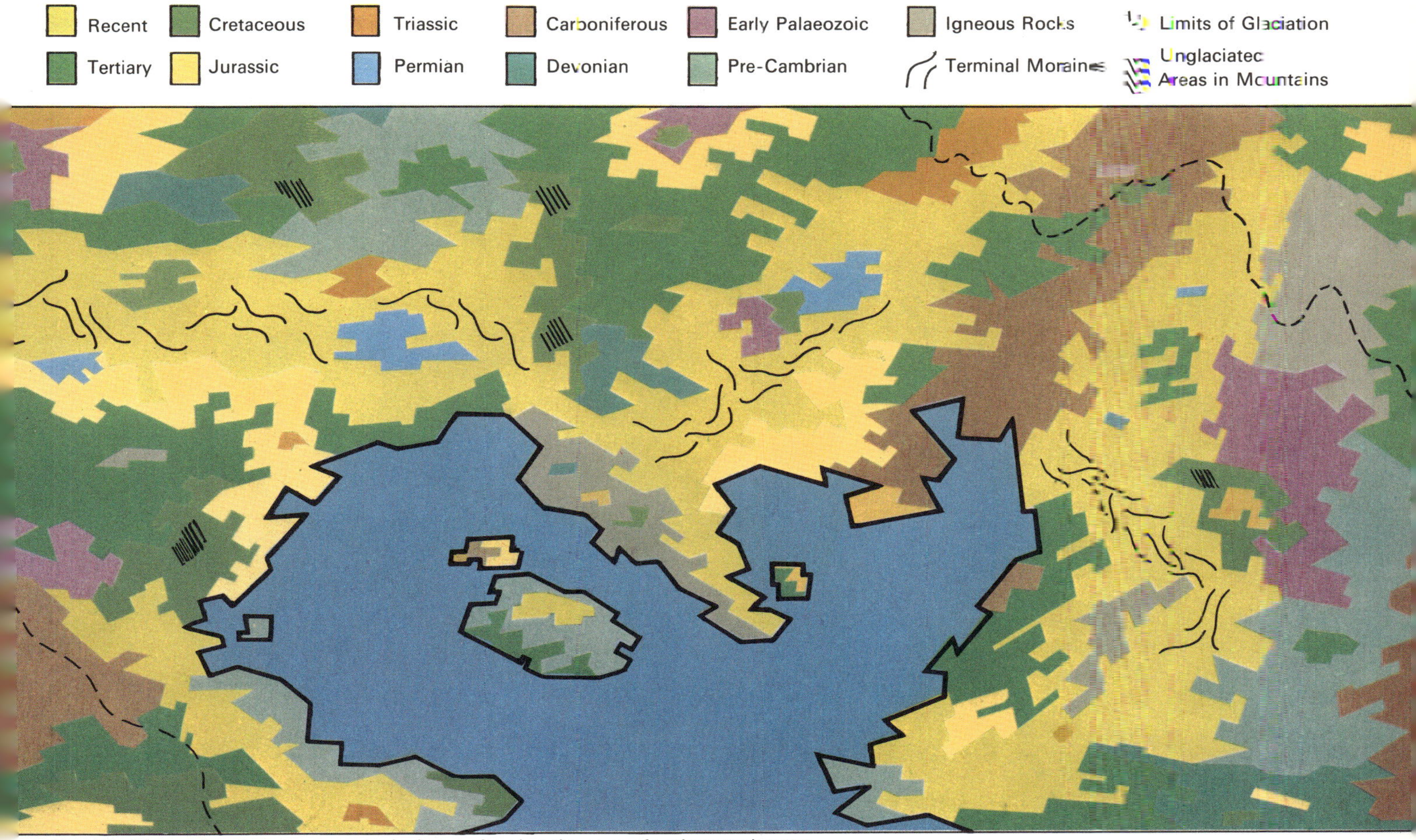

🟨 Recent	🟩 Cretaceous	🟧 Triassic	🟫 Carboniferous	🟪 Early Palaeozoic	⬜ Igneous Rocks	Limits of Glaciation
🟩 Tertiary	🟨 Jurassic	🟦 Permian	🟦 Devonian	🟩 Pre-Cambrian	Terminal Moraines	Unglaciated Areas in Mountains

Simplified form of an imaginary geological map showing the ages of various rock types.

Léopold Cuvier (1769–1832),
French anatomist

John Wesley Powell (1834–1902),
American geologist

Sir Charles Lyell (1797–1875),
Scottish geologist

Earth. It investigates the physical processes relating to the structure of the Earth and atmosphere. The various methods which have been developed for geophysical investigation are now used in civil engineering and in the location of water and oil. Geochemistry links geology with chemistry and is concerned with the distribution and migration of elements. This is a rapidly developing field and is of considerable value to the mineral and mining industry.

In view of the broad scope and many links with the other sciences, it is easy to understand why a new area of geology, called environmental geology, has become established. It provides valuable information for planners on a vast range of important topics from water supply to the siting of buildings.

Although geologists are professional workers and may use expensive equipment, there are still many opportunities for the amateur. Many of the specimens in museums have been collected and presented by 'weekend geologists'. Keen individuals can perform a valuable service to geology, which still relies to a great extent on observation in the field. An interest in the subject brings with it a realisation of the tremendous age of the Earth. It also brings the knowledge that once Earth's resources are used up they cannot be replaced and an appreciation of the need to exercise conservation if man is to continue to inhabit his planet.

Myths and Giants

Man's early interest in the Earth was forced on him in his struggle for survival. Even so he must have wondered about the forces which shake the Earth and about the great masses of liquid rock which pour from volcanoes. Early ideas on the Earth involved giants, mythical creatures and supernatural forces. Folklore is full of references to the Earth and its many features. The Greek philosophers held many different views. Herodotus (c. 485–425 B.C.) suggested that the finding of fossil shells in a rock indicated that the sea had once covered the area.

Theophrastus (c.372–286 B.C.) thought that fossils originated within the Earth as did the Elder Pliny (A.D. 23–79). Strabo (c.60 B.C.–A.D. 21) noted that earthquakes were less active when volcanoes erupted. During these early years of 'scientific investigation' and into the time of the Renaissance, interest was limited to minerals and gems, figured stones (fossils), mountains and their origin, rivers, springs and earthquakes. Geology did not exist as a subject.

Religious beliefs and the need for a literal interpretation of Bible stories seriously hampered the science of the Earth. However, Leonardo da Vinci (1452–1519) understood that fossil shells were the remains of animals long since dead, and that from such remains it was possible to tell the changes which had occurred in the relationship of land to sea. It was Georg Bauer (1494–1555), better known as Agricola, who brought a sense of realism to the study of minerals. He was a mining

The curvature of the Earth's surface was known to the ancients, but only when the first space vehicles moved away from our planet and photographed it 'in the round' could its shape finally be proved by observation.

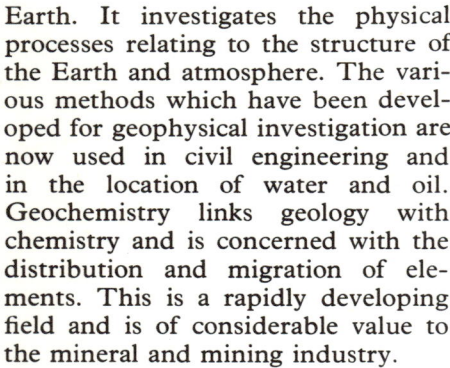

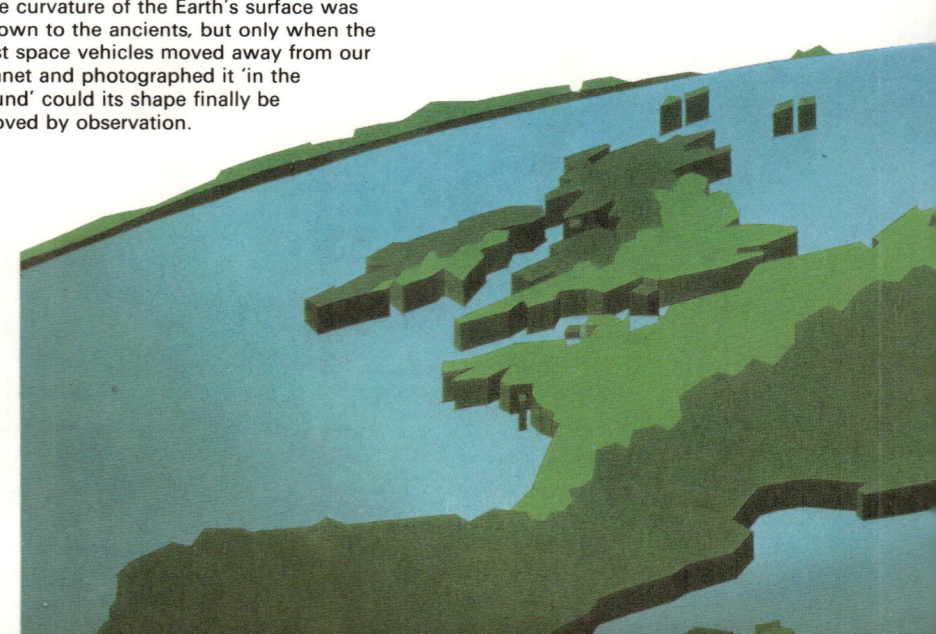

The Egyptian theory of creation features a flat Earth (the Earth-god Geb) beneath a sky vault formed by the sky-goddess Nut.

An old Hindu belief shows the Earth supported on the backs of elephants riding on a turtle which swims in the sea.

expert in Germany and did not classify minerals by their magical properties but on evidence which could be seen and felt, such as colour, shape, weight and occurrence.

The Nature of Fossils

Many scientists were interested in the strata of the Earth and its development. Once the true nature of fossils was established then came suggested explanations of the rocks themselves. The birth of stratigraphy and stratigraphical palaeontology were near. Robert Hooke (1635–1703) had indicated the uses of fossils while Nicolaus Steno (1638–87) went one step further and interpreted the geological history of an area from the rocks he discovered there. Progress was slow because there was still a large number of people who supported the idea of a universal deluge, a world completely submerged during the Flood.

As more and more learned people went into the countryside they began to examine the rocks for themselves. Jean Étienne Guettard (1715–86) produced some of the first geological maps on which the distribution of stones, minerals and metals were shown by means of symbols. The idea of the succession of strata was born, the lower rocks in a succession being older than those above.

The Origin of Rocks

Before the origin of rocks was finally settled there was a fierce argument between two rival theories. Abraham Gottlob Werner (1750–1817) of the Academy of Freiburg thought that all rocks were derived from the sediments on the ocean floors. This is true for many but not for those such as granite and basalt. The followers of Werner became known as the Neptunists, after Neptune, God of the Sea. They were violently opposed by the followers of James Hutton (1726–97), the Scottish geologist, who has often been referred to as the Father of Modern Geology. The followers of Hutton were known as Plutonists, after Pluto, God of the Underworld. In his work published in 1795 and called *Theory of the Earth, with proofs and illustrations*, Hutton stated his belief in the origin of some rocks from the oceans but also thought that many more were of volcanic origin. He observed for himself how granite had become intruded into other rocks and how heat and pressure may change rocks. He also realised that the erosion of the rocks and the transport of sediments to the sea was all part of one great cycle. He realised that the present is the key to the past.

It was the English geologist William Smith (1769–1839) who was to use fossils in the identification and correlation of rocks. In his time the science of geology was thus firmly established. It has continued to grow and it is extremely important to man, but still it owes much of its development to accurate observations in the field.

The Earth's Surface

The Earth is unique in our solar system, although it is possible that similar worlds may exist elsewhere in the universe. When seen from space the Earth presents a vivid changing picture of white and shades of blue. It contrasts strongly with the greys and other dull colours of the Moon. Even without plants and animals, the mountains, plains, rivers and seas present scenes which are not shared with any of the other planets. The sunrises and sunsets, rain and snow, blue skies and white clouds are all unique to the Earth. Even the volcanic activity with its associated geysers and hot springs

Water is the life-giving force. Life itself originated in the seas and it is water in one of its forms which has sculptured much of the Earth's surface.

A number of different concentric zones make up the Earth. Surrounding the solid Earth is a thin layer of gases and water: this is the atmosphere. The layer is about 1,000 kilometres (620 miles) deep. The lower part, that nearest to the surface of the Earth, consists mainly of the gases nitrogen, oxygen, argon, carbon dioxide and water vapour. This layer has an average thickness of about 11 kilometres (7 miles) and is called the troposphere. It is the zone of the weather.

Above this lies the stratosphere which is mainly thin, almost cloudless air. It is within this layer that many of the dangerous ultra-violet rays from the sun are absorbed and the majority of meteorites burn up. Still higher lies the ionosphere with layers which can conduct electricity. It is from here that radio waves are bounced back to Earth, making possible the transmission of such waves around the world.

Land forms on the Earth's surface range from the fields and shorelines of northern Europe to the grandeur of Alpine scenery and the American canyons.

seem to be best developed on the Earth. It is only on our planet that the rocks 'can be read' and their history interpreted.

Support of Life

Life has been able to develop on Earth because of a suitable atmosphere and it is the existence of life which really sets the planet apart from its neighbours. Earth is not subjected to the great ranges of temperature experienced by other members of the solar system. The mean is about 11°C. Mars has a mean temperature of about −30°C. The Moon can claim a similar mean temperature to that of the Earth, but life as we know it could not survive the extremes of −170°C. to 100°C. Of all the planets the Earth's atmosphere is the only one with the abundant oxygen and nitrogen which are essential to living organisms.

One more unique feature makes the Earth able to support life. It is the presence of water in a liquid form.

The atmosphere cannot escape from the Earth because of the force of gravity. Although it is usually quoted as about 1,000 kilometres (620 miles) thick, there is really no upper layer. The density of the atmosphere decreases rapidly with increasing height. At a height of 96 kilometres (60 miles) it is only one millionth of the density at ground level. The decrease of density is even noticeable in the mountainous regions of the Earth, and this is why mountaineers in the Himalayas and other high mountains have to wear breathing apparatus.

Below the atmosphere lies the Earth's next zone, which is not continuous, the hydrosphere. This includes the waters of oceans, seas, lakes

The age of the Earth is generally assumed to be about 4,600 million years, although modern dating methods progressively tend to push back the date of the planet's formation. The Earth is not a sphere but what is called an oblate spheroid, that is flattened on opposite sides, in the case of the Earth at the poles. This means that its polar diameter is approximately 12,700 kilometres (7,900 miles) and its equatorial diameter is approximately 12,750 kilometres (7,925 miles). The greatest circumference of the Earth is at the equator which is 40,000 kilometres (24,900 miles). The Earth's mass is calculated to be 5,880,000,000,000,000,000,000 tons, its density 5·5 times that of water, and its volume about 1,066,000,000,000 cubic kilometres (256,000,000,000 cubic miles). As the average density of the crustal rocks is only about 2·8, the rocks beneath the crust must be much heavier. The central core of the Earth is believed to be of iron and nickel and if this is so then iron is by far the most abundant element in the Earth. The crust of the Earth varies greatly in depth, averaging 6 kilometres (3·7 miles) under the oceans, while the land masses have an average of 35–40 kilometres (21–25 miles). Beneath the oceans none of the rocks appears to be more than 200 million years old, while on land some are as much as 3,800 million years old.

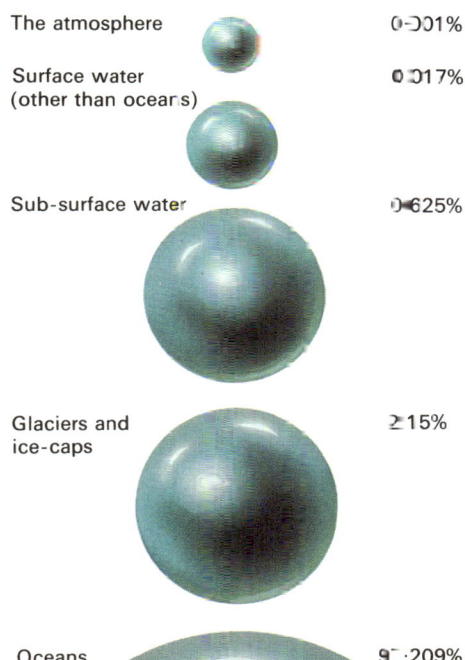

The atmosphere	0·001%
Surface water (other than oceans)	0·017%
Sub-surface water	0·625%
Glaciers and ice-caps	2·15%
Oceans	97·209%

The total volume of water on the Earth is about 1,340 million cubic kilometres, as seen in the diagram (not to scale) above.

Of the Earth's surface approximately 71% is water, 360,300,000 square kilometres (139,500,000 square miles), and 29% land, 148,300,000 square kilometres (57,500,000 square miles).

and rivers. Below this lies solid rock, the crust of the Earth. One other zone is usually included, which like the hydrosphere is not continuous. This is called the biosphere, the zone of life. It includes all the animals and plants above or below the ground, on land or in the seas.

A Flat Earth
For many years the Earth was thought to be flat. This was the view held by the ancient Greeks and during the Dark Ages in Europe, although the true shape of the Earth had been established by the Greek philosophers, Thales (sixth century B.C.) and Anaximander (611–547 B.C.).

Several simple observations prove that the Earth is a sphere. When ships sail away they gradually disappear, the last point to vanish being the highest part of the ship. If the observer climbs to a cliff top he can then view the ship for a little longer before it disappears. Increased height provides an increased view into the distance.

When looking across the sea the horizon is seen to be circular. Further evidence of a spherical Earth can be seen at the time of an eclipse, when the Earth's shadow is in the form of part of a circle.

Around the Globe
The Earth was finally proved to be round in 1522 when Magellan's ships completed their voyage round the world. It was Isaac Newton (1642–1727) who established the reason for the shape of the Earth, and also proved that it is not a true sphere but has a slight flattening at the poles and a bulge at the equator.

The reasons for these irregularities are connected with forces acting on the Earth. Gravity tends to pull everything to the centre, while the centrifugal force created because of the rotation of the Earth acts in the opposite way. At the equator the apparent value of gravity is reduced, while at the poles the reverse is true, hence the bulge and the flattening.

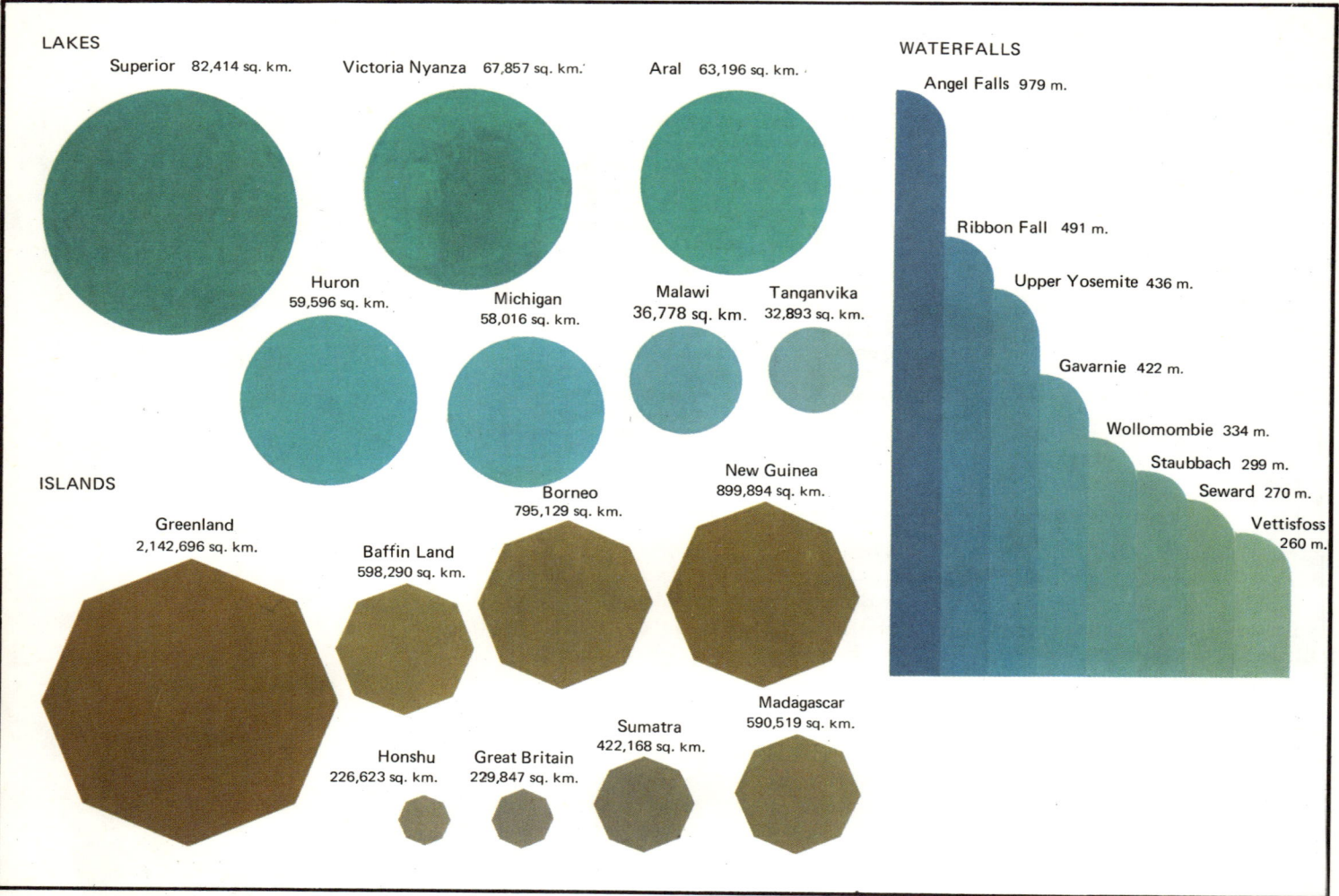

LAKES

Superior 82,414 sq. km.   Victoria Nyanza 67,857 sq. km.   Aral 63,196 sq. km.

Huron 59,596 sq. km.   Michigan 58,016 sq. km.   Malawi 36,778 sq. km.   Tanganyika 32,893 sq. km.

WATERFALLS

Angel Falls 979 m.
Ribbon Fall 491 m.
Upper Yosemite 436 m.
Gavarnie 422 m.
Wollomombie 334 m.
Staubbach 299 m.
Seward 270 m.
Vettisfoss 260 m.

ISLANDS

New Guinea 899,894 sq. km.
Borneo 795,129 sq. km.
Greenland 2,142,696 sq. km.
Baffin Land 598,290 sq. km.
Madagascar 590,519 sq. km.
Sumatra 422,168 sq. km.
Honshu 226,623 sq. km.
Great Britain 229,847 sq. km.

Land and Sea

A quick glance at any world map is enough to show the clear division of the Earth into land and sea. The land masses fall into four groups. First there is Eurasia (Europe and Asia) linked to the African continent at Suez; next is Australia and New Guinea; then North and South America with their slender connection through Central America; and finally the ice-clad continent of Antarctica.

The land masses, unlike the oceans, are not joined. The oceans of the world are the Pacific, Atlantic and Indian. Sometimes the Pacific and Atlantic are divided into North and South and the Arctic and Southern Oceans added. The Southern Ocean encircles the world, and all of the waters intermix.

Distribution of the Land

The actual distribution of the land is also uneven. It is mostly north of the equator, in the northern hemisphere. The only parts of the four groups to be completely south of the equator are the relatively small land masses of Australasia and Antarctica. The southerly tapering sections of Africa and South America also cross into the southern hemisphere. Of the northern hemisphere 39·4 per cent is land while only 18·6 per cent of the southern hemisphere is land.

There are many other differences between the oceans and land. The rocks on land are often very old, the oldest being 3,800 million years, while the oldest rocks yet discovered under the oceans are only 200 million years. In many ways the oceans with their mid-ocean ridge system are more symmetrical. The ridge system can be traced in the Atlantic, Indian and Pacific Oceans.

The continents seem to consist of very ancient core areas known as shields. On to these have been welded the younger rocks. These cores are made up of very old rocks which have been altered by the pressure and heat created by many millions of years of Earth movement. Examples of the core areas are found in Canada and Scandinavia. In some parts the edges of the cores are overlain by sedimentary rocks which are still in their original horizontal layers, showing that they have not been subjected to any great movements. The Baltic Shield (Scandinavia) has its extension in the Russian Platform. In Canada, the Canadian Shield is covered to the south by rocks which underlie the Great Plains.

All of these differences are due to the structure and evolution of the Earth.

Lowering of the Sea

Many of the land areas are relatively small and surrounded by sea, for example the British Isles and Newfoundland. If the sea level was to be lowered by about 200 metres (650 feet), some of these islands would be joined with the mainland, for example the British Isles to Europe, Newfoundland to North America, Tasmania and New Guinea to Australia. Even such a seemingly remote group as the Falkland Islands would be rejoined with South America. These islands are really extensions of the main landmasses and are called continental islands. The sea bed between them and the land is the continental shelf.

Even if the sea was to be lowered by 2,000 metres (6,500 feet) many other islands would remain unattached. These are the oceanic islands and there are two types. By far the most common are those of volcanic origin. Most of these occur in the Pacific Ocean, but others are linked to the mid-oceanic

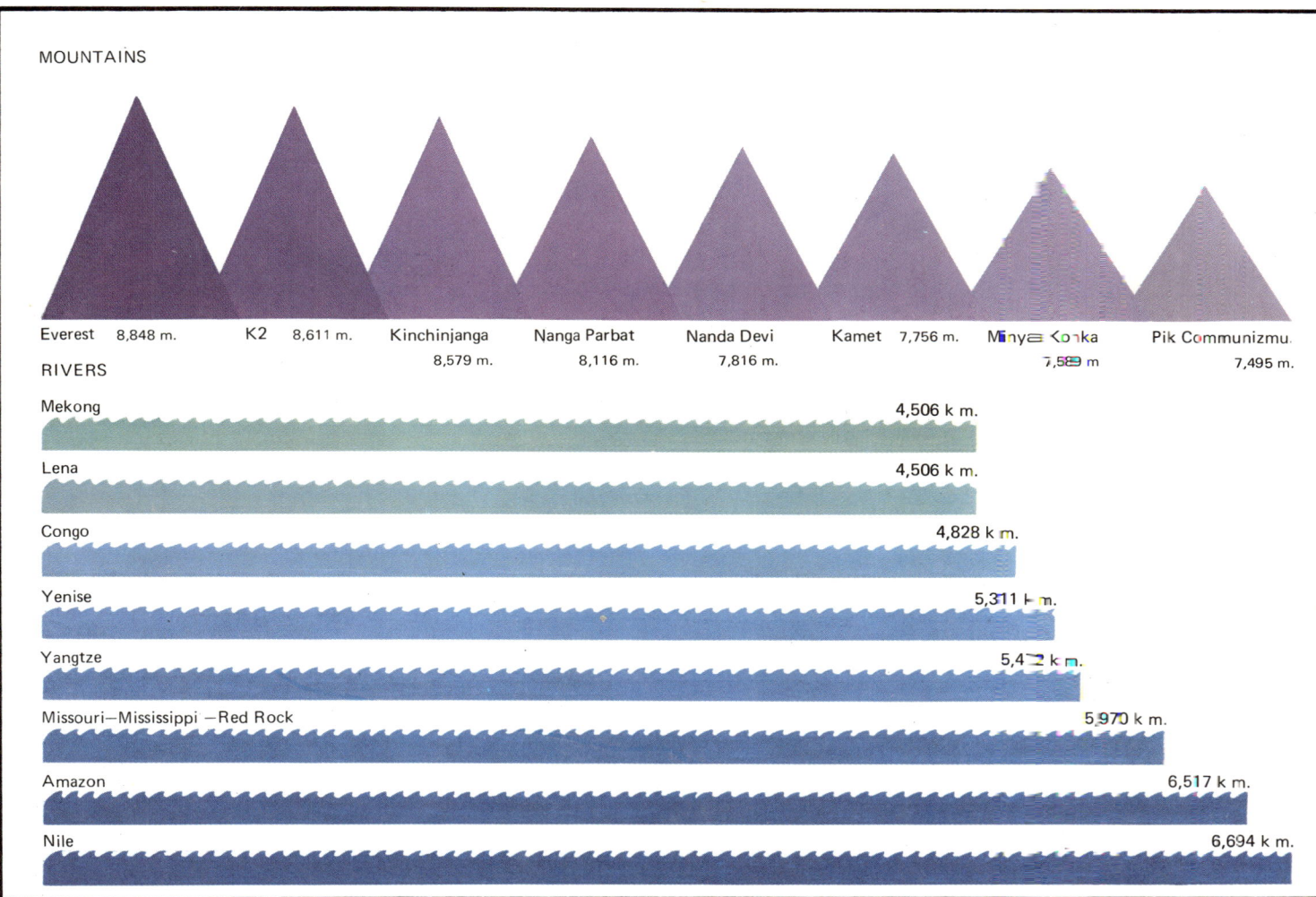

MOUNTAINS

Everest 8,848 m. K2 8,611 m. Kinchinjanga 8,579 m. Nanga Parbat 8,116 m. Nanda Devi 7,816 m. Kamet 7,756 m. Minya Konka 7,590 m. Pik Communizmu 7,495 m.

RIVERS

Mekong 4,506 k.m.
Lena 4,506 k.m.
Congo 4,828 k.m.
Yenise 5,311 k.m.
Yangtze 5,472 k.m.
Missouri—Mississippi—Red Rock 5,970 k.m.
Amazon 6,517 k.m.
Nile 6,694 k.m.

ridges, for example Iceland, the Azores and Tristan da Cunha. Even the peaceful coral islands and atolls were once volcanoes. There is a whole group of islands in the Pacific which show the range from coral islands through dormant volcanoes ending in the spectacular Hawaiian Islands.

To geologists, however, it is the smaller group of oceanic islands which provide the most interest. These include the Seychelles and Madagascar. They have beneath them typically continental crust, and yet they are clearly oceanic islands. The solving of such mysteries will provide much information about the way in which the continents have changed their positions, for the oceanic islands could be fragments which have broken off during continental drift.

There are also considerable differences between the land and oceans in their average heights and depths. The deepest point of the ocean would easily take the highest mountain. The majority of the oceans are between 3,000 and 6,000 metres (9,800 and 19,600 feet) deep. In fact ocean levels between these depths cover half the surface of the Earth. The deepest parts occupy only 0·2 per cent. The higher parts of the land masses, above 3,000 metres

(9,800 feet) occupy only one per cent of the land surface. Of the surface of the Earth 20 per cent is taken up with the continental platform, which is land below 1,000 metres (3,300 feet). The average height of the land is 825 metres (2,707 feet) against the 3,797 metres (12,460 feet) average depth of the oceans.

Asia

Asia is the largest of all the continents, covering 44,000,000 square kilometres (16,993,000 square miles). It covers one third of all the land on Earth, and includes areas well within the Arctic Circle and the tropics.

Included within its boundaries are some of the wettest and driest places and some of the highest and lowest. Much of the north and central part is only sparsely populated although this is more than compensated for in the southern countries of China and India.

The average height of Asia is over 3,045 metres (10,000 feet) and it includes within its borders such great mountain ranges as the Himalayas, Hindu-Kush, Tien Shan, Elburz and Taurus Mountains. More than 50 of the highest mountains of the world are contained within the Karakoram-Himalaya massif.

The rivers of Asia are no less impressive than the mountains and include the Yangtse-Kiang 5,520 kilometres (3,430 miles), which is the longest in the continent, the Hwang-Ho 4,600 kilometres (2,900 miles) and the Mekong 4,160 kilometres (2,600 miles).

The largest inland sea in the world is the Caspian which covers 370,000 square kilometres (143,350 square miles) and has a maximum depth of 980 metres (3,215 feet) This compares with Lake Baikal which is the deepest lake in the world, plunging down to 1,615 metres (5,300 feet).

Two main deserts, the Arabian in the east and the Gobi in Mongolia and China, cover a total area of 2,300,000 square kilometres (900,000 square miles).

Africa

The African continent covers 30,233,000 square kilometres (11,673,00 square miles). The coastline is relatively free of major indentations and there are few off-shore islands. However, Madagascar lying off the eastern coast of Africa, is the fifth largest island in the world. The high mountains of Africa are found mainly in the coastal areas.

Lake caused by warp in Earth's crust.

Lake caused by a fault in a valley.

Lake caused by a landslide in a valley.

The highest mountain is Kilimanjaro at 5,900 metres (19,340 feet) in Tanzania. This, along with the other major peaks of Mount Kenya and the Ruwenzori group lies along the Great Rift Valley of East Africa. In the north is the largest desert in the world, the Sahara, which occupies 8,420,000 square kilometres (3,250,000 square miles). Flowing to the north is the longest river in the world, the Nile, which is 6,670 kilometres (4,145 miles) long although its basin area is not as large as that of either the Amazon or the Mississippi-Missouri.

The rivers of Africa are made even more spectacular by the waterfalls. The Zambesi flows for over 3,200 kilometres (2,000 miles) and plunges over the famous Victoria Falls. Because of the quantity of material carried by the Congo river 4,600 kilometres (2,900 miles), the reddish-brown waters can be traced into the Atlantic for 48 kilometres (30 miles).

The lakes of Africa range from the second largest in the world in Lake Victoria 69,484 square kilometres (26,828 square miles) to Lake Chad, which has an average depth of only 1·5 metres (5 feet), but covers

Lakes are formed by bodies of water lying in basins, the bottoms of which are below the surrounding water table.

between 11,000 and 22,000 square kilometres (4,250 and 8,500 square miles), according to the season.

The Americas

The land mass of the Americas covers 42,043,000 square kilometres (16,233,000 square miles) made up of North America 21,500,000 square kilometres (8,301,000 square miles), Central America 2,750,000 square kilometres (1,062,000 square miles) and South America 17,793,000 square kilometres (6,870,000 square miles).

South America is a continent of extremes. To the west is the mighty range of the Andes rising to 6,960 metres (22,834 feet) in Cerro Aconcagua. Within the Andes group are the highest volcanoes in the world. Some 11,800 square kilometres (4,600 square miles) of South America are glaciated and to the south there are glaciers which reach the sea along the fiord coast. A little north of the

Ullswater, a typical scene in the Lake District of Britain.

area of ice on the eastern side of the mountains is the Atacama Desert.

Any map of South America is dominated by the mighty river Amazon which flows 6,400 kilometres (4,000 miles) from one side of the continent to the other and has a basin area larger than any other river in the world. The amount of water arriving at the sea is so great that it makes the water fresh for many kilometres out into the Atlantic Ocean. It is possible for ocean-going ships to travel up the Amazon from the coast to Peru.

There are relatively few large lakes in South America with the exception of Lake Titicaca which has an area of 9,000 square kilometres (3,500 square miles). Waterfalls, however, abound and include some of the highest in the world, for example the Angel Falls with a total drop of 980 metres (3,212 feet).

North America consists of a number of distinct regions. To the north is the Canadian Shield which is one of the oldest parts of the Earth's surface. To the south and east of this is a zone of mountains and to the west and south are the central plains. Like

South America the western coastal zone is mountainous. These ranges include the Rocky Mountains and the highest point in North America, which is Mount McKinley, the only peak to rise more than 6,095 metres (20,000 feet).

In the north is a whole series of lakes from Great Bear Lake and Great Slave Lake to the Great Lakes themselves—Superior, Michigan, Huron, Erie and Ontario. Lake Superior is the largest lake in the world covering 82,400 square kilometres (31,820 square miles).

The whole continent is well endowed with extensive river systems including the mighty Mississippi–Missouri, the third largest river in the world, which drains a large basin and ends in a famous delta.

Europe
Europe covers 10,523,000 square kilometres (4,063,000 square miles). In the south is a great mountain range including the Cantabrian, Pyrenees, Jura, Alps, the mountains of Yugoslavia and those of the Black Sea area. To the north the mountains of Scotland are continued on the other side of the North Sea in Scandinavia. Europe ends in the east at the Urals. The highest peaks are

Erosion of the coastline is caused by the combination of sea and wind forces over a long period of time.

found in the south-east while the Alps rise to 4,800 metres (15,770 feet). There are a number of notable volcanic peaks including Vesuvius, Stromboli and Etna.

In between the mountain masses of the north and south are the great plains, including the Plain of France, the North German Plain and the Great Rumanian Plain. Locked in between the Carpathians and the Serbian Highlands is the Hungarian Plain.

Some of the deepest cave systems in the world are to be found in France, Italy and Spain including the Gouffre de la Pierre Saint-Martin in the Pyrenees and the cave system at Holloch in Switzerland. The world's largest cave system is in the United States in Kentucky.

Europe's longest river is the Volga which flows for 3,686 kilometres (2,292 miles) in Russia, finally emptying into the Caspian Sea. The second longest river is the Danube which flows from Germany to the Black Sea.

Antarctica and Oceania
Antarctica covers about 13,598,000 square kilometres (5,250,000 square

miles) and forms the largest glaciated area in the world. Although a continental ice sheet, individual glaciers are up to several hundred kilometres long. It includes a number of mountains over 4,265 metres (14,000 feet) high and the world's most southerly active volcano, Mount Erebus.

Oceania is normally taken to include Australia, New Zealand, New Guinea and other smaller islands. It covers 8,960,000 square kilometres (3,460,000 square miles). Australia itself would be the largest island in the world but it is customary to regard it as a continent. The island of New Guinea, which is now politically divided into two areas, covers 823,000 square kilometres (317,000 square miles) and is second only to Greenland which has an area of 2,175,000 square kilometres (840,000 square miles).

Australia is dominated by the great desert which covers 1,550,000 square kilometres (600,000 square miles) in western, southern and central Australia. The highest mountains of the region are found in New Guinea, while the highest in New Zealand is Mount Cook at 3,763 metres (12,349 feet). Lake Eyre in Australia is one of the larger lakes of the world, but like Chad in Africa, it varies greatly in its extent.

The Cycle of Erosion

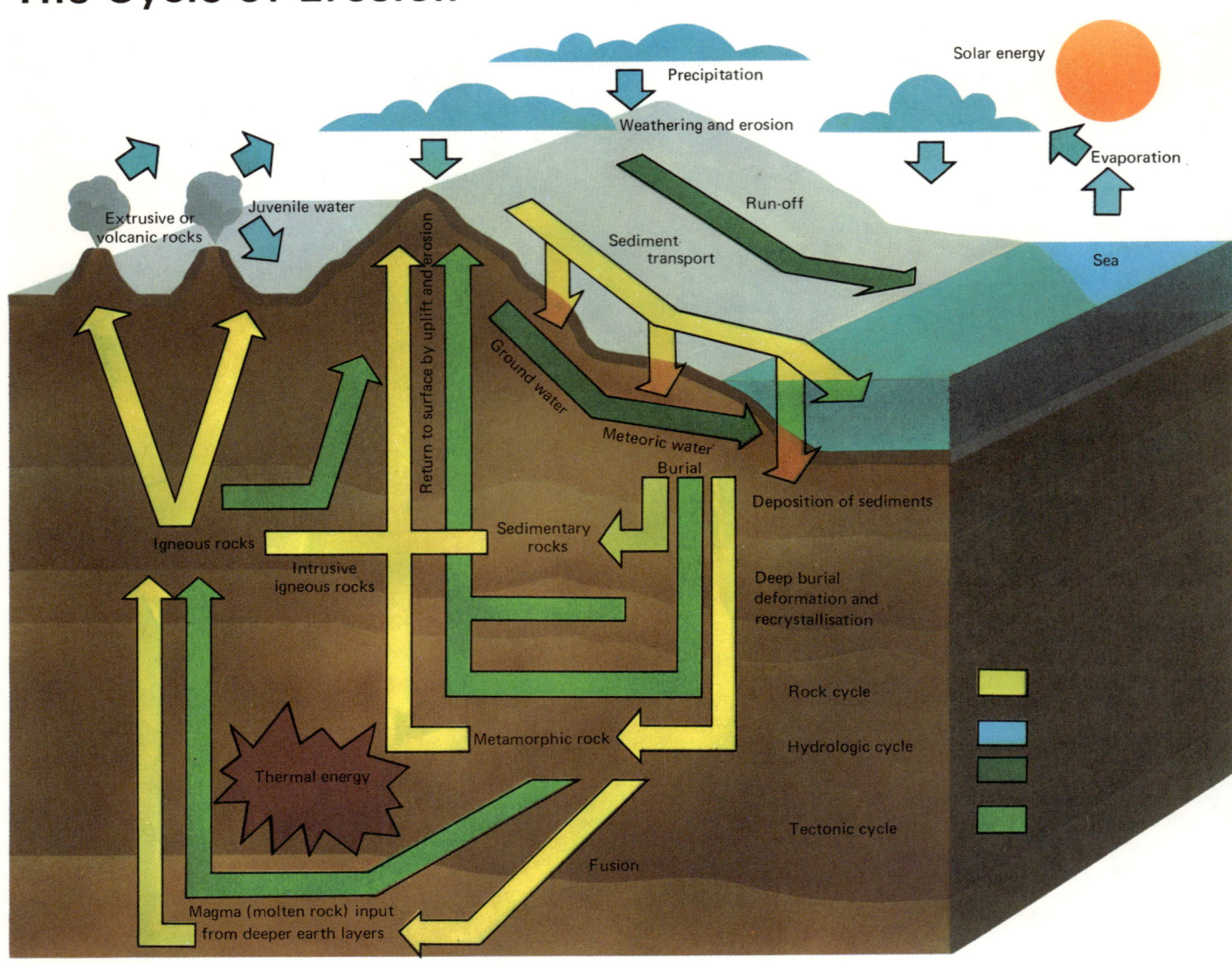

Illustrated in this diagram are three geological cycles whereby materials at or near the Earth's surface are broken down and later reformed. The rock cycle shows the formation, alteration and destruction of rocks by various means. The hydrological cycle demonstrates the circulation of water between the atmosphere and the seas, either by direct action or through the land. The tectonic cycle shows the formation and destruction of the Earth's major structural features.

The surface of the Earth is under constant attack. The present scenery is built on the wreckage of former worlds. The rain falling on the land loosens some fragments of rocks and alters others. It finds its way into cracks and crevices, gradually widening them and shattering the rock.

Frost is a potent breaker of rock as are changes in temperature. Animals and plants all act to break up the Earth. Burrowing animals throw up quantities of soil, and trees and other plants which grow on rock push their roots down to break up the surface. The decay of rock material produced by all these agencies is called weathering.

Movement of Debris

As time goes by the broken material will find its way to lower levels. Gravity plays a considerable part in this,

helped by rain and landslides. Much of the debris will end up in the rivers, where it is carried away in a solution or as solid particles. More will be rolled along the bottom, sometimes stopping for weeks and months in one place only to head downwards again in a time of flood. Glaciers carry vast quantities of debris on their surfaces and within the ice. In glacial regions frost action on the walls of the valley will break off considerable quantities of rock fragments. Both glaciers and rivers use the material they have collected to modify their own valleys. Gradually the rock fragments are broken into even smaller particles, and the wind may remove vast quantities of sand and dust. The destruction which occurs during transportation is called erosion from the Latin word *erodere*, to gnaw away.

The dual processes of rock weather-

ing and erosion are called denudation, a word again derived from the Latin, *denudare*, to make bare. Gradually the land masses are being worn away by denudation. It has been calculated that, in some areas, they lose about 30 centimetres (12 inches) every three to four thousand years.

Water works both chemically and mechanically on the surface of the Earth. Moist air and rain decompose the surfaces of the rocks by dissolving and breaking up certain of the mineral constituents or by removing the cementing medium. The principal agent in this process of decomposition is carbon dioxide which is dissolved in the water and gives a weak acid. The minerals mainly affected by these processes are the aluminous silicates containing such bases as potash, soda, lime or iron. These are found in all igneous rocks and in many sandstones and metamorphic rocks. The rocks removed or broken up by the direct dissolving action of the carbonic acid are the limestones and calcareous sandstones.

When a limestone contains impurities these may be left behind as a residue. The red earths, called *terra rosa*, in Yugoslavia have accumulated because of the traces of iron compounds in the original limestone. In igneous rocks the feldspars are broken down into clay minerals.

In well-jointed rocks such as basalt the water is able to attack individual blocks from all sides at once. The main force of the action is on the edges and at the corners which gradually split, allowing the process to go deeper. The whole block is slowly rounded and becomes rather like an onion in its layers. This action is known as spheroidal weathering.

Falling of Rain

Rain falling on the surface of the Earth also acts mechanically to break up the ground. Loose particles of soil and rock are washed out. Where much of the rain falls in heavy showers, gullies will be cut into the hillsides. The whole land is gradually cut up into a large number of such gullies and ravines. In North America these areas are called badlands and stretch from Alberta to Arizona.

Where water rushes down the slopes of boulder clay deposits, it will soon wash away the surrounding soil and leave large boulders which are more resistant to the action of water. Eventually a pillar will be built up, and where these are located in sheltered positions they have reached over 21 metres (70 feet) in height.

Changes in temperature also destroy rocks. When water freezes it expands by about 10 per cent of its volume and can exert extreme pressure. Fragments are broken off as the water thaws and these fall downwards. In some upland regions there are deposits of such angular material at the base of the hills. These accumulations are called screes.

Rocks can be cracked in desert regions by the cold nights or the occasional shower of almost freezing rain which may follow a period of intense heat. In some cases the rock begins to peel, and this is known as exfoliation.

Erosion by Animals

Plants and animals also contribute to the breaking up of rocks. In a single year the earthworms in one hectare (two acres) of land will bring to the surface between 20 and 30 tons of material. The roots of plants can exert enormous forces as they find their way downwards, while all plants extract some goodness from the rocks

below. The bacteria in the soil also attack both the soil and rocks. Plants help too in preventing the removal of soil. This is why when soils are allowed to become worked out or forests are suddenly cut down, the almost immediate result is a massive erosion of the soil itself. This can result in the destruction of a whole area. The effects of poor farming are to be seen in the great land areas of the United States and elsewhere. Man himself is now a most important agent of erosion, but unlike natural forces he is not limited by climatic controls.

In equatorial regions which are hot and experience heavy rains, there is a type of rotting degradation. The tropical regions share some of the erosion patterns of both equatorial and desert regions. In the latter the main force is the wind. Only in the temperate regions is there a great variety of types of erosion due to frost, ice, rain, rivers and the wind. In the Arctic regions the action is almost entirely due to frost and ice.

In many places rocks are covered by a less coherent mass. Sometimes, for example in soil, this mass will grade downwards into the rock from which it has developed. Soils usually show different horizons (layers) according to the type of climate and vegetation. The top layer contains the humus and the smallest particles while the next consists of larger particles and

Ben Lomond, a mountain in Scotland. The Highlands of Scotland are old fold mountains, formed 250–500 million years ago.

The sediments which formed the Appalachian Mountains in eastern North America are up to nearly thirteen kilometres (eight miles) thick.

The jagged peaks of the Alps reveal the fact that in geological terms they are young mountains not yet worn smooth.

Soil is the product of weathering caused by the effect of climate and by the activity of the many organisms it contains. This cross-section from northern Europe shows the several layers of sandstone, shale and slate rubble which exist beneath the surface of loam and matted grass.

and also part of Western Australia provide numerous examples. The largest rock outcrop in the world is Mount Augustus in Australia, 1,105 metres (3,627 feet) above sea level. It is about eight kilometres (five miles) long and three kilometres (two miles) wide. More famous than this is Ayer's Rock which is half the size and located 400 kilometres (250 miles) south-west of Alice Springs in the heart of Australia. A similar type of residual hill is the famous sugar-loaf of Rio de Janeiro in Brazil, and there are other examples of inselbergs in North America and Asia.

All the material which is carried by rivers and glaciers must eventually be deposited. When a glacier melts, its load will drop. Some will be moved on again by the action of rivers and streams and the wind. Perhaps the most important site of deposition is the sea. Here the waste of the land transported by the rivers meets that removed by the sea. The heaviest particles are dropped first while the finer material may be carried to the depths of the oceans. Gradually over millions of years the sediments will build up. Earth movements eventually occur that alter the pattern of land and sea. The sediments on the sea floor are raised up again into great mountain chains. The sediments now compacted have lost their water content, for the grains have become cemented together and they are now rocks ready to begin on the same journey again.

less vegetable matter. The sub-soil is made up of broken rock almost unaltered from the underlying bed-rock. Soils may develop because of the transportation of loose deposits by all the agents of erosion.

Soils vary in their structure and in their ability to grow plants. An ideal soil, for agricultural purposes, should be well aerated and not too permeable. There should be a balance between the humus and the smallest particles, called colloids.

A podsol (ash beneath) is a forest or heath soil. The upper layer consists of decomposing vegetation and raw humus with a white or bleached layer. This is followed downwards by a brown-black-red soil the colouring of which is the result of nutrients being drained out of the top horizon.

In a brown forest soil the top layer is black-brown with a well developed humus content. This also extends down into the next layer. This mildly acidic soil is typical of deciduous forests. If the vegetation cover is removed, the soil degenerates into a podsol.

A chernozem (black earth) consists of a uniform layer of black soil for a metre or so and there is no distinction between the top two horizons. It is a neutral soil and supports grasslands.

Island Mountains

Even though some rocks have a covering, in some places weathering still goes on and gradually material is removed to lower levels. Climatic conditions have a considerable effect on the cycle of erosion. Under very dry conditions a region can be reduced to a flat plain. The massive upstanding mountains which remain are termed inselbergs (or island mountains). The most outstanding examples are found within the tropics and they are well developed in Africa—where they were first named—and in Arabia. In Australia, the borders between Northern Territory and South Australia,

In many places the sea is working to destroy the coastline, causing it to retreat inland. In others the coastline advances as rock debris and sand deposited by the sea extends the beach platform.

The Work of Water

Water forms into microscopic droplets as it is condensed from vapour in the atmosphere. It builds up into bigger and bigger drops until its weight can no longer be supported by the air currents and rainfall results.

Rivers begin in high ground and cut fast-flowing narrow channels which become wider and slower on lower ground. Material deposited by rivers sometimes causes them to meander across flat plains, ending in deltas where the water enters the sea.

Water and wind work to erode rocks into many strange forms. Where the rock is particularly hard isolated formations called mesas and buttes stand out above the level of the surrounding landscape.

Water is the most effective sculptor of the landscape. It works above the ground and beneath. Majestic rivers carve for themselves great valleys and canyons, and leap over layers of rock to form waterfalls. They carry vast quantities of sediment to the sea. When frozen, water splits rocks, and as great streams of ice, the glaciers quickly change a rugged landscape into one of rounded hills and U-shaped valleys. The sea has a dual effect in changing the shape of the land. In places it attacks and removes vast quantities of rock and soil. Cliffs crumble and buildings near the edge may be undermined and slip down into the waves. In other places, the sea deposits the results of its destructive action as spits and bars. It builds up deposits of sand and gravel.

Because of the interest in springs and rivers, there have always been a number of fascinating theories to account for their origins. One of the first people to record the true origin of springs and rivers was the famous potter Bernard Palissy (c.1509–89). He recorded in a book published in 1580 that 'I have learned definitely that these (springs) take their origin in and are fed by rain and rain alone'. He realised that snow also had a part to play. However, over eighty years later Athanasius Kircher (1602–80) in his famous book *Mundus Sub-terraneus* (1664) still suggested that

there were holes in the bottom of the sea, marked by whirlpools, through which the waters of the ocean drain. By means of a series of underground channels, he said, the water finds its way up inside the mountains and issues from the tops as springs and rivers. It then returns to the sea to complete the cycle.

Much of the rain which falls on the land soon evaporates back into the atmosphere. Plants and animals use some and a quantity drains through the soil and into the rocks below. Some runs on the surface to form streams which grow to become rivers. The way in which water drains the land will depend on the type of rock present. Once through the soil it will quickly soak into a sandstone-type of rock. Here the connecting pores allow a considerable quantity of water to collect. Clays however will not allow the passage of water, and hence it tends to collect in the soil leading to water-logged roots and crop failure.

The Water-table

No matter what the conditions are on the surface of the Earth, somewhere below will be water. As the water drains downwards, further movement may be prevented because of an impermeable rock (a rock which will not allow water to drain through). The upper level of the water-saturated rocks is called the water-table. When a well is sunk, water first appears in the shaft when the water-table is pierced. To provide a water supply at all seasons the well must be driven deeper. This is because the water table varies in its depth below the surface according to how much rain there has been. Its level is also much affected by man pumping water from the great reservoirs. A shallow well

Earth pillars are created where fingers of rock are protected from erosion by hard rock caps.

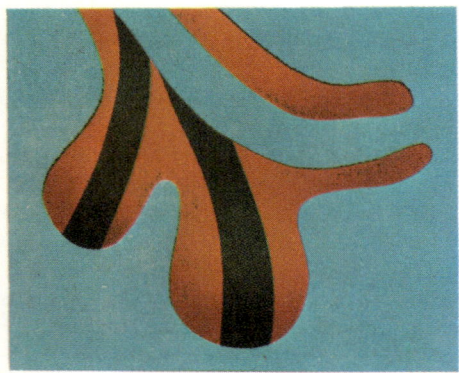

In delta areas sediments carried by rivers sometimes build up to force the water into a new channel.

Where water falls over a top layer of hard limestone the ground beneath is eaten away by the action of the water.

easily becomes polluted with sewage and other waste.

A special type of well is called an artesian well after the Artois region in France where such wells in Europe were first sunk. Although very deep, the water rushes up the boring to pour out at the surface without any pumping. Such a well is only formed where certain geological conditions are fulfilled. The water is trapped between two impermeable layers of rock and is fed from an outcrop of rock which is at a much higher level than the top of the well. The largest artesian basin in the world covers part of Queensland, New South Wales and South Australia.

Where the formation of rocks dips, the water will soak down to a layer of impermeable rock and then run along the junction. If a valley or gorge cuts through this particular group of rocks, the water may well issue as a spring. Where the rocks have been fractured, sometimes a permeable rock is brought next to an impermeable one. The pressure of water builds up in the former and may force its way upwards at the junction of the rocks to issue as a spring. In some cases a whole line of springs is created.

Formation of Caves

Rainwater is not pure, for it contains in it dissolved oxygen and carbon dioxide. This acts in a very noticeable way on limestone rocks. It dissolves away the rock along the joint lines, gradually widening them into what are known as grikes. Sometimes the

water concentrates at just one point for its entry into the rock and this is widened into a funnel-shaped depression called a swallow-hole. The water will gradually find its way down through the limestone until it encounters an impermeable rock. On its journey it will act on the joint lines and lines of weakness, in many cases creating caves. In all caves there is a considerable opportunity for the growth and development of stalactites and stalagmites. In the former case water droplets on the roof evaporate, leaving a deposit of calcium carbonate. This is added to little by little and over hundreds or thousands of years the stalactite will develop. Stalagmites, which grow up from the floor of the cave have similar origins. Sometimes the two will meet, forming a column. In many cave systems there are spectacular displays of stalactites, stalagmites and columns, many of them coloured due to various minerals and other impurities in the rock.

Sometimes a whole cave system will collapse leaving just a gorge. In limestone regions rivers often disappear below ground only to reappear miles away at a lower level. This is also due to the action of water on the rock.

Where the water-table is always near the surface, swamps, bogs and marshes will form. In a swamp the land is saturated with water, while in tropical areas masses of vegetation grow above. Some of this lies rotting in shallow pools. Swamps are often found in delta regions, for example, the

Niagara Falls in North America, perhaps the most famous falls in the world, are gradually wearing away and in geological terms will be short-lived.

Rocks, particularly limestone, are weathered by rainwater, and in a limestone area water seeps through the rock finding its way freely until it reaches an impervious layer. This creates holes, caverns and underground streams. Where the roof of an underground channel collapses a gorge is created.

Ganges. Perhaps the most famous swamps are the Everglades of Florida and the Dismal Swamp of North Carolina and Virginia. Bogs develop where a moss known as sphagnum moss grows out from the edges and leads to masses of decaying vegetation on the bottom. This decaying mass is continually being added to, and gradually the weight on the lower layers forces out the water and peat will form.

From usually humble beginnings rivers grow into great highways for the transportation of fragmented rocks. In removing this debris they carve for themselves deep valleys. Once the river reaches the sea, the crushed rocks may be deposited to form new land around the lower reaches of the river or be deposited in the sea, to be swept away by the tides and currents to another shore, there to extend its limits.

River Scenery

Much of the scenery best loved by man owes its origins to the work of rivers. High up near its source the stream will rush along, tumbling over rocks and stones. A great deal of its energy will be taken in overcoming the friction of the bottom and sides, but enough will remain to enable it to cut down into its own bed. Where it meets a more resistant layer of rock it will swing round it. Gradually other streams will join the main one, the volume of water thus increasing, and

enabling the river to transport more material.

The scenery of this first stage is characterised by narrow steep-sided valleys. The stream swings between the hills leaving a series of interlocking spurs of land. In flood, perhaps after the melting of the winter snows in the high hills, it will be able to carry considerable amounts of debris in solution and suspension, while even larger boulders and stones will be rolled along the bottom. The movement of such large rocks can cause the river to become blocked. Disastrous floods will occur. Sometimes the rocks, each weighing many tons, will be swept the length of the stream to crash on some unsuspecting coastal village.

Often the gorges which rivers carve for themselves have only enough room at the bottom for the swirling mass of water. In some cases, such gorges have been turned into tourist attractions and visitors are able to walk along narrow paths of steel which cling to the rock wall. One example is the Aare Gorge in Switzerland, the path of which is above the wild and foaming waters. The gorge varies in depth from 98–198 metres (320–650 feet), and at places the walls almost meet overhead. At these points the water is forced, seething and bubbling, through a mere crevice.

Waterfalls

When the river flows over a layer of hard rock, beneath which are other

rocks more easily eroded, a waterfall will tend to form. The development depends on how the rocks themselves dip in relation to the water. If the slope is in the same direction as that of the flow of the river, all that will result is a stretch of rapids. If the hard layer is horizontal, or almost so, then a waterfall is most likely to develop. As the water plunges over the edge it will create currents which cut back into the rocks beneath the fall-producing layer. There is a constant cutting back; gradually great lumps break away from the hard layer and the falls retreat a little further upstream. The river works constantly to remove a waterfall, which geologically has only a very short lifetime.

Perhaps the most famous falls in the world are the Niagara Falls on the Niagara River between Lake Erie and Lake Ontario. These falls, on the boundary of the United States and Canada, are divided into two by a small island, called Goat Island. The Horseshoe Falls are on the Canadian side while the others are the American Falls. The former, as its name suggests, is shaped like a horseshoe, and because more water flows on this side, it is receding faster than the American Falls. The average height of the falls is 49 metres (162 feet).

Often behind waterfalls there is a ledge and sometimes it is possible to walk behind the great wall of water. This was once the case with Niagara but it has now been stopped because of the size of the rocks which crash down. Some of these lumps may weigh up to 185,000 tons. The force of the water as it hits the floor of the river beneath the falls causes a deep pool to be excavated. Some idea of this force may be gained by the figures for Niagara. Every minute 417,000 tons of water go over the falls. The Iroquois Indians certainly gave it the right name, for Niagara means 'thundering of waters'.

The Guaira Falls on the Parana River in Brazil have developed where the river plunges over the edge of a great basalt plateau. No less than eighteen falls are grouped around the main gorge. This is itself cutting back into the floor of the lake which is on the plateau above the falls.

The 'greatest river wonder of the world' also owes its origins to a river spilling over a basalt plateau. The Zambesi in Africa, where it plunges an average depth of 92 metres (304 feet) along a width of 1,700 metres (5,580 feet), forms the Victoria Falls. The first outsider to view this spectacular sight was Dr David Livingstone in 1855. Below the falls is a 96 kilometre (60 mile) long gorge

Tropical swamp area where the vegetation is thick and lies rotting in stagnant pools.

showing how the falls have retreated over the years.

The highest waterfall in the world is the Angel Falls in Venezuela, with a single drop of 807 metres (2,648 feet) and a total fall of 979 metres (3,212 feet). In the South Island of New Zealand the Sutherland Falls drop 580 metres (1,904 feet) in three sections, while the Gersoppa Falls on the Sharavati River, India, leap 253 metres (830 feet).

Where the water flows quickly over the rocks, currents will be set up and small whirlpools created. Because there will most likely be particles of rock suspended in the water, or being rolled along the bottom, they will cut into the bed making a round hole. These are called pot-holes and may be several metres wide. All the time the river is working on its channel, other forces of erosion are joining in to wear away the banks. Wind and rain will wash particles down into the river. Animals and plants will also help in this destruction.

Tributaries

As the river continues on its journey to the sea, the valley floor becomes wider and the cliffs on either side less steep. The flow of the river is slower. Other tributaries continue to join the main stream and vast quantities of sediment are transported. Lower downstream the river tends to meander. This means it swings from side to side in great curves. As it turns thus the main mass of water is thrown against the outside bank. This tends to be undercut and steep cliffs result, while on the inside of the curve the slower moving water deposits some of its load as banks of sand and gravel. The great loops made by the river tend themselves to move downstream. Sometimes in the lower reaches the river cuts through the outside

Where the water-table is always near the surface, swamps, bogs and marshes will appear, such areas being saturated with water and never properly drying out.

bank and joins two loops together. A crescent-shaped depression is left which, when filled with water, is called an ox-bow lake.

Also in this stage the river is moving very sluggishly and is gradually beginning to deposit its load. During floods, material dropped at the edge of the river may form banks, called levees. Mud, sand and silt deposited on the stream bed tend gradually to raise the river above the level of the surrounding landscape. The Mississippi River in the United States and the Hwang Ho in China are examples of rivers which have become raised above the countryside. Should the banks break or the river level rise above them, disastrous floods affect great areas of land.

When the river enters the sea its carrying power comes to an end. Where no strong currents sweep along the shore the river will build for itself a triangular-shaped piece of land called a delta. It is named after the Greek letter Δ. First, the heavy material—the pebbles and gravel—will be laid down, while the lighter sandy material is carried farther and the clay particles may even reach the

Flood-tides raise the water level evenly in most rivers, producing no more than a series of rolling waves. Certain estuaries, however, produce a freak large wave called a tidal bore which may rush up river for some distance.

Along rocky coasts the sculpturing effect of the waves can be seen in stacks and arches which are evidence of a retreating coastline.

When a coastline is in the process of subsiding, land is worn back to a new point.

A coastline is extended when river silt accumulates offshore.

depths of the ocean. The land will be pushed out into the sea. It will be criss-crossed by a multitude of dividing and rejoining streams. It looks just like a river entering the sea across a sandy beach.

There are a number of famous deltas in the world. The Mississippi in the United States adds to its own delta at the rate of 140 million tons of minerals, 400 million tons of sand and silt and 60 million tons of rock material each year. The delta has changed its shape and position many times during the last hundred years. The Nile Delta in Egypt is the most famous in the world and was the first one to be studied. Its fertile land is of vital importance in growing food for the Egyptian people. Other deltas are situated at the mouths of the Ganges and Brahmaputra in Bangladesh, the Hwang Ho in China and the Po in Italy. Deltas offer attractive conditions

for agriculture, wildlife and industrial plants and ports.

Changes in the sea level can cause river valleys to become invaded with salt water. Such valleys are said to be drowned. A special type of drowned valley which is found in Norway, Finland, Greenland, New Zealand and many other places is called a fiord. When the sea level was lower, during the last ice age, great glaciers found their way down the river valleys to the sea. They scoured out the rock creating the typical U-shaped valley. When conditions became warmer the ice melted and the sea level rose and drowned the valley.

In the Himalayas and some other regions rivers seem to have cut right through the mountains. In such cases the river has been able to keep pace with the slowly rising land mass. Great gorges and canyons are created. The Grand Canyon, on the Colorado River

Fiords are scenic features particularly associated with the countries of Scandinavia. They were formed by the action of glaciers during the Ice Ages, when river valleys were deepened and widened by the ice and eventually filled by water from the sea.

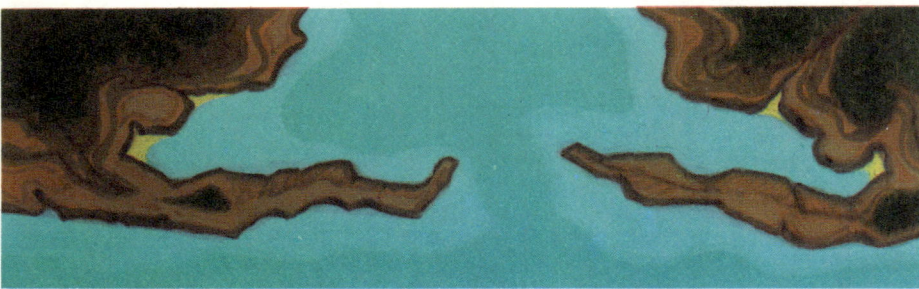

Bars of land are built up by the accumulation of sand at the break point of waves offshore. The sand bar is added to both from its landward and seaward sides.

The projecting pieces of land known as spits are created gradually by waves that sweep sand inland along a beach from the direction of the sea.

still 2,400 metres (8,000 feet) thick while in Antarctica it may reach even greater depths. Glaciers remain, however, in many parts of the world, even in the tropics where they are found in the high mountains.

In the mountainous regions the snows of hundreds and thousands of years pile up. The lower layers are subjected to great pressures and change into ice. The process takes longer in colder climates. The weight of the snow above causes the glacier ice crystals to become deformed; they are forced out of the hollow in which the original snow collects and gravity does the rest. For the glacier to move, it is essential that there is a thin layer of water between the ice and the rock. Just like the rivers, the ice flows down the valley rather like toothpaste squeezing out of a tube.

Once underway the ice attacks anything which stops its progress. It tears and plucks at the rocks. Masses of fragmented rock become embedded in the glacier. In some areas it is possible to walk inside a glacier, and in the ice walls the lumps of rock which have been carried down the valley can easily be seen. The rocks form an effective agent in the attack on the valley sides and floor. The speed at which glaciers move varies greatly; up to 12 kilometres (7·5 miles) in a few months is not unknown. Sometimes it will cease forward movement and retreat, only to advance again.

As the glacier travels on its way, it will meet obstacles which cannot be removed. It will tend to rise up over these causing the surface of the ice to crack and split under the strain. This is how crevasses appear. Sometimes where it falls over a ledge of rock the ice will be completely shattered and the jagged blocks will make an ice-fall. At some points tributary glaciers will join the main one. Here the masses of ice will be under considerable stresses and strains and many cracks will develop.

In some areas where the snowfall is considerable, the glaciers will combine and form one great sheet covering a vast area. Such is the case in Antarctica and in Greenland. During the last ice age such sheets covered much of Scandinavia, Scotland and North America.

As well as tearing the rocks away, glaciers eventually deposit much of their load to form scenic features which nowadays provide valuable clues as to the original ice cover and its direction of movement. Other features

in the United States is the most famous canyon in the world.

Lakes

Lakes are scenic features which man finds very attractive and useful. They provide natural reservoirs for the storage of water and many opportunities for various kinds of sport.

Lakes, like waterfalls, have geologically short lives. There are many ways in which they can be formed. A river valley may become dammed by a landslide. In limestone areas lakes may form in swallow holes. The ice of the past is also responsible for many of the lakes. The glaciers pushed masses of material to block streams and carved out basins in the rock which filled with water when the ice melted.

The Work of Ice

Water in the form of ice has created many of the present land forms. The surface of the Earth has been carved and gouged by the masses of ice which covered 30 per cent of the land areas during the last ice age. Today glaciers still cover 10 per cent of the land surface but most of this is due to the ice-clad continents of Greenland and Antarctica. In Greenland the ice is

During the Ice Ages, 'U'-shaped valleys were carved in pre-glacial rock (left). When the glacier (centre) melted, the landscape showed evidence of its action in the structure of the valley peaks and in the broken rock debris at the foot of the valley (right).

are produced by the action of the glacier itself—for example, the U-shaped valleys tell where a river of ice once existed. Sometimes hanging valleys are created where a river is now left to plunge over the edge of the valley side. High in the mountains, circular shaped depressions, often now filled with water, mark the birthplace of the glaciers of past ages.

Icebergs

A glacier is not just a mass of solid ice. Beneath it flows a stream. On top of the ice there may be other streams which suddenly disappear down a crevasse. All of these, just like other streams, carry rock waste and once the glaciers melt, or they change their courses, various deposits are left. Eskers are ridges formed of melted water deposits. In Finland they meander between the lakes ranging from 10–100 kilometres (6–62 miles) in length and 5–30 metres (16–98 feet) in height. At the very front of the glacier is a mound of unsorted rock debris. If an ice sheet or glacier reaches the sea great lumps will break off and float away as icebergs.

Glaciers will sometimes transport blocks of rocks great distances from their original source and leave them perched precariously. Such perched blocks tell geologists much about the directions of ice movement.

Where the glacier meets a very resistant mass of rock, the ice may be diverted. On the downward side the original sediments will remain untouched. Such a feature is called crag and tail. Drumlins are small rounded hills which often appear in swarms and create what is known as a 'basket of eggs topography'. Their origin is obscure but may be connected with the action of ice on a boulder clay deposit.

Roches moutonnées are formed when the ice travels up and over hard resistant rock and causes it to be smoothed on the one side and plucked on the leeward side. The resulting shape is considered to resemble a resting sheep or a wig.

Kettle holes are formed when the ice is pushed down into the ground and remains there long after the main glacier has retreated. Some of these depressions are still filled with water.

Waves and Currents

Waves are usually thought of as destroyers of cliffs and beaches. Even when the sea is calm they hit the beach, churning up sand and small stones. They also slap against the cliffs. In a storm great quantities of sand and gravel are removed while lumps of rock are torn from the cliffs. However, not all the work of the sea is destructive, for all the material that it collects must be deposited again. Often one section of the coast is being eroded while only a matter of a few miles away sand and gravel are being deposited.

In its work the sea relies on two forces, the waves and the currents. As a wave hits the rock, the air which is compressed in the cracks and joints forces them open. As the wave retreats, the air is released and some debris is washed away. In some places the sea is constantly attacking the cliffs, while in others it only reaches them at high water or even during storms. The upper parts of the cliffs are under constant attack from the wind, water and animals.

The nature of the beach area will also have a considerable effect on the action of the sea. Sometimes there is a wave-cut platform, with sand and shingle on the landward side. In such cases the waves break a long way from

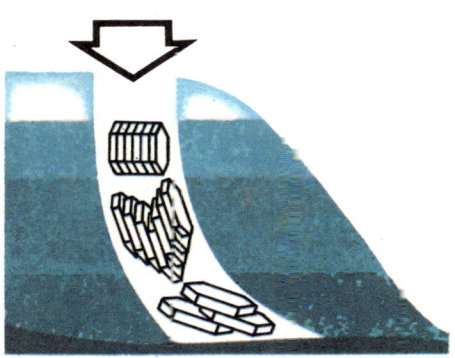

Glaciers are in constant movement because of the great weight of the ice. The top layers compress the lower ones and alter their molecular structure causing them to slip slowly downwards. Icebergs (below) are parts of glacier walls that have broken free to drift in the seas.

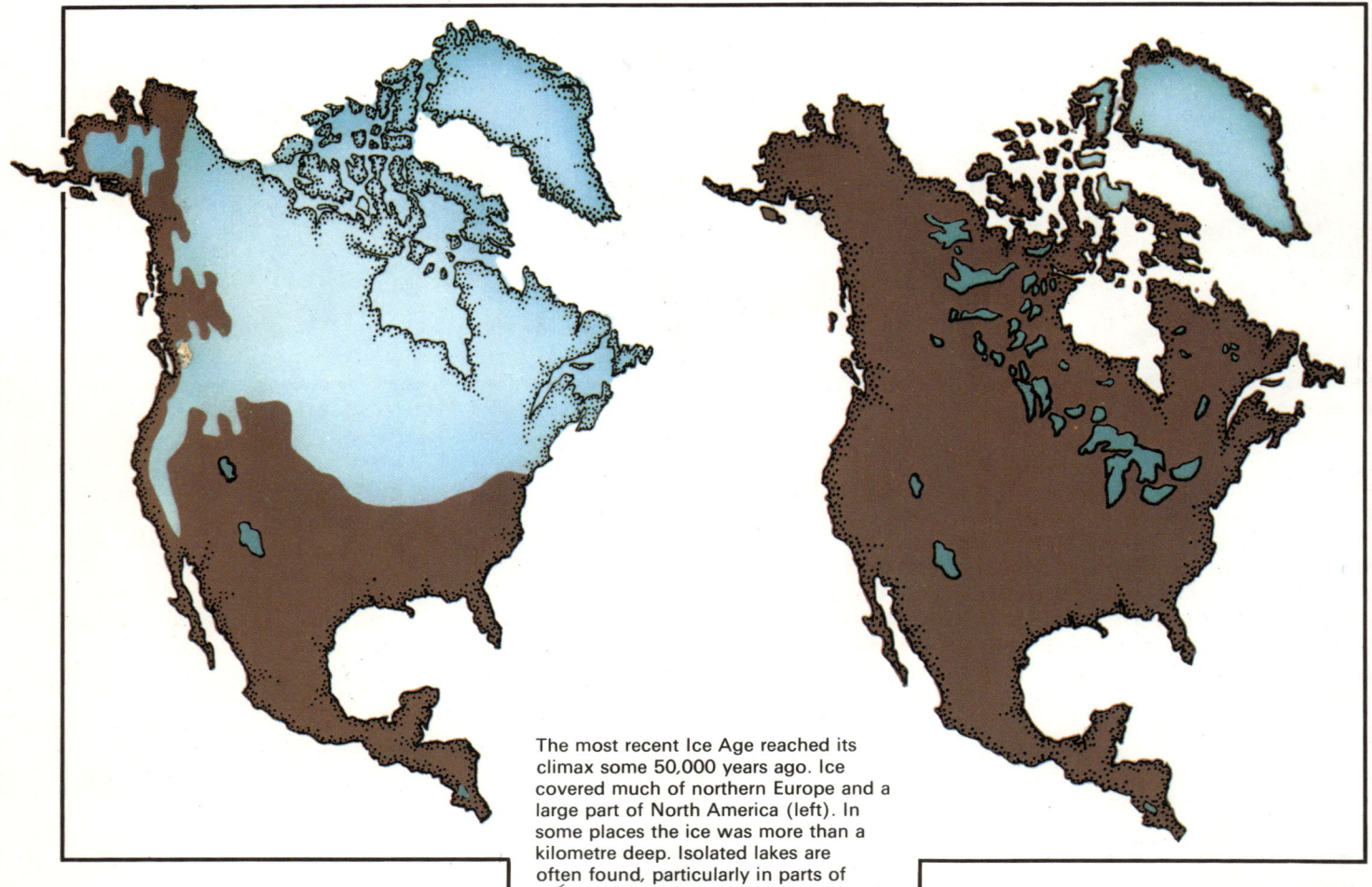

The most recent Ice Age reached its climax some 50,000 years ago. Ice covered much of northern Europe and a large part of North America (left). In some places the ice was more than a kilometre deep. Isolated lakes are often found, particularly in parts of Canada (right) and these were formed by large areas of ice that remained frozen for a considerable period after the rest of the glacier had melted away.

the cliffs and therefore there is little destructive action. As a wave breaks it will tend to wash material up the beach, but in turn the backwash will draw it down again. It is obvious that the balance, or lack of it, between these two forces is important in building up or destroying the beach deposits.

Waves are also affected in their action by the way in which they reach the shore. Where there are headlands and bays, waves will tend to erode the outstanding masses and deposit sediments in the bays. There will be a tendency to straighten the coastline.

Cliff Rocks

The type of rocks which make up the cliffs and the way in which they dip are also important to cliff development. The unconsolidated glacial deposits are quickly eroded, while granite and other igneous rocks are not. Erosion will be rapid where layers of soft and hard rock alternate.

Where the strata are horizontal, high cliffs will develop. However, the sea will cut into the lower layers resulting in rock falls. Landslides will be common when the rocks dip towards the sea. Where there are clay layers overlain by other well-jointed

rocks, even more spectacular slides will result.

A well-jointed rock offers many opportunities for the development of various land forms. Sometimes the sea will force its way into the joints and attack a line of weakness to the surface. When the sea rushes in it will appear like a fountain some yards inland from the cliff edge. Such features are called blow-holes. Collapse will create a very narrow steep-sided inlet.

Caves often develop in the bases of cliffs. These sometimes partially collapse to form arches which in the end are reduced to just a single lump of rock called a stack. Where hills and valleys run parallel to the sea coast the underlying rocks are often alternately hard and soft. Should the sea break through the outer hard layer it will quickly erode the soft rocks and create coves.

Tidal currents and waves remove the shattered rock material. When the waves reach the shore at right angles,

a number of shingle ridges will be produced. The one nearest to the land will be made up of the largest pebbles and may well only be added to during storms. Where the waves hit the shore at an angle, the sand and shingle will gradually move along the beach. In such cases, where man has erected wooden fences out into the sea, it will tend to pile up the beach on the windward sides.

Mention has already been made of the building of deposits in bays. If material is drifting along the shore a sand and shingle ridge will be built up. Such spits may also develop across the mouth of rivers. In such cases the river may be diverted and run parallel to the sea for many miles before being able to enter it.

Where the sea-level relative to the land is changing, two types of coast will result. These are called coasts of emergence or submergence. In the former case the old line of cliffs is eventually found some way inland and it will have on the seaward side a raised beach. Submergent coasts are characterised by drowned valleys. These deep inlets provide excellent harbours. When highland regions are submerged high cliffs will result.

The Work of the Wind

Almost everyone has witnessed the action of the wind. After a long dry spell even light winds will whip up dust from roads and pavements and make walking unpleasant. In the fields, a long dry spell after ploughing often results in the wind moving quantities of the smaller particles of soil. In some regions of the world whole areas have been devastated because of poor farming methods. The great plains of the United States were particularly affected by this action in the 1930s. Other areas have also suffered erosion by wind action when forests were cut down and the soil exposed. Once attacked by the wind the loose earth is also subject to rapid gullying by stream and river action.

In many areas where such erosion has occurred, great efforts are now being made to reclaim the land. In some areas in Turkey where over-grazing was the initial cause of the break-up of the soil, dunes 6–9 metres (20–30 feet) high had built up and were threatening the good agricultural land which remained. Windbreaks made of canes bound together with wire were erected. Rye grass and about 3 million trees were planted and to supply the necessary water wells were sunk.

Desert Winds

Wind action is most noticeable where the climate is dry, and it is not surprising therefore that it is in the deserts of the world that the best examples of wind-made landscapes occur. Even so, in performing its task, wind will carry the smallest particles of dust for many miles. Dust particles have a diameter of less than 0·06 millimetres. Winds blowing from North Africa are often laden with such minute debris and it frequently falls over southern Europe and has even been known to reach England. There are sand dunes on the Canary Islands which are completely made up of sand from the Sahara. In America dust from the western states has been deposited in the east. Other deposits are built up in the areas adjacent to the main deserts.

The smallest of the particles can be moved easily by the wind. The larger sand grains, about 0·02 milli-metres in diameter, move by a series of leaps and bounds. A stronger gust will pick up quantities and as the wind loses velocity they will be dropped again to resume their journey at a later time. Air holds thousands of tons of dust. In a really large dust storm millions of tons will be moved. The wind's action is therefore selective. It can never, unlike a river or glacier, remove the larger pebbles or boulders, although when sand-laden it is able to act as an abrasive.

The wind acts most effectively a short distance above the ground. This is where the sand grains are carried and the effect is like that of sandpaper. During desert storms people have to protect themselves from the abrasive action of the wind. Telegraph poles in these regions of the world wear collars of metal at their bases or piles of stones and rocks

The dramatic effects of wind and rain erosion are shown in this picture of the Arches National Monument, a natural feature at Utah in the United States.

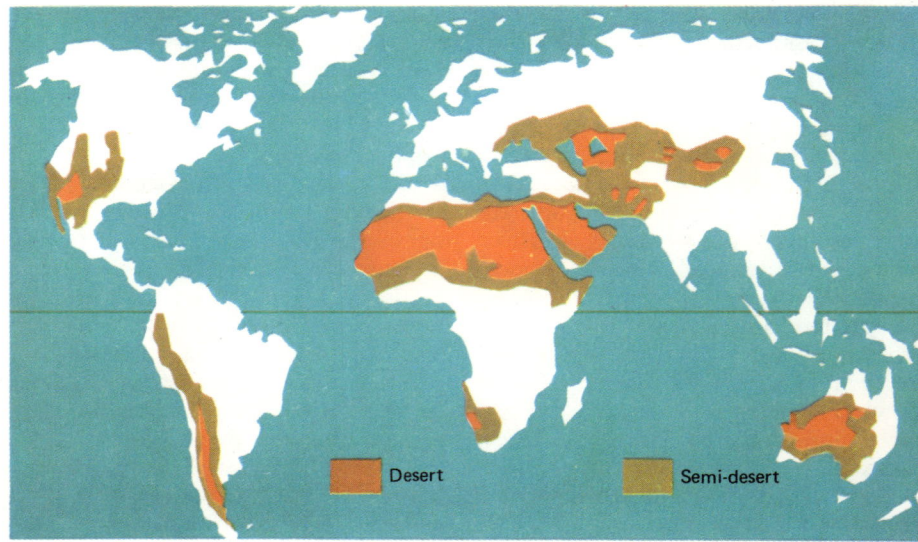

surround them to protect them against the cutting winds. Vehicles which traverse the arid regions frequently have their paint stripped off.

As the wind blows, it is constantly moving material and the tendency is gradually to lower the whole landscape. The only thing which can prevent the action continuing is when the water-table is reached. In desert areas this is often well below the ground. Once the water-table has been reached, however, the particles are bound together by the moisture. Vegetation will develop and also help in stabilising the soil or sand. This process of lowering is called deflation after the Latin word *deflare,* to blow away.

Many of the depressions of the deserts are due to such action by the wind. Perhaps the most famous is the Qattara depression to the west of Cairo which has been excavated to a depth of 128 metres (420 feet) below sea level. Many an oasis owes its origins to the wind cutting down to the water-table. Soft shales are the most likely rocks to be attacked by the wind. Other examples of depressions occur in Asia and South Africa.

Shaping the Landscape

The wind, either by removing material or depositing it, is responsible for creating three types of desert landscape. A rock desert is where the wind has removed all the sand and only the bare rocks remain, often much smoothed by the abrasive action of the wind. In some cases the smaller material is swept away leaving the larger stones and pebbles to create an appropriately named stony desert. Where deposition occurs a sandy desert will be the result.

The wind is a most effective sculptor where the barrier it hits is made of alternating layers of soft and hard rock. Bizarre shapes will be created particularly if the wind direction is fairly constant. It will also attack, as do other agents of erosion, any weakness in a rock, such as joint lines or cracks. Where the cementing medium of the rock is relatively soft, this will quickly be etched out and a honeycomb-like structure left. As the main action of the wind is near ground level, caves may be cut into the rock. Often pinnacles of rock are left. Where the capping rock is harder than that below, a mushroom shape is left.

The sand which is actually breaking up the rock face will also be broken and rounded. Sometimes the pebbles

left on the desert floor are packed close together. The continuing action of the wind planes off the upper surface, leaving a desert pavement. Stones are often transformed into shapes which resemble Brazil nuts, that is, they are three-sided. These polished stones are called *dreikanter* (after a German word meaning three-sided).

Sand Dunes

Dunes are perhaps the best known features associated with the wind. Often on a beach the wind will pick up particles of dry sand near the high-water mark. If the prevailing direction of the wind is on-shore it will gradually move some of this material away from the coast and inland. Gradually the sand will pile up. Some is swept over the crest and comes to rest at the natural angle of repose on the other side. Coastal and sand dunes can reach heights of over 30 metres (100 feet). If they are allowed to march inland unmolested they can cause considerable damage. There are cases known where houses have been overwhelmed by the advancing sand, only

In desert areas the wind is constantly changing the appearance of the landscape. The extent to which it does this varies with the hardness of the rock below the sand. Dunes which the wind moves slowly forward with points leading are called barchan dunes (left). Stronger winds will blow sand along in reverse crescents (1 and 2 above) or in longitudinal ridges (3).

Seen through a microscope loess deposits are revealed as individual particles averaging 0·025 millimetres in diameter.

In order to stop the advance of dunes in coastal areas, bent or marram grass (above) is planted to bind the soil together.

to reappear years later as ruins when the dunes have passed on their way.

In some places the dunes stretch inland for up to 8 kilometres (5 miles). In order to stop the advance bent or marram grass is planted, fences erected and trees planted. In countries with very well defined dry seasons dunes may form when the rivers dry up. If the valley is sufficiently wide the sand will be scooped up from the river bed and piled on the surrounding land.

The process of dune formation is very complicated and relies on a number of factors including the site of accumulation, direction of the wind and its force, size of the sand grains and the rate of erosion. Nevertheless dunes of 430 metres (1,410 feet) have been recorded in Algeria. Desert dunes originate when the wind is forced to drop some of its load. The heap gradually grows with the windward face building into a long slope in contrast to the relatively steep leeward face. The sand is swept up the incline, topples over the crest and comes to rest on the other side. There is therefore a constant movement forwards. Where the prevailing direction of the

wind is relatively constant the lower sides of the dune offer less resistance and tend to move forward at a faster rate than the higher central part. This leads to a crescent-shaped dune, called a barchan. Often the surface between the dunes is swept clear of sand. This is because the eddies, which are set up in the air currents climbing the dunes, tend to pull the sand particles on to the dune's windward slope.

The width of such dunes rarely exceeds 30 metres (100 feet) and they move forward at a rate of about 6 metres (20 feet) per annum.

Where the wind blows from several directions barchans will not develop and the result is long ridges of sand.

Loess Deposits

A very special type of wind deposit is called loess (from the German word for loss) in the western world and yellow earth in China. The Chinese name originates from the fact that one of its mightiest rivers, when flowing through the region of very fine deposits, carries so much in suspension that it appears yellow in colour. Hence the names yellow earth, and Yellow River.

Although best developed in China where deposits 90 metres (295 feet) thick are known, loess is widely distributed throughout the world, being found in North and South America, North Africa and central Europe.

The unique feature of loess is the diameter of the individual particles which average only 0.025 millimetres, making it as fine as talcum powder. It is made up mainly of quartz (60–70 per cent), carbonates (10–20 per cent) and clay minerals (10–20 per cent). The smallness of the particles has caused considerable discussion in geological circles and an extra-terrestrial origin was even suggested.

For many years it was considered that the origin of loess was in the deserts of the world. Although in many respects this would seem correct, it cannot account for the small size of the grains. The only forces capable of grinding material so small are the glaciers, and it would appear that a great deal of loess has originated from this source. When the ice melted the loess has been removed from the material deposited.

Violence from the Past

The reminders of past violence are not only contained in the scenery but also in the records of casualties to human life and property. For example over 800,000 people died in the earthquakes in Shansi Province in China in 1556.

As we shall see, volcanic activity has affected almost all of the Earth's surface at some time in the past. Reminders of this activity still linger on in some dramatic landforms. Many of these areas look so much like the surface of the Moon that they have acquired such names as the 'Craters of the Moon' and 'Moon Land'.

(Above) A chapel in France built high up on top of the hardened plug of an old volcano.

The Giant's Causeway in Northern Ireland formed from six-sided basaltic columns of once molten lava.

Perhaps the most famous area of recently extinct volcanoes is the Craters of the Moon area in the United States, covering 215 square kilometres (83 square miles) in Idaho. These are cone-shaped hills of cinder along with black barren wastes of lava. They were not violent eruptions which caused this landscape. Big Cinder Butte rises to 240 metres (800 feet) and is the highest, while Sunset Cone, Grassy Cone, North Crater Butte, Silent Cone, Crescent Butte and Fissure Butte all rise to a height of over 120 metres (400 feet).

Within this area 27 lava flows and some 35 vents have been located. Several vents would have been active at any one time and no doubt many others will have been buried under later lava flows. The craters are aligned along what is called the Great Rift. There are two main types of lava and both are represented in this area.

Types of Lava

Both of the types of lava surface are given Hawaiian names. Those which cool to ropy or pillow-like masses are called *pahoehoe*, while the jagged masses of broken blocks are known as *aa*.

Great caves and caverns are found in the *pahoehoe* flows. In some, notably Indian Tunnel, Great Owl Cavern and Buffalo Cave, lava stalactites have grown. Horizontal ridges on the walls of the tunnels show the levels of the lava which flowed through the tunnels, while the vertical ridges represent the last drops of lava which trickled down the wall. Roof collapses leave natural arches and bridges. Indian Tunnel Bridge has a height of 18 metres (60 feet) and a span of 23 metres (75 feet).

A similar landscape is found in the Canary Islands especially on Lanzarote. On this island alone there are 300 large crater mountains and many smaller ones. In some cases several are built on top of each other while others line up along cracks in the surface of the Earth. Some of the cones have been attacked by the agents of erosion, the water removing the unconsolidated material. The colours are black, grey and rusty brown. The north of the island has the largest lava-cave system in the world. The Cueva de los Verdes has a total length of 6·1 kilometres (3·7 miles) although in some places the roof has fallen in. Its height reaches 15 metres (48 feet) and the width 24 metres (78 feet).

Volcanic Eruptions

It is possible for whole islands to be removed during a volcanic eruption leaving just a ring of smaller islands. The mightiest eruption witnessed by man in recent years was that of Krakatoa which is situated in the Sunda Strait between Sumatra and Java. The

The Craters of the Moon in Idaho (inset left) compared with the true surface of the Moon (above).

The fall-out from an active volcano leaves behind a landscape covered by ash and cinders.

eruption blew away two-thirds of the island. Five times as great as this eruption was that of Santorini in the Mediterranean Sea. This eruption was thought to have caused the destruction of the great Minoan empire on Crete and gave rise to the legend of Atlantis.

Once the activity stops, the volcano will be attacked by the forces of erosion. What remains will depend on what the volcano is made of. Where the majority of the mountain consists of lava flows it will offer considerable resistance. In many other types of volcano, however, both lava and fragmented rock material goes to form the cone and these will be attacked more easily. Smaller volcanoes are built up of ash and other loose material, but without the addition of lava they do not reach more than about 450 metres (1,500 feet) in height, and are quickly broken down.

Plugs and Plateaux

A particularly resistant part of a volcano is the lava which may solidify as a plug in the main conduit. The wind, rain, frost and snow gradually wear away the surrounding hill, which may well be made of very loose material which is easily removed. An example of an old volcanic plug now standing out as a hill on its own is the Ship Rock in New Mexico, which is 500 metres (1,640 feet) high. A similar example from Nigeria is the Wase Rock. In France in the Auvergne district of the Massif Central many chapels and castles are built on volcanic plugs. The plugs and small volcanic cones in this area are called puys. Many of them, like the one on which the chapel of St Michel d'Aiguille, Le Puy is built,

stand up like fingers in the landscape. This particular puy is 89 metres (290 feet) high and the chapel was built in the eleventh century.

There are many remnants of once great lava fields. In Scotland various hills around Glasgow and Edinburgh are all that remain of the great carboniferous lava out-pourings. In Glencoe, hills called 'The Three Sisters' are composed of lava which flowed 370 million years ago.

Eruptions from fissures have created lava plateaux. In southern India, the Deccan is made up of flow upon flow of lava which advanced over the land in early Tertiary times. Today some 260,000 square kilometres (100,000 square miles) are left of the lava which once covered twice this area. In South America and Parana basalts which are of Jurassic age are in parts more than 3,000 metres (10,000 feet) thick. The lavas of the Columbia and Snake River Plateau which cover parts of Washington, Oregon, Idaho, Nevada and California have an area of about 520,000 square kilometres (200,000 square miles). They are of Miocene to recent age. Great mountains were buried under these mighty lava flows which in places are more than 1,820 metres (6,000 feet) deep.

Great Tertiary outpourings of lava formed the vast plateau of the north stretching from Scotland, through Northern Ireland, the Faroes, Iceland and away westward to Greenland.

The wrecks of some of the volcanoes which contributed to this plateau are to be found in Mull, Ardnamurchan and Skye in Scotland, while areas such as Iceland are still active. The depth of the lava has been measured in some

placed it. Further activity on the floor of the lake has given rise to a new cone which now pokes its head through the waters and is called Wizard Island.

In the Eifel region of Germany a number of formerly explosive vents are to be found. Long silent, they are thought to have been places where hot steam and gases spurted into the air, for little or no debris is to be found nearby. Many have become filled with water. The name maar (lake) has been applied to these but it should really be used for all such circular holes, no matter where they are found or whether or not they contain water. Other maars are found in New Zealand, the Philippines and Italy.

Not all the magma which wells up towards the surface of the Earth pours out as lava. Some of it solidifies a long way below ground. Some ends up as a volcanic plug. Maybe years of erosion will wear away all the overlying rocks and even the deepest seated intrusions will be revealed.

When magma forces its way between the layers of rock a sill is formed. In northern England the Great Whin Sill is a prominent feature on which part of Hadrian's Wall is built. Sills vary in thickness from a few centimetres to many metres. Perhaps the magma cools as wall-like masses. These are called dykes and again vary in thickness from centimetres to hundreds of metres. Some dykes stretch for several hundred kilometres and are at certain points very wide. Erosion of the surrounding softer rocks often leaves dykes as upstanding masses.

Laccoliths and Batholiths

Other features associated with such activity are laccoliths and batholiths. The former are formed when the upper surface of the magma bulges upwards. In the United States, the La Sal Mountains in Utah are almost entirely made up of laccoliths, and many are also found in the Henry Mountains of Utah. Very large masses of cooled magma are batholiths. These often form the core of mountain ranges and it takes millions of years for them to become exposed at the surface.

Earthquakes also affect the landscape but the results of their activity are quickly annihilated by the action of weathering. Landslides also leave their mark but again water and wind soon alter them. Both of these forces can, however, cause the damming of valleys and the development of lakes as well as causing considerable loss of life and damage to property.

places as 1,820 metres (6,000 feet). Perhaps the most famous feature of this great area of lava which can still be seen are the gigantic columns of basalt. Their hexagonal shape is due to contraction during cooling. They make up the Giant's Causeway and Fingal's Cave on the Isle of Staffa.

Craters and Calderas

On the top of many volcanoes is a depression, called a crater. In vulcanology the term crater is usually reserved for the smaller depression: larger depressions are called calderas.

In Japan there are depressions which have widths of up to 27 kilometres (17 miles) while in North Africa they range in size from 6·5–18 kilometres (4–11 miles). In Sumatra a great depression occupied in part by Lake Toba, is over 95 kilometres (60 miles) long. In Oregon in the United States is the most famous caldera, now filled with water, called Crater Lake. The original volcano called Mount Mazama was 3,650 metres (12,000 feet) high but during a mighty eruption much of this was removed and a caldera 9·6 kilometres (6 miles) in diameter re-

The Anatomy of the Earth

Some 4,900 million years ago the Earth-to-be was encased in a gaseous envelope.

The origin, shape and age of the Earth have provided the basis for discussion throughout historical time. The origin of the Earth is that of the solar system, the planets and the Sun. Many theories have been suggested.

In the early years they were very speculative and involved the act of a god. However, even some of the early theories included aspects of thought and imagination which now seem to be correct. With the increasing knowledge of the universe and in particular of the Earth's satellite the Moon, it should become possible to come to a better understanding of the origins of our world. The origin of the Earth cannot be investigated as a laboratory experiment, for one could not be conducted on such a grand scale. At present it is only possible to check the various theories against the known laws of physics and dynamics.

Immanuel Kant (1724–1804) published in 1755 a little book which provided the idea of the evolution of the solar system from a gaseous mass. The theory of Pierre Simon, Marquis de Laplace (1749–1827) added to that of Kant. The Laplacian gaseous nebula hypothesis, as it became known, was generally accepted in the nineteenth century. It assumes that the Sun, planets and satellites were all once part of a glowing and rotating mass. In 1904 T. C. Chamberlin (1843–1928) and F. R. Moulton (born 1872) published their Planetesimal Theory which was based on the dominant form of nebula known to exist, the spiral nebula.

For many years it was considered that the production of a planetary system was a rare event since there would seem to be little chance of two stars passing each other at the required distance in the void of space. Once the immense age of the system was discovered, it was also realised that many stars might have systems of planets around them.

Gradually it has been assumed that an extension of the theories of Kant and Laplace provides the most likely clues to the origin of the Earth. In general the idea of a cold origin is favoured. According to this theory the mass, or nebula, consists of gas and dust. This vast revolving mass is hot enough in the central part for various thermonuclear reactions to take place which lead to the formation of the Sun. The surrounding mass condenses into the planets. Such clouds have been located in space, some of which are in the process of forming new stars.

The Earth's Age

Just as the origin of the Earth has fascinated man so has its age been the cause of heated discussion. The most precise, if inaccurate, date must be that given in the sixteenth century by Archbishop James Usher who set an exact time for the origin of the Earth as the year 4004 B.C. Various civilisations have made attempts to calculate the age of the Earth. The astrologers of the Babylonian empire thought that man first appeared on Earth 500,000 years ago, whereas the Chaldeans believed the Earth to have emerged from chaos about 2 million years ago. The Brahmins of India considered the Earth to be eternal.

With increasing geological knowledge it became apparent that the Earth must have taken a considerable time to evolve. Hermann von Helmholtz (1821–94) suggested that it was 68 million years old. He arrived at this figure by studying the original temperature of the Earth and its rate of cooling.

Other ideas based on the cooling of molten rocks gave different results. K. G. Bischof (1792–1870) had melted lumps of basalt and then observed their cooling rates. He reached the conclusion that the Earth must be

The atmosphere around the Earth was formed about 4,400 million years ago.

The violent eruption of the volcano Paracutin in Mexico seen at night. The lava peak grew to 137 metres (450 feet) in only two weeks.

Antoine Henri Becquerel discovered radioactivity in 1896.

Four types of rock, pitchblende, orangite, orthoclase and torbernite used in radioactive dating.

about 350 million years old. It was Lord Kelvin (1824–1907) who thought that the Earth was not less than 20 million or more than 400 million years old and favoured a figure of about 100 million years.

Gradually the age of the Earth has been pushed back. Using the most modern methods available, it is now assumed that it was formed 4,600 million years ago.

The name given to the study of methods of dating is geochronology, and geologists recognise two types. One is called relative dating. This as its name suggests, means correlating one rock with another. It does not give an exact age. The other type of dating, which is very much more dramatic, is absolute dating. In this case an age, often in millions of years, is given for a particular rock or fossil.

Relative dating is of more use to geologists and archaeologists than absolute dating. Over many years of investigation geologists have built up a knowledge of the fossil content of the various rocks. In some rocks certain animals, such as trilobites, graptolites and ammonites, are used to identify the various zones. Many of the divisions of the Jurassic system are named after various types of ammonites. Each division is characterised by a particular animal or group of animals which do not occur in the rocks above or below. By studying the fossil content of the rocks it is possible to correlate them on a world-wide scale.

The Tools of Early Man
The same type of dating takes place in archaeology, using the tools made by early man. There have been so many excavations and such a wealth of material has been collected that many museums have large reference collections of tools. When a new discovery is made, as soon as tools are found it is possible to date them relatively. As an example flint tools become increasingly refined the more modern the site. The earliest ones were rough and ill-shaped, while later, flaking went all round the edges of the flint giving the typical pear-shape. Later still edges

were straighter. Therefore even if the human bones discovered are fragmentary it should be possible to assign the find to a definite culture.

There are other methods which are helpful in establishing a relative date for the various finds. Particularly useful to the archaeologist are the pollen grains and spores found in many sediments. The study of these has become a subject in its own right and the person who undertakes such work is called a palynologist. By examining the pollen grains and spores it is possible to deduce the type of vegetation which grew at a particular time. As the growth of plants is dependent on the climate, it is possible to interpret the climatic conditions which existed.

Again of value to the archaeologist is the use of fluorine analysis. Because the fluorine content of water varies it cannot be used for absolute dating. However it can be used to discover whether or not all the bones found at one site have been there for the same amount of time. If all of them have, they will have absorbed the same amount of fluorine.

This method is particularly useful in testing material in which a fraud or hoax is suspected. It was by using this method that the Piltdown Man hoax was uncovered. This fragmentary skull 'discovered' in 1912 was long believed to be of the oldest human species found in Europe until proved a fraud in 1953.

Nitrogen may be used in the same way as fluorine, except that instead of absorbing nitrogen, bones tend to give it up as they age.

Dating Deposits
An early method of absolute dating

The study of tree rings is called dendrochronology. The growth rings show annual growth and can also give information about past climates.

The inside of the Earth can be divided into layers. First there is the crust, a thin skin of rock.

Next is the mantle, possibly a reservoir of molten matter, a layer of very hard rock about 2,900 kilometres (1,800 miles) thick.

Then there is the outer core, probably made up of nickel and iron in liquid form, about 2,100 kilometres (1,300 miles) thick.

Finally comes the inner or centre core, a ball of immensely hot liquid iron and nickel about 2,600 kilometres (1,600 miles) in diameter.

was to use the deposits which built up on lake floors. The main idea was to estimate the time which had passed since the last ice sheet had retreated from northern Europe. The layers of the sediment in the lake are rather like the rings of a tree in that they show alternations between the seasons. In the summer the rivers ran quickly, bringing down vast quantities of sediment to be deposited in the lake. In winter, when the ground was frozen, little or no material reached it. It was therefore possible to count the layers and arrive at a figure for the passing

of the ice. The result of this calculation was 8,500 years. Later figures based on a radio-carbon dating gave 11,000 years.

Another method, although mainly concerned with the recent past, is the study of tree rings. This is called dendrochronology. The growth rings show not only the annual growth but may also provide clues to the past climate. Many of the larger museums have a massive tree-trunk in cross-section. By counting the rings important dates in history can be positioned and noted on the tree section.

A well-known method of absolute dating is that which uses radiocarbon. Carbon dioxide in the atmosphere contains radioactive carbon-14. This is generally absorbed into living plants and into the animals which feed on them. Once the animal or plant is dead no more radioactive carbon can be taken in. In fact after death the amount of radioactive material in once-living matter declines at a rate which is known. For example, after 5,568 years only half the carbon-14 remains. This figure is called the half-life of carbon-14. By measuring the quantity of radioactive carbon in the remains of an animal or plant it is possible to discover its age.

The method can be used to date remains which are up to 70,000 years old, but it is more reliable and requires less specialised equipment when dealing with material which is not older than 40,000 years.

Radioactive Rocks

Rocks which contain radioactive elements decay at known rates. It was Ernest Rutherford (1871–1937) who first used this knowledge to date rocks. He dated a specimen of pitchblende (a volcanic rock) as being 700 million years old.

The uranium-238 contained in a specimen is radioactive and gradually decays to lead. It has a half-life of

Continental Crust   Oceanic Crust

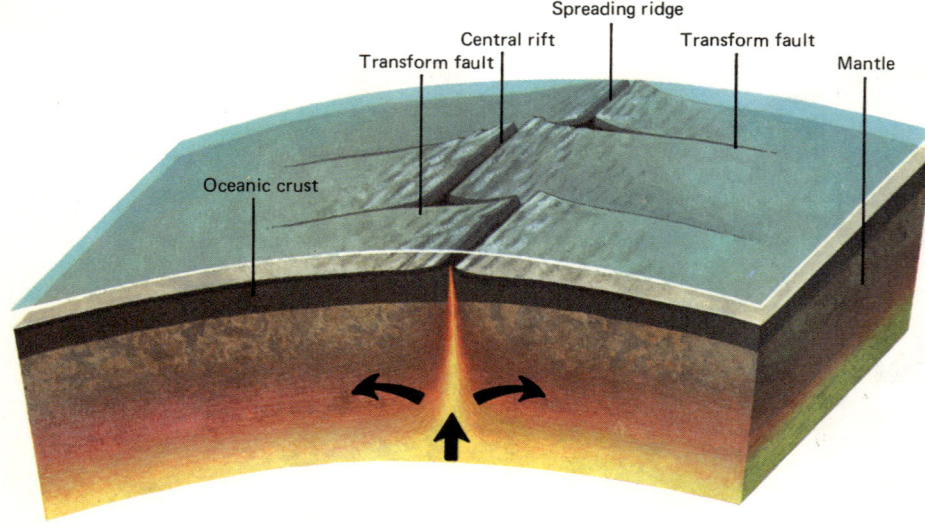

In studying the formation of the oceanic crust it has been found that it is above the ocean ridges where the greatest flow of heat comes from the inside of the Earth. Here new material is added to the ocean floor.

4,510 million years. It was by measuring the ratio of lead to uranium in the specimen that Rutherford calculated its age.

Another method of dating is based on the decay of the radioactive isotope potassium-40 into the gas argon. The isotope occurs naturally in potassium. The half-life of this is 1,350 million years. It has been used to determine the age of some of the oldest rocks. Because volcanic rocks provide material which is particularly suitable for analysis by this method, it has been useful in dating the rocks of Olduvai Gorge in East Africa where so many specimens of early man have been discovered.

The study of fission tracks is one of the newest methods of absolute dating. When radioactive material decays it splits up. This is called fission. As the particles shoot off they leave tracks, called fission tracks. By using certain acids on a specimen of rock and viewing it under a microscope, it is possible to count the tracks. By subjecting the specimen to X-ray bombardment it is then possible to calculate its age.

Below the Crust
We cannot see inside the Earth. All our knowledge of what lies below the crust has been gained by methods other than direct observation. One of the earliest of such observations was that the temperature increases with depth. Away from the areas of volcanic activity the average increase in temperature is 30°C. per kilometre. In some areas it has been found to be as low as 9° to 10°C. per kilometre. It also

differs with different types of rocks. It increases quickest in the soft shales and slowest in rocks like granite.

Most of the measurements on temperature increase have been made in mines. At a depth of 3,288 metres (10,788 feet) in a Transvaal mine the temperature is about 51°C. In the deepest well ever sunk, in Oklahoma in the United States, the temperature at the bottom of the 9,159 metres (30,050 feet) boring was 214°C.

Some idea of the interior of the Earth may be gained from the density. The average density of the planet is 5·5 but it has been calculated that the crustal rocks have an average density of only 2·8. The rocks beneath the crust must therefore be much heavier. Density is the term used to describe the closeness with which the particles of a substance are packed. It is measured by comparison with water with a density of 1·0.

There was an idea of American origin to bore through the crust of the Earth into the next layer, called the mantle. This project was known as the Mohole. The idea was abandoned in 1966 through lack of funds. However, during the initial work much experience was gained in the sinking of bores in deep water. This was extremely valuable to the project which followed the Mohole. This was the Deep Sea Drilling Project, launched in 1966 and still going on. A highly sophisticated and well equipped vessel, the *Glomar Challenger* was constructed. The aim of the investigations is to discover the history of the oceans. The vessel can drill in water of up to 6,000 metres (19,700 feet) in depth and can take sample bores 1,000 metres (3,280 feet) below the ocean floor.

Earthquake Waves
It is by the study of the waves produced during earthquakes that most of the

Bogoslof Island is a volcanic island in the Aleutians.

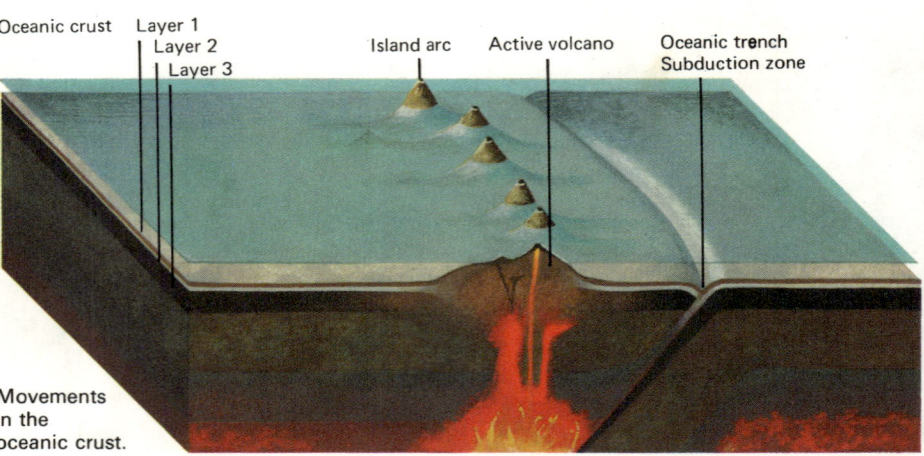

Movements in the oceanic crust.

information about the interior of the Earth has been obtained. Depending on the type of rock through which the waves pass, they may be speeded up or slowed down or bent or stopped altogether. When they are received again after their journey they are recorded on an instrument called a seismograph. By checking the records at several stations it is usually possible to find out exactly where the earthquake originated. By measuring the time taken for the waves to travel from one point of generation to the recording device, it is possible to learn something about the rocks which the waves have passed through.

Originally the instruments used were not sufficiently sensitive to record all the data necessary for a detailed interpretation of the structure of the interior. The need to monitor underground nuclear explosions has led to new, highly sensitive seismographs and also the development of seismic arrays. Their impact on studies of the Earth have been similar to the impact of radio telescopes on astronomy.

Two main waves are generated by earthquakes which travel through the rocks. They are called P and S waves. The P (primary) waves are like sound waves and are able to be transmitted through both solids and liquids. The S (secondary or shear) waves cannot pass through liquids. The speed of both types of wave is affected by the properties of the rocks through which they pass. Particularly important are the density and elasticity of the rocks.

Although work had been carried out earlier, the first feature to be discovered, in 1909 was the change in rocks between the crust of the Earth and the

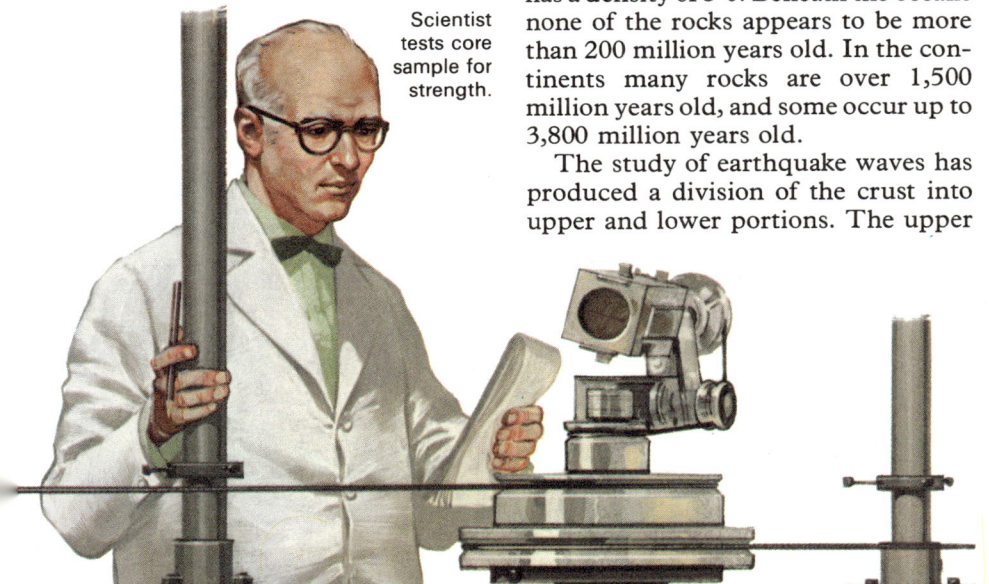

Scientist tests core sample for strength.

mantle. It was found by the Croatian seismologist Andrija Mohorovičić. To this day it bears his name as the Mohorovičić discontinuity or Moho for short. The next main division to be located was that between the mantle and the core. This was based on the time taken for the P waves to reach the

The Mohole project was an attempt to drill through the crust of the Earth under the sea to the next layer.

recorder. It was calculated that the boundary between the mantle and core was at a depth of about 2,900 kilometres (1,800 miles). S waves have not been recorded for at least 2,000 kilometres (1,240 miles) below the boundary with the core. It is therefore suspected that the outer part of the core, at least, is liquid.

The major divisions of the Earth were thus established. Further investigations have led to sub-divisions and a much greater knowledge of each of the layers.

Depth of the Crust

The crust of the Earth varies greatly in depth. Under the oceans it is only about an average of 6 kilometres (3·7 miles), while under the land masses it is an average of 35–40 kilometres (21–25 miles) and even reaches a depth of 60–70 kilometres (37–43 miles) under the very high mountain ranges. The average density of the upper part of the crust is 2·7 while the lower part has a density of 3·0. Beneath the oceans none of the rocks appears to be more than 200 million years old. In the continents many rocks are over 1,500 million years old, and some occur up to 3,800 million years old.

The study of earthquake waves has produced a division of the crust into upper and lower portions. The upper

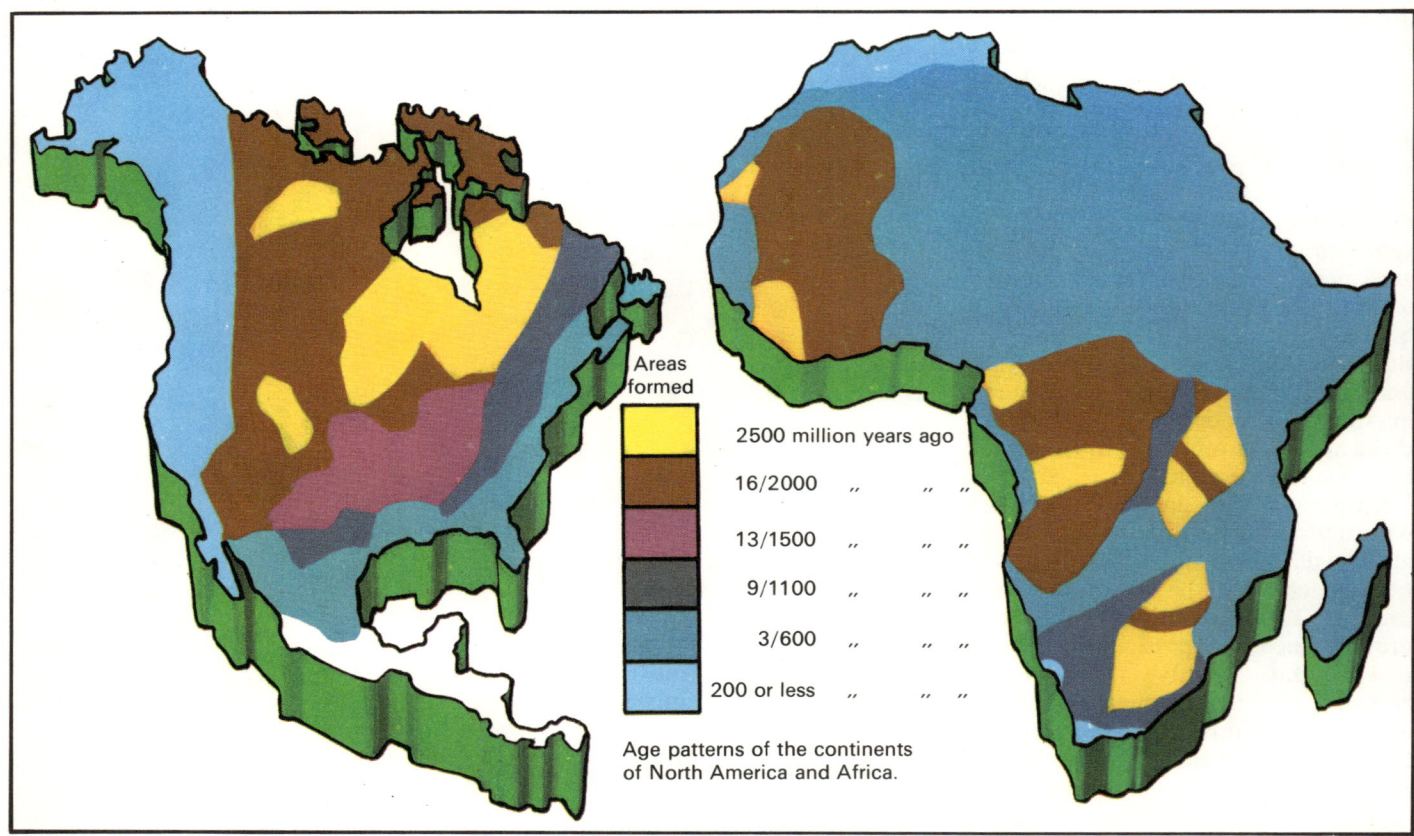

consists mainly of granite-like rocks with some sediments. The layer below, which is not well known, would appear to be basaltic. The crust beneath the oceans, unlike that below the continents, is of simple structure. The uppermost layer consists of unconsolidated sediments which are in turn underlain by consolidated deposits with solidified lava flows and a much denser rock which leads down to the Moho.

It would appear that the various parts of the crust are floating rather like rafts on water. One way of describing this is to imagine blocks of wood of different sizes floating in water. The larger blocks will float with their bottoms deep into the water, while the smaller and lighter ones will not sink so far. Somewhere below the surface there will be a point at which the pressure is equalised. Perhaps in the case of the Earth this layer is within the mantle.

It could be argued that there can be no such layer from the interpretation of the earthquake waves, as the S waves have not been prevented from passing through. It is now thought that there is a layer within the mantle which acts as a solid to the short, sharp earthquake waves but behaves as a liquid to the persistent and constant forces taking place over long spans of time—rather as sealing-wax will bend if left

unsupported. The confirmation of such a layer has been made by a detailed examination of the earthquake waves. This plastic layer about 100–200 kilometres (60–100 miles) below the surface was first suggested in 1926. Although it took a long time for its existence to be confirmed, such a layer is suggested by volcanic eruptions, the rate of increase in temperature and the idea of a point of equal pressure. It is now also thought that this layer may allow the movement of the great masses of the Earth's crust.

The Mantle and Core
The mantle is made of a rock called peridotite. It is essentially solid and its density ranges from 3·3 to 6·7 and the temperature from 600°C. to 2,500°C. It stretches to about 2,900 kilometres (1,800 miles) and the pressure at this depth is 1,400 kilobars.

Even though it might be possible one day to examine the rocks of the mantle—indeed geologists think they have discovered mantle rocks in at least four parts of the world—it is unlikely that samples of the core will ever be examined in the laboratory.

In order to understand the nature of the core, three main areas of investigation have been followed. By the study of meteorites, which are thought to be fragments of a shattered planet, information has been obtained about the

materials which make up the core.

The most profitable line of investigation has again been the detailed study of earthquake waves. It was, however, in experimental work that it was discovered that pure iron when subjected to the great pressures of the Earth's core had a 10–15 per cent greater density than the core of the Earth when interpreted by seismic observations. Further experimentation with an alloy of 90 per cent iron and 10 per cent nickel gave a result much nearer the one expected. This also agrees with the analysis of most of the meteorite fragments.

The core of the Earth consists therefore of iron and nickel. Further investigations have led to the conclusion that the centre of the core is solid with a density of about 13·5. It has a radius of about 1,216 kilometres (755 miles) which means that it is just a little larger than the moon. This solid core is surrounded by a transitional zone of about 500 kilometres (310 miles) followed by a liquid outer core of 1,700 kilometres (1,050 miles).

The pressure at the centre of the Earth has been calculated as 3,400 kilobars and at the upper boundary of the core as 1,400 kilobars. Estimates of the temperature of the core vary from 2,500 to 3,500°C., although the figure of 10,000°C. has also been quoted for the inner core.

Movements Large and Small

The Earth is constantly being attacked. The rocks are worn away by the action of the air, water and wind. Even so, the Earth is far from flat. Mountains tower to nearly 9,150 metres (30,000 feet) and the average height of the land is still 825 metres (2,707 feet) above the sea. Forces must therefore be at work which keep pace with the erosion of the rocks. Sedimentary rocks are laid down in layers and yet often when seen in quarries they are twisted and folded. What forces are at work to cause these movements?

Drifting Continents

It has been explained that the crust is kept in a state of balance and this will cause it to rise up when great weights have been removed, for example after the retreat of the ice of the last ice age. There are even greater forces at work. Forces that move whole sections of the Earth and cause the continents to drift.

A look at the map of the world shows how well the facing coastlines of Africa and South America would fit into each other if pushed together. It was in 1912 that Alfred Wegener (1880–1930) the German meteorologist and geodesist, first put forward his theory of continental drift. In 1915 came his book, *The Origin of Continents and Oceans.*

The theory was not at first accepted but gradually over the years, with increasing geological mapping, it became clear that there are links between the now widely separated land masses. The study of ancient life through fossils, again pointed to the fact that the continents had once been joined.

Techniques have been improved, and from the study of past climates and past magnetism, more data have been obtained. The result is always the same: there was a time when the continents—the Americas, Europe, Africa, India, Australia and Antarctica—were joined.

During upheavals of the Earth's crust rocks are subjected to vast strains causing fractures called faults (top). When rocks are folded into an arched shape the structure is called an anticline. When strata are folded to form a basin this is called a syncline (above).

A great land mass existed 200 million years ago, called Pangaea. By the end of Triassic times, about 180 million years ago, the continents had started to drift. To the north was the mass of Laurasia (North America, Europe and Asia), to the south Gondwana (which consisted of South America and Africa joined together, India separate and Australia and Antarctica joined). By Jurassic times, 135 million years ago, South America had started to break away from Africa and the South Atlantic Ocean was born.

Drifting continued until finally the continents assumed the positions we know today. But drifting has not stopped. The forces are still going on and in 50 million years from now the world may look different again. Geologists think that East Africa, to the east of the Great Rift Valley may have broken away. The Atlantic and Indian oceans will continue to grow and Australia will move northwards. The Arabian Peninsula will move north closing the Persian Gulf. Part of California and Lower California will cut itself away from North America and be taken northwards.

Ocean Ridges

The mechanics of the movement of the continents had long been regarded as impossible. However, just as meteorology had to wait for the development of the aeroplane in order to advance, so the theory of continental drift had to await a detailed survey of the oceans. Since the 1950s there has been an ever increasing interest in the oceans of the world. The great system of mid-oceanic ridges has been discovered and examined in some detail.

These ridges hold the key to the evolution of the oceans. It is above the ridges that there is the greatest flow of

It is now believed that the Earth's crust consists of a series of rigid plates which 'float' on top of the fluid mantle. Where plates meet, some are moving apart. Deep ocean trenches are formed when oceanic plate underlies a continental plate, forcing land upwards to form mountains.

as far as 100 kilometres (60 miles). This is as far as the layer of the mantle, which may be plastic and which could allow movement.

The creation of new oceanic crust takes place at the edge of the plates, which are gradually separating as new material is added. In contrast to these areas are the so-called subduction zones. Here plates meet, with the result that one plunges down below the other and is gradually eaten up as it passes into the mantle. It may well not be totally destroyed until it reaches a depth of almost 700 kilometres (430 miles). Sometimes plates meet and slide past each other.

If the world distribution of earthquakes and volcanoes is examined, it will be seen that they occur along these lines of activity, that is, along the margins of the plates. Both volcanoes and earthquakes are experienced in great numbers along the ocean ridges. Where one plate dives below another, the centres of the earthquakes are found to lie in an inclined plane, following the plate downwards. At these points both shallow and deep earthquakes are recorded.

Another feature of such a zone is the forcing upwards of material to create volcanoes and island arcs. Examples of the latter are the Kuriles and Aleutian Islands. Earthquakes, with their foci (points of origin) at shallow depths, are encountered where plates slide past one another. Those originating in the San Andreas fault zone in California are examples of this type.

One other type of earthquake is linked to plate movement. The collision of two plates, both carrying continental masses, can occur. One is forced down below the other, but the continental material is too light to be carried downwards, and it tends to bob up under the other mass. A great chain of mountains may be formed in this way and it is thought that the Himalayas are due to this type of activity. The Mediterranean and Black Seas may be remnants of a once much larger ocean. The earthquakes associated with these regions are all shallow ones and are due to the enormous forces of compression caused by the collision of the plates.

heat from the Earth and it is from them that new material wells up from the mantle and adds an average of 10 centimetres (4 inches) a year to the ocean floor.

To find proof of all these happenings much research has been devoted to the ocean ridges and surrounding ocean floors. It has been found that on either side of the ridge the rocks are older as their distance from the ridge increases. The youngest sediments are also found nearest to the ridge. The study of ancient magnetism (palaeomagnetism) on the basalts on each side of the ridge also reveals the same pattern.

A rift valley (seen in the picture and also in diagrammatic form) is formed when a section of the Earth's crust is forced downwards between two or more parallel faults.

number of plates. Some are very large, one covering almost all of the Pacific, while others are quite small. In all, there are not less than fifteen plates. Their thickness is not just that of the crust of the Earth for they stretch down

Plate Tectonics

It was the bringing together of the theories of continental drift and those concerning the spread of the sea floor which led to the theory of plate tectonics. This is the most up-to-date area of geology. Almost daily, and certainly weekly, new facts are published which have a bearing on this important phenomenon. The whole world is considered to consist of a

The collision of two plates carrying continental masses can occur.

Convection Currents

Although the theory of plate tectonics is now well established, much has still to be discovered about the mechanism of movements. Convection currents may offer the answer. These currents

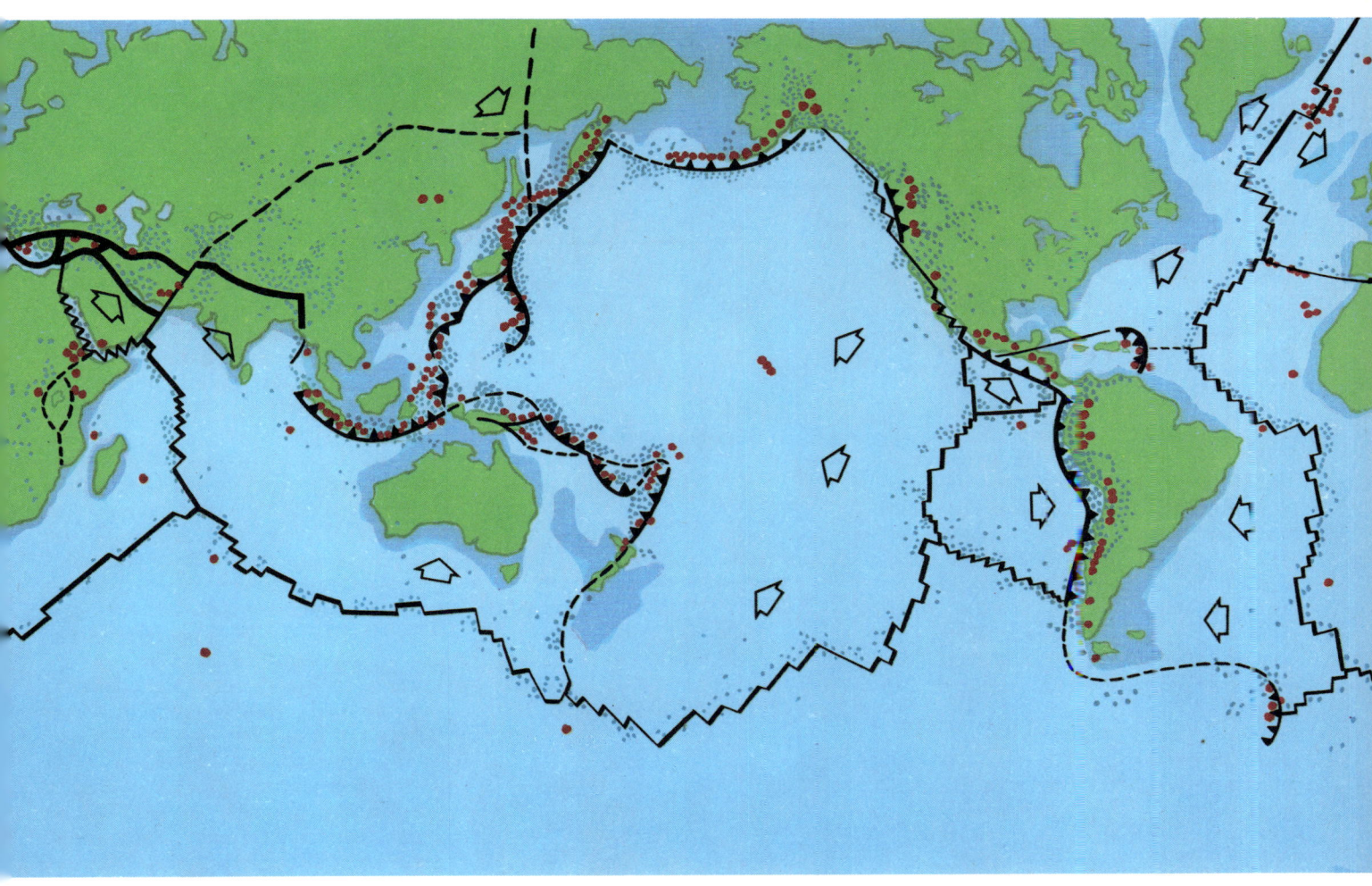

are set up because of the differences of temperature in the mantle. The lower layers are hotter than those above and this causes currents to rise upwards. These cool on reaching the upper part of the mantle and descend again. The result is a stirring action. The currents acting through the mantle's plastic are able to move the plates, and they will have different effects on the Earth according to whether they are rising or falling.

Where the current is rising there will be a tendency to split. This might be the case below the oceanic ridges, for the flow of heat from these points is high. Other interesting areas for this study are the Gulf of Arabia and the Red Sea. Here an ocean is thought to be in the making. This is an extension of the Indian Ocean ridge system and links also with the great rift valleys of eastern Africa. As we have already noted, it has been suggested that Africa, in the region of the rift valley, is being split. Again in Iceland, which sits astride the Atlantic ridge, there is evidence of splitting.

When the convection currents plunge downwards they would tend to anchor the overlying structures. They

The crust of the Earth is considered to consist of a number of plates, not less than fifteen. Some are very large and others quite small. The probable plate boundaries are shown by black jagged lines. It will be seen that where the plates meet, earthquakes and volcanoes (red and blue dots) occur. These are particularly common along ocean ridges and in such areas as the San Andreas fault zone in California. The continual movement of these plates over a long period of time will considerably alter the shape of today's map of the world.

would also tend to fold and raise the surface. Such movements would be very slow but they could account for the different features of the Earth's surface.

Folded Rocks

With all this activity it is easy to overlook smaller movements. Smaller, that is, in relation to the movements of the continents. However, some of the ways in which rocks are deformed are due to the movements of the larger masses.

When sedimentary rocks are first laid down the various beds are usually horizontal. The same will apply to most of the lava flows. Over vast periods of time the rocks are gradually

altered, in some cases being folded in, others fractured or faulted. In very stable areas of the crust very old rocks can still be found in which the beds are horizontal, just as they were when first laid down as sediments on the ocean floor.

When the rocks are folded into an arched shape the structure is called an anticline. The reverse of this, when the strata are folded to form a basin, is called a syncline. There are many different types of folding depending on the pressures which are put on the rock. Some are very small and others occupy many miles. In some cases the rock has been completely turned over.

Most of the great mountain systems are made up of folded rocks, although in many places the folds have become broken and great wrenches have occurred. The Alps, Himalayas, Rockies and Appalachians all show considerable degrees of folding.

During the process of manufacture and drying out many rocks develop cracks and joints. During upheavals of the Earth's crust, rocks are subjected to vast strains and may well fracture. Where it is possible to measure the

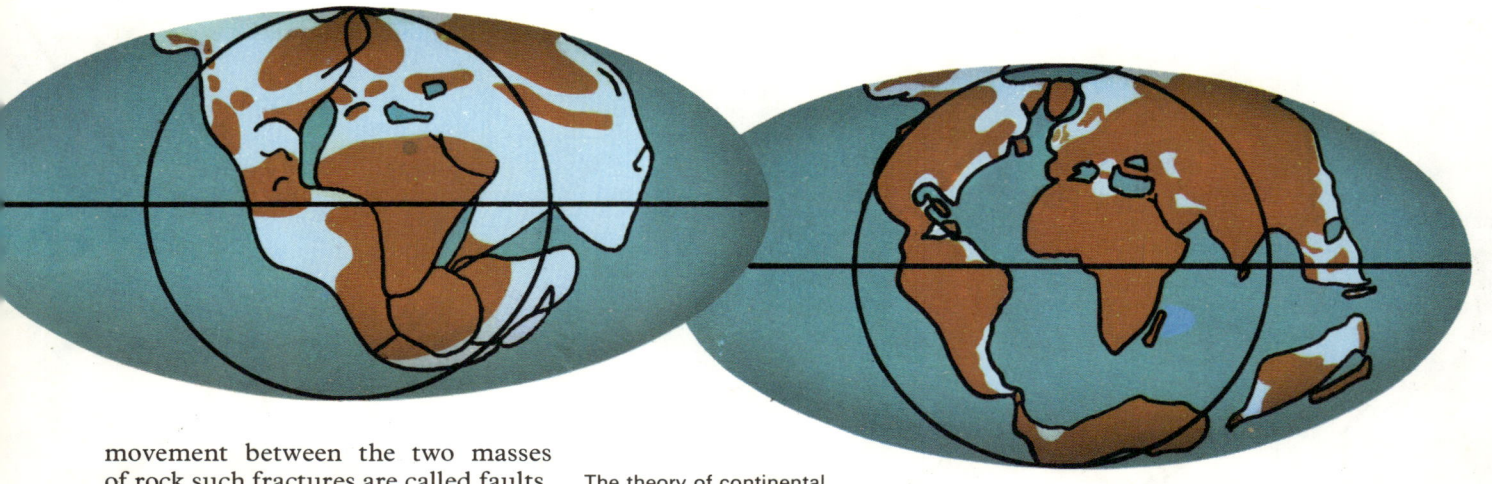

movement between the two masses of rock such fractures are called faults. Rocks may move horizontally or vertically. One mass may be moved horizontally many kilometres and vertical movements of thousands of metres are known. Movements along such active faults are often the cause of earthquakes. Some of the great faults, particularly those in which horizontal movements take place, are connected with the movements of the plates.

San Andreas Fault
Perhaps the most famous of these is

The theory of continental drift was put forward by the German scientist Alfred Wegener in 1915. It is now believed that all the continents were originally one land mass which various forces have pushed apart and which are still moving.

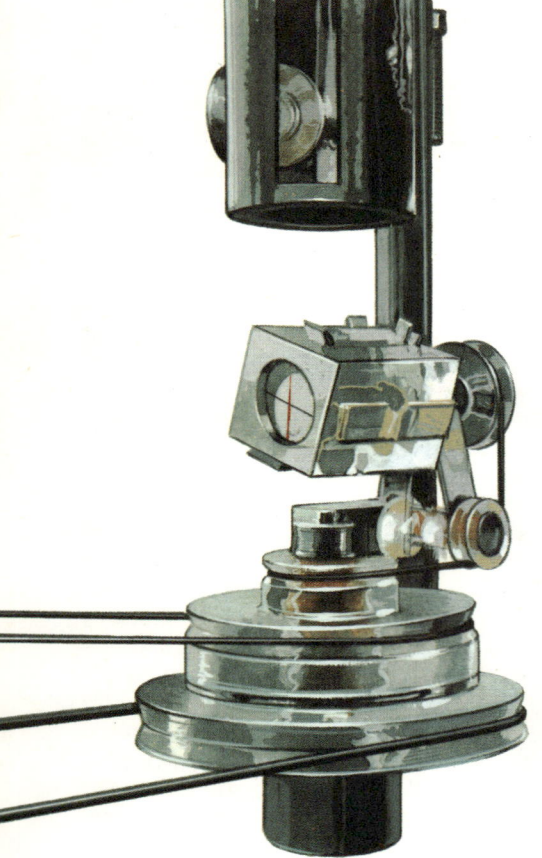

Astatic magnetometer, an instrument which measures the palaeomagnetic property of rocks.

The north magnetic pole appears to have drifted since Cambrian times. Its position and that of the continents have changed relative to each other and palaeomagnetic measurements of rocks suggest different pole paths.

the San Andreas fault which runs through California. It marks the edge of the Pacific plate. It was movement along this fault which caused the San Francisco earthquake in 1906.

Some of the major mountain ranges are made up of folded rocks, but faulting has also created mountains. The Vosges, Black Forest and Harz Mountains are all well known examples of horsts (raised blocks). In the United States the Wasatch Mountains in Utah and the Sierra Nevada in California are great faulted blocks. The Sierra Nevada is 640 kilometres (400 miles) long and 120 kilometres (75 miles) wide. The eastern scarp rises to over 3,900 metres (13,000 feet). Other typical horsts are the Little and Great Kharas Mountains in south-west Africa.

Just as faulting can make mountains so it can create valleys. Valleys which

result from the crust sinking down due to parallel faults are called rift valleys. These are sometimes connected with the evolution of the margins of plates. The best known rift valley is the one which runs from Jordan down through the Dead Sea and continues into East Africa. Its total length is about 3,000 miles and included in it are the lakes of East Africa. The valley ranges from about 35–37 kilometres (21–44 miles) in width and on either side are steep sides. Associated with it are many volcanoes, both active and dead. Earthquakes also occur in these regions.

The surface of the Earth is subject to constant change from above and even greater forces are pulling and tugging at the rocks beneath. New material is continually being added at the oceanic ridges, only to be consumed once again when one plate dives below another.

World of Activity

The constant changes and movement going on below the surface of the Earth manifest themselves above by earthquakes and volcanoes. In turn these cause landslides and tsunami (often wrongly called tidal-waves). All of these are very dangerous to man and his property.

The distribution of earthquakes and volcanoes is, as we have seen, related to the zones of weakness in the Earth. The study of the waves produced by the earthquakes has taught geologists much about the send masses of rock and gases high into the air. Lava will run over the sides and spread for many miles.

A typical volcano consists of a reservoir of magma, sometimes at a very shallow depth in the crust, and a pipe leading from this by way of which the magma reaches the surface. The summit may have a pit-like structure, called a crater. On the sides of the main cone there may be other smaller cones called parasitic cones. These may be erupting while only gases are being given off from the main vent. The way in which the magma originates is not yet fully understood. Magma is the name given to molten rock; lava is magma which reaches the surface. The plastic layer within the mantle has been thought to supply the volcano's magma reservoir at a shallower depth.

The magma contains gases and it is steam which is the main force in driving it to the surface. The type of eruption which occurs is governed by the make-up of the magma and its gas content. Where magma is very

The constant activity which goes on beneath the Earth's crust occasionally comes violently to the surface in the form of hurricanes and volcanoes and other acts of Nature which can be disastrous to man.

inside of the Earth, but still they are a long way from being able to control either the shaking of the Earth or the eruptions of the volcanoes.

Earth's Safety Valve

During the long history of the Earth almost all regions have been affected by volcanic activity. Their remains often form the well-loved scenic features of the present day. Volcanoes have been called the safety-valves of the Earth. A volcano is a point on the Earth's surface from which volcanic material is ejected. The name is also applied to the hill or mountain which is gradually built up around such a point. The volcano provides its own material for such a building operation.

Not all eruptions are by any means the same. Sometimes only gas is given off. At other times tremendous explosions with a roar like thunder

runny it escapes easily without any violent explosions. The reverse is true when the magma is sticky and will not yield. Here the gases force their way to the surface throwing lumps of the rock high into the air. Magma consists of the silicates (union of an oxide of a metal and silica) of potassium, sodium, magnesium, iron, calcium and aluminium. Gases include water as steam, carbon dioxide and monoxide, sulphur dioxide and hydrogen. Magmas which are rich in silica are called acid and are sticky and sluggish; the more basic ones (those with less silica) flow easily. The temperature of the magma varies between 700°C and 1,200°C.

Types of Eruption

Most of the volcanoes erupt through a central opening or vent. There are several types of eruption named after

A tsunami, a giant wave caused by an earthquake, threatens a coastal village in Japan.

Gray-Milne seismograph made in Glasgow in 1885. The tremors caused by an earthquake are recorded on rotating drums.

The longest earthquake on record is the Alaskan earthquake of 1964 when the shaking of the ground lasted for seven minutes. During an earthquake many injuries may be caused by falling masonry rather than by the earthquake itself.

who observed and lost his life in the eruption of Vesuvius in A.D. 79.

A different type of activity, although no less violent, produces clouds of hot gases which are heavily charged with droplets of lava. These clouds rush down the sides of the volcano. This type of eruption is called Peléan after Mount Pelée on Martinique. It was an eruption of this kind which killed 30,000 people in 1902.

Undersea eruptions provide some spectacular sights. Islands of volcanic origin have been known to appear and disappear again overnight. When one does become established, it provides scientists with a unique opportunity, not only to study an active volcano, but also to observe how plants and animals gradually colonise a new land area. The most famous recent example of the formation of an island is that of Surtsey, 20 miles off the south coast of Iceland. Iceland is well known for its intense volcanic activity, including not only volcanoes but also hot springs, geysers and boiling mud.

the various volcanoes. The Hawaiian type of eruption is characterised by the volcanoes of Hawaii which pour out masses of lava which spread over a wide area. Great cones are built up with lava lakes on the summit. The eruptions are quiet with few explosions.

A Strombolian eruption, named after Stromboli, north of Sicily (in the Lipari Islands) is where gases collect below the old solidified lava and other rocks and regularly burst forth. Stromboli has been called the lighthouse of the Mediterranean.

When the gases are released with a greater force than in the Strombolian eruption it is called Vulcanian, after Vulcano, another of the Lipari Islands.

An eruption similar to these but even more violent is called Vesuvian. Very gaseous magma is erupted and ash is distributed over a wide area. The most violent of these eruptions are called Plinian, after the great Pliny

Springs and Geysers

Other regions in which hot springs and similar features are found are in the United States, especially Yellowstone National Park, and in New Zealand. Often these aspects of volcanic activity have been wrongly interpreted as dying phases. Perhaps this is due to the fact that often nearby stands a long dormant volcano. Where only gases are emitted from the surface these vents are called fumaroles. The change in the gases often indicate a forthcoming eruption from a nearby volcano. Often chemical activity associated with these vents

gives rise to many deposits of various colours. Around the geysers great terraces are built up. The white colour is due to aluminium and ammonium chlorides, the orange to ferric chloride. The characteristic yellow heralding a sulphur deposit is unmistakable. Where the gases given off are mainly sulphurous the name given to a fumarole is solfatara. All of these events have the same origin. A mass of hot magma not too far below the surface provides the heat.

Hot springs are where water issues from the surface at a temperature higher than the annual mean temperature of the area. Not all hot springs owe their origin to the action of volcanoes. Some exist because of the great depths to which the water circulating in the rocks descends. Alteration of rocks around a spring may result in the formation of 'mud'. Thus arise the odd and grotesque plopping pools of hot or boiling mud.

Perhaps the most dramatic of these events are the geysers. Taking their name from the Great Geyser in Iceland (called Geysir) these eject great fountains of hot water into the air. A long channel, with many passages and cavities branching off, stretches down into the ground. The water gradually collects and is heated. The water becomes hotter and hotter and, if it were not for the pressure it is under, the water at the lower levels would boil. This superheated steam finds its way through cracks and eventually causes some of the water to boil. There is an overflow at the surface because of the rising steam. This causes a lowering of the pressure which changes the superheated water into steam and shoots it upwards.

The world's most famous geyser is Old Faithful in the Yellowstone National Park in the United States. Discovered in 1870, this geyser erupts every 37 minutes. The eruption lasts for about five minutes and the water is thrown 52 metres (170 feet) into the air.

Disaster Prevention

Geologists have long been convinced of the need to study continuously the activities of volcanoes. The Hawaii Volcano Observatory was established in 1911 and it has been in action ever since. The one on Vesuvius was created in 1847 and others exist in New Britain (Australia) and the Lesser Antilles (French). Japan has a National Centre for Disaster Prevention and there are other establishments in Russia.

Crater Lake in Oregon, in the United States is a volcanic relic caused by the collapse of the crater of Mount Mazama. The island in the centre is formed from a cinder cone.

It is only by closely monitoring their activities that scientists hope one day to be able to provide advance warning of volcanic eruptions.

Much has already been written about earthquakes. Every year there are approximately 500,000. Of these 100,000 can be felt by human beings and 1,000 cause some damage. Like the volcanoes they are linked to areas of activity and weakness within the crust and mantle. Sometimes, however, the movement of an old fault will cause an earthquake in an area which is otherwise stable.

The shaking of the ground during an earthquake lasts for less than a minute, although the longest on record is the Alaskan earthquake in 1964 in which movement lasted for seven minutes. Damage is caused to buildings, roads, railways and bridges. During an earthquake many people will be injured by falling masonry rather than by the quake itself.

By using an instrument called a seismograph it is possible to record the waves produced by the quake. There are two main types of wave which have already been described. By using the reports of a number of stations it is possible to locate the epicentre, or point on the Earth's surface directly above the source of the earthquake. The actual point of generation within the crust or mantle is called the focus.

The majority of earthquakes originate at quite shallow depths, less than 65 kilometres (40 miles), although they have been known to occur to depths of 650 kilometres (400 miles).

When an earthquake occurs under the sea there is a grave chance that it will set off a tsunami. Tsunami is a Japanese word for a storm-wave.

Erosion works upon the cone of a volcano until only the hard central plug remains.

These occur when the bottom of the ocean moves and displaces a large quantity of water. The waves created are very large, being 160–640 kilometres (100–400 miles) long but less than a metre or so high. They can pass under a ship without being felt. They travel at great speed, about 640 kilometres (400 miles) per hour.

On reaching the shore they are slowed down and an enormous wave results, which rushes onto the land causing considerable damage and loss of life. One wave 65 metres (220 feet) high was reported off Alaska during the 1964 earthquake, although lower heights are more common. Such waves can travel great distances. They have been known to cross the Pacific Ocean from one side to the other.

When an earthquake occurs in a mountainous region, landslides and avalanches can be generated. There was a considerable loss of life in Peru in 1970 during an earthquake which caused a large amount of snow and ice to slide down the valley, wiping out an entire village.

World of Water

Exploration of the oceans began in the 19th century with such voyages as those of James Clark Ross into Antarctica (1839–43) and the *Challenger* expedition of 1872–6. In modern times man has descended to the ocean depths in diving suits, submarines and deep-water craft such as the bathyscaphe.

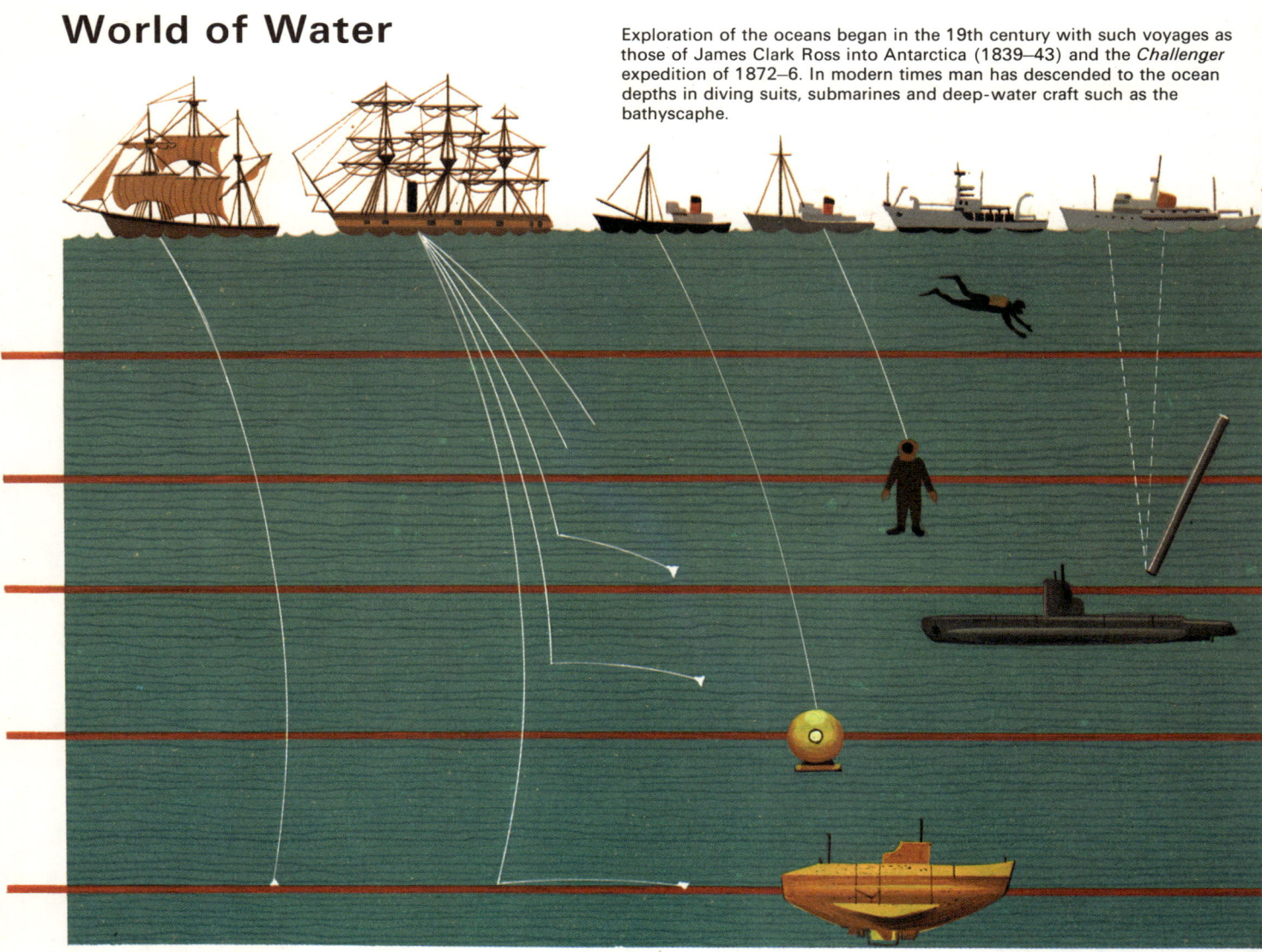

Water covers 71 per cent of the Earth's surface. The largest ocean is the Pacific with an area of approximately 164,500,000 square kilometres (63,800,000 square miles). The volume of the oceans is estimated at about, 1,285,458,000 cubic kilometres (308,400,000 cubic miles) and the mean depth is about 3,650 metres (12,000 feet). The oceans have points deeper than the highest mountains.

A number of claims have been made for the deepest point of the sea. They are based mainly on the study of the Mariana Trench off the island of Guam. It was in 1959 that the Russian research ship recorded a depth of 11,030 metres (36,200 feet). Figures in this same region, of 9,810 metres (32,190 feet) and 10,860 metres (35,640 feet) have been recorded by Japanese and British research vessels. In January 1960 the bathyscaphe *Trieste* descended to a depth of 10,900 metres (35,800 feet). It took two crew members Jacques Piccard and Donald Walsh, four hours forty-eight minutes to reach the bottom and three hours seventeen minutes for the return.

Oceanography

The science of the seas and oceans is called oceanography. It involves scientists from many fields of research, including chemists, geologists, meteorologists, botanists and zoologists. Many nations have for centuries relied on their knowledge of the sea for their prosperity. The oceans are in many ways closely connected with the land masses, not least through the rivers and shallow coastal waters. Man has always been affected by the oceans and the oceans in turn have a great effect on the world, regulating climate and supplying the vast reservoirs of water which eventually provide the rain and snow.

In the past man's only interest in the oceans was concerned with matters having a direct effect on his ships, for example, the tides and currents. In shallower waters he also needed to locate sandbanks and rocks. The measurement of distance was also important. Despite this limited interest, however, even by the fourth century B.C., a book had been written by Aristotle on sea animals and plants.

There has also been an interest in ocean currents, and like all aspects of oceanography, the study of them increased rapidly in the nineteenth century. The American statesman and scientist Benjamin Franklin had listed their surface temperatures and issued tables of them so that sailors might keep their vessels in the Gulf Stream, thereby resulting in faster passages across the Atlantic.

It was Fridtjof Nansen (1861–1930), the Norwegian explorer and oceanographer, who first tested the idea of currents in the Arctic Ocean. He had a specially built ship called the *Fram* which he allowed to become locked in the ice and drift with it. It drifted for three years and came to within 580 kilometres (360 miles) of the north pole. He then left the ship and went by sledge to a point within 363 kilometres (226 miles) of the pole. Since Nansen's time Russian oceanographers have made considerable use of floating ice stations in their study of the Arctic Ocean.

In 1855 Matthew Fontaine Maury (1806–73) published the first English

language textbook of oceanography, called *The Physical Geography of the Sea*. This gave information on the extent of the oceans and coastlines, the tides and currents, physical and chemical conditions of the water, and the animals and plants. It provided the first diagrammatic cross-section and map of the floor of the North Atlantic.

Challenger Expedition

The greatest spur to oceanography in the nineteenth century was the voyage of the British vessel HMS *Challenger*. This was the first attempt at a deep water oceanographic expedition. The voyage lasted from 1872–6 and the vessel sailed all the major oceans of the world. Thousands of specimens were collected and soundings taken. The many huge volumes of published results are still used by oceanographers of today. About the same time as the voyage of the *Challenger*, research was being undertaken by the German ship *Gazelle* and the American *Tuscarora*. The equipment used was the plumb-line, deep-sea thermometer and dredgers to bring up sediments and marine life.

From the voyage of the *Challenger* the science of oceanography can be said to have developed into a subject in its own right. But it was not until after the 1950s that the ocean floors became well known and partially understood. The advent of the theory of plate tectonics has greatly stimulated oceanic research.

A great deal has been learned about the oceans, their deposits and history from the work of the *Glomar Challenger*. This specially constructed vessel is able to take cores from the ocean floors by drilling. It has thrusters on the bows and stern which help to stabilise the ship, and it has been found that it can maintain a position to within 40 metres (130 feet) of a set point in a 30-knot gale. Sonar beacons are dropped to the ocean floor near the drill hole and the signals transmitted by these are picked up by hydrophones placed under the ship. A complex computer system links these signals to the motors which keep the vessel reasonably stable.

Because oceanographic ships are very expensive to operate, many other methods have been used to study the oceans. Buoys help to measure surface and subsurface temperatures, salinity (saltiness) and wave size. Often they transmit recorded information by radio, using satellites to the shore station. Off-shore towers are also used, as are lightships, to record information. Aircraft and satellites with special sensors also collect information about the surface waters.

Before the 1920s the bottoms of the oceans were considered to be rather flat and featureless. Exploration since then and particularly in the last fifteen years has proved this to be entirely wrong. There are three major areas to the oceans. First there is the continental shelf. This is really an extension of the land, where the depth of the sea above averages about 200 metres (650 feet). This area ends with the continental slope which dips moderately steeply towards the deep oceans. The shelf and slope often have great canyons cut in them. A famous one is the Hudson Gorge which runs out to sea from the mouth of the Hudson River in the United States. There are other similar gorges at the mouths of other great rivers, for example, the Congo. Parts of these gorges have been cut when the sea level was much lower than at present, possibly during the last ice age. It would seem that the excavation of the lower parts is due to the action of currents which are heavily loaded with sediments and possess great cutting power.

Ocean Mountains

Geologists have estimated that there are more than 10,000 mountains rising from the floor of the Pacific which are over 1,005 metres (3,300 feet) high. Many do not reach the surface of the water as the average depth of the ocean is 4,260 metres (14,000 feet). Not all have the typical cone shape associated with volcanoes. Some are flat-topped and these are called guyots. It is thought that these volcanoes once stood above the water, but, when no longer active, were attacked by the sea and gradually worn down. The

Diagram of an ocean floor, showing deep oceanic trenches, typical mid-ocean ridge with volcano and oceanic islands.

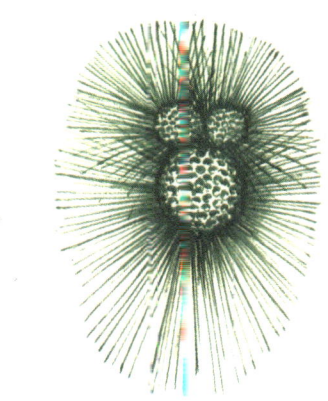

Globigerina, a common planktonic animal.

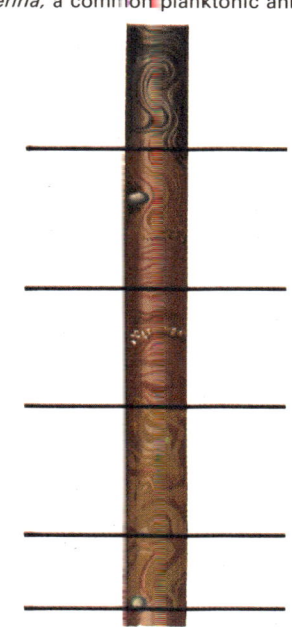

Core taken from the sea bottom beneath the Atlantic. Study of the content of the sediment layers enables conditions at the time when each layer was made to be reconstructed.

Close-up of limestone layer in the sediment partly formed by skeletons of such animals as *Globigerina*.

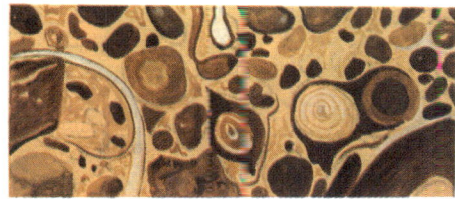

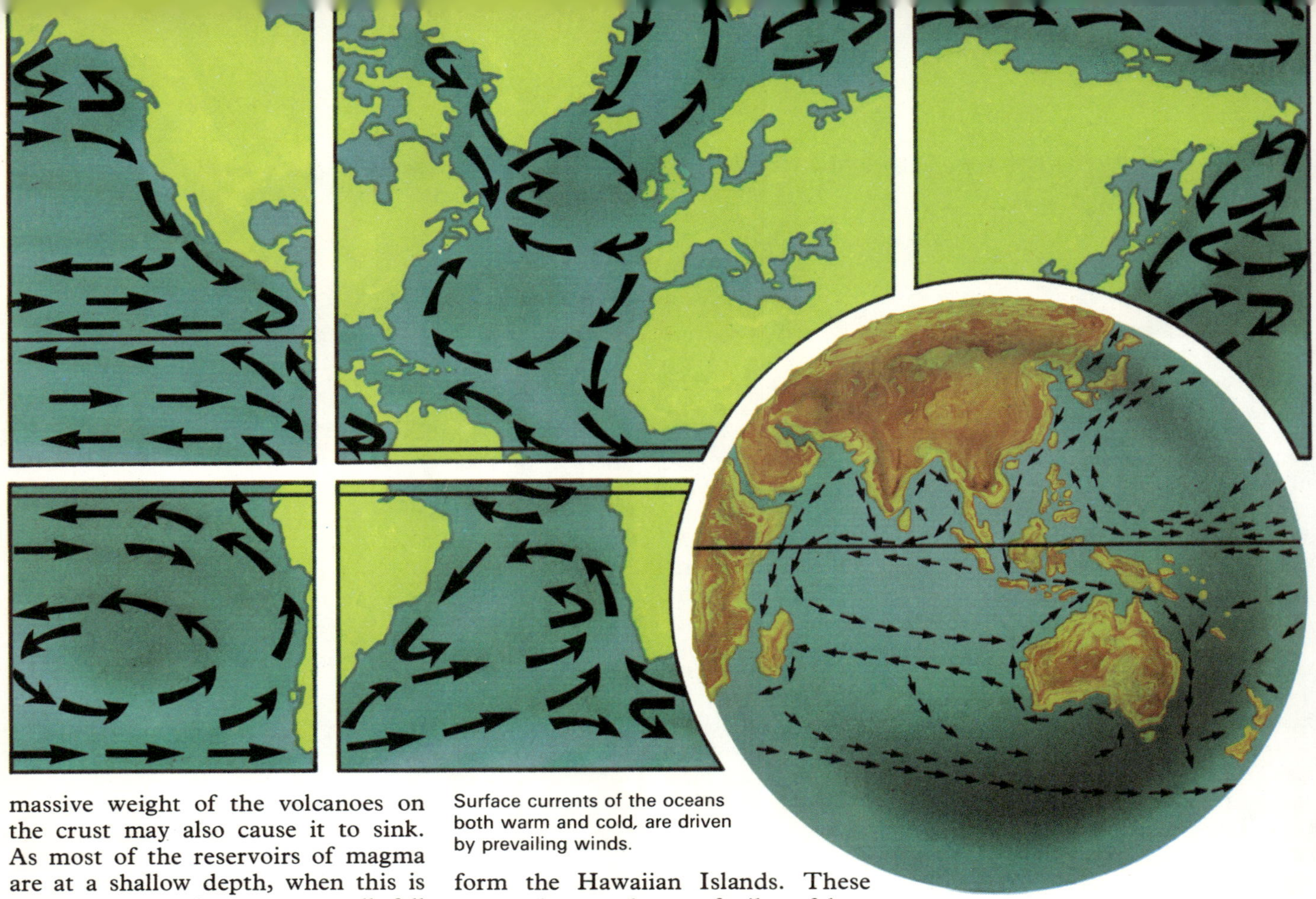

Surface currents of the oceans both warm and cold, are driven by prevailing winds.

massive weight of the volcanoes on the crust may also cause it to sink. As most of the reservoirs of magma are at a shallow depth, when this is used up the volcano may well fall back into the void. Material has been dredged from the top of some guyots and study of the fossils they contain shows them to be as old as 100 million years.

The Pacific Ocean is famed for its coral reefs and atolls. Even these peaceful locations have had a fiery history. While the volcano is above the sea the coral will grow as a reef around it. Corals are tiny animals, and with their hard skeletons they form a colony of sharp and jagged rock. They need very exact conditions to thrive. The temperature must not go below 20°C and they will not be found below 45 metres (150 feet) as they require sunlight. As the volcano ends its life and gradually sinks, so the coral will continue to grow upwards and towards the area originally occupied by the top of the volcano. Eventually all that is left is a ring of coral. Some of the atolls have great thicknesses of coral, as much as 1,200 metres (4,900 feet) in some places.

The tallest mountains in the world are found in the Pacific and their tops form the Hawaiian Islands. These mountains, made up of piles of lava flow, rise to 9,150 metres (30,000 feet) from the sea floor and form a chain of islands 2,500 kilometres (1,600 miles) long from north-west to south-east. Their origins go back 25 million years.

The Salty Seas

The oceans and seas are salty, as every swimmer knows, but some parts are more salty than others. Sea water is salty because of dissolved salts received from rivers which pour material into them, and from their own basins. The evaporation of the sea water itself in the regions of higher temperature must also increase the saltiness.

It has been calculated that the amount of salt in the sea, if dried, would cover the land masses to a depth of 150 metres (500 feet). Throughout the world there is in general a great uniformity in the salinity of the oceans ranging from 3·3 per cent to 3·7 per cent. Most oceanographers express salinity in parts per thousand, therefore the average salinity would be given as 33 per cent to 37 per cent. The Atlantic

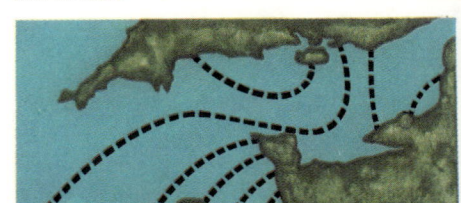

Atolls are formed by calcareous corals, the skeletons of tiny marine animals.

Tidal ranges between the coasts of England and France.

A bird sitting on the surface of the water demonstrates the circular movement of the waves.

is the saltiest of the oceans especially in the northern subtropical region. The Pacific Ocean is less salty and the Arctic and Southern Oceans least salty of all. Local conditions sometimes have a great effect on the salinity. The Baltic Sea, which is almost landlocked, is nearly fresh water, while the Red Sea and Persian Gulf have salinities of 42 per cent, and there is one particular spot in the depths of the Red Sea and Persian Gulf which has a salinity of 270 per cent plus. This is almost saturation point.

Most of the deposits on the continental shelves are sediments brought down by rivers and eroded by the sea itself from nearby land masses. Some of this material, particularly the finer particles, finds its way to the deep oceans where it is joined by the remains of tiny animals. Those animals with a calcareous, or chalky, shell are called foraminifers (single-celled animals), and there are also coccoliths and a type of mollusc called pteropods. When the remains are dominantly those of foraminifers the term globigerina ooze is used. Siliceous (containing silica) remains come from radiolarians (also single-celled animals), sponges and diatoms (minute plants). These siliceous deposits are

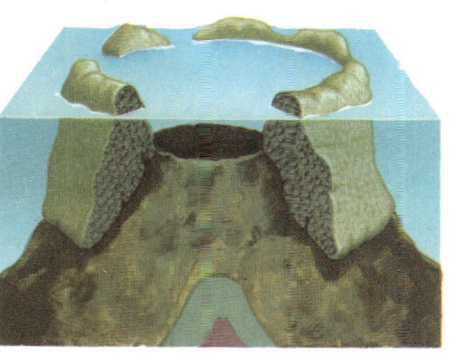

As a sinking island is gradually submerged by the sea an upward growth of coral forms an atoll.

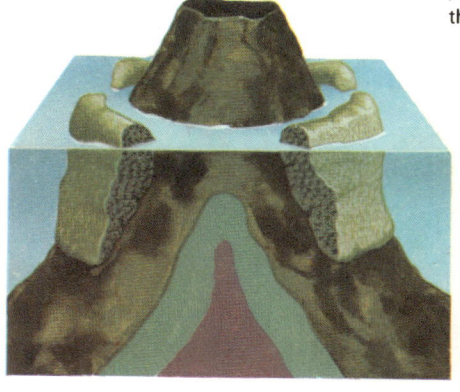

Tides are caused by gravitational attraction of the Moon which pulls the water away from the Earth on one side of the planet and the land away from the water on the other.

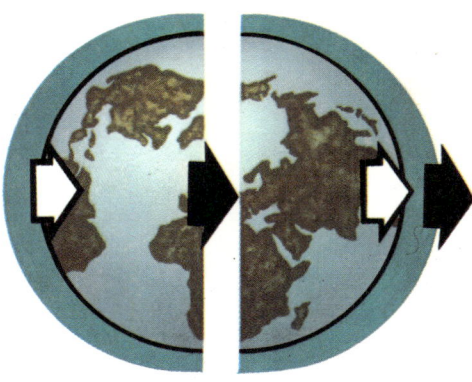

Surface water from the sea is evaporated by the Sun to form clouds which fall on land as rain. Water runs off the land carrying mineral-rich sediment back to the sea.

which are the result of undersea earthquakes. Ordinary waves usually travel at a speed which is less than half the speed of the wind. Most waves are less than 3·6 metres (12 feet) high and it is only in severe storms that those measuring 15 metres (50 feet) are recorded. The highest wave on record comes from the Pacific Ocean and was measured as 34 metres (112 feet) high. The size of the waves depends on the strength of the wind and how much sea it has passed over. The water itself does not move but the wave passes through it. On reaching the shore the drag of the bottom in the shallow water causes it to topple forward and break.

The winds are also in part responsible for the ocean currents. It is these currents which have such a marked effect on the climate of the countries on whose shores they wash. The sun causes changes in temperatures, and hence density, which also plays its part in helping the circulation of the oceans.

In the northern hemisphere the motion is clockwise, south of the equator it is anti-clockwise. The most famous current is the Gulf Stream. This is formed by the coming together of the North and South Equatorial Currents in the Caribbean. It flows out across the Atlantic, taking the course of the westerly winds, finally reaching the British Isles and Scandinavia as the North Atlantic Drift. The colder currents coming from the north tend to sink below the warmer water and where a meeting takes place, for example off Newfoundland, the sea is rich in nutrients and hence a good fishing ground.

Most coasts of the world experience two tides every day, two high water and two low water levels; these are the flood and ebb tides. The tides are generated because the gravitational forces of the Moon, Sun and other bodies overpower that of the Earth so that the water is pulled away. Two great masses are produced, one facing the Moon, the other facing away.

found mainly in the higher latitudes and in the equatorial regions of the Pacific.

Also accumulating in smaller quantities are the remains of the vertebrate animals, along with the ash and debris of volcanoes and clay minerals. There are also nodules and concentrations of various materials with coatings of manganese and the iron oxides. The depth of the sediments varies greatly and is usually more in the Atlantic than in the Indian and Pacific Oceans. The layer of unconsolidated sediments averages

about 1,500 metres (4,900 feet) in depth, and this lies over consolidated sediments about 1,750 metres (5,740 feet) thick.

Wind and Water

The oceans are in constant movement. The waves are always crashing on the shore, the tides always in action. Throughout the oceans of the world currents carry enormous quantities of water from one place to another.

The main cause of waves is the wind. Mention has already been made of the giant waves, called tsunami,

Rocks and Minerals

The collection and identification of rocks is a popular hobby with many people and requires only simple equipment.

All rocks are hard: at least that is what most people believe. When a person wants to describe something which is strong and long-lasting he may use the words rock hard to describe it. Geologists would not agree with this, for they regard as rocks not only granites, sandstones, limestones and marbles, but also soils, sands and gravels. Some rocks are very hard and resistant to wear, but others are very soft and easily worn away or altered.

Rocks are made up of minerals. Sometimes many minerals go to make up one rock. Granite is made up of quartz, feldspar and other minerals, while sandstone consists mainly of just one mineral, quartz.

Just as with many other natural events, rocks and minerals are made, broken down, carried away, deposited and turned into new materials. Their nature is cyclic, in just the same way as the process of water. Deep within the Earth molten material called magma wells upwards along lines of weakness. Some cools before it reaches the surface while the remainder will flow as lava beneath the seas and down the slopes of volcanoes. The type of rock which results after cooling will depend on the make-up of the magma and its temperature. It will also be affected by how quickly the magma has cooled. The magma which cools below ground does so slowly, allowing large crystals to grow. The reverse is true of lava. This rock is usually very fine-grained or glassy in appearance. Rocks which are formed by such activity are called igneous rocks, from the Latin word *igneus* meaning fiery.

Igneous Rocks

Igneous rocks are divided into groups according to how much silica they contain and their appearance. The amount of silica present in the rock can be estimated roughly by the types of minerals present. It is only possible to estimate the types of minerals in coarser specimens, and in the case of many lavas a more detailed laboratory analysis is required. In general the lighter coloured the rock the more chance there is that it is an acid one.

Many households have a lump of volcanic rock in the kitchen or bathroom. It is grey in colour, full of holes and will float on water. It is called pumice and results from volcanic explosions in which the lava is heavily laden with gases. It may also result from undersea eruptions. Obsidian is an acid rock which is like a

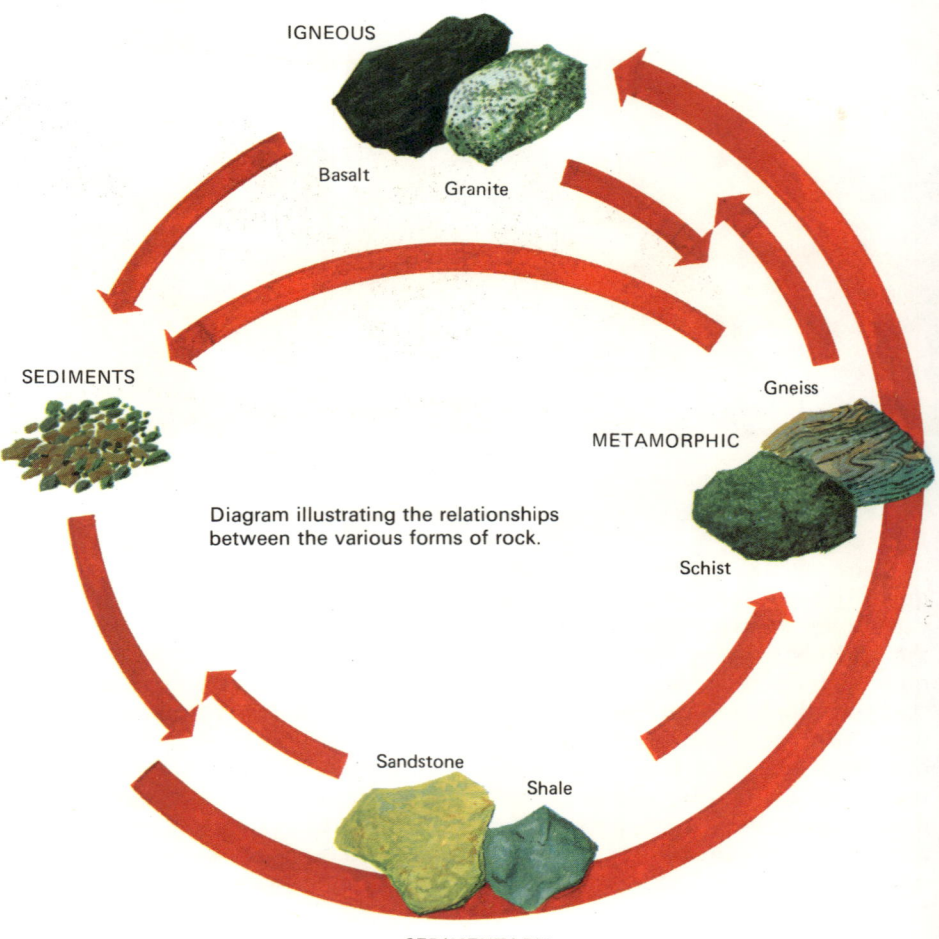

Diagram illustrating the relationships between the various forms of rock.

IGNEOUS

Basalt

Granite

SEDIMENTS

Gneiss

METAMORPHIC

Schist

Sandstone

Shale

SEDIMENTARY

black glass. Pitchstone is rather like obsidian but, when examined under the microscope, is seen to contain more crystals.

Basalts are among the most widespread of all the rocks of the Earth's crust. Basalt varies in its make-up but it is known mainly as a dark, heavy and finely grained rock. It forms the major part of lava flows.

Perhaps the best known of all the igneous rocks is granite. It varies considerably in its colouring and mineral content. Unlike basalt, granite does not appear in lava flows but as great masses. They are found only as parts of the continental crusts, not being present beneath the ocean floors. There has been much debate about the origin of granite and many scientists believe that at least some granites are derived from the original crustal rocks rather than from the cooling of magma.

Igneous rocks underlie the surface everywhere. When they appear as surface rocks they are often broken down by the action of the air and water. Chemical changes take place and new minerals are formed. In other cases grains are broken off and carried away by gravity and water to lower levels. In time they are deposited, these remnants of a former world, as sediments. This is the first stage in the making of a new type of rock, which because of their origin, are collectively called sedimentary rocks.

Sedimentary Rocks

These provide the geologist with a vivid picture of the past conditions of the Earth. He can read them like the pages of a book. Consider a lump of sandstone as one example to show why this is possible. If such a lump is crushed, the grains look exactly like those that could be found on any sandy beach or in the desert. It is therefore logical to assume that when a sandstone is located, it represents a time when a shallow sea beach or desert covered the area.

As the sediments pile up, in a river valley or on the floor of a lake or sea, so the lower layers are subjected to a greater pressure. The water is squeezed out of them and the sediments become harder. The spaces or pores which remain are often filled by a cement. Gradually, over a long period of time, the unconsolidated masses of sand, mud and silt are transformed into rocks. A change in sea level will result in the rocks becoming dry land.

Another characteristic of sedimentary rocks is that many of them contain fossils. Some are almost entirely made up of the remains of plants and animals. In others, for example sandstones, they are very rare. This does not mean that sandstone never contains fossils but that the rock is so porous they have been washed away. Fossils are important in the study of rocks, as we shall see.

The sedimentary rocks which result from the destruction of other rocks are called clastic, from the Greek word *klastos*, meaning broken. Those made of coarse fragments include the breccias, conglomerates and boulder clay. These rocks are made up of material which has often travelled only a short distance from its origin. Scree deposits found at the foot of cliffs and in steepsided valleys are made up of large angular blocks which when consolidated form breccias. The stones and pebbles on a beach vary greatly in size, but the action of the sea rolling them together has caused them to become smooth and rounded. These form a rock called a conglomerate. Such deposits also occur in the valleys of fast-flowing rivers and streams.

Boulder Clay

Glaciers move great amounts of rocks, boulders and debris along with much finer sediments. When glaciers melt and retreat back up a valley, a deposit called boulder clay is left. Should this be subjected to the process of lithification (the driving out of the water and cementing together of the grains), it

One of the commonest of all minerals is quartz, used in the electrical and optical industries.

Beryl is the most common beryllium mineral and has valuable metallurgical properties.

Chalcopyrite is a copper mineral, the most widespread ore of copper.

Amethyst is a crystallised quartz and its colour is due to the presence of manganese.

Agate is a distinctive and decorative mineral.

The beautiful silica mineral opal is prized for its attractive colours.

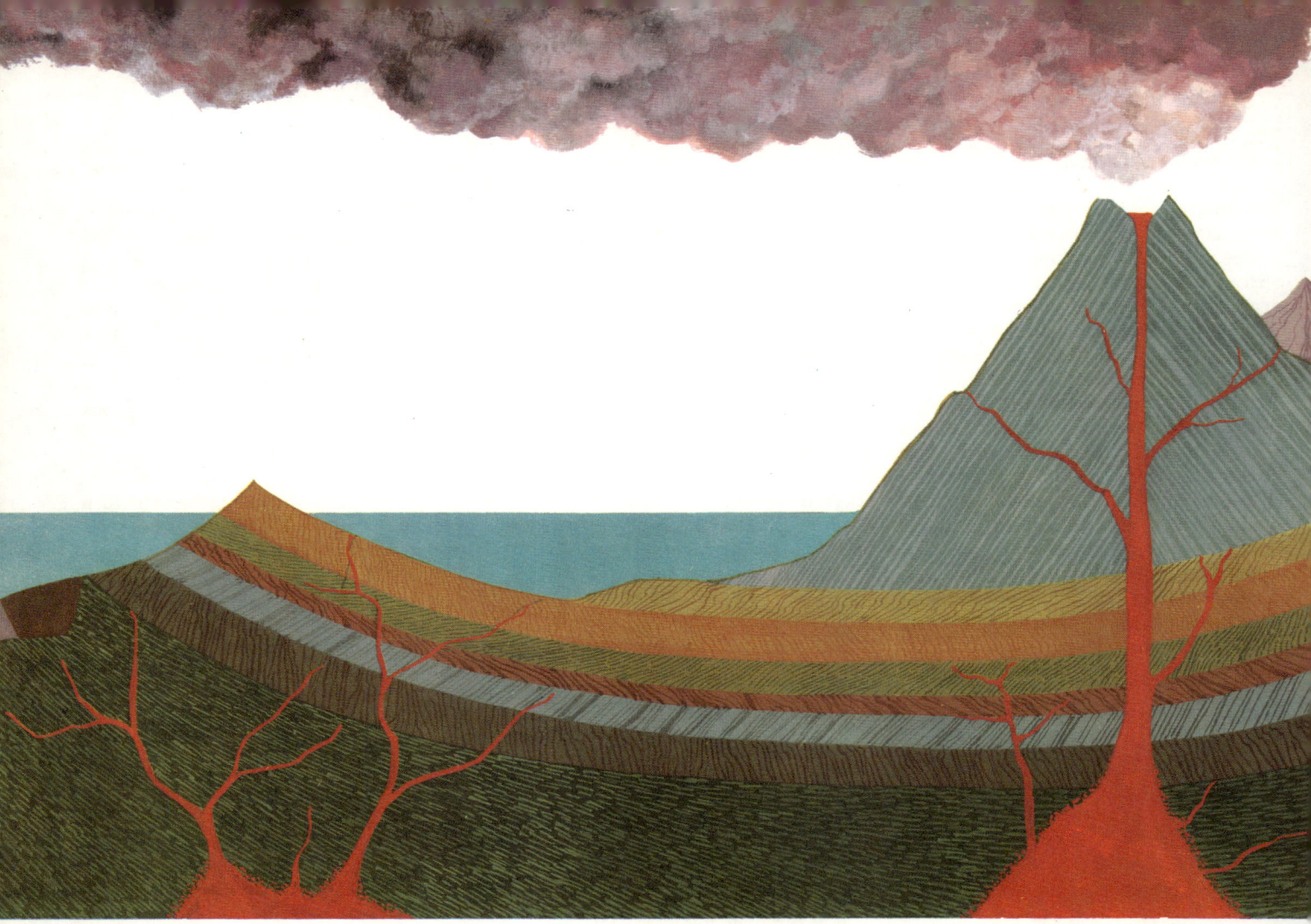

becomes what is called tillite. When discovered in a sequence of rocks, tillite clearly indicates the existence of a former glacier and glacial action.

Sandstones are made up of grains which are between $\frac{1}{16}$ millimetre and 2 millimetres in size. These result from beach deposits and deserts. They are made up of material which has been transported farther away from its source than in the case of the breccias. Most sandstones are made up of quartz grains. Sometimes very important deposits are found in which quartz is not the main mineral. Gem-, chromite-, magnetite- and tin-bearing sands are all known to occur.

Some sedimentary rocks are produced because of the activity of plants and animals or by the direct precipitation of matter from water. Limestones may be entirely made up from fragments of animals, the shells of which sink to the ocean floor when they die. Limestone is mainly calcium carbonate and originates in still, warm seas. The coral reefs of today are found in fossil form making up a limestone. Chalk is a limestone made up of the remains of tiny single-celled animals.

When the sea is found in shallow areas in which the sun causes much of it to evaporate, the salts remain

Some of the basic substances called chemical elements come from the magma which rises up from the interior of the Earth.

as a deposit. Rock salt and gypsum are both formed in this way. There are also rocks which are rich in iron. In some instances the iron is due to chemical action at the time of the settling of the sediments, in others it has originated in swampy conditions. One other group of sedimentary rocks is called carbonaceous. These rocks provide the seams of coal, peat and oil.

Metamorphic Rocks

The presence of renewed heat and pressure may alter both sedimentary and igneous rocks into metamorphic rocks. Metamorphic is derived from the Greek words, *meta* and *morphe* meaning change of form. It is by such action that shales can be turned into slate, limestone into marble and sandstone into quartzite.

All sorts of variations of metamorphic rock can be found. Occasionally some features of the original rock remain. Rocks are metamorphosed on a local scale when a mass of magma finds its way upwards. The rocks nearest to this intrusion will show the greatest degree of change, while those further away may be only partly

affected. The movement of rocks along a fault line deep within the Earth can also lead to rocks being changed. Sometimes, perhaps due to mountain building or other catastrophic changes, whole areas are subject to considerable increases of both temperature and pressure. In such events rocks are changed over vast areas. Slate may go on to be changed into schist and then gneiss (pronounced nice).

Minerals and Elements

Minerals make up rocks and in turn they are made up of a chemical combination of the elements which occur naturally. There are over a hundred elements, many of which are rare, but they include iron, copper, sulphur, oxygen and hydrogen. Ice is made up of oxygen and hydrogen; quartz of silicon and oxygen. Other minerals may consist of a combination of as many as five or more elements. Other mineral characteristics are a constant chemical composition, recordable as a chemical formula, and a definite atomic structure.

The type of minerals discovered in any one area will depend on the type of rock present. In the case of igneous rocks this depends on the type of magma. When there is a collection of substances which are usually found scattered throughout the rocks, it is called a mineral deposit. Ore deposits are those from which a metal of value to man can be economically retrieved. Mineral deposits are found in fissures, in masses or as beds.

The two great groups of minerals are the silicates and the non-silicates. The former are those in which silicon and oxygen combine with other elements in varying proportions to form different minerals, including garnets, hornblende and quartz. The non-silicates include the native elements, sulphur, gold and carbon (both as graphite and diamond)—the sulphides, pyrite and galena—the sulphates, gypsum and barytes—the chlorides and fluorides, rock-salt and fluorspar–the oxides, magnetite, hematite and cassiterite—and the carbonates, calcite and dolomite. These are particularly important to man as a major source of ores. Gem stones are merely minerals which man holds in high esteem. They are notable for fine colours, a certain degree of rarity and their hardness. Gem stones include

Stalactites are formed by the evaporation of water droplets on the roof of a cave leaving deposits of calcium carbonate. Stalagmites grow upwards in a similar way.

the diamond, ruby, sapphire, topaz, garnet, agate and many others.

Collecting Minerals

Altogether there are about 2,000 minerals. The collecting of minerals has become a fascinating hobby for many people. The first step towards the identification of a mineral is to assess its characteristics. Colour is not a good guide as many minerals appear in a wide range of colours. However, if a mineral is scratched on a piece of unglazed porcelain, the colour of its powder (the streak) will be revealed. This is of considerably more value than the colour of the actual specimen. The hardness of a mineral is important. A scale was devised by the German mineralogist Friedrich Mohs (1773–1839) to determine the relative hardness of different minerals. The scale is:

Hardness	1 (softest)	talc
	2	gypsum
	3	calcite
	4	fluorspar
	5	apatite
	6	feldspar
	7	quartz
	8	topaz
	9	corundum
	10 (hardest)	diamond

A penknife will scratch minerals of hardness less than 6 while a finger-nail will scratch those of hardness 1 or 2. Two minerals which are often confused are calcite and quartz. It is easy to tell them apart using the hardness scale.

Other properties are also useful in identification. Some always tend to split in the same direction. This is called cleavage. Mica and biotite are both minerals which split easily and they are referred to as having a good cleavage. A mineral may have a characteristic feel, for example, soapy as in talc; or taste, for example, rock salt. Lustre or brilliance, the way a mineral fractures and its specific gravity (the relative weight of the mineral when compared with the weight of the same amount of water), are also important in identification.

The examination of other properties requires laboratory equipment. The atomic structure may be important in identifying a mineral and its crystal structure is one of the most useful aids. Crystallography is the name given to the study of the form, property and structure of crystals.

Rocks are made of minerals, substances formed naturally out of the basic elements.

Peridotite

Granite

Crystallised malachite

Limestone

Schist

Shale

Coal, Oil and Natural Gas

Man owes his existence to plants. His present state of development is largely due to the abundant supplies of energy which are available in the form of fossil fuels. Plants are responsible for coal and natural gas and have contributed to the formation of crude petroleum.

When plants die they are quickly attacked by the various agents of destruction, such as bacteria and fungi. As long as oxygen is present, cellulose, which is the basic substance in plant tissues, is eaten away. In swamps and bogs there is little or no oxygen available and the bacteria are limited in their work. Gradually a mass of humified tissues collects together. In this process carbon dioxide, water and methane are given off.

feet) in depth. In the Ganges delta the densely forested swamps have been compared with the swamps of the Carboniferous period, some 250 million years ago. The plants themselves are not of the same type but the environmental conditions are the same. Sometimes the sea invades the delta, laying down sediments which later consolidate into sand and clay.

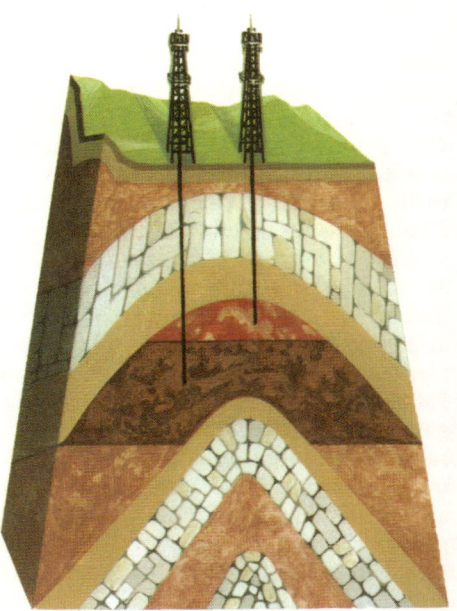

Different strata of the Earth produce gas (top) and oil (below).

During the Carboniferous period the land was subjected to slight rises and falls. Luxuriant growths of vegetation and swamp conditions existed for thousands of years. The vegetation died and lay rotting in shallow water. First the sea would invade the sinking land and then the land rose to return to swamp.

Methane, more commonly known as marsh gas, is found at such locations. It is also encountered when mining for coal and can cause explosions.

For the resultant peat to develop there must be a supply of moisture and the plants themselves must constantly be adding to the decaying mass. They must grow more quickly than the wastage occurs. In tropical areas the growth and decay rates will both be very high. Such masses of decaying vegetation are often found in swamp areas of the tropics. Such swamps are common in the great river deltas.

In Virginia and North Carolina in the United States, there are vast deposits of peat covering as much as 3,880 square kilometres (1,500 square miles) and averaging 2·1 metres (7

Coal Deposits

If peat becomes even more compacted the end result will be coal. To become so compacted, sediment must be deposited over the peat to provide the extra weight. The rocks of the coalfields provide the best indication of the events which must have occurred. The land was subjected to slight rises and falls, allowing first a luxuriant growth of vegetation and swamp conditions for thousands of years. The vegetation would die and lie rotting in the shallow water. Finally a slight sinking of the land would cause an invasion by the sea. A rise would cause it to retreat bringing back swamp conditions.

All of these events are reflected in the rocks above and below a single

seam of coal. Below the seam itself is the 'seat-earth'. This clay is used for making refractory bricks and has in it numerous plant rootlets. The seam of coal itself is often widespread and uniform in thickness. However, in a delta area, the waterways are constantly changing their courses. These changes are shown in the coal seams by what the miners call 'wash-outs'. These occur when a seam of coal suddenly gives way to a sandy deposit. The seam itself represents the collection of plant remains over thousands of years. Above the coal are shales, often with freshwater mussels and leaves, and above these are the sandstones. This shows a gradual drowning of the land. However, the sandstones give way again to the 'seat-earth' showing that the cycle continues.

Lignite, or brown coal, has undergone the least compaction, while anthracite, which is a hard, brittle coal, is produced where the original coal seams have been subjected to extremes of temperature and pressure. Anthracite is associated with rocks which have experienced movements. In lignite the original stems and leaves of plants can often be seen. In some places the seams are up to 100 metres (325 feet) thick. The majority of the world's finest coal is of Carboniferous age while lignite is found in Cretaceous and Tertiary rocks.

Another type of coal is derived from spores, pollen, algae and pulped remains of plants. These are called sapropelic coals and include cannel coal and boghead coal. The latter is mainly made up of algae and both are valuable sources of gas and oil.

Petroleum

Crude petroleum is a mixture of liquid, solid and gaseous hydrocarbons. Hydrocarbon is a chemical compound consisting of carbon and hydrogen. The main hydrocarbons present are paraffin wax (solid), hexane and octane (liquid) and methane (gas). Oil, unlike coal, gives no indication of its origin. Neither is it found in the position of accumulation for it migrates to the other rocks.

The origin of oil is still not fully understood. It was originally thought to have accumulated through inorganic action; possibly the action of water on

As the sediments become compacted the water and oil are squeezed out of the pores and the oil migrates. It flows like groundwater following the porous rocks. It migrates upwards particularly into sandstones and limestones. Unless it is to be lost at the surface, as much must have been, there has to be a suitable capping rock, perhaps a shale or clay.

Certain geological structures favour the accumulation of petroleum, for example, domes and anticlines. Salt domes are particularly favourable to the collection of oil. Salt deposits within the Earth tend to well up in great plugs which are roughly cylindrical in cross-section. With the development of salt-domes, the ends of the rocks which they pass through are dragged

Emerald

Diamond

Amethyst

Turquoise

Garnet

Ruby

rocks. It is now considered that the main constituent in the origin of oil are micro-organisms such as algae and diatoms. It is also thought that microscopic animals may play some part.

The remains of these minute creatures accumulate in a mud where there is very little free oxygen. Bacteria are probably responsible for the first stages in the evolution of oil. The rest of the cycle is not understood, but obviously the weight of the sediments which continue to accumulate on top plays some part.

Gem stones are simply minerals which man values because of their comparative rarity. They exhibit fine colours, particularly when cut and polished, and a high degree of hardness.

upwards. Oil and gas tend to rise and collect in these traps. The rocks above are arched and hence suitable for the collection of crude petroleum and gas.

Natural Gas

Natural gas is mainly methane, although its make-up varies from field to field. Other common constituents are ethane, propane and butane along with nitrogen, helium and other gases. It is possible that natural gas is derived mainly from microscopic plants. Gas occurs with crude petroleum, dissolved in it and on its own. When it is located on its own, the gas is often associated with coal seams and could be linked to the process of coal formation. It accumulates in the same way as petroleum.

The Long Journey Through Time

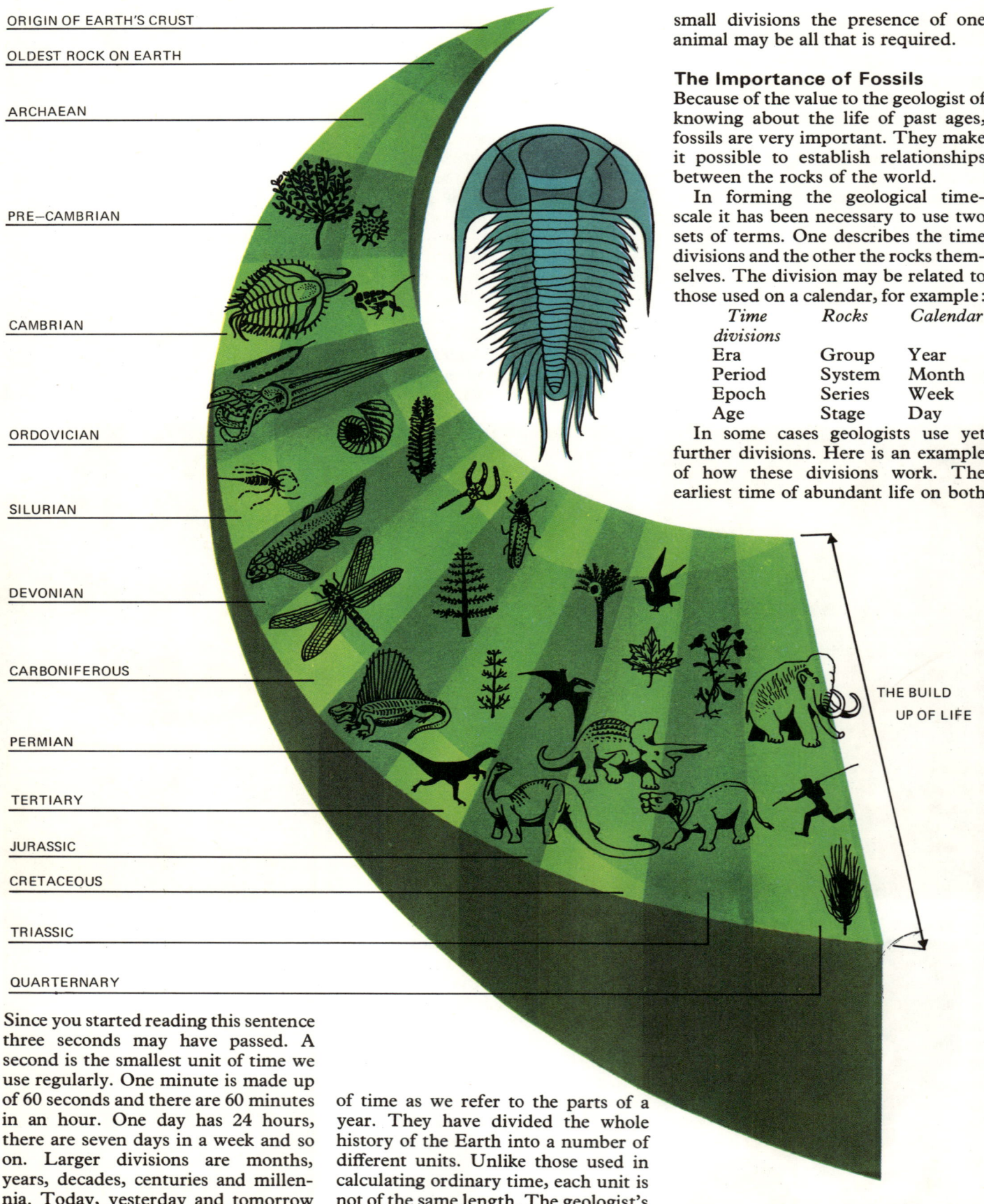

ORIGIN OF EARTH'S CRUST

OLDEST ROCK ON EARTH

ARCHAEAN

PRE—CAMBRIAN

CAMBRIAN

ORDOVICIAN

SILURIAN

DEVONIAN

CARBONIFEROUS

PERMIAN

TERTIARY

JURASSIC

CRETACEOUS

TRIASSIC

QUARTERNARY

THE BUILD UP OF LIFE

small divisions the presence of one animal may be all that is required.

The Importance of Fossils

Because of the value to the geologist of knowing about the life of past ages, fossils are very important. They make it possible to establish relationships between the rocks of the world.

In forming the geological time-scale it has been necessary to use two sets of terms. One describes the time divisions and the other the rocks themselves. The division may be related to those used on a calendar, for example:

Time divisions	Rocks	Calendar
Era	Group	Year
Period	System	Month
Epoch	Series	Week
Age	Stage	Day

In some cases geologists use yet further divisions. Here is an example of how these divisions work. The earliest time of abundant life on both

Since you started reading this sentence three seconds may have passed. A second is the smallest unit of time we use regularly. One minute is made up of 60 seconds and there are 60 minutes in an hour. One day has 24 hours, there are seven days in a week and so on. Larger divisions are months, years, decades, centuries and millennia. Today, yesterday and tomorrow are all words used to describe time.

Geologists are dealing not with thousands of years but with thousands of millions of years. They need to be able to refer to parts of this vast span

of time as we refer to the parts of a year. They have divided the whole history of the Earth into a number of different units. Unlike those used in calculating ordinary time, each unit is not of the same length. The geologist's calendar is based on the various characteristic forms of life present in the form of fossils in the rocks. For the larger divisions of time, broad characteristics are used, while for the very

This diagram charts the successive stages of the 'Long Journey Through Time'. The build-up of life has taken many millions of years but man's share in the journey is extremely short, representing only a tiny slice of the geological time-scale.

land and sea was the Palaeozoic era. This span of time is made up of a number of shorter periods, of which one is the Carboniferous. It was during Carboniferous times that the coal seams were formed. One coal seam is a formation. This seam together with others and the rocks such as sandstones and shales are known as the Coal Measures. In many areas there are two other series of rocks which altogether make up the Carboniferous system.

Another way of imagining life's long journey through time is to relate the whole span of Earth history to a single day. The first forms of life would have appeared by eight in the morning. By about nine o'clock in the evening it would be the Cambrian period. There would be no land plants and no animals with backbones. At about a minute and a half before midnight, the earliest forms of man would have developed, and modern man would appear about two seconds before the end of the twenty-four hour day.

Apart from the use of fossils in correlating the various rocks, our whole knowledge of the development of life and the process of evolution is gained through them. The word fossil is derived from the Latin word *fodere*, to dig. Originally the word fossil was applied to anything which was dug out of the Earth including minerals. For many years now its use has been confined to remains of plants and animals and traces of their activity. Fossils also provide information about past climates and geographical conditions.

What makes a Fossil?

For an animal or plant to become a fossil, a whole sequence of events must take place. When an animal dies its remains are quickly seized by others. Some will tear at the flesh while bacteria may rot away what is left. Sometimes the bones will be taken and eaten, but more likely they will be scattered by the weather. It is an unusual event for a fossil to be formed. If the animal does not have any hard parts, for example, a shell or skeleton, its chances of being fossilised are even less likely.

There is a greater chance of fossilisation for the sea and lake dwellers. When their remains fall slowly to the bottom they may be quickly covered in mud and saved from the attentions of scavengers.

The hard parts which usually remain to become fossils include the shells of molluscs and other animals without backbones, the bones and teeth of the vertebrates and the stems and branches of some trees. Often information about the soft parts of the original animal may be provided by markings on the fossil which show their attachment to the skeleton or shell. Sometimes the process known as carbonisation will also preserve the impressions of the soft parts. The impression which remains is a thin film of carbon – the oxygen, hydrogen and nitrogen having escaped after the breakdown of the original tissues.

Where the sediments laid down are very fine, extraordinary detail will be preserved. The Jurassic limestone from the Solenhofen area of Germany has impressions of jelly-fish and the fine wings of insects. It is from these rocks that the earliest bird has been discovered, the feathers being perfectly recorded in the stone.

Usually, however, fossils are formed because mineralisation takes place, that is, the original material is replaced by other minerals derived from percolating waters. Often the remains of trees are completely replaced by silica and the cell structure can still be seen. A famous example is the petrified forest in Arizona in the United States. Sometimes the remains are gradually dissolved away leaving only an internal cast or a hollow mould.

Preserved Animals

Very rarely whole animals are preserved. Insects are often trapped in the resin of pine trees. When this resin is fossilised it is known as amber. The animals that were originally trapped are also preserved. In the frozen wastes of Siberia mammoths have been found in the ice, the remains of their last meal still in the stomach. In the tar pits of Rancho La Brea, California, many animals have been well preserved. The skin of a giant ground sloth has been discovered in South America in a mummified form because of the dry climate.

Although fossils allow the reconstruction of the evolution of life, the story they tell is incomplete. Many animals and plants will remain forever unknown to man because they have left no traces. Many gaps are still to be filled in the existing record but no one can doubt the value of fossils. If they do, let them remember that all our coal, oil and natural gas originated from plants and animals: these are known as fossil fuels with good reason.

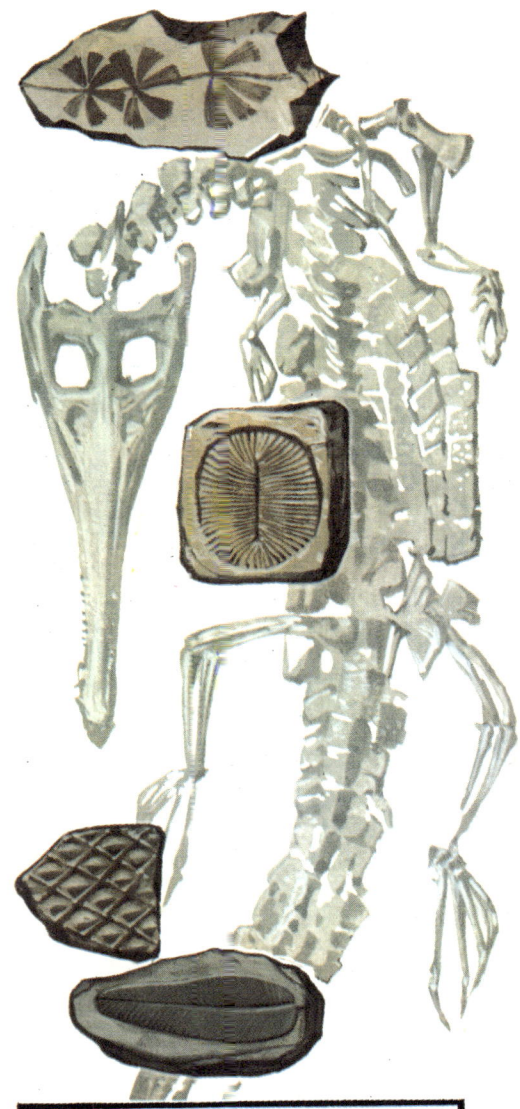

Fossils are important to the geologist who wants to know about the life of past ages. His knowledge of the development of life and the process of evolution is based upon the study of fossils

The Early Years

The Pre-Cambrian era covers a vast and unimaginable span of time. It stretches from the origin of the Earth 4,600 million years ago until about 600 million years ago. This is more than three-quarters of the whole existence of the Earth. During Pre-Cambrian times the Earth's crust was formed, the atmosphere was lost and remade, the first sedimentary rocks were manufactured and life began.

It has been calculated that there were at least nine periods of mountain building during these years. Mighty ranges of mountains must have been slowly uplifted only to be worn away again by the action of the weather and running water. There were periods of glaciation and during these times great ice sheets and glaciers spread out across the land. Because of their great age and periods of Earth movements in Pre-Cambrian times and since, many rocks have been altered by heat and pressure. In some cases it is impossible to discover their original nature. These factors have delayed the investigation of the earliest period of Earth history. The oldest rocks so far discovered are those in western Greenland and they have been dated as about 3,800 million years old.

Early in Pre-Cambrian times the molten Earth solidified and the solid crust was formed. This must have been made of igneous rocks, perhaps basalts and, later on, granites. The world would still have been torn apart by

In the process of cell development, bacteria (1) absorbed by larger cells (2) which in turn absorb algae (3) produces chloroplasts (4). Animal cells (5) contain no chloroplasts.

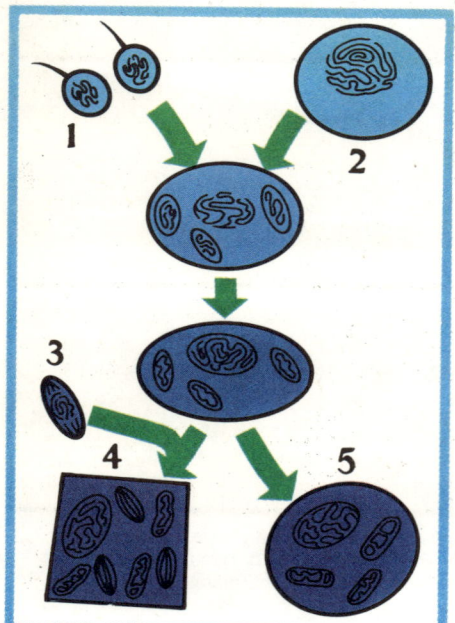

mighty eruptions and great lava flows would have spread out and created a rugged landscape.

Initially there would have been little weathering of the rocks. The hills would have had a more jagged outline, like those of the Moon. There would have been no 'soft' rounded views to be admired. The landscape was barren—no soil, no plants and no animals. There would have been wide variations in the temperatures between day and night.

The Coming of Rain

As cooling continued, water vapour in the atmosphere condensed and fell as rain. Still the volcanoes continued to add vast quantities of gases and water vapour to the air. Once the rains came, the rocks were attacked. Pieces would be dislodged to find their way to lower levels. The water running on the surface would carry other particles. The streams would rush to the lower regions and collect as the first seas and oceans. The oceans would quickly become salty as minerals were removed from the rocks which made up their basins and yet others were added by the rivers. Sediments would be deposited, providing material for the sedimentary rocks.

The original atmosphere of the Earth was quickly lost in space. All that remains today are the traces of rare gases. The evolution of the new atmosphere and of life are intimately linked. The Earth created its own atmosphere from gases emitted from the surface during cooling and from volcanic eruptions. The process is still going on. At that early stage the atmosphere was primarily made up of hydrogen, carbon dioxide and water vapour. Very little, if any, oxygen was present. The surface of the Earth would not have been protected from the harmful effects of the Sun's ultra-violet rays. Today, life as we know it depends on oxygen but the origin of life depended on there being very little of it.

The actual origin of a living cell still remains a mystery. One of the first stages must have been the combination of the original elements to make compounds. The next step must have been the appearance of organic compounds. These are mainly composed of carbon. The amino acids and proteins essential for life are organic compounds. In the laboratory, ammonia, methane and water vapour have been subjected to electrical discharges. The result was the production of complex organic

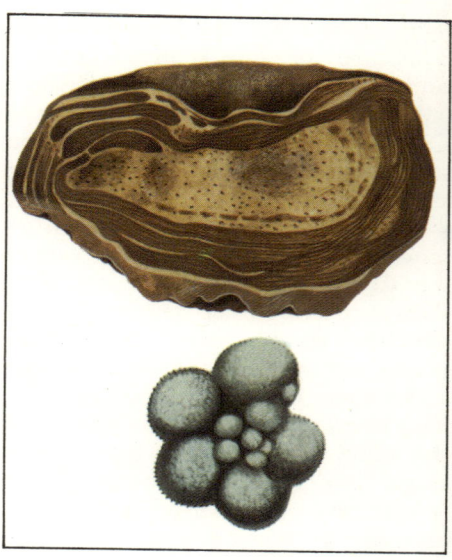

Fossils from Pre-Cambrian times are particularly important in establishing accurate information about the period when the Earth's crust was formed.

compounds. In nature such a discharge could be in the form of lightning.

These organic compounds may have collected in sheltered areas of the sea. The idea of a sort of soup or broth has been suggested by some scientists. At this time the land surfaces and the shallow water would still have been bombarded by ultra-violet radiation. It seems, therefore, that the chance joining of the organic compounds to form a living unit must have taken place under water. This first phase of evolution, called chemical evolution, took about 1,000 million years.

Single-celled Life

The first living being was of microscopic size, consisted of a single cell and would use as food the organic molecules in the 'soup' in which it originated.

Development must have been quick after this as all the available food would soon have been eaten. The next barrier for life to cross was to allow the living creature to make its own food from inorganic material. Judging by the chemical fossils which have been found, this could have occurred as long ago as 3,200 million years. These creatures were like bacteria and blue-green algae. They could break down water into two elements, hydrogen and oxygen, using only sunlight. The hydrogen is used in converting carbon dioxide to sugars, which are then used to provide and make other substances necessary for growth. In this way the first plants arrived. The action of making their food is called photosynthesis. During the process a gas is

liberated into the atmosphere, and this gas is oxygen.

Life gradually developed. Oxygen was continually being added to the atmosphere by the primitive plants. Eventually an ozone layer would be built up in the stratosphere to shield the surface and shallow waters from the harmful radiation of the sun. The earliest fossils found have been dated as 3,200 million years old and come from rocks in the Fig Tree Formation in southern Africa. Each animal con-

An imaginary picture of the Earth during the time when the first continent Pangaea was created about 4,200 million years ago. It was a hot, barren land with much volcanic activity. Pangaea subsequently split into two sub-continents, Laurasia in the north and Gondwana in the south.

sists of only one cell. The cell itself is very simple, having no nucleus and being sexless.

Life still had to cross the most important barrier. The rocks of northern Australia—the Bitter Springs Formation—have yielded evidence of

the crossing of this barrier. Fossils recovered from these rocks appear to be similar to the green algae of today. The cells now possessed a nucleus. This means that they were capable of sexual reproduction. With the recombining of the genetic material, variations will occur. Because of this, evolution will proceed, for genetic variability is the raw material of evolution. The way was clear for all the many forms of life which exist now and have existed in the past.

Life in the Seas

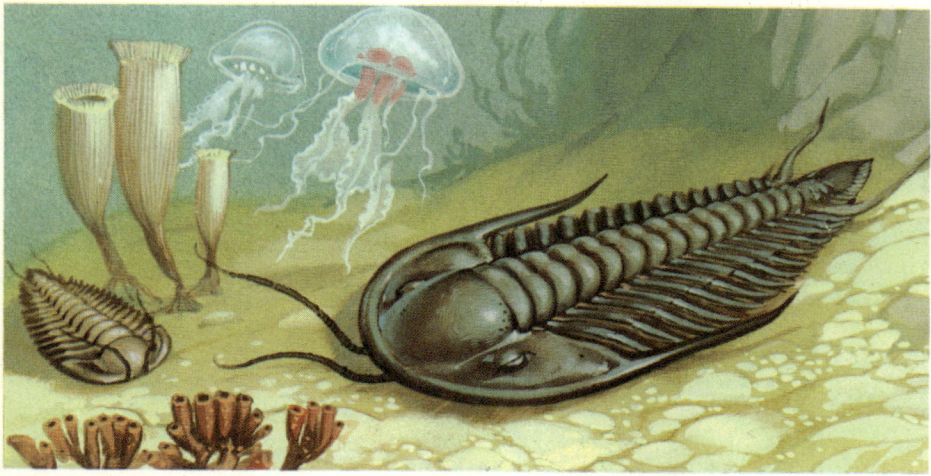

Among the most important animals of Cambrian times were the trilobites.

■	Sea in L. Carboniferous and at present.
■	Sea in L. Carboniferous but now land.
■	Land in L. Carboniferous and at present.
□	Land in L. Carboniferous but now sea.
●	Land plants

Map showing the geography of the Lower Carboniferous period.

The Palaeozoic era stretches from about 600 million years ago to 225 million years ago. Palaeozoic means 'old life'. It is divided into a number of different periods. The oldest is the Cambrian, named after the Roman name for Wales—Cambria—where the rocks were first described. The Ordovician and Silurian periods followed. Both of these names are derived from Celtic tribes, the Ordovices and Silures, who lived at one time in the area of Wales where the rocks of these systems were first studied. The Devonian period is so called because the rocks of these times are well developed in Devon, England. The many thick coal seams found in the rocks of the

next period give the Carboniferous its name. The final period is named Permian after the Russian province of Perm in the Ural Mountains.

The Palaeozoic era is one in which the seas team with life. All the major groups of animals without backbones (invertebrates) were found. It is also a time when the plants gradually colonised the land. Once this colonisation had begun it progressed rapidly, for in Carboniferous times there were great forests and masses of decaying vegetation which were eventually to form our major deposits of coal.

Animals with Backbones
The most notable event of the era must

be the evolution of the animals with backbones, the vertebrates. First they inhabited the seas, the forerunners of fish and later the fish themselves. Gradually they struggled ashore. By the end of the era both amphibians and reptiles had developed and the scene was set for the first mammals.

With the beginning of Cambrian times there was a great number of animals and plants although the land remained barren. The great diversity of fossils found in Cambrian rocks is due to the animals having hard protective shells and skeletons. These factors increase their chances of being preserved as fossils and therefore of allowing the palaeontologist to reconstruct the life of past ages. This sudden abundance of life has been interpreted in many ways. The increase of oxygen in the atmosphere may well have provided a greater chance for increased activity.

In the seas were the single-celled protozoans, jelly-fish, primitive members of the sea urchin group, brachiopods (lamp-shells), molluscs (snails and clams) and arthropods. The name of this last group means joint-footed, and today includes insects, crabs, lobsters, centipedes, millipedes and spiders. In Cambrian times the most important arthropods were called trilobites. They looked rather like the wood-lice of today, although they ranged in size from tiny creatures to others about 45 centimetres (18 inches) in length.

The Ordovician period was again a time of developing sea life, with the appearance of animals called graptolites. They were like the trilobites, by then extinct, although their remains are useful in the classification of some of the early rocks. The oldest fragments of fish-like creatures have been found in rocks of this age.

The origin of the vertebrates has provided palaeontologists with a tremendous puzzle. It is now generally

Monsters of the Silurian seas were the eurypterids, or sea scorpions.

In the Devonian period the early, leafless forms of plants were replaced by an abundant growth of ferns and horsetails.

assumed that their line of development is from the same ancestors as those of the echinoderms (sea-urchins). Cephalopods became more abundant and their shells although usually small, grew in some cases to as long as 4·5 metres (15 feet).

The Silurian period is noted for its coral-reefs, indicating warm, shallow seas. The rocks of this period have also yielded the first land plants, which it would seem, developed in Ordovician times. Just as the animals had to overcome a number of barriers in colonising the land, so did the plants. They would have had to be able to stand upright, without the help of water, and their tissues would need to be thick enough to stop too great a loss of moisture. Also they needed to evolve a way of getting water and minerals from their root systems to those parts above ground.

Monsters of the Silurian seas were the eurypterids. These sea-scorpions, which are only remotely related to the land scorpions, grew to a length of about 3 metres (10 feet). They lived in estuaries and coastal lagoons. They had large pincers and undoubtedly preyed on other animals.

An intense period of mountain building brought the Silurian period to a close and affected most of the following Devonian period. The world had changed, mountain ranges had been slowly uplifted and in many cases desert conditions prevailed. Plants had become more abundant, spreading out to occupy different sites on land.

Gradually the early, leafless forms of plants were replaced by ferns and horsetails. The land itself, once the plant cover was established, was invaded by many different types of animal, including mites, insects and millipedes. Spiders existed but did not yet make webs. The freshwater streams and lakes had mussels in them.

The Age of Fishes

The greatest development of this period was in the backboned animals. The Devonian period has been called the Age of Fishes. The early fish-like forms gradually evolved into true fish. Some had their bodies covered in plates while others already had scales. A great step forward was taken with the evolution of jaws and paired fins. Some of the fish were enormous, growing to 9 metres (30 feet) in the case of *Dinichthys*.

It was during the Devonian that the first sharks appeared. Living at first in the fresh water they eventually became sea dwellers. The true bony fish also developed and from the very beginning there appeared to have been two divisions. The one remained insignificant in Palaeozoic times but later diversified and led to many of the fish of the Mesozoic era and of today. The other group included the fish with lungs and others which were more powerfully built and had the characteristics of early amphibians. This latter group was thought to have become extinct during the Mesozoic times but the discovery of the coelacanth disproved this. Lungfish are still found in Australia and South America. Some are able to survive out of water, and others can even burrow in the mud. In some types the fins are strong enough to enable them to move on land. It is easy to see why the ancestors of these two groups may have fathered the first land animals.

The Carboniferous period is the time of the great evergreen forests. The scale trees grew to nearly 30 metres (100 feet). Their great leafy shoots would have had cones on the end of them. Today there are only about 25 different types of horsetail, none of which grows to more than 75 centimetres (30 inches) high.

The Days of the Dinosaurs

The Triassic period saw the development of reptiles, some of which have survived unchanged.

Map showing the geography of the Cretaceous period.

About 65 million years ago, at the end of the Cretaceous period, after millions of years of drift, the present-day continents began to form into their familiar shapes.

The Mesozoic (middle life) era stretches from 225 to 70 million years ago. It is divided into three periods. These are the Triassic period, named after the three-fold division of the rocks in Germany; the Jurassic period named after the Jura Mountains; and the Cretaceous period named after the Latin word *creta*, for chalk.

This was the time when life finally arrived on land in force and began to fill the many different habitats. Plants took on a modern appearance by the end of the Mesozoic. It was also the era of the great reptiles of enormous size and weight. Never again were reptiles going to be so important and diverse. Gradually mammals developed but did not have a great influence on the fauna.

Although originating at the end of the previous era, the gymnosperms (naked seed-plants) now began to be the most important of the plants. Many had short, cylindrically shaped stems while others were tall and slender. The gymnosperms include some of the forms that were present in the Carboniferous but cover also the cycads and the ginkgoes. Of the latter the only living survivor is the maidenhair tree.

The evolution of the gymnosperms was a great advance in the development of plants, for it enabled them to reproduce independent of water. Also with the advent of seeds there was a better chance of survival and of colonising new areas. The next great step forward in the plant kingdom was the evolution of flowering plants. As remains of these have been discovered in rocks of the early Cretaceous age, it would seem likely that they developed in Jurassic times. The earliest of these included shrubs and trees like the fig, magnolia and japonica of today. By the end of the Mesozoic era the gymnosperms were in decline and flowering plants were beginning to dominate the plant world.

The Triassic saw not only changes in plant types but also in animals. In the seas a whole new group of corals appeared. The ammonites (coiled shells) became increasingly important and the first lobster-like crustacean evolved. But in the seas there were also large reptiles with the agility of fish. The giant ichthyosaurs (fish-lizards) were the scourge of the seas. Fish-shaped and with many teeth they preyed on all sorts of animals. They reached their maximum development in Jurassic times and died out by the end of the Mesozoic. These animals were not egg-laying but the young developed inside the mother, although their nourishment was obtained from an egg. Remarkable fossils have been found in which the young are seen inside the mother.

The Great Reptiles

The Triassic also saw the development of reptiles. The first tortoises and turtles arrived. They have survived almost unchanged until the present day. The ancestors of the dinosaurs had developed while the mammal-like reptiles had evolved into a number of different forms and from their ancestors were to come the first true mammals.

The dominant land animals of the Jurassic period are the dinosaurs. These tend to overshadow all the many other interesting events which

Among the dinosaurs of the Jurassic period was the *Styracosaurus*.

The largest dinosaur of the Age of Reptiles was the *Diplodocus,* which spent much of its life in swampy regions.

were taking place. On land, plants looked much like those of the Triassic, but the fauna included beetles, termites and flies. The amphibians, although no longer large, now included frogs and toads among their number.

As well as the dinosaurs there were flying reptiles, the pterosaurs (winged reptiles) which included the pterodactyls. The vertebrates had begun to conquer the air. These early forms looked rather like bats—which are mammals—although they did not fly as efficiently. Retaining all the reptilian characteristics, the largest had a wing span of 7·5 metres (25 feet). The Jurassic forms were generally smaller than those of Cretaceous times. The first birds must have evolved from a similar ancestor. By a thousand-to-one chance the fine Solenhofen limestone of Bavaria has preserved a number of remains of the earliest bird. It has been called *Archaeopteryx* (ancient wing). This first bird was about the size of a magpie. Although it had feathers, its reptile ancestors had left their mark in the teeth and claws. It was not the most efficient of fliers.

Among the Jurassic dinosaurs was *Stegosaurus* (roof lizard). This had a double row of plates along its back and grew to about 6 metres (20 feet) in

length. It fed on plants. This same period can claim the heaviest animal of all times—the mighty *Brachiosaurus* (arm lizard) which grew to a length of 21 metres (70 feet) and could have weighed up to 80 tons. The brain of the dinosaurs was extremely small and in the large forms must have been limited to controlling the muscles and giving warning of food or danger. Some of these monsters had a 'second brain' which helped, through its attachment with the spinal column, to control the tail and hindquarters. The largest dinosaur was *Diplodocus* which was about 25 metres (80 feet) long. This was characterised by its very long neck and tail. These larger forms spent their lives in swampy regions and often their footprints have been preserved.

There were also the flesh-eating dinosaurs, *Megalosaurus* and *Allosaurus*. These walked on their hind legs and used the shortened front ones to hold or capture their prey.

Jurassic Mammals

The mammals of the Jurassic were generally small, about the size of a rat. They already showed adaptations to various ways of life, some eating insects, others small creatures and plants.

The Jurassic seas had not only the ichthyosaurs but also the generally longer-necked plesiosaurs. These grew to over 3 metres (10 feet) in length. Among the animals without backbones were the ammonites.

In Cretaceous times the dinosaurs still dominated the land. Perhaps the best known of all the dinosaurs comes from this time. *Tyrannosaurus* (tyrant-lizard) grew to a height of 6 metres (20 feet) and was over 12 metres (40 feet) long. It moved on its hind legs while the front ones were extremely small. Its teeth measured up to 15 centimetres (6 inches) and were well equipped and shaped to tear at the flesh of the other dinosaurs on which it undoubtedly fed.

Remarkable finds have been made in Mongolia of dinosaur eggs. However, at the end of the Cretaceous times the dinosaurs were to die out. What caused the reptiles' decline is not known. The changes of climate which occurred may have affected them. Perhaps it changed the vegetation and thus caused the plant-eating dinosaurs to die out. With nothing on which to feed, the meat-eaters would also have quickly died out. It is possible, too, that the swamp lands disappeared.

Development of the Modern World

These Eocene animals are (from the left) *Eohippus, Phenacodus, Tritemnodon* and *Diatryma*.

Sea in Eocene period and at present.

Sea in Eocene period but now land.

Land in Eocene period and at present.

Land in Eocene period but now sea.

● Mammals

Map showing the geography of the Eocene period.

The Cainozoic (later life) era consists of a maximum of seven periods. The last two, which make up the shortest span of time, are often grouped together as the Quaternary era while all the rest go to make up the Tertiary era. The Quaternary era is the time of the ice ages and the coming of man. The earliest period of the Cainozoic is the Palaeocene followed by the Eocene (dawn of recent life), Oligocene (few recent forms of life), Miocene (less recent forms of life) and Pliocene (more recent forms of life). The whole era to the present day covers the span of time from seventy million years ago.

It is characterised by a number of important developments, not least among them the considerable development of mammals and in particular of the primates. Primates are the group to which man belongs. Not only were mammals developing, but plants took on a more modern appearance with the rapid evolution of the many forms of flowering types.

Also showing rapid development and occupying a number of different environments were the birds. Possibly they were aided by the increase in flowers, which in turn caused a dramatic rise in the insect population. The development of one type of creature was often therefore dependent on others.

At the beginning of the Tertiary era the main groups of mammals already existed. They included the carnivores (meat-eaters), the insect-eaters, the primates, rodents, rabbits and whales. Hoofed animals were the most numerous in the early years of the era. They lived in great herds. The hoofed mammals (ungulates) soon divided into the odd-toed and the even-toed. Examples of the former are the rhinoceroses, tapirs and horses, and of the latter, pigs, camels, cattle and sheep.

Some ungulates did not survive Eocene times. The massive *Uintatherium* lived in North America. It had three pairs of 'horns' on its head. It was in Eocene times that the ancestors of the elephant appeared. They are thought to have originated from *Moeritherium* whose remains have been discovered in North Africa. This animal did not have a trunk and was about the size of a tapir.

There were also flesh-eating mammals at this time and early primates. Some of the latter resembled the present-day lemurs, others the tarsiers.

At the end of the Eocene times many of the mammals disappeared as new forms developed and spread over the land. Many of the animals of Oligocene times are therefore the forerunners of those of today. The elephant-like forms continued to develop. Short trunks were in evidence and some forms had tusks in both the lower and upper jaws.

Primitive camels also began to develop together with pig-like animals. The flesh-eaters of the period included *Hyaenodon*. There was a considerable development of the families which now include the dogs and cats. However, before the ice age, many of the cats were of the sabre-tooth variety. In

Two mammals of the Miocene period, *Merychyus* and *Stenomyius*.

Pleistocene animals such as the sabre-tooth and the mammoth resembled their modern counterparts, the tiger and the elephant.

these the top canine teeth were long and curved.

Evolution in Action

There are a number of examples of 'evolution in action' provided by the mammals. The evolution of the elephants is one, but the most famous is that of the development of the modern horse. Horses began in late Palaeocene or early Eocene times in the form of *Hyracotherium* which was about the size of a fox-terrier. It lived on leaves and other matter found in the forest. It had four toes on the front feet and three on the hind. The evolution goes on through the forms known as *Mesohippus* and *Merychippus*. The latter has three toes but the central one was best developed. The animal stood about as high as a donkey. The modern horse has evolved from *Pliohippus* which was the first true horse to have one toe. The evolution of the horse shows how animals become adapted to different environments. The earliest representative was a forest dweller but the final product lived on the plains. There was a gradual increase in the brain size, and because of the need for changes in diet, the shape of the face altered to accommodate a different arrangement of the teeth.

Modern Fauna and Flora

Gradually, therefore, the fauna and flora (animals and plants) became increasingly modern in their appearance. There were, however, exceptions to this in Australia and South America.

Because of the changing distribution of the land masses and the gradual break-up of the original continent, the only animals to reach Australia were the more primitive ones, the monotremes (platypus) and the marsupials (the koala and kangaroo). These became the dominant mammals of that continent until the introduction of the more advanced forms by man. Being isolated, the primitive animals' territory was not invaded by more advanced forms and therefore they survived for millions of years.

South America was joined with North America at the beginning of the Tertiary but then split away until Pliocene times. Again the mammals evolved in isolation. Many unusual forms arose. Among them was the giant sloth, *Megatherium* which was the size of an elephant, and the giant armadillo, *Glyptodon*. Once the land bridge was again established, these forms were overrun by those from the north, although some of the southern animals also moved northwards and colonised what is now Mexico and the southern United States.

The First Primates

It was during Tertiary times that the primates evolved. Among their characteristics are the ability to grasp, forward-looking eyes and the fact that in most claws have been replaced by nails. The whole group shows a gradual increase in brain size. The primates evolved from the insectivores. A hedgehog is a modern insectivore. The primates which lived during the Palaeocene times do not seem to have lived on into the Eocene, when a relatively new line of development emerged. These Eocene animals had shorter noses and forward-looking eyes.

Egypt has yielded some of the remains of the early primates. In Miocene times there were many types of apes. These are often grouped together as *Dryopithecus*. From these the gorilla and chimpanzees of today have developed, while yet another line of descent may have been through *Ramapithecus*. It is from this creature, only known from fragmentary remains, that man himself may be descended, but there is a long gap between it and the first hominids.

Earth in the Age of Man

Man has become a powerful force in changing the landscape. He changes the Earth both directly and indirectly. From prehistoric times he has turned his attention to creating environments which are suitable for his needs at any given time. Early man used the technique of fire to drive wild animals into his traps. With the coming of agriculture, land and forest would be burned to make way for the plough. Forests were later cut down to provide fuel for the various industrial enterprises and for the making of ships.

The Industrial Revolution made great changes in man's effect on the environment. Suddenly great factory complexes were built. Mines were quickly exploited and increased in size. Dirt and grime became synonymous with industry. The atmosphere became heavily polluted and sulphurous. Canals and railways were constructed to carry people and material from one end of the world to the other. They were built, not with mechanical diggers and shovels, but by human effort. Great gangs of men dug out cuttings, constructed embankments, drove tunnels through the mountains and built endless bridges and viaducts. The landscape was altered considerably by the ribbons of water and steel.

The need to transport goods and people was to have an even more dramatic impact on the world in the twentieth century. Airports cover a large area of land. Roads, especially motorways, cut great slashes across valleys and hillsides. At interchange points land is used up to help the flow of traffic. Often such roads are built on good agricultural land and pass through some of the most beautiful scenery.

Population Increase

There are two major reasons for man's continuing and dramatic impact on the world. One is increasing population and the other the need to sustain technological advance. It is estimated that at the present time there are 4,000 million people in the world. But the increase has not been a steady one. The first great impetus to population increase was given when man ceased being a hunter and became a farmer. Before this time the whole world may have contained only 5 to 10 million people; by 2,000 years ago it had risen to 250 million; by 1,000 years ago to 350 million; by 500 years ago to 450 million; by the year 1800 to 1,000 million; by 1900 to 1,650 million. By the end of the twentieth century it will have reached 6,500 million,

four times the number of people who were living on the same planet 100 years before.

To keep pace with these increasing numbers more and more food has to be grown. Early on, the burning of forests caused considerable erosion of the land. In this century poor farming methods have led to the same disasters. In many countries hedgerows have been torn up and fields made larger to accommodate machinery used on the farm. In areas such as South America and the Far East man has constructed terraces to make the best use of the gently sloping valley sides. The fields there rise in a series of gigantic steps, each tier of which is held by an earth or stone wall. Terracing of such slopes goes back thousands of years.

The continuing need for water for agricultural purposes has led to vast irrigation projects. Rivers are dammed and diverted. In the upland regions dams are used in the generation of hydroelectric power. But good does not always come from such activities. The Aswan Dam prevents the annual deposition of vast quantities of silt over the land, thereby making them less fertile. The gradual infilling of sediment into a reservoir can make it less effective. It has also been

Brasilia

established that the creation of very large reservoirs in geologically unstable areas can cause earthquakes which may have disastrous results.

Mining

Perhaps more than any other activity, mining has altered the landscape, often leaving ugly scars which take years to heal. Mining goes back to Neolithic times when man first dug into the Earth to obtain flint. Advanced technology in the form of larger and more efficient machines has led to larger and larger mines and opencast workings.

The largest quarry in the world, the Bingham Canyon Copper Mine, is in the United States at Utah. The quarry has been worked for over sixty years and every day now some 321,000 tons of material are removed. This one example shows what it is now possible for man to achieve.

Mining underground presents the environment with two hazards. In digging the shafts and tunnels, quantities of rock are brought to the surface and dumped, creating hills of broken rock material and dust. Subsidence due to mining and to drilling for oil

Land Reclamation

Modification of the sea shore by the construction of sea walls, jetties and harbours are old practices. In some areas, mainly in the Netherlands, thousands of hectares have been reclaimed from the sea to create new farmland. The whole of the western

must continue to use the resources of the Earth, he must have more respect for the planet. There can be no escape to the Earth's satellite or the other planets. In the coming years there will have to be more recycling of industrial material.

There is evidence that man has

Man's power to change the face of the landscape is amply demonstrated in the dense forests of Brazil, through which roads have been driven to the complex of government buildings in the modern capital city of Brasilia.

and natural gas is more widespread than is often realised. In three sites in California 6,500 square kilometres (2,500 square miles) were affected. To prevent subsidence, salt water under pressure is pumped into the oil reservoir.

part of Holland would be under the sea if it were not for the dams and dykes. In 1,000 years from about A.D. 900 the Dutch have added more than 405,000 hectares (1 million acres) to their country. Ambitious schemes are still proceeding to provide even more land. The islands off the coast are to be linked by sea defences and by 1980 another 405,000 hectares (1 million acres) will have been added.

Although it is indisputable that man

begun to learn to care more for his environment. When the Alaska pipeline project was agreed upon by the United States Congress, it was only after many environmental safeguards had been built in. The permafrost (permanently frozen subsoil) will not be affected by the pipe-line, and the caribou will still be able to migrate. There will be no driving over the virgin land nor will any hunting of the animals be tolerated.

The Coming of Man

In 1726 Professor Johann Scheuchzer of Zurich discovered a fossil which he named *Homo diluvi testis* which means, man, witness of the flood. He described it as a 'rare relic of the accursed race of the primitive world', and added rather piously, 'melancholy skeleton of an old sinner, convert the hearts of modern reprobates'. The fossil was later found to be the skeleton of a giant salamander.

It was not until the mid-nineteenth century that the question of fossil man was taken seriously. Even then, many refused to believe what the various finds of fossil bones clearly indicated. For years, religious prejudice and general ignorance had led the people to believe that man was created in his present form. Even the great naturalist Georges Cuvier (1769–1832) declared that fossil bones of man did not exist.

Piltdown Man

It was also ignorance coupled with strongly held, but preconceived, ideas of fossil man, which led to the acceptance of one of the greatest hoaxes of all time. In 1912 a labourer at the East Sussex village of Piltdown in England dug up some bits of a skull and jaw. The skull was large enough to give a brain capacity equivalent to that of modern man while the jaw had the appearance of an ape. This fitted exactly with the current theories of ape-men. However, finds in other parts of the world in following years began to make it difficult to accept the fossil man of Sussex.

Between 1949 and 1953 an intensive examination of the remains began, during which fluorine dating was used as well as chemical and physical investigations. The hoax was uncovered. The skull turned out to be that of a modern man who had lived about A.D. 1330, and the jawbone that of a young orang-utan of about A.D. 1450.

Gradually, from the end of the nineteenth century, more and more of the world began to be geologically examined. Fossils of creatures akin to man were found in South Africa, China and the Middle East. The main story of man's evolution can now be told, although it still contains many gaps.

The development and characteristics of the primates in Tertiary times have already been described. Before it is possible to understand the evolution of man itself, it is necessary to be aware of his place in the animal

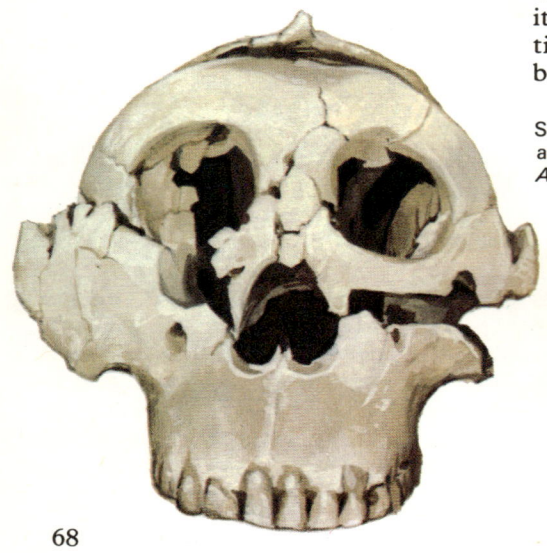

Skulls, jaw-bone and hip bone of *Australopithecus.*

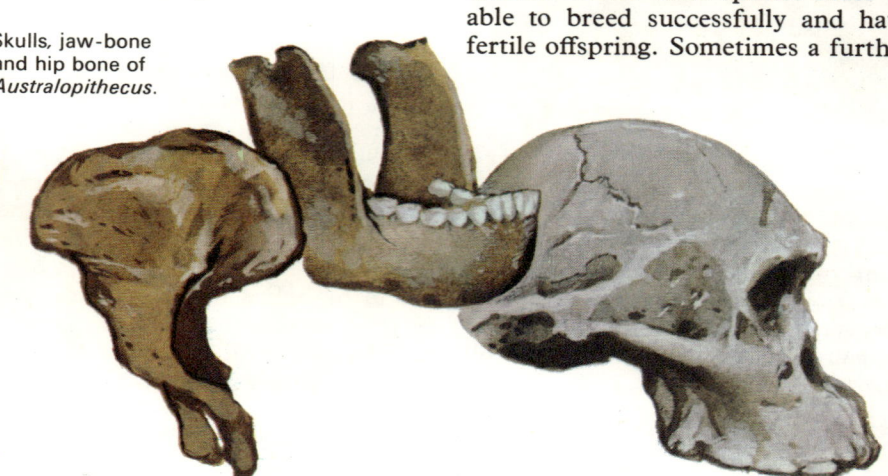

kingdom and also the skeletal framework of modern man.

The Animal Kingdom

All living forms have a place in one of the two great kingdoms of animals or plants. Within the animal kingdom there is a very clear division between those with backbones and those without. The former are called chordates. Man certainly has a backbone and must therefore be within this group. The next subdivision brings together those animals which are warmblooded, have hair and suckle their young, and during their lifetime most have two sets of teeth: these are the mammals. The characteristics of the primates, which form a group within the mammals, have been detailed. The primates include the lemurs, bush babies, tarsiers, monkeys, baboons, gibbons, orang-utans, chimpanzees, gorillas and man himself.

Animals which possess a number of the characteristics of man are grouped together in one family, called the Hominidae. This family includes not only man of today but a number of fossil forms as well.

Scientists give two or even three Latin names to each animal. The two most commonly given refer to the genus and species. All the plants or animals in the same species must be able to breed successfully and have fertile offspring. Sometimes a further

One of the most important sites for the discovery of early modern man is the Olduvai Gorge on the Serengeti Plain in Tanzania, East Africa.

subdivision is made by the creation of sub-species. Classification, or taxonomy, is a very difficult area in which to work. Those who study fossils have to examine large numbers of specimens and read many scientific papers to enable them to classify individual specimens. They attempt to place each organism in its correct place on the 'tree of life'. It is rather like constructing a family history.

Man, therefore, may be classified as follows. The names in the left hand column are those given to each of the divisions of the animal or plant kingdoms.

Kingdom	*Animalia*
Phylum	*Chordata*
Class	*Mammalia*
Order	*Primates*
Family	*Hominidae*
Genus	*Homo*
Species	*sapiens*
Sub-species	*sapiens*

Modern man is referred to as *Homo sapiens sapiens*.

Modern Man

Modern man possesses a number of characteristics which it is vital to understand in tracing his evolution. It is usually the hard parts of animals which are preserved in fossil form, and therefore the bones which make up the skeleton are usually found in excavations. The different shapes and arrangements of the 206 bones in man tell much about the way he lives. His teeth indicate what type of food he eats. Bones may also reveal diet, disease and injury.

Bones are relatively uninteresting to look at and one may wonder why they are of such value in interpreting how their owner lived. A simple

example will resolve this. A tall person will have large bones. Therefore, by averaging out the sizes of bones found at different sites of the same age, it is possible to provide a relatively accurate figure for the average size of the people involved. There are also marked differences in the pelvic region between males and females which help to identify skeletons.

The skeleton not only protects the softer organs from damage, but it also provides points of attachment for the various muscles. At these points there are grooves and impressions which on fossil bones tell a valuable story.

The most important parts of the body in the study of fossil forms are the skull, teeth, backbone, foot, hand and pelvis. It is by studying the changes in these structures in the fossils which have been found, that our knowledge of man's ancestors has been gained.

Today man has a considerable brain capacity which is reflected in the size of the skull which protects it. The teeth and jaw are characteristic

and affect the shape of the skull. Because man walks upright, the joining of the skull to the backbone and the shape of the spinal column itself are distinctive.

Some of the features which man presents are in fact remnants of his past way of life. Everyone is familiar with the different movements it is possible to make with the arms and legs. Arms can be swung right round. The structure which permits this is relatively simple. It is a legacy from a time when man's relations lived in the trees and swung from branch to branch.

The reason for the development of bipedalism (walking on two feet) in hominids is not fully understood. It is likely that several factors contributed to their descent from the trees. The lush forests of Tertiary times had by the Pleistocene period given way to more open landscapes. Extensive observations of chimpanzees and other primates have revealed that many spend some time on the ground and also walk on their hind legs. Some

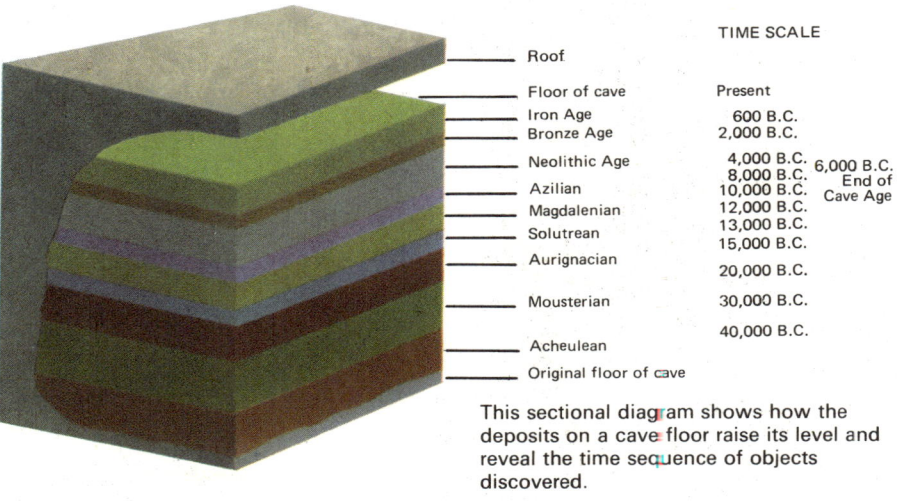

	TIME SCALE
Roof	
Floor of cave	Present
Iron Age	600 B.C.
Bronze Age	2,000 B.C.
Neolithic Age	4,000 B.C. — 6,000 B.C.
Azilian	8,000 B.C.
	10,000 B.C. — End of Cave Age
Magdalenian	12,000 B.C.
Solutrean	13,000 B.C.
	15,000 B.C.
Aurignacian	20,000 B.C.
Mousterian	30,000 B.C.
	40,000 B.C.
Acheulean	
Original floor of cave	

This sectional diagram shows how the deposits on a cave floor raise its level and reveal the time sequence of objects discovered.

even use 'tools'—sticks to prod into the holes of insects, or rocks to break open other finds. Once on the ground, development of primates could have been due to a change of diet. Meat-eaters need to capture their prey, which may mean stalking it for many kilometres. Other reasons for such developments may have been due to the added protection given to the young if they are carried rather than forced to hang onto their mothers. The development of tools might also have influenced the early hominids.

Body Structures

Man's upright stance is reflected in many structures in his body. The spine is curved and allows the head to rest on the top in a position of perfect balance. Because of the curves, some of the blocks of bone (vertebrae) making up the column, are wedge-shaped. The pelvic girdle also is much shorter than in the other primates. Certain bones of the foot are distinctive in a creature which walks upright, in particular the structure of the big toe.

These are all important when examining fossil remains. The difference, or degrees of difference, between early and later man are reflected in the structure and shape of the bones. The hand has remained a simple structure, but a significant change has come about to allow hominids to touch the tops of the fingers with the thumb. This allows man to perform a number of delicate and intricate movements.

The skull itself also shows change. An increase in brain size means an increase in skull size. Brain capacity has certainly grown over the years but this in itself does not mean an increase in intelligence. The various finds of tools and the development of other activities show clearly, however, that intelligence has also evolved.

Apart from indicating brain size the skull also presents a number of other features which are valuable to the palaeontologist. Where the skull joins the spine there is a large hole. The position of this hole varies. In man it is well to the front and opens downwards. In the apes it is placed further back and its opening is directed backwards.

In gorillas there is a large crest of bone on the skull roof. This is used for the attachment of muscles to operate the massive jaw. Because the head is not well balanced there have to be massive neck muscles which also need areas of attachment. The evolution of teeth has had a profound effect on the shape of the face. Presumably the changes in teeth reflect a change in diet. In the case of the gorilla, the shape of the dental arch is rectangular, while in man it is U-shaped.

Man's Ancestors

The different types of primates living today are useful for comparing the functions of the different structures of the body. It must not be thought, however, that man developed from creatures such as the present-day apes and gorillas. All may have had a common ancestor but if so, it existed millions of years ago. Since then the groups have evolved in their own way.

Although it would seem that there are many features which enable man's evolutionary progress to be charted, the first requirement is to locate suitable specimens. Any animal which lives on land is less likely to be preserved as a fossil than those which live in the sea. Under some conditions,

Australopithecus

Peking Man

for example in wet, acid soil, bones completely disappear. Once dead, an animal is attacked by scavengers and the bones which remain are quickly scattered by the weather.

Once on the plains, early man would have lived close to streams and lakes and sheltered in caves. All of these sites provide a reasonable chance of fossilisation. In the case of a river or lake, a flood may quickly deposit fine mud over the bones, while in a cave the remains are safe from the ravages of the weather.

There were many fluctuations of climate during the evolution of man, for it was the time of the great ice ages. The ice advanced and retreated in four major phases. Between these there would have been many smaller advances and retreats. Much of North America, northern Europe and Asia was covered with ice. The glaciers moved farther down the mountains of the Alps and Himalayas and in New Zealand. The total area covered was 30 million square kilometres (11·5 square miles). Changes in the climate

would have had considerable effects on plants and therefore on the animal population. A fauna consisting of elephants, rhinoceroses and lions would be replaced by one of woolly rhinoceroses, bison and mammoths. Forests would be transformed to a few stunted trees.

All of the climatic changes would have considerable effects on the sea level. When the ice was at its height the sea would be much lower than at present. Land bridges would connect otherwise remote areas. Alaska was joined to Russia, England to Europe and many other islands would be linked with nearby mainlands. These links would allow the spread of man to otherwise inaccessible areas.

Fossil Hominids

It is in Africa that the most important finds of fossil hominids have been made. Even so there is a very long gap between *Ramapithecus* described in the section on Tertiary times and the first true hominids. From the very beginning there appear to have been two types. Some scientists consider them to have sufficient differences to be placed in different genera. They are, however, both far enough removed

from the men of today and other fossil forms to be placed not in the genus *Homo* but in one called *Australopithecus* which means southern ape.

These early hominids lived in groups and hunted as well as collected berries and fruit. They could not walk with the striding action of modern man. They were more likely to jog along. Of these two forms the lighter one stood about 1·4 metres (4·5 feet) tall and weighed 30 kilos (66 pounds). A plains dweller, this early man sheltered in caves and many have manufactured tools.

The more robust form, sometimes given the name *Paranthropus*, stood about 1·5 metres (4·8 feet) high and weighed about 45 kilos (99 pounds). It is likely that *Paranthropus* lived in the forests and had a mainly vegetarian diet.

Three areas have become particularly important for the remains of prehistoric man. Olduvai Gorge, situated on the Serengeti Plain in Tanzania, was created by a river cutting through lake and volcanic deposits to create a gorge 91 metres (300 feet) deep. Lake deposits are excellent for the preservation of fossils, and the various layers of lava which

Neanderthal Man

Cro-Magnon Man

71

Skull of *Australopithecus*.

Skull of Peking Man.

are encountered in the succession are most useful for dating purposes. A number of australopithecine remains have been recovered. A site in Ethiopia called Omo has yielded a number of important remains. In Kenya, australopithecine remains reckoned to be almost five million years old have been discovered.

There are also a number of important localities in South Africa. Those at Sterkfontein and Taung are about two million years old and yielded remains of the smaller australopithecine. Others, less old, are Makapansgat (smaller australopithecine), Swartkrans and Kromdraai which have yielded remains of the robust australopithecine. The last site is dated at one million years old. It is from the finds at Sterkfontein that a pelvis with the characteristics of both modern man and the gorilla has been obtained.

Although the East African finds have greatly increased our knowledge of man's development, they have in some cases created problems. One find from here appears to be of a hominid more advanced than the australopithecines, although coming from layers of rock about the same age. It is considered by some to be advanced enough to be counted within the same genus as modern man. It has been called *Homo habilis*, which means able or skilful man. It may be no more than a variation of the australopithecines, for by comparison, there is plenty of variation between the various races of modern man and yet they are all considered to be of the same genus and species.

Homo Erectus

For the next development of man,

finds in the Far East are very important. Fossils discovered in Java and China are now considered to belong to the same group called *Homo erectus* or erect man. Older names, often still used, reflect where specimens have been discovered, for example, Java man and Peking man. These people are thought to have lived between 350,000 and 1,000,000 years ago. Their brain size shows an increase over that of the australopithecines, and although shorter than modern man, they still had massive brow ridges (ridges over the eyes) and the chin was not well developed.

Man had now taken a great step forward—he could control fire. It must have been tended with great care and respect. Perhaps when the band moved from place to place the fire was taken too. This new discovery enabled man to cook meat, warm his cave and provide light during the long dark nights. It would also have been of value in keeping wild animals away from a cave.

Other finds which have been made in Java may indicate that the australopithecines also reached those areas. Other remains of Middle Pleistocene men have also been discovered in South Africa, Algeria and Morocco. A European example may be provided by Heidelberg man. The jaw of this creature has affinities both with *Homo erectus* and later forms.

Early remains of *Homo sapiens* have been unearthed at a number of sites, although a query still hangs over some of the finds. Hungary, England and Germany all provide examples either of earlier members of the *Homo sapiens* group or very close relatives.

Neanderthal man is everyone's idea

of prehistoric man. In fact it has now been proved that the original description giving a picture of a slumped, shuffling cave man, was based on a specimen which in life had been crippled with arthritis. In fact, although thickset, a little shorter and with fairly heavy brow ridges, Neanderthal man was very little different in appearance from modern man.

His brain size was often greater than that of man today and he was an expert hunter, often going to elaborate lengths to catch his prey. He used both snares and pits and would drive game over cliff edges or canyons. Cooperation between individuals was now very well established. When the animals were caught they were cut up and taken back to camp. During the warmer periods such camps would be out in the open, but in the winter or during colder periods caves were used. Neanderthal man wore clothes which were fashioned out of the hides of animals. It can be assumed that they were worn not out of modesty but out of the need to keep warm.

Social development had also advanced considerably from that of *Homo erectus*. The dead were buried and not simply left to scavenging animals and birds. It would seem that these people related death to sleep, which shows a sense of logic. One find at Le Moustier in France revealed a man laid in his grave in a sleeping position.

Neanderthal Burials

Perhaps a religion had developed and Neanderthal man believed in magic. The cave bear was a central figure in his rituals. At Drachenloch (Dragon's Hole) in Switzerland, bear skulls were

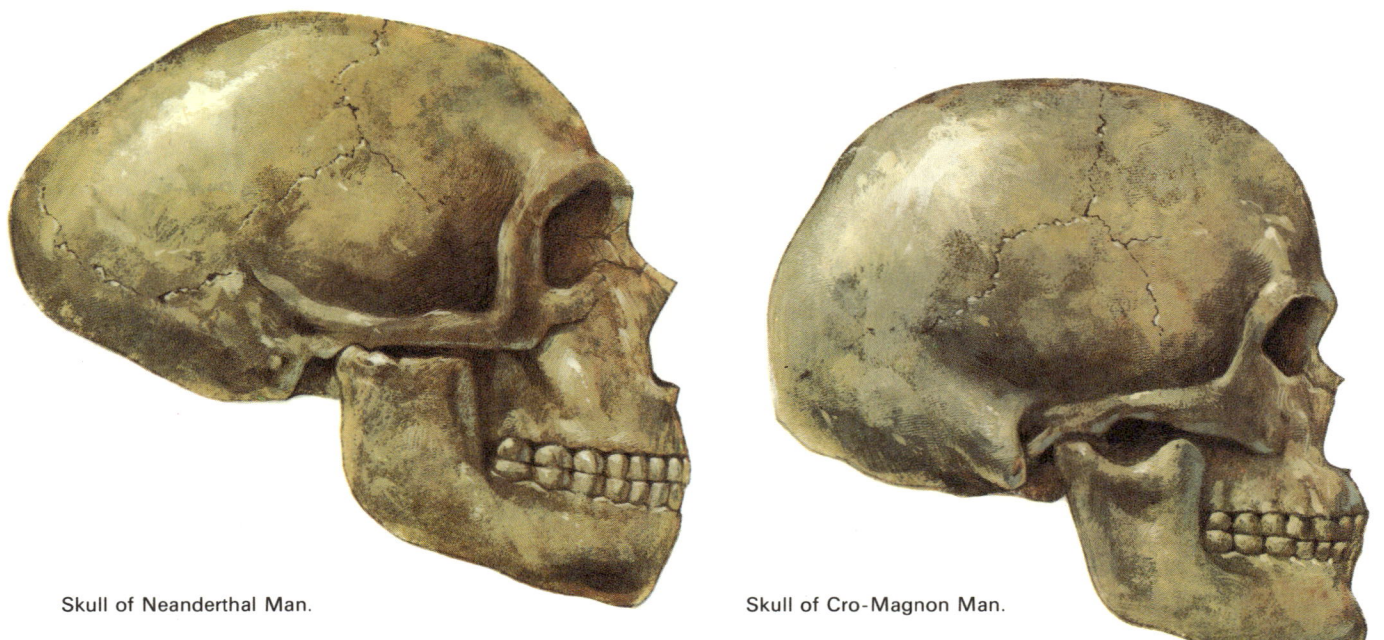

Skull of Neanderthal Man.

Skull of Cro-Magnon Man.

discovered along with other bones in set arrangements. Other similar finds have been made in Austria and Germany. The cave bear was a fearsome creature and would have been much taller than Neanderthal man. Perhaps the rituals grew out of a need to protect himself from the attacks of the bear. About 35,000 years ago these men vanished without trace. The reason for their disappearance is uncertain. Maybe they were exterminated by another race of man or perhaps they simply interbred with other migrants.

In the first instance many of the finds were in Europe, and because of this, only a partial understanding was gained about Neanderthal man. It has since been discovered that there were really two types—the 'classic' one described in the sections above, who lived in western Europe, and one called 'progressive'. The two types had many features in common, but the 'progressive' possessed some characteristics which heralded modern man. This group is known as the neanderthaloids.

In the Middle East some interesting finds on Mount Carmel in Israel have provided more information about these different types. The older of two caves excavated there is called Tabun. Here the neanderthals have features which link them with other finds in Africa and Europe. At the other cave, at

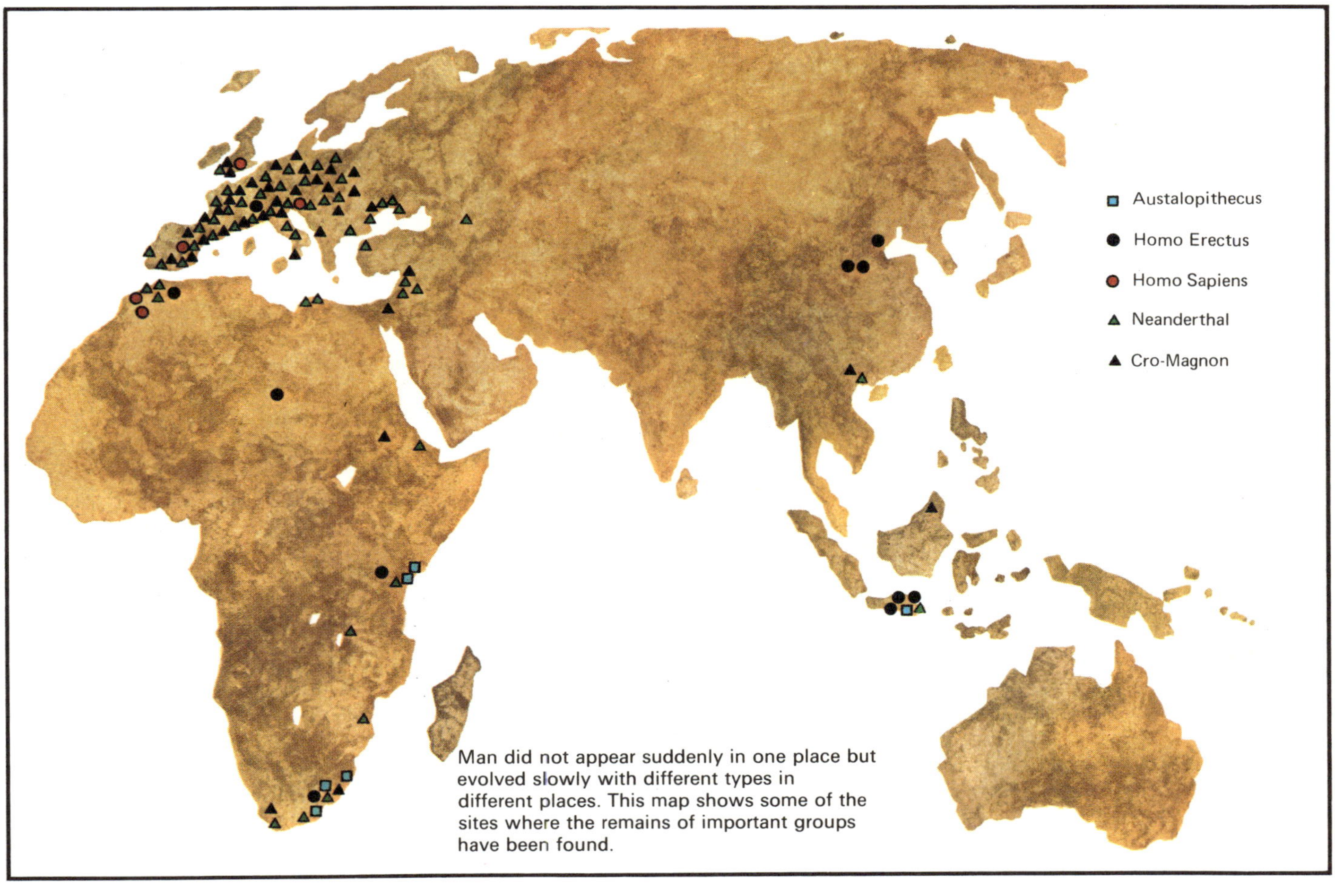

- ◻ Austalopithecus
- ● Homo Erectus
- ◉ Homo Sapiens
- ▲ Neanderthal
- ▲ Cro-Magnon

Man did not appear suddenly in one place but evolved slowly with different types in different places. This map shows some of the sites where the remains of important groups have been found.

73

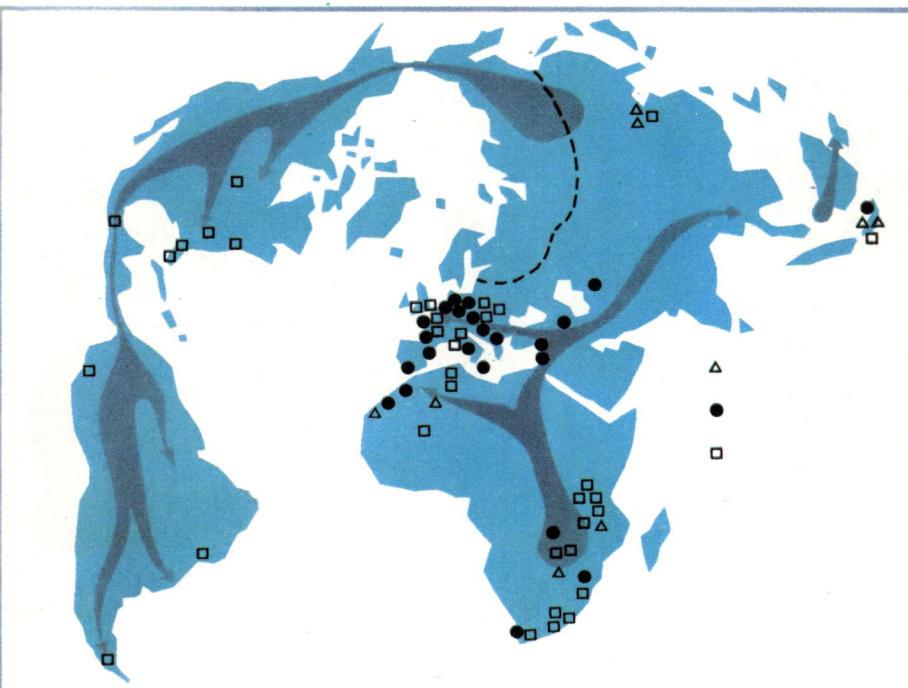

Man's migrations (above) took him across land bridges into the Americas and Australia. Some later migrations are shown in the map below. Green routes indicate voyages of exploration from Spain and Portugal in the 16th and 17th centuries; orange routes the slave trade; pink routes movements of Indian labour; and black routes other voyages of exploration.

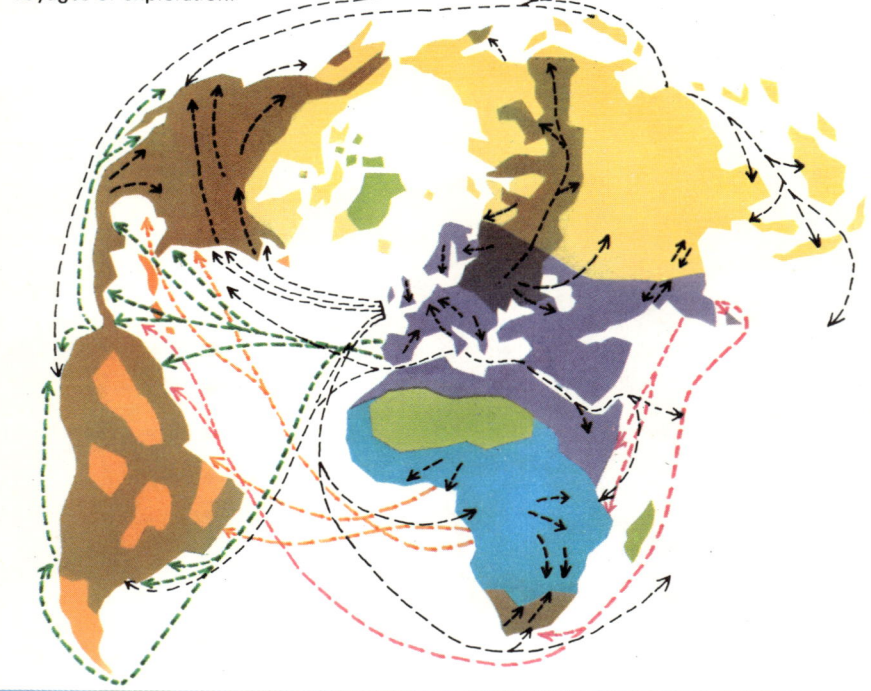

Skuhl, many have resemblances to modern man.

Homo Sapiens
Coinciding with the disappearance of the neanderthals is the appearance of modern man, *Homo sapiens sapiens*. All at once many different races seem to be represented. The most famous is the Cro-Magnon group named after the site at which they were first discovered in the Dordogne in France.

These have very few differences from modern man, although the skull is longer and narrower than at present. They were a tall and powerful people. They produced fine tools and were expert hunters. They were succeeded in the next period—the Neolithic—by a people with rounder skulls whose bones still tended to be thicker than those of present-day man.

Man was now established in the world. He was to break away from the

need to track after animals and was to settle down and farm the land. Neolithic times saw the beginning of agriculture. Villages grew into towns and towns became cities. The early forms of crops were developed and included wheat and barley. Animals, such as sheep, goats and cattle, were domesticated. The centre of this development was somewhere in the middle East.

Although the story of man is known in some detail, many gaps remain to be filled. Different groups of scientists place different emphasis on the various changes. Perhaps *Homo* first appeared one and a half million years ago, and from this stem arose the populations of Middle Pleistocene China and Java, while another line of development was Neanderthal man. Both were doomed not to survive. Other scientists consider that modern man developed from the neanderthal group in the Middle East. Yet other ideas stress that from Middle Pleistocene times onwards, a whole succession of forms arose, some of which have died out, while others live on in the many races of the world of today.

Man's Migrations
All the discussion on fossil man has so far concentrated on the land masses of Eurasia and Africa. How did man reach the Americas and Australia? The changes in sea-level must have made available land bridges to allow migrants to cross from one area to another. These changes would have allowed man to cross from Asia into Indonesia and later into Australia. It may well turn out that, whereas Australia was in the past considered to have been populated in relatively recent times, the first aborigines reached its shores more than 20,000 years ago.

The unfolding of the story of man in the Americas is one of increasing age. Recent discoveries in Peru show that man lived there 22,000 years ago, which indicates that he must have arrived in North America as long ago as 30,000 to 40,000 years. No one really doubts that his line of entry into the western world must have been from Russia across the Bering Strait and into Alaska. Although at almost all times the conditions in this region would have been harsh, the people making the trek would have been used to the cold and snow. There may have been several waves of invasion in view of the diversity shown by the many Indian tribes.

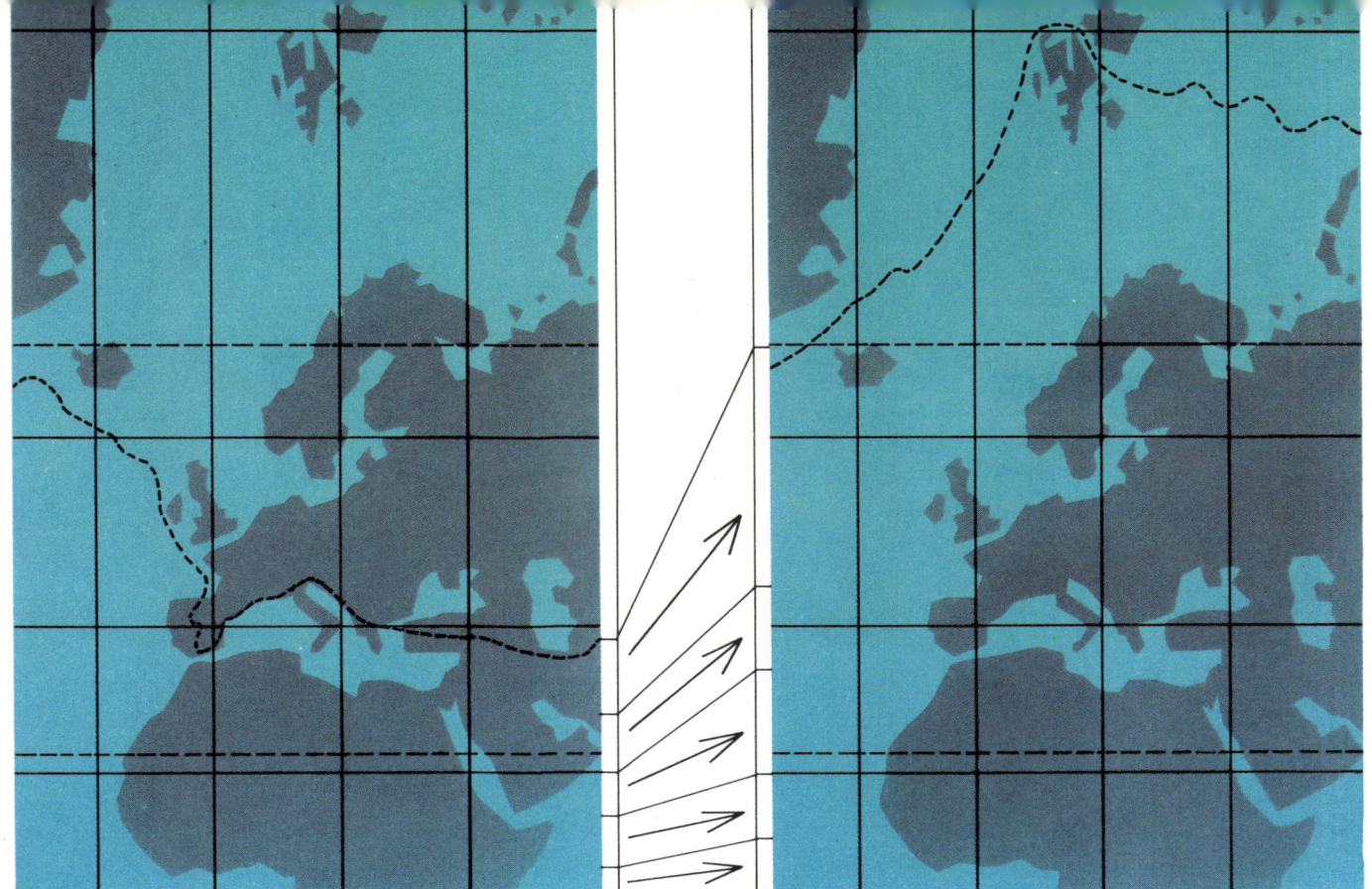

World Climates

As the ice retreated after the last of the Ice Ages the climate of Europe became progressively warmer.

During the past hundreds of millions of years, the surface of the Earth has experienced great changes in climate. At least four times in the last two million years vast ice sheets have spread out from various centres, covering the plains and filling the shallow continental seas. There have been other periods of somewhat less intense climatic stress too, when only small glaciers were able to develop among the high hills. These episodes have been of great importance in the development of the Earth's living beings. Always, however, they have been brief in terms of geological time, and after them the Earth has returned to more genial conditions, which have lasted for long periods.

The composition of the Earth's atmosphere has also varied throughout geological time. The total volume of nitrogen has increased, for that gas is so inert, that once it becomes a part of the air it is almost certain to remain there. The proportions of oxygen, carbon dioxide and water vapour have also fluctuated considerably. Carbon dioxide, for example, is produced mainly by living organisms, the natural decay of organic elements in the soil and the burning of fossil fuels. It is in turn absorbed by plants and dissolved by the sea where it produces carbonate of lime. The balance of the amount of carbon dioxide in the atmosphere at any one time is therefore delicate. Between 1900 and 1940 the total quantity of world carbon dioxide is estimated to have risen by ten per cent, due largely to the increased burning of fossil fuels.

Weather Records

Much of the available information on climatic change is based on archaeological evidence, analysis of vegetation history by means of pollen remains preserved in peat bogs, and for more recent periods only, documentary sources. Reliable weather records have only been kept during the last 100 years or so, and therefore it is only the recent climatic fluctuations which can be investigated in detail. General patterns of change are nevertheless clear since the end of the last glacial period.

Following the final retreat of the continental ice sheets from Europe and North America between 10,000 and 7,000 years ago, the climate rapidly improved in middle and higher latitudes. A thermal maximum was reached about 5000 to 3000 B.C. when summer temperatures are known to have been several degrees higher than today. Thereafter a decline set in with cold, wet conditions in Europe around 900–500 B.C.

Although temperatures have not since equalled those of the thermal maximum, there was certainly a warmer period in many parts of the world between A.D. 1000 and 1250, during the period of Viking colonisation of Greenland.

A further deterioration in climate followed and severe winters between A.D. 1550 and 1700 gave a 'Little Ice Age' with extensive arctic pack-ice and glacier advances. The warming trend which ended the 'Little Ice Age' began early in the nineteenth century and reached a peak in the 1920s. The effects of the temperature rise are apparent in many ways, notably the retreat of most of the world's glaciers, a raising of the snowline and a retreat of the tundra margin.

The latest evidence suggests that the warm period of the 1920s and 1930s has come to an end. Cooling has taken place in Arctic regions, but perhaps in compensation, slight winter warming has at the same time affected the United States, Europe and Japan. In very recent years too there has been a change in tropical rainfall patterns, with repeated unseasonal droughts occurring in large areas of tropical Africa and increases in precipitation reported in equatorial regions.

Many reasons for climatic change have been proposed, principally depending upon the changes of intensity of solar radiation received by the Earth. The intensity received depends upon the output of radiation by the sun, and also on differences in the Earth's atmospheric composition which alter the amount of the sun's energy absorbed at different times. Thus, increases in the carbon dioxide content of the atmosphere and periods of frequent great volcanic eruptions between 1800 and 1930 have been suggested as reasons for the warming that occurred in the nineteenth century.

Climatic Changes

No general agreement has been reached as to the primary cause of climatic change. It is, however, universally accepted that the climate is constantly changing, and that the present climate of an area is not the only climate that has been experienced there in the past.

A knowledge of past climates leads to a better understanding of much of the history of living beings on the planet, for the climate of an area and the type of life it can support are intimately linked.

Climatic changes during the last five or six hundred years appear, at some times, to have allowed sufficient vegetation for men and animals to travel across what are now deserts. This applies also to areas of North

Equatorial climate occurs in the Zaire Basin and southern parts of West Africa.

Africa, central Asia and the region of northern Mexico and south-western United States of America which are now largely uninhabited. At other times these routes of trade and migration have been cut off.

The evidence of climatic change given by the racial migrations depends on the principle that, during a period of increased rainfall, there is a movement of peoples from regions which are naturally moist to regions which are naturally dry. During the drier periods, the direction of movement is reversed, the naturally moist regions being occupied and the dry regions more or less abandoned.

The Thames river seems to tell its own story of climatic change too. The river in London does not seem to have frozen over more than once or twice in a century until the 1500s. But during the sixteenth century it froze four times, in the seventeenth century eight times and in the eighteenth century six times. The only year since 1800 that it froze was 1814. But it seems likely that if embankments and

bridges that speed up tidal flow had not been built, and tributaries closed over by pipes and culverts, it would have frozen over more often.

Present day seasonal changes of climate account for annual migrations of many birds and animals. Vast movements of birds take place from one continent to another in search of climates and habitats suited to their needs throughout the year. From evidence supplied by ringed birds, it appears that the majority of birds that summer in Europe, winter in the African continent. Swallows, for example, winter in the extreme south-east of Africa and journey to Great Britain and Germany for the summer. Not all migrants however penetrate so far into Africa, the Sahara proving too inhospitable for species such as blackcap and chiffchaff. As the summer visitors are leaving Britain for the south, other birds from the vast tracts of the Arctic, northern Europe and Siberia come to winter in the milder, relatively snow-free British Isles.

The climate of an area is made up of the characteristics of such things as temperature, rainfall and wind which lead to the different natural conditions of cold, wet and dry.

Present Climates

This contemporary painting shows a fair in progress on the River Thames in 1684.

The words weather and climate are not synonymous. Weather changes from day to day, whereas climate goes on all the time and is the summing up of all the changes of weather. The climate of an area gives a description of the generalised characteristics of phenomena such as temperature, rainfall and wind experienced over a period of time in the area.

It is difficult to define exact boundaries between different types of climate, but certain generalisations can be made and broad areas described as having similar climates. Species of animals and plants only thrive under limited conditions of temperature and precipitation. Therefore, as the climate changes over the surface of the Earth, so does the vegetation found.

Tropical and Equatorial

The limits of tropical climates north and south of the equator vary greatly with longitude and season. Tropical weather conditions reach well beyond the Tropics of Cancer and Capricorn on occasions up to 30° north and 30° south. Of the surface of the globe, 50 per cent lies between these latitudes and over a third of the world's population inhabits tropical lands.

Equatorial climate occurs in the Amazon Basin, the Zaire Basin and southern parts of West Africa, and the lowlands of Malaya and Indonesia. The heat and moisture in these areas is oppressive, and there is very little seasonal variation as the noonday sun is always high in the sky. Continuous high temperatures and heavy rainfall permit the growth of lush forests which are composed of a wide selection of trees and climbing plants. The trees are tall and their tops form a canopy of leaves allowing little sunlight to reach the forest floor. Plants can grow throughout the year and so the forest is evergreen. This type of equatorial forest is known as selva in South America.

When areas in these forests are cleared they need constant attention if they are not rapidly to return to forest. The most successful example of clearing to date is found in Malaya, where vast areas are given over to the cultivation of trees from which rubber is obtained.

Savanna and Monsoon

Areas experiencing savanna climate adjoin the equatorial rain forests in Africa and South America, with an additional area being found in northern Australia. The climate is dominated by seasonal changes brought about by the movement of the sun. When the sun is overhead the weather is hot and rainy, but when the sun moves to the other hemisphere, temperatures fall slightly and there is very little rainfall. In the hot season the temperatures rise higher than in the rain forest. The total rainfall received in a year in these areas decreases away from the Equator.

The vegetation is commonly of tall grasses interspersed with small trees. The trees are adapted to the seasonal drought, shedding their leaves at the end of the rains and having thorny leaves to reduce the loss of water by evaporation. The South American savannas have individual names, being known as the campos in the Brazilian highlands and the llanos in the Orinoco basin of Venezuela.

Monsoon climate is found in Southeast Asia. Very marked seasonal changes in climate occur, brought about by changes in pressure over the land and associated changes in the winds.

In the winter months, when the

Climatic extremes can cause a waterfall to freeze, or disastrous floods or even the proverbial frying of eggs on hot pavements.

sun is situated over the southern hemisphere, the land surface grows cold. High pressure develops in the chilled air above it, and dry winds blow outwards towards the ocean. In summer the land is heated, the air above it is warmed and low pressure systems form. In consequence moist, rainy winds are drawn in and a wet season results.

In the very wet areas, forest vegetation occurs which is deciduous to enable it to survive the dry season. Agriculture is practised widely and depends upon the monsoon rains or the floods that result from them. As the monsoon rain is unreliable however, areas are equally liable to flood or famine.

Desert Climates

A desert is defined as an area receiving less than 25 centimetres (10 inches) of rain per year, and many areas receive rain only a few times a century. The chief hot deserts of the world are the Sahara of North Africa, the Middle Eastern deserts that extend into Iran, the great American desert of south-western United States and Mexico, the Atacamba desert of South America, the Kalahari desert of South Africa and the Australian desert.

The desert lands become very hot in summer, but as there is no cloud cover, they are also very cold at night. That is to say, the daily range of temperature is great.

Some plants such as cacti are adapted to the prolonged periods of drought, being able to store water, whilst others such as the date palm develop long roots enabling them to reach water deep underground. Due to the lack of water and sparse vegetation cover few people inhabit desert regions.

Temperate Climates

Temperate climates occur in latitudes between the Tropics and the Arctic

Microclimates are those changes which occur just above the surface of the ground, for example alongside a wall or at the base of a tree, or in the presence of ground mist (right).

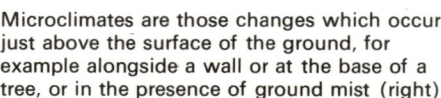

and Antarctic circles. The majority of the world's population experience these climates as most developed countries lie in the temperate zone.

Mediterranean climate is found in the coastlands of the Mediterranean Sea and also occurs in California, central Chile, the tip of South Africa and south-western and south-eastern Australia. The climate is characterised by its seasonal pattern of hot dry summers and cool wet winters, the regions being subjected to high pressure and dry winds in summer and to mild oceanic westerly winds in winter.

There is enough warmth to allow plants to grow all the year round, if there is enough water. The natural vegetation of the regions is evergreen scrub forest, composed of drought-resistant trees. The trees are adapted to the seasonal drought by having long roots to reach water underground, or by having thick bark or waxy leaves to reduce losses by transpiration. Plants which have long been cultivated in the Mediterranean climate include the olive, vine and fig. Citrus fruits are now commonly grown, such as oranges, lemons and limes.

North-west continental climate is experienced in areas on the poleward side of the regions of Mediterranean climate, where westerly winds dominate throughout the year. It is therefore found in the extreme north-west of Europe (including the British Isles), British Columbia, southern Chile and New Zealand. Summers are never really hot, the mean temperature being only 22°C. The winters are very mild for the latitude and rain occurs at all seasons. The weather is very changeable and is seldom the same for many consecutive days.

The rainy climate favours the growth of forest. In many areas, however, especially in Europe, this has been cleared, and cultivated crops such as wheat, oats, and grass for pasture and hay are found. In other parts of the world with similar climate, settlement has been more recent and consequently more of the forest survives. In mild situations the trees are deciduous hardwoods such as oak, ash, elm and beech. In more rigorous conditions of high ground, poor soils or proximity to the poles, evergreen conifers replace the hardwoods.

Semi-arid climates are experienced in continental interior locations and give rise to some of the largest grassland areas of the world. In the northern hemisphere, the prairies of Canada and United States and the Russian steppe receive this semi-arid climate, and in the southern hemisphere the grassland of Patagonia, the veldt of South Africa and the Darling Downs of Australia display similar characteristics. The chief feature of the climate is the large annual range of temperature, the summers being hot and the winters cold. This is due to the fact that continents gain and lose heat at a faster rate than do oceans. Interior continental locations therefore receive more extreme climates than do coastal locations at the same latitude. The grass grows best in the spring and autumn, but now vast areas of grassland have been given over to cultivation and ranching, neither of which is an intensive form of agriculture but demands considerable areas of land.

The climatic type known as warm eastern margin is found on the eastern coasts of continents in the latitudinal range from the tropics to about 35° north and south. This includes the Gulf Coast of North America, the

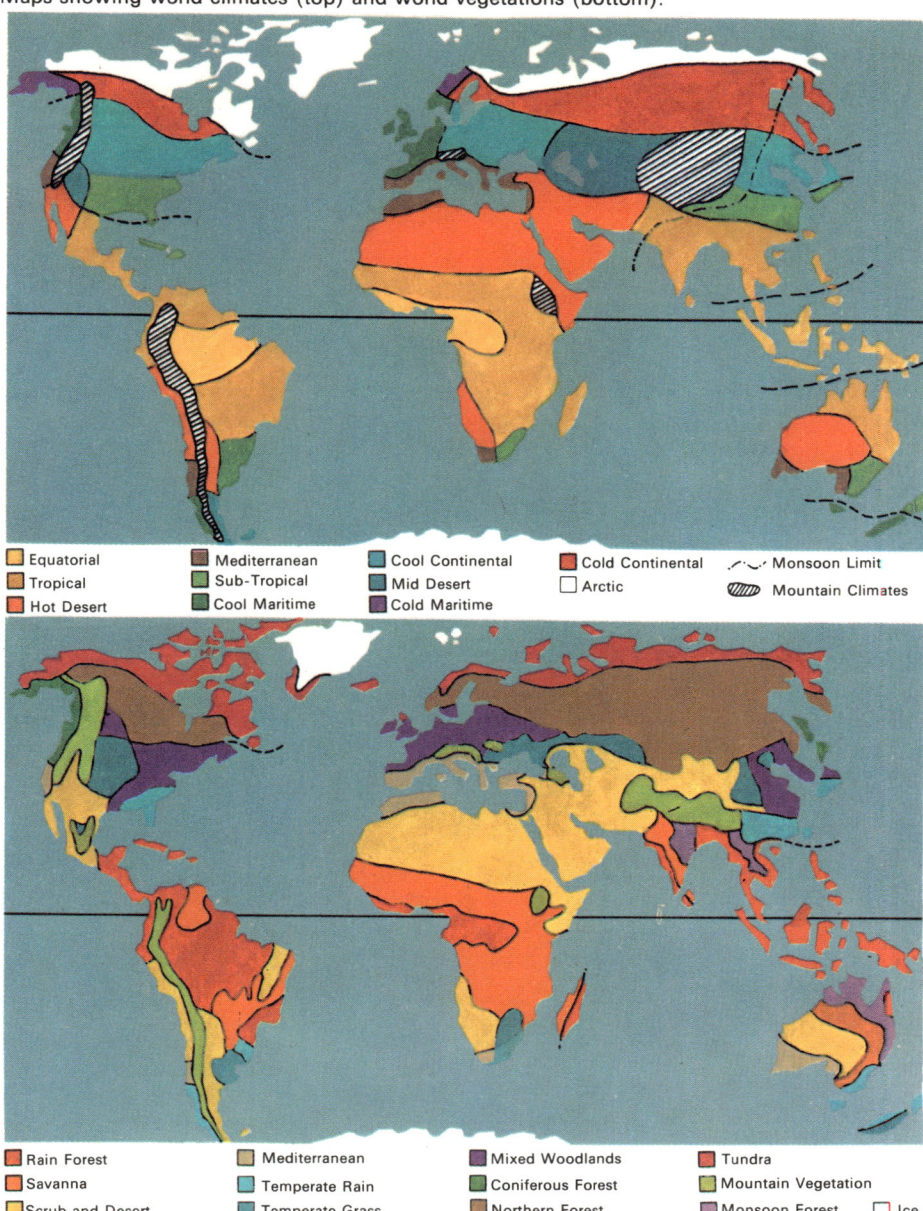

Maps showing world climates (top) and world vegetations (bottom).

Equatorial	Mediterranean	Cool Continental	Cold Continental	Monsoon Limit
Tropical	Sub-Tropical	Mid Desert	Arctic	Mountain Climates
Hot Desert	Cool Maritime	Cold Maritime		

Rain Forest	Mediterranean	Mixed Woodlands	Tundra
Savanna	Temperate Rain	Coniferous Forest	Mountain Vegetation
Scrub and Desert	Temperate Grass	Northern Forest	Monsoon Forest	Ice

pampas grasslands of Argentina and areas of Australia and South Africa. Summers are hot with average temperatures of about 28°C. Thunderstorms, tornadoes and hurricanes affect some areas due to the intense heating. The winter seasons by contrast are quite cool and again subject to rainfall, but of a less intense nature. The annual rainfall is therefore well distributed throughout the year. These areas are suitable for cultivation, and most of the original grass and woodland have been destroyed, especially in North America where cotton, maize and tobacco flourish.

Areas of cool eastern margin climate lie poleward of the warm eastern margins. They are found only in the northern hemisphere, there being no land masses at these latitudes in the southern hemisphere. Summers are

warm, average temperatures being about 20°C., but winters are cold with approximately three months having temperatures below freezing. Rainfall is moderate in amount and well distributed throughout the year. Areas of eastern Europe experience similar climates, although these cannot truly be described as continental eastern margins. The natural vegetation of the climatic type is forest, with deciduous hardwoods in the lowlands and more tolerant conifers on the uplands. Much has now been cleared, as areas are heavily populated and the land given over to mixed farmland and orchards.

Polar Regions

The polar regions extend from 66·5°N and 66·5°S to the north and south poles respectively. The climates are

Siesta time in the hot Mediterranean afternoon.

cold and many areas are largely uninhabited.

Boreal climate is experienced in a large area of North America and Eurasia. It is characterised by cool, short summers and cold winters, when the average temperature drops well below freezing. Precipitation is not heavy and comes partly as snow which lies on the ground during the winter months.

The most general form of vegetation is the coniferous forest, which is able to withstand the severe climate. The forest obtains enough moisture despite the low precipitation, as evaporation losses at the low temperatures are small.

The boreal forests often possess timber composed of a single type of tree covering many square kilometres. This is of great commercial value and lumbering is an important industry in the boreal regions.

Tundra climate is experienced in a zone north of the boreal regions. Summers are cool and very short, and average temperatures are often below freezing for nine months of the year. The ground is permanently frozen at depth and only the topsoil melts even in summer. This condition is known as permafrost.

The natural vegetation consists largely of mosses and lichens. Any conifers that manage to survive exhibit very stunted growth.

The coldest climate of all is called ice cap and occurs over the ice caps covering the majority of the Antarctic continent and Greenland. The average temperature for the year is below freezing point and precipitation always falls as snow. The ice is many thousands of feet thick and vegetation virtually non-existent.

Mountain and Local Climates

Climates found in areas of high altitude do not conform to those of the latitudinal zone in which they are located. Mountains and hills create their own climates.

The height of an area above sea level has a direct effect on the temperature experienced, as the temperature drops 1°C. per 150 metres (500 feet) above sea level. In equatorial mountainous regions of the world such as the Andes, the temperature at the summits can be below freezing point, whilst at the foot tropical conditions prevail. Mountains also affect the amount of rainfall received, for if they lie in the path of moisture-bearing winds, they force the damp air to rise over them and produce precipitation. On the lee side of the mountain, however, when the air descends from the peak, there is often a dry area known as a rain-shadow.

On a smaller scale than the mountain climates, hills and valleys are responsible for producing variations within any of the climatic types. Local temperature and wind difference result from the flow of colder air from hill tops into valley bottoms at night, and a reversal of the flow during the day. The accumulation of cold air in valley bottoms can cause the formation of frost hollows and pockets of fog. Also the aspect of a particular location is important, as south- and north-facing slopes receive different amounts of sunshine.

Weather

Warm air rises before a cold front.

Cumulus clouds are thick and develop upwards.

Stratus clouds resemble fog and lie on hills.

Wave clouds are blown in ridges across hills.

A description of the climate of a country or a town is based on an average of all the different conditions day by day, year by year. Meteorology, or the study of the atmosphere, is concerned, among other things, with explanations of these day by day conditions. The atmosphere surrounding the Earth is made up of a number of layers. Only the lowest of these, the troposphere, has any relevance to the study of weather.

Most of us are not greatly affected if it rains one day and is sunny the next, but there are groups of people to whom an accurate weather forecast is essential. Those particularly concerned with receiving weather reports include farmers, the aviation and public transport authorities, river boards and all those concerned with the sea and shipping.

Weather Forecasting

There are two types of forecast prepared, an immediate one covering approximately the next 24 hours, and another which tries to predict conditions for about one month in advance. The first step in preparing a forecast is to discover all the various movements of air within the atmosphere. These are then plotted onto a chart. The task of making a weather map is not unlike that of the ordinary mapmaker. But the weather forecaster needs to examine the charts of several previous days so that he can see what weather changes have occurred and how the various masses and pockets of air have moved. Having identified all the various phenomena, the forecaster must then decide what sort of weather may be associated with them.

Many countries have central agencies responsible for weather forecasting and meteorological research. In areas which frequently experience violent weather, such as tornadoes and hurricanes, there are permanent departments whose job it is to locate and track such storms.

They are also responsible for issuing warnings to the public which may include the need to evacuate whole areas. Many countries also have flood-warning systems which work on similar lines. Most people's acquaintance with the work of meteorological offices is through the daily weather forecasts given in newspapers and on radio and television.

The importance of long-range forecasting grows as it becomes more accurate. Forecasters use information gathered from all over the world. Some comes from weather ships and buoys carrying recording instruments. Details of cloud formations are provided by satellite pictures. The collection of data is co-ordinated on an international scale by the World Meteorological Organisation. Also used in the preparation of long-range forecasts are the charts of conditions for the same period and area over past years. The various meteorological conditions present at any given time are described by reference to a number of elements, all of which can be accurately measured and recorded.

The Atmosphere

The dry air of the lower atmosphere is composed of nitrogen (78 per cent), oxygen (21 per cent), argon (less than 1 per cent) and carbon dioxide (0·03 per cent). There are also quantities of the rare gases. The atmosphere contains dust and pollution of various sorts. Vivid sunsets, for example, result because of a scattering of the Sun's radiation by dust particles. The most variable constituent of the atmosphere, and the most important so far as the weather is concerned, is water vapour.

The temperature of the atmosphere is ultimately due to radiation received from the Sun, and it is unequal heating which causes the general movement of the air. Of the radiation received through space from the Sun, it is estimated that 43 per cent is returned

The atmosphere consists of the troposphere (nearest to the Earth), the stratosphere, the ionosphere and the exosphere.

Diagram (right) represents in code the weather conditions around a weather station.

as reflected sunlight, while of the remainder, 14 per cent is absorbed, due primarily to the water vapour content. The rest is absorbed by the Earth's surface, the land being more efficient in this process than the sea. The Earth re-radiates some of this heat and therefore it is the Earth which heats the atmosphere. There is a complex reaction between this radiation and the atmosphere, due primarily to the carbon dioxide and water vapour present. It is the trapping of this out-going radiation by the atmosphere which enables the surface of the Earth to be so warm and not subjected to the enormous ranges of temperature experienced by its satellite, the Moon.

Temperature is measured by means of a thermometer. It is important that the instrument being used is not placed in the direct sunshine. It is usually housed in a small box with louvred sides and is raised off the ground to allow the air to circulate around the bulb of the thermometer.

The symbols below are used by meteorologists to indicate forms of precipitation, cloud types and degrees of cloud cover.

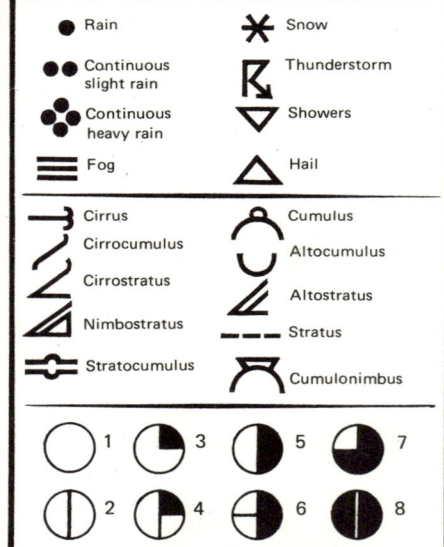

A special type of thermometer is used to measure the maximum and minimum temperatures which are experienced in any period of twenty-four hours.

Humidity is the term used to describe the water vapour content of the atmosphere. There are a number of forms of condensation which may be recorded. When the water vapour in the air is cooled, it will condense into very small, but visible, droplets which together form clouds.

Cloud Formations

The highest clouds are those of the cirrus group ranging between 6,000 metres (19,000 feet) and 14,000 metres (46,000 feet). These appear as wisps of grey and white. The clouds of the middle group, from 2,000 metres (7,000 feet) upwards are altostratus and altocumulus. The lowest of the cloud formations are stratus, nimbostratus and stratocumulus.

Cloud cover is estimated in eighths of the sky which can be observed. Thus a clear blue sky is zero and a completely overcast one is given the rating eight-eighths. Various symbols are used for the different cloud types on weather maps.

Condensation may also cause fog. When the warm moist air which is next to the ground is cooled quickly the water vapour will be condensed into drops of water. When the air is clear the land cools quickly and this is why fog often results on clear, cold nights. It will also occur over the sea, particularly in areas where cold and warm currents meet.

Dew forms on the leaves of shrubs and plants and on the grass when the air is cooled against the ground and forced to unload some of its moisture. A hoar frost results when the dew-point is below freezing. In contrast to this type of frost there is air frost which occurs when the air temperature is also below freezing point.

Precipitation

When condensation is sufficient to cause particles to fall, precipitation results. This term includes rain, snow, sleet, hail and freezing rain.

Raindrops have diameters of from 0·5 millimetres to 5·5 millimetres. The latter is the largest size possible, for above this the drops will break into smaller ones. The formation of raindrops is an extremely complex process. The cooling of a mass of air to cause rain can occur under a number of circumstances. When the surface of

Radio-sonde equipment

Rain gauge

Teleprinter

Cup anemometer

Sunshine recorder

Radar reflector

Some of the equipment used by meteorologists to record weather conditions.

the Earth is heated the air rises and begins to cool. Eventually condensation will occur and rain results. This type of rain often falls as very heavy showers and will frequently occur on warm afternoons. In the tropics nearly all the rainfall is of this type. It is called convection rainfall.

Particularly fierce upward movement will cause thunderstorms. Lightning is produced because of the static electricity which is present. There are many different types of lightning, although the most familiar are sheet and fork lightning. The former is the light produced by the flash while the stroke itself is seen as a branched streak, or fork lightning. It is lightning which causes thunder. While passing through the air lightning creates considerable heat which causes the air suddenly to expand and contract. This can be heard as thunder. Not all thunderstorms are due to a local heating of the Earth's surface. Some are the result of vigorous activity within a depression. This type usually occurs in winter.

Rain which is associated with a depression is termed cyclonic. Sometimes moisture-laden winds are forced to rise by a range of hills or mountains. Cooling occurs and rain falls. Once over the range, the air descends and warms and there is little or no rain. The windward sides of many of the mountain ranges which are aligned at right angles to the prevailing winds have a very heavy annual rainfall, while the leeward side may be dry enough to produce desert conditions. The name given to this type of rain is orographic and the leeward side of the hills is said to be in a rain shadow.

Extremes of Weather

Different parts of the world have very different amounts of rainfall. The greatest annual rainfall was 2,646 centimetres (1,042 inches) recorded in Assam in 1860–61, although 30 centimetres (12 inches) are recorded to have fallen in one hour in Missouri in 1907. The driest place on Earth is the Desierto de Atacama in Chile which had, until 1971, experienced about a 400-year drought.

A rainbow is caused when raindrops reflect and refract the Sun's rays. The colours seen are the visible ones of the spectrum from violet on the inside to red on the outside.

A particularly hazardous type of rain is called freezing rain or glazed frost. This occurs when rain falls on to the Earth's surface when it is below freezing point. Trees and shrubs, and even telephone wires, may become coated with ice. Roads are very dangerous and railways are unable to operate. The covering on roads under such circumstances is often referred to as black ice.

Rain is measured by means of a rain gauge which is really a funnel directing the water into a small container. The contents of this are then poured into a special calibrated measuring glass. Strict precautions are taken in the setting up of the rain gauge so that it records accurately the amount of precipitation received. Usually the gauges are read every 24 hours. It is not uncommon for 2·5 centimetres (1 inch) of rain to fall in a day in many localities and this is equivalent to about 40 tons of water per hectare (100 tons of water per acre). Usually 25·5 centimetres (10 inches) of uncompacted snow is taken as the equivalent of 2·5 centimetres (1 inch) of rain.

Snow is formed by the joining together of many ice crystals. The clouds in which the original formation takes place are naturally below freezing, but the type of snow which falls depends on the temperature of the air through which the flakes pass. As long as the ground temperature is below 4°C., snow will occur. However, the colder the temperature the smaller the flakes. Hence the expression 'it is too cold for snow'. When driven by the wind, snow can be piled into great drifts which seriously hamper transportation of goods and people. Whole towns and villages can be cut off.

Hail is made up of pellets of ice and is often associated with thunderstorms. The hailstone may be subjected to several phases of sudden rising due to strong up-draughts. This results in a typically layered structure.

Air Movement

We feel the movement of the air as wind. In studying the wind, its strength or force is recorded according to the Beaufort scale, also the direction from which it blows. Its speed can be accurately measured by means of an instrument known as an anemometer.

Many areas of the world experience local winds due to irregularities in the local topography, or to the effect of mountain ranges on the prevailing wind. An example of a local wind known to almost everyone is the sea breeze. During the early afternoon, the heating of the land raises the air temperature above the land higher than that above the sea. This air then rises and cooler air from the sea flows on to the land. In late evening the reverse is true, for the land cools more quickly than the sea and the air is drawn from the land towards the sea. Air moves from a region of high pressure towards one of low pressure.

Other local winds include the sirocco which blows along the south and east Mediterranean. As it comes from the desert it is hot and dusty. The opposite is true of the mistral which affects the Rhône Valley. This is a bitterly cold wind from the Alps. The chinook of Canada can have a dramatic effect on snow, altering the temperature from −34°C. to plus 10°C. in a matter of hours. Other similar winds occur in

The Beaufort scale of wind force was devised by the British admiral Sir Francis Beaufort in the 19th century.

South Africa, India, China and New Zealand.

The most violent of all winds are the hurricanes and tornadoes. Although they are short-lived and affect a relatively small area, tornadoes are the more violent. They originate in warm, humid, thunder-like conditions, several thousands of metres above ground. These winds, which rotate at high speeds, can move forward at up to 112 k.p.h. (70 m.p.h.) and are usually about 25 kilometres (16 miles) long and 400 metres (1,320 feet) wide. They occur all over the world but cause most damage in the United States. Where they pass over water a water spout will be formed.

A violent depressional storm is given the name hurricane. In a hurricane the wind speed often exceeds 120 k.p.h. (75 m.p.h.). Its circular motion causes the hurricane to be very destructive. Although they thrive over the sea, hurricanes frequently come ashore where they do considerable damage to property and can cause loss of life. The area most frequented by these violent storms is the Caribbean, although they are also known in the

FORCE	0	1	2	3	4	5	6	7	8	9	10	11	12
DESCRIPTION	CALM	LIGHT AIR	LIGHT BREEZE	GENTLE BREEZE	MODERATE	FRESH	STRONG	MODERATE GALE	GALE	STRONG GALE	WHOLE GALE	STORM	HURRICANE
EFFECT													
WEATHER SYMBOL													

84

The recording instruments in a meteorological station.

Weather ships play an important part in making regular reports.

Philippines, and in the Indian and Pacific Oceans.

Depressions

So far only local systems of weather have been described, but there are much larger units, such as depressions, which give characteristic weather over thousands of square kilometres. There are, within the atmosphere, great masses of air with uniform temperature and humidity. Any alteration to the conditions will cause the whole mass to react. The original characteristics will depend on the source of origin of the mass.

Source regions are areas where the air remains stationary for some time, that is, an area of high pressure. There are two zones—the tropics and the polar areas—and within each of these there is a division into maritime and continental. When two air masses meet, there is only a very limited mixing and the zone of contact is called a front. Fronts are usually associated with depressions (areas of low pressure), in which winds circulate anti-clockwise in the northern hemisphere. The origin of depressions is obscure, but in general the warm air is trying to over-ride the cold while the cold air undercuts the warm from behind.

Another major pressure system is the anticyclone, which is a region of high pressure. A warm anticyclone often results from local heating of the land or in the tropical high pressure zone. In general the weather associated with anticyclones is dry and settled. In winter they may bring very cold air to a large area.

A ridge of high pressure may occur separating two depressions or as an extension of an anticyclone. Other features are troughs which are associated with depressions and cols which separate two depressions and two anticyclones arranged alternately.

Wind Systems

The so-called general circulation of the atmosphere is arrived at by averaging out the various wind systems. If the Earth were merely a globe of water, which did not rotate, the circulation would be very simple. The equatorial regions receive the most solar radiation. The air in these areas rises and gradually sinks towards the poles as it becomes cooler. At the same time this movement will cause the colder air on either side of the equatorial regions to be drawn into them. But a number of forces are at work to complicate this simple system. The rotation of the

Earth deflects winds to the right in the northern hemisphere and to the left in the southern hemisphere. The distribution of land and sea also plays a considerable part in influencing the wind systems.

It is, however, still possible to generalise. The hot air rises in the equatorial region while cooler air is drawn in. The lack of wind in these areas, particularly over the sea, caused sailors to call them the doldrums, as sailing ships could become becalmed there for days, or even weeks. Gradually the upward moving air cools and descends.

The airs being drawn into the tropics are called trade winds, a name derived from the old German word *trede*, meaning the ability to keep a definite track.

At about 30° north and south the air from the tropics descends, giving an area of relative calm. These are called the horse latitudes, a name again taken from nautical experience: ships often carrying horses became becalmed and the livestock had to be destroyed. It is from this region that the westerlies develop. These winds are very variable in the northern hemisphere but in the south they circle the globe unimpeded by land masses.

Man and the Earth

For thousands of years man remained in balance with nature. He fitted into the environment without disturbing it. There was no destruction of the vegetation, no mining of the resources of the Earth. However, his inventiveness led to the production of more and more tools. The raw material for their manufacture could no longer be found on the surface and a conscious effort had to be made to locate it. So the first mines developed. For years, although the population of the world increased, man made do with relatively small quantities of gold and copper, tin and iron. His requirements for coal were reasonable. He had, however, begun to use the Earth's resources—resources which could not be replaced.

The population steadily increased over the years, but still man was a rural creature making do with what he could grow. There were few fertilisers to help him increase production. The factories used water power to drive primitive machinery.

Sources of Energy

The Industrial Revolution of the nineteenth century affected the whole of Europe. Steam power had arrived, and the need to locate suitable sources of energy assumed an importance which in the next 100 years was to dominate the developed nations. It was in 1712 that Thomas Newcomen's steam engine powered the first Cornish mine pump. Improvements were made by James Watt which made it possible for the steam engine to drive machinery. Such stationary engines were soon to develop into the early railway locomotives. Transportation of people and goods was to be accomplished more quickly and comfortably than had ever been thought possible. At the end of the nineteenth century came the internal combustion engine. Already the days of steam power were numbered as the petrol engine developed rapidly. With it came the need to locate and exploit the deposits of oil. Other inventions quickly followed and the standard of living of the people of Europe and America increased rapidly.

Refined medical techniques meant that people lived longer and there were fewer deaths at birth. So the population increased as did the demand for

In the quest for gold man has brought into play all the sophisticated devices of modern engineering. This scene in an African mine is based on actual conditions created by man's assault on the Earth's resources.

manufactured goods and the energy to drive and operate them.

Man's only sources of energy come from the earth and include solar energy, the tides, the heat of the Earth, fission and possibly fusion fuels and fossil fuels. Industry demands an increasing use of minerals and rocks. Once extracted none of these can be replaced. Gradually the resources of the Earth are being used up, and one day they will all be gone. It is to be hoped that man can remain one step ahead in devising new materials and energy sources.

It is already true that mines which were uneconomic to work a few decades ago are now being reopened. Improved techniques of refining and smelting make this possible. In some cases the spoil put back into the mines is now being taken out and used. Advances in metallurgy allow for the better use of the metals themselves. There are many other instances where man has found substitutes.

Mineral Deposits

The deposits of metals and other rocks and minerals valuable to man are not evenly distributed throughout the world. It is true that some countries have richer resources than others, but none is self-sufficient. Even the United States with all its vast reserves has no deposits of tin. Civilisations have depended on the ability of their people to discover new sources of minerals. Often lengthy wars have been fought to colonise new areas believed to offer rich resources. The Romans incorporated Britain into their Empire so that it might have access to the lead, iron and tin. Earlier still the Phoenicians had sailed from the Mediterranean to the south-western tip of England to trade in tin. In later years the lure of gold caused people to traverse continents.

A very recent example of a continent whose destiny has been altered by the discovery of vast mineral deposits is Australia. Its rich resources have affected both its social and economic development. In Western Australia enormous resources of iron ore have been discovered, but one of the most famous mineral localities in the world is at Broken Hill in New South Wales. The development of its great mineral wealth was due to one man, Charles Rasp. He started prospecting in 1883 and mining started soon afterwards. In the 34 years following 1885, vast quantities of lead, zinc concentrates, silver and gold were extracted. The

company operating the site began to open other mines farther away, exploiting coal and iron deposits in South Australia and New South Wales. Although the original Broken Hill mine closed in 1939, silver, lead and zinc are still worked nearby. The town which has grown up at Broken Hill now numbers over 30,000 people and offers all the amenities to be found in any well developed urban area in the twentieth century. The contribution of the original mining company and its subsidiaries to the economy of Australia is considerable.

Earth Resource Satellites

In the search for new deposits of minerals, satellites have played an important part. These new items of technology are already making significant contributions to meteorology and communications. Suitably equipped they are able to produce data for the construction of maps of all types. This is essential, as geographical, geological and hydrological maps of many parts of the world are either non-existent or out of date.

The remote sensing by satellite enables the mineral content of soils and rocks to be determined by reference to the type of vegetation present. Fitted with radar and other sensors, satellites are able to penetrate the crust and therefore obtain more detailed geological information. Structural conditions may also be revealed which could lead to the location of new oil and natural gas deposits.

One of the most important tasks of the Earth resources satellites is the evaluation of the water resources of the world. Valuable data may be provided for irrigation schemes, and even the quality of the water can be measured. Sedimentation in harbours and estuaries can also be monitored as can fishing grounds by means of satellites.

Many elements are concentrated in sea water and they are an indication of the importance of the Earth's water resources.

Element	Tons per cubic mile
Chlorine	89,500,000
Sodium	49,500,000
Magnesium	6,400,000
Carbon	132,000
Nitrogen	2,400
Iron	47
Tin	14
Uranium	14
Silver	1
Lead	0·1
Gold	0·02

Folklore and Myth

Since the time of prehistoric man giants and gods have been invoked as the source of many of the majestic land forms. The 'productions' of the Earth have been considered to have magical properties. This is particularly true of fossils, many of which have been claimed to be remedies for illnesses. Much of this folk medicine is based on sympathetic magic. For example a twisted fossil shell will be considered valuable in the treatment of rheumatism and arthritis.

Fossil Mythology
Fossils were gathered early on in man's development. They were no doubt collected as they became weathered out of the rocks or were picked up from the ground. In some areas fossils still play an important part in the lives of the people, and for thousands of years the original conceptions of the value of fossils have lingered on in folklore.

Amber, which is the fossilised resin of pine trees and mainly found in the Baltic Sea area, is still used for adornment, as it has been since Bronze Age times. This transparent yellow-brown material often encloses insects and other small creatures. Amber was highly prized by the ancient Greeks and Romans and was the basis of considerable trading.

Fossils are also still used in the coats of arms of many towns. During the Industrial Revolution in Britain there was considerable quarrying of the limestone at Dudley in Warwickshire. One of the commonest fossils found was a trilobite and this has been incorporated in the coat of arms of the town. The fossil mollusc *Gryphaea* is found in Jurassic ironstone rocks. The prosperity of another British town, Scunthorpe, is closely linked to the iron industry, and so the fossil shell finds a place on its coat of arms.

Fossils often occur in advertisements and provide dramatic pictures. In the world of the film-maker, dinosaurs occur in the most unlikely settings alongside 'prehistoric' man. In many countries of the world there are thriving clubs of collectors of rocks, minerals and fossils. One famous site in the United States has been named Dinosaur National Monument. Even the nearby town is now called Dinosaur and the streets have such names as Tyrannosaurus Terrace and Stegosaurus Freeway. A café specialises in 'dinosaurburgers'.

The remains of ancient life still hold a considerable interest and fascination for modern man, but in the not so distant past they were the 'givers' and 'takers' of life.

Much has been discovered about the uses and folklore of the various fossils. Of the vertebrates it was sharks' teeth which were most widely used. These remains are fairly common at some locations and provide ideal material for necklaces. There may have been some link with vicious animals, for many modern tribes adorn themselves with the teeth of animals. Shark-teeth necklaces have been discovered in the upper Palaeolithic cultures.

The medical uses of the teeth were many and included protection against rheumatic disorders and more generally the warding off of the evil eye.

Toadstones are in reality fish teeth, but unlike sharks' teeth, which are sharp and pointed, these are found as stud-like forms. The stones were considered jewels which had formed on the head of a toad.

Giant's Graveyard
It is easy to understand the belief in the existence of giants when the bones

Primitive man has always invested the 'productions' of the Earth with magic powers. Magic symbols of folk art are common in every part of the world. Often these use the actual objects found in Nature, such as teeth and shell necklaces. At other times man has employed his skill to fashion objects of special magic significance.

Owl water vessel.

Pueblo kachina doll.

Palaeolithic necklace of wolf and fox teeth.

Necklace of gastropod shells.

Animal head on a fragment of reindeer antler.

North-west-coast Indian mask.

of the larger reptiles and mammals were discovered. This is particularly true where masses of bones are found together. The remains of mammoths were once used in the Ukraine to form a framework for huts. Later people inhabiting the area found the ruins of these and they thought they had discovered a giant's graveyard. It is also interesting to note that the giant fossilised trees found in parts of the United States were regarded by the Indians as the remains of giants.

China has long been the source of many tales about the use of fossils. So-called dragons' teeth and bones have been mined and sold to chemists to be crushed. Many of the bones and teeth are derived from the early form of horse called *Hipparion*. When the crushed fossil is sold it is thought that the purchaser will be helped by his patron dragon. Such material is also claimed to have a medicinal value.

It was the purchasing of dragons' teeth by Professor von Koenigswald which eventually led to the discovery of Peking Man. The teeth that were first obtained are now known to belong to the largest ape ever to have lived, *Gigantopithecus*.

Because of the greater availability of invertebrate fossils, many more of these feature in folklore. Some have assumed only a local importance while others have been widely used. Some have always been just bringers of good luck while the function of others has changed considerably over the years.

Of the fossils most commonly found the most spectacular must be the ammonites. Showing a wide range in size these coiled creatures were once compared with the horns of a ram. Rams were sacred to the ancient Greeks and linked with the god Jupiter Ammon. Specimens became known as 'Ammon's Horns' and hence ammonites. To many they conjure up the picture of a coiled snake, and have therefore assumed the name snake-stone. In at least one locality, specimens have had a head carved on them to make the story a little more plausible. The action of saints is invoked in the original killing of the snakes and turning them to stone. Part of the process of this ceremony involved the destruction of the head.

Belemnites, which are the remains of animals distantly related to the cuttlefish, are often called devils' fingers or thunderbolts. They are slender shapes with a point at one end. They have been used in curing illness in horses.

African ritual witch doctor performs a magic ceremony to induce rain.

Molluscs have long been used for ornamental purposes, being strung together into bracelets, necklaces and headdresses. Upper Palaeolithic finds of all these have been made. There often seems to have been a considerable trade in fossil shells set up over long distances. Gastropods (snail-like shells) were always more highly valued than the univalves (mussels and clams), presumably because of their shapes.

Magic Cures
The value of fossils to early man is proved by the carving of fossil shells by Neolithic people. Limestone was used to create the fossil replicas. It has been suggested that the larger scallop shells may have had a more practical purpose, being used to hold food.

Mention has already been made of *Gryphaea* or 'the Devil's toe nail'.

All ancient peoples have creation myths as part of their folklore and this drawing illustrates the creation of man in the tradition of Babylonian myth.

adderstones because the fossils appear coiled. Such rocks when suitably carved may well have had a ceremonial function. Corals of the compound type are often called starry-stones and have been discovered with Neanderthal remains. Some fossil corals have also been used to create necklaces.

In country areas, fossil sea-urchins have always been called shepherds' crowns and fairy loaves. They are still placed on the larder shelves to keep dairy produce from going sour. They have also been used in the treatment of stomach upsets and sea-sickness. In one Bronze Age burial more than 100 specimens were found placed in a circle around the bodies.

Crinoids, or sea lilies, belong to the same group as the sea-urchins. The stems are made up of a number of small blocks which have a hole through the centre. These are therefore most suitable for necklaces and are known from the Bronze Age. The individual discs have also been called fairy money. Also used for necklaces is one type of fossil sponge which is round and has a central hole.

The Work of the Devil

The more dramatic features of the landscape are often attributed to the work of the devil or giants. Giants are credited with piling up masses of rock to form islands just offshore. Even man-made features, such as Bronze Age barrows, have become incorporated into folklore.

Boulders and various other erratic blocks, often the result of glacial action, are interpreted as missiles thrown by giants in combat. The stone circles and single standing stones of previous cultures have entered folklore as the remains of people turned to stone.

Many other peculiar geological phenomena, such as stones with holes through the centre and rocking stones, are considered to confer good luck on those who visit them.

In view of the conditions under which miners worked, and have worked in the past, it is to be expected that there are many mythical creatures thought to live underground. Often they were considered the spirits of workers of hundreds of years ago. Such 'spirits' have been 'recorded' from mines in many European countries. In some cases they were said to lead men on to a rich lode, while in others their presence heralded the closing of the mine.

This mollusc has a left valve which has become very strongly incurved. Specimens have long been used as a cure for rheumatism, a particularly good instance of sympathetic magic.

Brachiopods once abundant in the seas are often found as fossils. Some of the forms have a 'winged' appearance. These have long been known in China as 'stone swallows'. In other places the same forms are called butterflies. Brachiopods have been used in the treatment of skin disease and eye troubles.

The belief in adderstones is widespread and of long standing. Rocks which include corals and worm tubes have always been associated with

Stone and Rock

The only way we have of studying how early man lived and worked is by examining the items made by him. Such things are called artefacts and may be made out of bone, stone, wood or other material. It is, however, only stone tools which usually survive from the earlier periods. It would seem that from the time of the australopithecines man has manufactured tools. Great collections have been made throughout the world and many museums house thousands of specimens. This alone proves that man must have manufactured such items with great speed. Times were hard and life would depend on the ability to kill game and prepare it.

Man must have sought suitable rock for tool manufacture from very early times. A number of properties were essential. The rock should be hard but capable of being fashioned. Sharp edges had to be created to cut up the meat and skin animals. The most suitable rock was found to be flint which is fine grained and made of silica. Flint is found mainly in the chalk of northern Europe and was not therefore available to all. Man's preference for this rock is shown by the active trading which occurred in flint in Neolithic times. Where flint was not available, other rocks such as chert, diorite, granite, quartzite and obsidian were used.

The Stone Ages

It is man's fashioning of the 'stone' which has provided the material for the division of time into the Palaeolithic or Old Stone Age, Mesolithic or Middle Stone Age, and Neolithic or New Stone Age. In the first two periods man was a hunter roaming from place to place. With the advent of the New Stone Age he settled into communities and became a farmer.

The development of tools shows an increasing dexterity and intelligence in the manufacturer. Before describing the evolution of the tools themselves, some of the techniques used in their fashioning must be outlined. In working a lump of flint, pieces were chipped off to get a suitable tool. In some cases the curved pieces chipped off were used and made into flake tools, while in other instances the lump remaining was used as a core tool. The earliest way of fashioning the material would have been by direct percussion. This would simply involve hitting one stone with another. A later development was the technique of indirect percussion. In this case a

piece of bone or wood was held on the stone and hit with another. This would be rather like using a hammer and chisel. Further development still took place with pressure flaking. Here, an object less hard than the material being worked was used to cut off fragments, gradually creating a very thin but sharp instrument. The overall effect of these different methods was for the tools themselves to become finer and more adaptable to performing different tasks. It was in Neolithic times that tools were first polished.

Oldowan Tools

Some of the earliest tools found are those from Olduvai Gorge and the name given to the culture is appropriately Oldowan. These early tools are obviously the work of direct percussion, the intent being to produce a point. The first crude hand-axes were next to be developed. On these the flaking

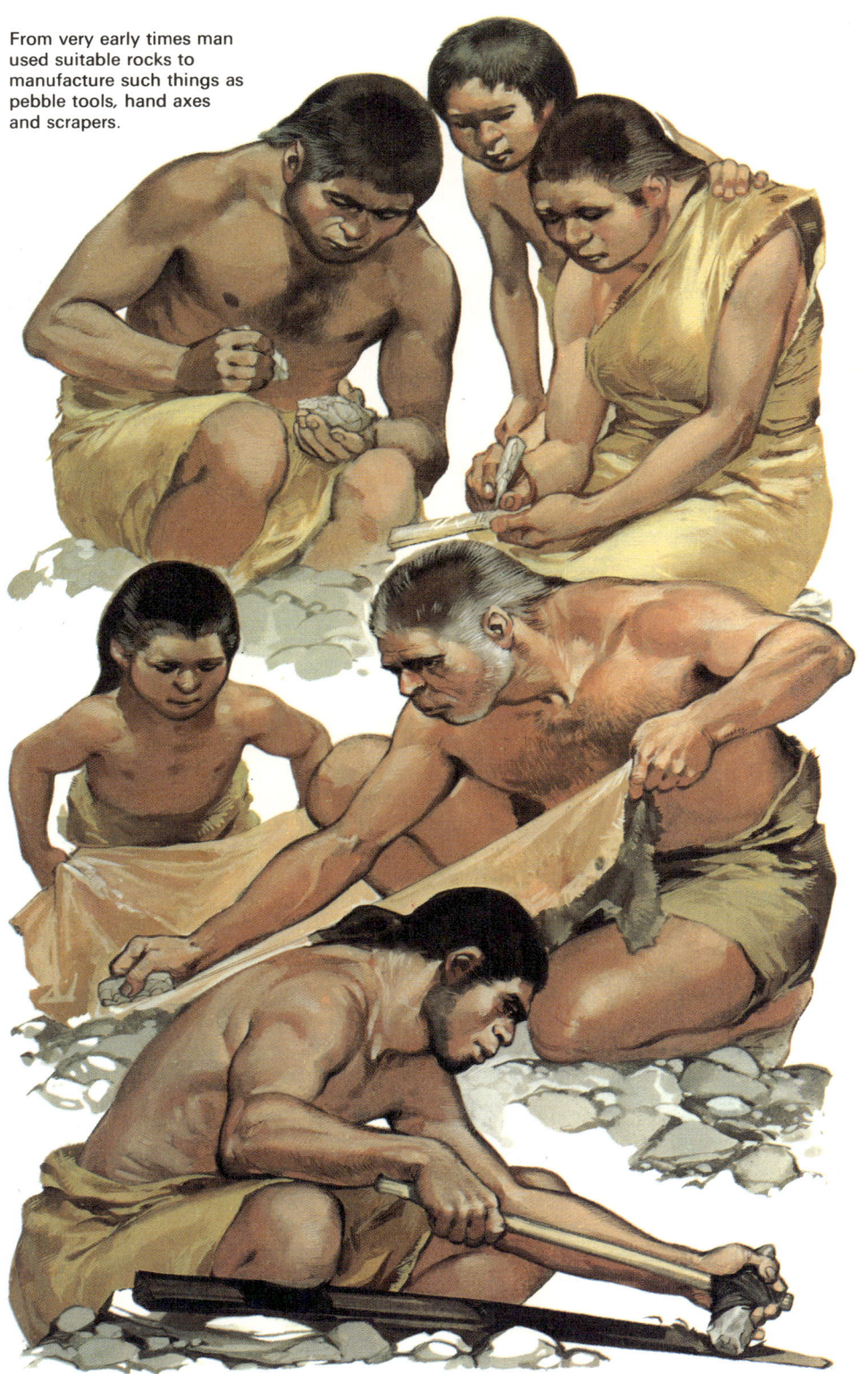

From very early times man used suitable rocks to manufacture such things as pebble tools, hand axes and scrapers.

goes all round the edge and the result was a pear-shaped axe. This culture is called the Abbevillian from Abbeville in northern France. These axes had rather a blunt point, whereas those of the following Acheulian culture (from St Acheul, near Amiens, France) had a distinct point and much straighter edges.

Neanderthal man's culture is called Mousterian after Le Moustier in the Dordogne in France. It has been discovered in Asia, Africa and Europe. The tools of these times included side-scrapers and points in the shape of a triangle. Maybe these were used for the scraping of skins and for cutting up the meat. Certainly Neanderthal man also had wooden tools, including spears.

Just as we have seen that Neanderthal man disappears from the scene, so does his culture. Suddenly, tools, now known to be characteristic of the Upper Palaeolithic, appear in various deposits. Here also are found tools for engraving on bone and wood, called burins or gravers. Art forms are included in the Aurignacian culture (from Aurignac, Toulouse in France)

which is that of Cro-Magnon man. The earliest cave paintings date from these times. Triangular flint points were attached to shafts to produce spears. Pins and awls were also used.

Although flint tools continued to be manufactured, there were now others made of bone, ivory and antler. The final culture of the Palaeolithic has often been equated to that of the present day Eskimos, for it included harpoons and many other bone implements. Many items of sculpture have also been discovered in deposits of this age.

The following Mesolithic cultures are characterised by tiny flints called microliths. At this time there is now increasing information about the everyday life of man. The heaps of refuse, called kitchen middens and well known from Denmark, show that men of the Middle Stone Age had a varied diet. We know too that trees were used to make dug-out canoes.

Neolithic Implements

Although still a hunter, Mesolithic man was soon to change his way of life, for in the succeeding Neolithic

period, hunting was to give way to farming. Fishing developed on a wide scale with the use of nets and traps, hooks and harpoons.

More and more good implements were needed for the increasing population and their range of activities. Good quality flint was at a premium. To obtain the necessary quantity man began to mine it. A pit was sunk from the surface often with several galleries at the site of the flint bands. The digging was undertaken not with spades and shovels but with antler picks. Once the supply was exhausted or the working became too dangerous the spoil was tipped back.

Quarrying was also carried on in these times, not only for material for the manufacture of tools but also for building. The oldest known cities date from Neolithic times.

For thousands of years stone had helped man in his struggle to keep alive, but now the age of stone was nearly at an end. It was to be followed in quick succession by the three ages of metal—copper, bronze and iron. It could be argued that the iron age is still going on.

Copper and Bronze

The first age of metal, the Copper Age, spread slowly, and although some blades may have found their way to the remoter parts of the world, stone continued to be used. Often the stone tools were made into shapes which imitated those made of copper. The Copper Age, because it was so limited in distribution, has yielded little about the people who first heated the native metal and poured it into moulds.

It was almost certainly by accident that man learned about copper. It is one of the few metals which is found in its natural form. No doubt during the heating of fires some nodules of the material became hot and melted. This would introduce man to the new material. Once melted, it would quickly be realised that by pouring it into moulds implements could be made.

Tin is another metal which can be smelted at a relatively low temperature. This was to be of considerable importance to the early metal worker. Many of the ores from which man obtains his metals are in the form of oxides, carbonates or sulphides when found in nature. In the case of tin the ore is an oxide. This means that in order to obtain the pure metal, oxygen must be driven off. The simplest way to do this is to combine the oxygen with carbon to form carbon dioxide which is then given off as a gas. When wood is burnt carbon forms and this provides a way of reducing tin ore to the metal.

Man soon discovered that by bringing together tin and copper a much harder metal, called bronze, was made. The Bronze Age began about 5,000 years ago and the metal was first used in the Middle East. It now became possible to manufacture many different kinds of weapons together with ornaments and armour. Although in many cases the blades of these new tools and weapons were no sharper than the old flint ones, they were less brittle and could be re-sharpened by grinding.

The Age of Iron

The next development was the smelting of iron. Iron was in use in the Middle East about 1400 B.C. As iron does not occur in its native state it has been suggested that the first iron smelted by man was derived from meteorites. High temperatures are necessary to smelt iron and therefore a furnace is required. Perhaps the earliest one consisted of stacking up the layers of ore alternately with charcoal and covering the whole mound with clay. Holes would have been left at the bottom and top to allow a draught of air. People of the Iron Age built many forts on the tops of the hills. Each one was surrounded by a number of concentrically arranged high banks.

Man had thus begun to make full use of the resources of the Earth. He was also beginning to control his environment, cutting down trees to make room for his crops and to provide him with boats. Mining and quarrying were both making their mark on the landscape. Man was no longer in balance with his environment. He had few enemies and his intelligence and ability enabled him to control his destiny. Man's greatest threat at that time, as now, was himself.

Marble quarry in the Apuan Alps with (inset) four examples of polished marble.

The Wealth of the Earth

The phrase 'energy crisis' is one which keeps occurring in newspapers and television reports. The political uncertainty in the main oil-producing regions of the world also heightens the fact of man's dependence on certain types of energy to maintain his standard of living. There are a number of sources of energy, but currently oil is the most important and also the one which will be the first to be used up. Other sources include coal, peat and running water, which have been used for thousands of years, and natural gas, geothermal power and nuclear power. In some parts of the world other forms are important in localised situations—for example the use of wind to drive small generators in remote farmsteads. Also, in India cow-dung is used for heating and the amount burnt each year is equivalent to 40 million tons of coal.

When an assessment is made of the energy balance of each of the countries of the world, great differences are revealed. The United States produces less crude petroleum than it needs but is self-sufficient in natural gas, coal and lignite. Many countries, however, are seriously deficient in crude petroleum, for example those of western Europe. This of course may change with the exploitation of North Sea oil and gas fields. Other areas, such as the Middle East, produce vast quantities of crude petroleum and use very little themselves.

The Mining of Coal

Coal has been a major source of power for at least 200 years and has been used for about 3,000 years. There are still vast reserves of coal of all qualities although some of it is in thin seams or at great depths, which at present make it uneconomic to mine. It is even possible to manufacture petroleum from coal but the cost is very high. It has been estimated that there is sufficient coal to last for 1,000 years, although with increasing populations and the industrialisation of more and more countries, perhaps 300 years would be a more realistic estimate.

There are two ways of obtaining coal, by mining below the surface and by opencast workings. In the case of the latter the overburden—soil and rock—is removed and then the seams of coal are quarried. Some of the deepest mines go down 1,200 metres (4,000 feet) and in some cases extend for a long way under the sea although the entrance shafts are always on land.

Mines have never been pleasant places in which to work, being cramped and damp. The dust of the coal causes infections of the lungs. There is always the possibility of sudden death by explosion, caused by methane gas, or a roof fall or flooding. Often in intensively mined areas a new shaft will pierce an older and now flooded working. The result is a sudden rush of water and the probable drowning of those miners working at the face.

The industry is now highly mechanised although the seams of coal are still too thin in many mines to allow the full use of cutting machinery. The coal is hewn from the seam by mechanical cutters and is automatically loaded on to moving conveyor belts for transportation. In some mines jets of water are used to break up the coal and flush it to the bottom shafts for collection.

Coal with a high carbon content is the best heat producer. Anthracite is 90–95 per cent carbon and ranks first, followed by bituminous or household coal, with 80–90 per cent carbon. The deposits of both these types of coal are of Carboniferous age. Lignite, or brown coal, is much younger, having originated during Tertiary times. Lignite has only 65–70 per cent carbon and is about half as effective as bituminous coal as a heating source. It is, however, mined in China, East and West Germany, Hungary and Russia.

A granite quarry in the United States with (below) three samples of different types of granite. It was at one time believed that granite was the original rock of the planet Earth but it is now thought probable that it is sedimentary rock that has undergone a process of metamorphosis.

Rocks have almost limitless uses for man. Shown here are some of the more common rocks and the products made from them.

Not all the coal mined is used as a source of energy. Much of it is turned into coke which in turn creates gas and tar. The derivatives of coal are used in the chemical industry, fertilisers and many other manufacturing industries. Coke is used in households as a smokeless fuel and also in the smelting of iron and other ores.

Oil and Petroleum

The first oil well was drilled in Pennsylvania in 1859 and the oil was struck at a depth of 21 metres (70 feet). But petroleum has been known to man for hundreds, or even thousands of years, for it sometimes seeps from the reservoir rocks to lie on the surface. After a while all that remains is natural bitumen. Pitch Lake in Trinidad is an example of this.

It has been estimated that nearly 6,000 products are obtained from petroleum, including synthetic rubbers, paints, perfumes, soaps, plastics, insecticides and medicines. This shows a considerable development over man's first use of bitumen for the caulking of ships.

The deposits of crude petroleum at the surface were in the early years sufficient to fulfil demand. But with the advent of the petrol engine at the end of the nineteenth century, it became necessary to begin exploration, and since the early years of this century man has always sought new oil fields. Initially only land areas were surveyed and fields developed, but in recent years attention has been diverted to the continental shelves under the sea. This has required a considerable advance in drilling technology. Barges were first developed which could drill in about 9 metres (30 feet) of water and were used in swamp areas. In the 1950s came the 'jack-ups' which could drill in 90 metres (300 feet) of water. The legs of these rigs are let down to the ocean floor and the platform then jacked up above the waves. In 1961 the first of the semi-submersibles went into action and was capable of operating in 181 metres (600 feet) of water. This relied on pontoons which float in the calmer water beneath the waves. The next development was the self-propelled semi-submersible weighing 25,000 tons and over 90 metres (300 feet) long. This can drill in 300 metres (1,000 feet) of water. For really deep sea work, ships which can drill up to

Crushed Limestone

Crushed Shale

Red Clay

Grey Clay

Gypsum

Pottery

Cement

Piping

Gypsum

Firebrick

Plaster of Paris

Building Construction

Land Plaster

Sand, Gravel and Crushed Rock

Crucible

Graphite

Pencils

Brushes

Lubricant

1,800 metres (6,000 feet) are used. *The Glomar Challenger* did much to aid the development of such vessels.

In exploiting the North Sea deposits the production platforms rise 146 metres (480 feet) from the ocean floor. The 12,000-ton base is fixed in place by 32 steel piles of 1·8 metres (6 feet) in diameter and driven 60 metres (200 feet) down into the sea bed. The top of the drilling derrick is about 220

metres (740 feet) above the sea bed. The whole structure is built to withstand 30-metre (100-foot) waves and 250 k.p.h. (160 m.p.h.) gales.

Oil Producers

The main producers of oil are Russia, the United States, Venezuela and the countries of the Middle East and North Africa. There are constant reminders that the reserves of oil will be exhausted

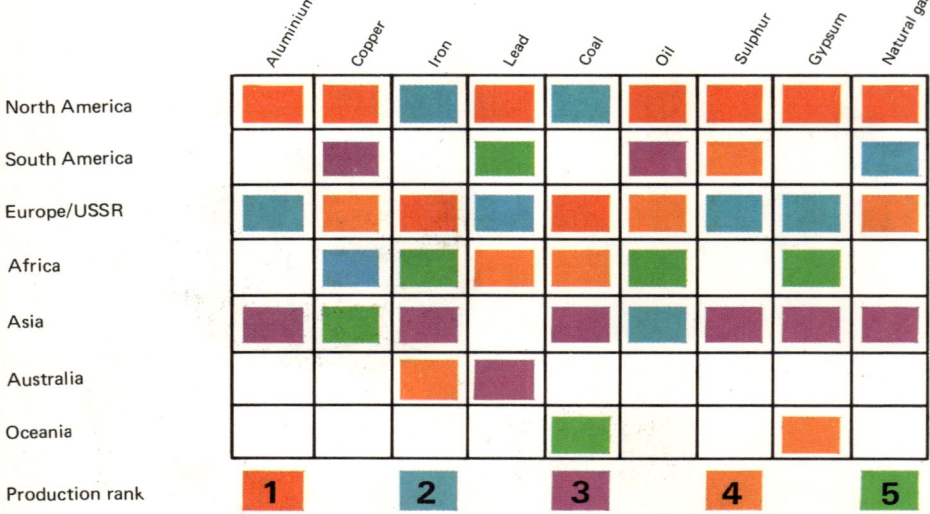

Natural gas (top), oil (centre) and coal (bottom) are the natural resources essential to the industrial nations. The chart below shows world production of essential minerals.

	Aluminium	Copper	Iron	Lead	Coal	Oil	Sulphur	Gypsum	Natural gas
North America	1	1	2	1	2	1	1	2	1
South America		3		5		3	4		2
Europe/USSR	2	1	1	2	1	1	2	1	1
Africa		2		4		5		5	
Asia	3	5	3		3	2	3		3
Australia			4	3					
Oceania					5			4	
Production rank	1	2	3	4	5				

within 50 years. It is certainly a fact that with most of the world now geologically surveyed, the chances of finding new large reserves is unlikely. Perhaps those of the North Sea and Alaska are the last. It is certain, however, that many smaller fields await exploitation.

The demand for oil is not static but is constantly increasing and this is what poses the threat. It may become economically possible to use the oil shales and sands which will extend the production of oil for some years. There are vast deposits of such rocks, the most important being the Athabaska tar sands of Alberta, Canada and the Green River oil shales of Colorado, Utah and Wyoming. Maybe sophisticated technology will enable the development of more oceanic fields or work in inhospitable regions.

Natural gas is closely associated with oil deposits both geologically and in production. Users of such gas receive gas straight from the gas field to their appliance.

Geothermal Energy

There is an increasing interest in geothermal energy. The use of geothermal energy is by no means new but it has not until recently been actively exploited. It has long been used in Iceland for the direct heating of homes, while in northern Italy, at Larderello, an electricity generating station was established as long ago as 1904.

Several factors have limited the use of geothermal energy. Only those fields in which there were surface manifestations in the form of geysers and hot springs were considered suitable. But with the advent of geophysical surveying by air using infra-red photography, a number of new sources have been found. It was often considered that the existing fields would be so short-lived as to be uneconomic to develop. It has now been shown that so long as there is enough ground water present, the life of the fields will be long enough to repay development.

It has also been found that the energy may be used in several ways. Apart from the generation of electricity, steams and hot water can be used in desalination plants and minerals may be extracted from the water itself. In Chile there is an elaborate experiment in progress in which electricity will be generated and the hot water from this will be used in a desalination plant. Valuable minerals will be extracted from the waste.

Geothermal energy is utilised in many areas and there are a number of types of field. Dry steam fields furnish steam which can be used directly for the generation of electricity. Wet fields are more numerous than dry ones. In these steam is used and the water discharged. The third type of field is called a low temperature field because the water temperature is below boiling point.

Such reserves of power are certainly going to be used by man in future years, and it has been predicted that there will be a four-fold increase in the amount of electricity generated from such sources in the present decade.

Nuclear and Solar Energy

The rise of nuclear energy means an increasing demand for uranium, the ores of which are pitchblende and uraninite. These are often discovered in association with copper, silver, nickel and cobalt.

Because all sources of energy originally come from the Sun, it is not surprising that great efforts are being made to use this source directly. There are a number of difficulties, however, not least among them the fact that solar radiation is not constant at any given point on the Earth's surface. It

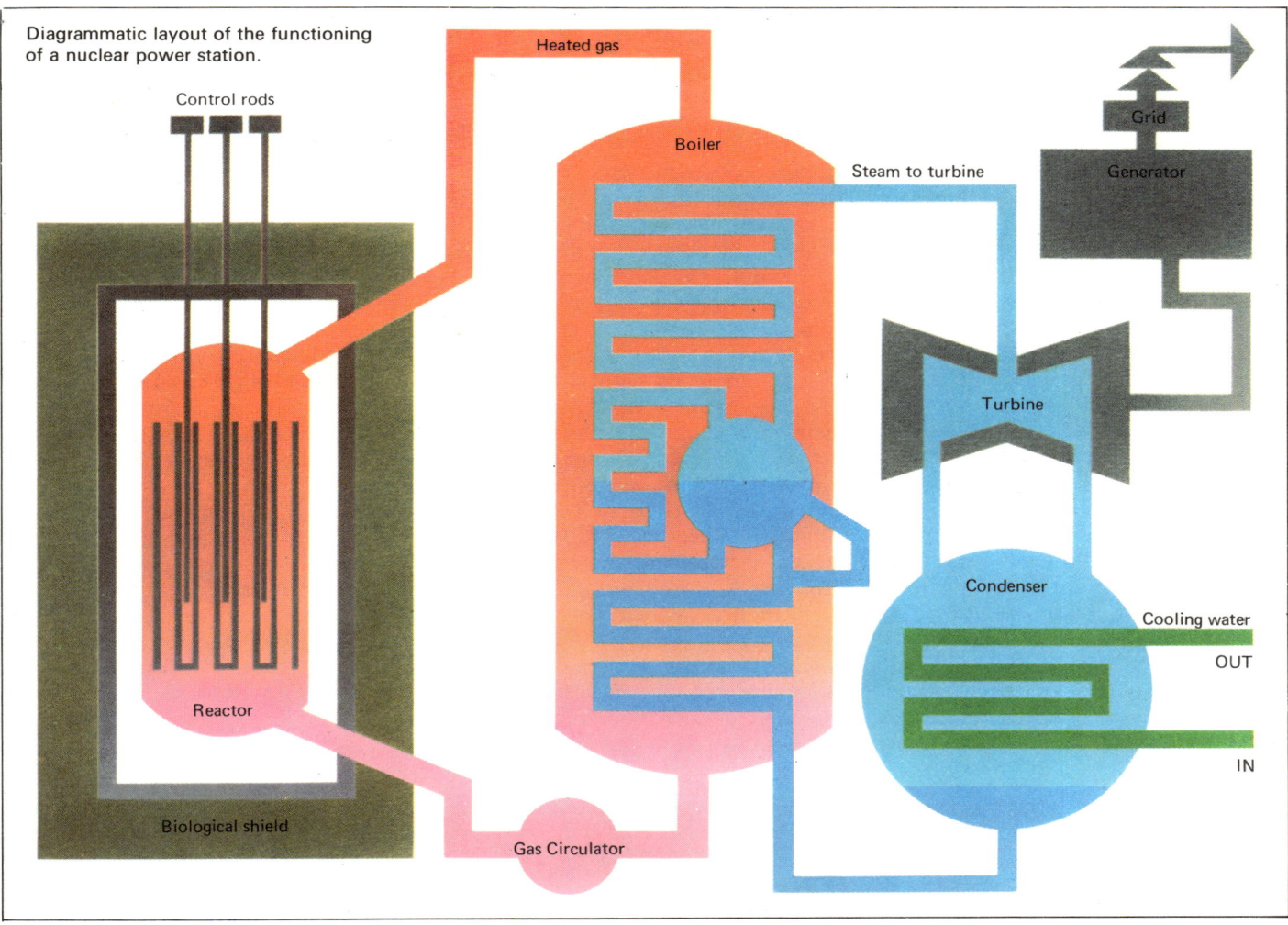

Diagrammatic layout of the functioning of a nuclear power station.

Control rods

Heated gas

Boiler

Steam to turbine

Grid

Generator

Turbine

Condenser

Cooling water

OUT

IN

Reactor

Biological shield

Gas Circulator

has been calculated that the best sites for plant are between 35° north and south of the equator. Assuming the efficiency of the apparatus to be about 10 per cent, it would need a collection area of at least 24,500 square kilometres (9,500 square miles) to provide electricity for the United States alone.

Rivers have long been dammed to create reservoirs and provide energy to drive the turbines of hydroelectric stations. A more novel way of generating electricity is by using the tides. At present only one such installation exists, at La Rance in France. It may be possible to develop other sites where there is a large tidal range.

Water Resources

The Earth's most precious resource, and the one most often wasted, is fresh water. Many areas of the world need water for irrigation to produce crops, and many more could be developed if only sufficient water was available.

In the years to come there will have to be a stricter control on the use of water. Conventional water closets use appoximately 11 litres (19 pints) of water each time they are flushed, and

yet a perfectly sound model has been developed which uses only 0·3 litres (0·5 pints). It has been estimated that this change in a city the size of Los Angeles would save some 181,694,700 cubic metres (237,747,600 cubic yards) of water each year. The control of pollution and the re-cycling of water used in industrial processes would also help in the conservation of water resources.

One of the most famous irrigation projects is the Snowy Mountain scheme in the states of New South Wales and Victoria in Australia. Here an entire river system has been diverted. Originally flowing eastward, its course has been altered by a series of tunnels and dams to flow to the arid interior in the west. It now supplies an entire region with adequate water. Engineers have cut through mountains, constructed sixteen large dams, 160 kilometres (100 miles) of tunnels and 128 kilometres (80 miles) of aqueducts. A number of power stations have also been built.

A continental approach to the water resources of North America has been suggested. This would divert the

flows of the Canadian rivers southwards. The whole scheme, made up of 370 different projects, would cover an area from Alaska to Mexico. The scheme if fully commissioned would include the building of enormous dams and reservoirs. It is claimed that there would be considerable benefits to agriculture particularly in the west and south-western United States.

Any scheme of this size, if carried out, would have considerable effects on the climate. The storage of vast quantities of water in reservoirs in a geologically unstable area has already been proved to cause earthquakes.

There have been similar schemes in Russia in which the northward flowing streams have been diverted southwards, but the environmental effects have been serious.

Rocks and Ores

For thousands of years rocks have been quarried for building. They are still used for the construction of roads, bridges and buildings of all types. Although we now live in an age of concrete, even this material depends on the Earth's resources in the form of limestones, for cement production, and sands and gravels.

Some igneous rocks such as dolerite and andesite are crushed for aggregate in concrete, ballast and road metal. Granites and syenites (coarse-grained plutonic rocks) are used in building. Marble is used both as a building stone and in sculpture.

Clays provide the raw materials for tiles, bricks and pottery, while slate was for hundreds of years an important source of roofing material.

One of man's most important discoveries was the use of metal. As we have seen, first copper and then gold were used, followed later by tin and iron. Today the most important metals are iron, copper, lead, tin, and zinc. Almost the whole of industry is dependent on the supply of iron, the most valuable of all metals.

There are four main ores of iron. Haematite (iron oxide), is sometimes called kidney ore, after the shape it assumes. Limonite is hydrated iron oxide and only contains about 60 per cent of iron. Magnetite is iron oxide and provides the richest source. At Kiruna and Gellivare in Sweden there

are whole mountains made of haematite. Naturally occurring magnetic magnetite is called lodestone and was used in the earliest marine compasses. The other main ore of iron is siderite.

In smelting the iron ore a blast furnace is used in which it is packed with alternating layers of coke and limestone. Hot air is blown in at the base of the furnace and the molten iron and slag drops down into a pit.

Copper was the first metal used by man and it is now in great demand in the electrical and chemical industries. It is found in its natural state but it also has more ores than any other metal. The most important are azurite (hydrated copper carbonate) and chalcopyrite which is copper-iron sulphide and malachite (hydrated copper carbonate). When alloyed with other metals, for example tin, copper forms bronze. A combination with zinc provides brass which has a number of major applications.

Lead is used mainly in coverings in telephone and electrical cables, bearings and general construction work. Lead does not corrode easily and cannot be penetrated by gamma rays. This

latter property makes it valuable in shielding personnel in X-ray units and nuclear reactor plants. It also has applications in the manufacture of batteries and as an additive to petrol. It is mainly recovered from galena (lead sulphide), cerussite (lead carbonate) and anglesite (lead sulphate).

Tin was also one of the earliest metals recovered by man and is now used in the manufacture of tin-plate, alloys and solder. There is only one important ore, cassiterite (tin oxide) which occurs in quartz veins in granite masses. Although some tin is mined it is mainly recovered from deposits in river gravels. The tin has been weathered out of the parent rock and redeposited.

Zinc is used mainly to produce alloys, for example brass and in plating. It is also used in ceramics, drug manufacture, textiles and floor coverings. Its recovery is often associated with lead. Blende (zinc sulphide) is the chief ore. It is often known as black jack. The other major ore is smithsonite (zinc carbonate) and deposits of zinc minerals are also known in the United States.

Oil drilling rig at sea.

Many other minerals are mined both for metallic and non-metallic substances. Aluminium, although abundant in the world is very difficult to extract. The only important ore is bauxite. Aluminium is extremely useful because of its lightness and resistance to corrosion. It is used in the construction of aircraft and motor vehicles.

Cobalt is used for colouring and in the hardening of steel. It is frequently found in association with copper ores, for example, in Canada and Zambia. Manganese is an essential element in the manufacture of steel and in the chemical industry. The only metal which, at normal temperature is liquid is mercury. It occurs in nature as cinnabar, and is used in dentistry and in scientific instruments and apparatus.

Two other metals of value to the steel industry are tungsten and molybdenum. Tungsten carbide is one of the hardest of all substances and is much used in the manufacture of drills.

Precious Metals

The three precious metals are gold, platinum and silver. Gold has always been highly prized by man and as it occurs in its natural form it was soon used for adornment. The largest nugget found is the Welcome Stranger which weighed 64,300 grammes (2,280 ounces) and was discovered in 1869 at Bathurst, Australia.

For many years the main deposits of gold were contained in rocks constantly subjected to weathering by rain. Because of its weight, the gold collected in pockets in the stream bed. The gold rushes of North America were based on gold located and gathered in this way.

Gold is now mainly considered as a form of international currency. Other uses are in dentistry and the manufacture of jewellery. Some of the most famous archaeological finds are made of gold.

Although originally considered to be worthless, platinum is now highly valued as a catalyst, in the chemical industry, in jewellery and in the production of electrical equipment.

Silver may be found in its natural form or recovered from argentite or cerargyrite. It is used in photography, electrical apparatus, solders, plating and jewellery.

There are a number of gemstones but the most famous must be the diamond. Because of their hardness diamonds are also very important as abrasives and for drill-bits and saw-edges. The main source of diamonds is the rock kimberlite which originates very deep within the Earth. The Kimberley area of South Africa is the most important diamond-producing region. Diamonds are also recovered from streams and the sea bed by dredging. Famous diamonds are the

Koh-i-Noor (Mountain of Light) from India and the Cullinan from South Africa.

Gem varieties of corundum are called rubies when red and sapphires when blue. The red colour is due to the presence of traces of chromium and the blue to titanium. Beryl when grass-green is the source of emeralds.

There are many other gems and semi-precious stones, some of which have already been listed, but apart from diamonds, none is as valuable as the other minerals to man's continuing development.

Natural Elements

With intensive agriculture there is a constant need to replenish the soil with such elements as phosphorus, calcium, potassium, nitrogen and sulphur. Raw materials for the fertilisers come from phosphates, limestones, sulphur and nitrates of sodium and potassium. Phosphate is obtained from the blast furnaces and from the mineral apatite. Sulphur deposits are often found in volcanic regions, being deposited by escaping gases, or in conjunction with salt domes.

The need for salt in our everyday diet and for preserving is readily acknowledged. It is also vital to the chemical industry. Rock salt is mined from beds which may be more than 18 metres (60 feet) thick. Such deposits often occur in domes.

rk on the construction of this nuclear
ctor goes on at night under floodlights.

99

Under the Sea

Seaweed and marine animals concentrate minerals from sea water.

Since earliest times man has used the sea, although it is difficult to discover whether he first used it for fishing or for transport. Another early use of the oceans was for the production of salt. Man still uses the water of the seas and oceans for all these activities. Although advanced technology means that he now constructs ships of 500,000 tons in place of hollowed out tree-trunks, the oceans of the world are still vital to communication and the transfer of goods.

Under the oceans are deposits of crude petroleum, natural gas and coal. Exploitation of these deposits has already been described. Sometimes they are obtained by drilling from above, in other instances, for example, in the extraction of coal and tin, mines stretch out from the shore. The oceans in recent years have received increasing attention from man. Often as a direct result of his quest for deposits of oil, geological knowledge of the ocean floors has increased rapidly. With the development of special equipment needed for work at sea, man's use of the oceans has also increased. Such developments are concerned with both rocks and minerals and with living resources such as fish and invertebrates.

The sea has always been used as a depository for waste material. Increasing concern is being shown with regard to the near-shore waters which, in many areas, have become heavily polluted with sewage and industrial waste. Even radioactive wastes deposited far out to sea pose a threat for the future.

Oceanic Resources

Full exploitation of the resources of the oceans is hampered by a number of restraints, among which are legal problems. Many of the oceanic resources lie beyond territorial waters. It would seem that the deep oceans will have to be developed by international agreement. Other difficulties arise between private companies and national governments over financing and the back-up research development programmes.

Many parts of the world suffer because of inadequate rainfall and surface water. Agricultural development, for example, is seriously hampered. It might be assumed that one of the chief sources of fresh water would be by the desalination of sea water. But in most cases the economic aspects of desalination plants do not, at present, allow their use on a wide scale. However, where the climate is dry, or the location an island, for example, in Kuwait or Ascension Island, it may well be worth while using sea water.

The sea also contains many other elements which may in the future provide valuable sources of metals. The only ones used at present are common salt, magnesium and bromine.

Diving saucer for undersea exploration.

Of the world's production of bromine 70 per cent comes from sea water.

The sediments of the ocean floor have considerable economic importance. Those on the continental shelf include sand, gravel, tin and diamonds. The recovery of such valuable rocks and minerals is undertaken by dredging. This is a very easy operation, although at the present time it has a number of limitations. Dredgers cannot operate in very deep water, being limited to about 60 metres (200 feet), nor can they endure rough weather. Technological developments in the future will undoubtedly increase their range and versatility.

This is important because the sediments of the continental slope are very thick and may well be important to man. Phosphorite nodules have been discovered at such locations and in the deeper water of the continental shelves, off Mexico, North and South America and South Africa. These are not at present mined but will be in the future.

Deposits under the Sea

The deep oceans offer very few resources except manganese nodules. These have been much publicised although they do not contain as high a percentage of manganese as the surface deposits being worked. They are made up of 24 per cent manganese, 14 per cent iron, 1 per cent nickel and 0·5 per cent copper. It would seem therefore that at least in the near future they may be used as a source of copper or cobalt. The nodules form as a result of precipitation from sea water around a fragment of rock or the remains of a dead animal. They occur mainly in the Pacific Ocean.

At present the most important section of the ocean is the coastal strip. It is in this area that many interests and uses vie one with another. Some of the most valuable resources of this area are in the form of sand and gravel deposits. With the gradual working out of the land deposits and the increasing building programme both are required in greater amounts. In many countries, developing towns and cities are near to the coast and therefore it is easy to transport sea-dredged sand and gravel quickly to their point of use. However, in many localities man is reclaiming land along the coastal belt to extend his houses, often building over the very deposits he wishes to use.

There are a number of problems with such developments. There are examples of severe erosion of beach material once dredging has begun. The fishing industry may also object as spawning and breeding areas could be damaged.

The in-shore area is also often used for recreational purposes and it is here that pollution problems are at their worst. It is a vital area in which a constant battle rages between different interests.

Marine Animals and Plants

It is perhaps the living resources of the oceans which are best known—the fishes, whales, crustaceans and molluscs. But it is not only the animals providing for man's need that are important, but also the plants such as seaweeds. Once used in the manufacture of soap and as a source of iodine, seaweeds still form a valuable source of fertiliser.

It is, however, on the microscopic plants which live in the upper layers of the ocean that the whole of oceanic life depends. These form the beginning of the food chains, for they can manufacture food by photosynthesis. In turn they are fed upon by minute animals which are preyed upon by larger ones.

The largest catches of marine animals are made up of familiar creatures like herrings, cod and mackerel. But because of man's increasing requirements, fisheries experts are attempting to locate new species of fish for human consumption. In other areas nurseries are being set up to rear young fish and especially to cultivate and market shell fish.

Fishery vessels are carrying increasingly sophisticated equipment and more research is being undertaken to improve nets and other fishing gear. At present fish is one of the very few foodstuffs which is produced in enough quantity to keep pace with the increasing population. But for how long?

Plant for the extraction of magnesium from the sea.

Mining the sea bed.

Man Explores His World

The urge to explore is easily satisfied in most people. The need to discover what lies beyond a strange door or across a new field is soon fulfilled. Very often, the world that we wonder about on the other side of the hill turns out to be little different from the one we already know. And there is much pleasure to be had from the warmth and security of familiar surroundings.

But for some there is always another hill to climb, another world to explore, another sea to cross. Away from homes and families and most of the things that the rest of us hold dear, a few special men have blazed a trail since the human race began, seeking always to discover the unknown places where none of their own kind has stood before.

The story of exploration is a story of many men, and if each has some special quality in common it does not mean that the men themselves are similar. To expect all great explorers to have been fired by the same idealistic motives is as unrealistic as to expect that only artists who lead saintly lives are capable of producing great works of art.

When Alexander of Macedon launched his attack on the Persians in 334 B.C. he was waging a war of vengeance. It was almost incidental that in defeating King Darius he conquered Asia Minor and Egypt as well, thereby vastly expanding Greek culture. Alexander's extraordinary journey into northern India six years later, during which he marched his army over the Hindu Kush's terrible Khawak Pass, is often regarded as an expedition of discovery. But if we disregard the fact that he was extending an empire greater than any the world had seen before, it is still true that the expedition would never have been started at all had Alexander not been engaged in crushing a rebellion.

Certainly to the Rajput King Porus, Alexander and his Macedonian army were looked upon as invaders rather than explorers. The Rajput culture which Porus sought to defend was older than that of the Greeks, their traditions even prouder, for the folk history of this warrior people reads down the centuries like the tales of some Eastern Arthurian legend. So how should we look at Alexander? As an explorer, or as a despotic conqueror who, according to an ancient tale, wept when there were no lands left for his armies to overrun?

Original Inhabitants

Most new lands found by the great explorers were already inhabited. The fact that in many cases the inhabitants were primitive tribes existing at a level far below that of their discoverers, does not seem, to modern eyes, any reason why they should be annexed.

We may read of Ferdinand Magellan's little ships making the first marvellous circumnavigation of the globe in 1522 with the reassuring thought that they were not interfering with anyone. But early explorers on land and sea were obeying an instinct as old as time and had little regard for the lives or feelings of people they 'discovered' and often dispossessed.

In the days before frontiers, man was a nomadic hunter, wandering like any other animal in search of his next meal. Some men settled down to grow crops and build up cities, but there were always those more restless who kept on the move, eventually settling in new lands among newly found people. The constant movement of early peoples across the world was as inevitable as the migration of birds, and for us the fascination of the story lies not in why, but how they accomplished their journeys.

The world of the early explorers was limited to immediately neighbouring lands and perhaps those areas a little farther off which travellers and traders described. To venture farther afield was to risk appalling danger and perhaps the wrath of the gods themselves.

The Shape of the Earth

For many centuries the Greeks, master travellers though they were, believed the earth to be flat in the shape of a circular disc—a huge island that contained seas, rivers and all known lands. Around it, like a vast moat, stretched Oceanus, a sea that ended with the fixed dome of the sky that covered everything in the manner of an enormous, transparent canopy. Sun, Moon and stars were thought to rise from the edge of Oceanus, move across the curved dome of the sky, then sink beneath the sea again. It was not an unreasonable theory and served to answer most questions that were likely to be asked. But it was one that held special terrors for those who had

Alexander and his armies were not only conquerors but explorers in a strange land.

thoughts of sailing beyond the known world to Oceanus itself.

For many years these reasons, as well as the technical limitations of early sailing ships and a total ignorance of such arts as sailing against the wind, kept even the most intrepid sailor within sight of a coastline. Easier by far for the soldier to strike out over the distant hills in the comforting knowledge that providing he did not meet a stronger enemy and the food lasted, he could with luck retrace his steps and live to tell the tale. Some marched for conquest, some in the hope of gold and many—much later—to spread a faith in their god. But all of them marched or sailed because they were driven by a need quite foreign to the majority of men who were content to tend the fields at home.

Magellan's little ships made the first voyage of exploration around the world.

The Ancient World

Egyptian traders took part in the expedition to Punt in 1500 B.C.

The civilisations of both Sumer and Egypt depended on great rivers, on the banks of which early settlers learned to farm the rich land. The Tigris and Euphrates in Mesopotamia and the Nile in North Africa were essential to the livelihood of the people and on these rivers men learned to sail and navigate.

The Sumerians may have been the first sailors to have ventured out into the open sea, spurred on to explore beyond their own lands by the desire for trade. It is believed that as long ago as 3500 B.C. their ships may even have penetrated as far as the Asian coast of the Indus.

The Egyptians

The ancient Egyptians do not appear to have taken to the open seas with any enthusiasm, despite the fact that their ships, barges and rafts had for centuries plied busily up and down the great waterway of the Nile. Like all lands in the ancient world of the eastern Mediterranean, Egypt was short of trees to provide timber for building. In a country that was largely desert, with a limited amount of vegetation, the first Egyptian boats were ingeniously constructed from papyrus reeds. The characteristic shape of the papyrus boat, familiar from many ancient wall paintings and models of Nile river boats, was continued in the first wooden boats, when trade with other countries, particularly the Lebanon, made possible the importing of short lengths of timber.

Some primitive craft: papyrus boat, a coracle, a kayak, and an inflated animal skin.

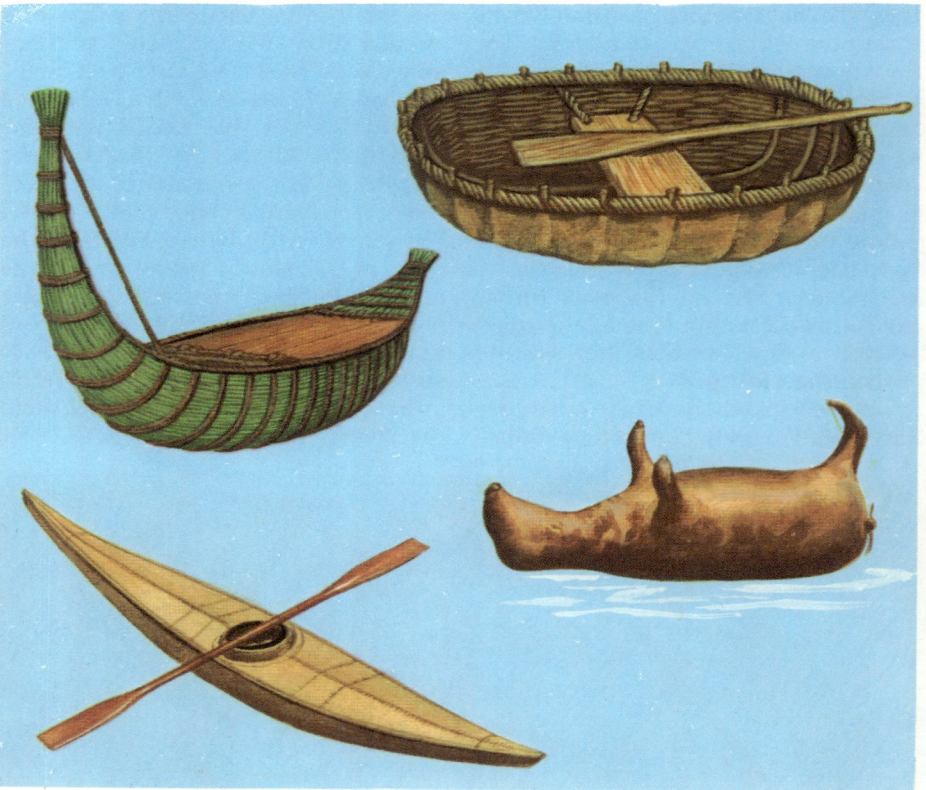

By the year 2000 B.C. there was much trade and interchange of ideas between the three principal nations of the Mediterranean—Egypt, Phoenicia and Crete. The pharaohs of Egypt were great importers, for many of the things essential to their way of life came from abroad, not only wood, but precious stones, ivory and, of supreme importance, the sweet-smelling gum called myrrh. The fact that myrrh was so important was due to the unique part played by religion in Egyptian life, where the ruler was also a god. Gods were said to like the smell of myrrh and great quantities were burned as incense in the temples during religious ceremonies.

Myrrh was normally obtained at enormous expense by the Egyptians from southern Arabia through a long chain of traders. The need to find a new source of supply was one of the principal reasons for Egypt's most celebrated trading voyage to the distant land of Punt. This was at the command of Queen Hatshepsut, then sole ruler of Egypt, about the year 1500 B.C. Hatshepsut also sought gold to supplement the dwindling supplies from Nubian mines. Her mission of five or more ships has been recorded in pictures and words, 'to bring back fragrant woods, myrrh, resin, ebony and ivory, gold and cinnamon wood, with apes, dogs and the skins of panthers, with natives and their children'.

Egypt's ships had been to Punt before but since the last Egyptian expedition there 500 years had passed. With only the record of tomb inscriptions and half-remembered traditions to guide them in the general direction of the north-east coast of Africa, Queen Hatshepsut's mariners set out. Exactly how they went and where, we cannot know for certain. Probably they carried timbers from Thebes, across the desert, to the shores of the Red Sea, where they built their boats and travelled south into the Gulf of Aden, before heading down the coast of Africa. Punt has been identified in modern times as Somalia but its location may have been as far south as Mozambique. It could have been a formidable journey of over 2,000 kilometres. Yet the Egyptian sailors undoubtedly again found Punt and continued to trade there, although the round trip took as long as two years.

The voyages to Punt were the Egyptians' greatest accomplishment in the field of exploration. But from about the first millenium B.C. their achievements were overshadowed by a

Greek war galley.

race of sailors whose courage and sheer dedication to exploration have not been equalled to this day. They were a Semitic race, called Phoenicians, and came from the eastern Mediterranean ports of Tyre, Sidon, Dor and Gaza. They established trading centres in Greece and Spain, made their way to India, Persia and China, and most probably reached the coasts of England where they traded for tin.

The Land of Gold
Just as we shall never know with certainty where Punt was, so we can only guess at the location of Ophir, the Land of Gold, to which the Phoenicians sailed on a great expedition ordered by King Solomon. It is recorded in the Old Testament that the men from Tyre and Sidon returned with 420 talents of gold, as well as silver, ivory, apes and peacocks. The Phoenicians were very secretive about their routes and left few records of their own behind them. Some think that Ophir may have been the strange, unexplained land of Zimbabwe in what is now Rhodesia, which could have been reached by the River Zambesi. Others think it was the same land of Punt visited by the Egyptians, but if the Phoenicians really did bring back peacocks it is more likely that they travelled to India or Arabia.

Of all the voyages made by the Phoenicians, none compares with the one described at length by the Greek historian Herodotus, in which Phoenician ships sailed 23,000 miles round the shores of Africa to circumnavigate the continent. Herodotus provides the

only record of this extraordinary voyage but there is a ring of truth in his account. In about 600 B.C. the pharaoh Necho is said to have commissioned the journey because he wanted to know if there was a possible trading route by sea from the Red Sea to the Mediterranean. Herodotus says that the Phoenician crews worked steadily down from the Red Sea to the Cape and then north to the Mediterranean. They stopped twice to plant corn, waiting until it could be harvested before resuming their journey.

Pytheas the Greek
For hundreds of years the idea of venturing north seemed to hold little appeal for the sun-loving Mediterranean voyagers. The great exception is Pytheas, a Greek astronomer and geographer, probably a contemporary of Alexander's. Pytheas left Massalia (present-day Marseilles) and struck north. Little is known of his quest, for apart from fragments, the book he wrote about his adventures has disappeared. We do not even know whether he went at public expense or his own. It is likely that he sailed in a galley, for the Greeks had great faith in oars, passing up the west coast of Britain, then north-east beyond Scotland to somewhere called Thule. *Ultima Thule*, or farthest north, is a phrase which we use still. Once again we have no certain means of identification. It may have been the Orkneys, Iceland or Scandinavia. Certainly Pytheas sailed all the way round Britain before making his way back home to Massalia overland.

The Roman army crosses the Alps during a winter campaign.

Eurasia

It was astonishing how swiftly the known world grew. People of the ancient civilisations had crept hesitantly along their coasts in frail boats, but as time passed, men returned with tales of a vast land mass to the north to balance that of Africa in the south. Alexander the Great had crossed the huge mountain ranges guarding India, crushing anyone who opposed him in that legendary land, and his armies had returned home. Now it was the turn of the Romans, never wholly at home on the water, to thrust outwards overland, conquering and colonising as they went.

The Romans expended both time and men in the search for new lands. In terms of history their conquests were accomplished with astonishing speed, but their achievements were those of whole legions, in days when populations were small. Life itself was short 2,000 years ago, and many men spent the greater part of theirs walking from one country to another and back again. Yet if we can believe their superbly literate accounts, these olive-skinned, disciplined soldiers went cheerfully into the unknown with much the same belief in their enterprise that had characterised the founders of the British Empire in the nineteenth century.

Roman Colonies

Because the Roman adventurers moved as a military unit, their impact on any land they came upon was immense. The Phoenicians had set up scores of trading posts that stretched along the whole coastline of North Africa as far as Tangier, but when Tyre came under Assyrian rule in the ninth century B.C. their virtual monopoly of the great sea routes ended. The same thing could not happen to the Romans, for where they marched, they established a culture that was in most cases to last much longer than the empire it represented.

The fact that the Romans took control of Greece, Macedonia and Egypt can in no way be considered exploration. It was the simple act of expanding within a known world. But when the legions headed north, crossed the Alps to overrun Gaul (France) and Britain, they were entering unknown territory. The emperor, Augustus, even launched an expedition of conquest from Alexandria south

A 'T–O' map of the 12th century which shows Asia, Europe and Africa within an O separated by the T of the Mediterranean and the rivers Nile and Don.

Skellig Michael, an island monastery off the coast of Ireland.

through the desert, east of the Red Sea as far as the borders of what is now southern Yemen, before the appalling heat drove his men back.

The desert set a southern limit to Roman colonisation, just as the aggressive Germanic and Slavic tribes had halted it to the north and as the Persians had blocked the way to the east. But it did not stop the Romans probing still farther in the course of trade. About A.D. 45 the Indian king, Kadphises, actually sent an embassy to Rome to inform the emperor Trajan that he had conquered the whole of India's north-west province. This first political connection between east and west was by no means without motive. It was, in fact, an admission that Kadphises—a remarkably ambitious and far-sighted ruler—was looking forward to a continuance of the

After satisfying their wanderlust by voyages of exploration around Europe, the Vikings ventured out across the Atlantic in their longships and reached the coast of America.

flood of gold that had poured into his country in exchange for the gems, dye-stuffs and spices that Roman traders eagerly loaded aboard their ships at Indian ports.

Not all men sailed with the solid purpose and method of the Romans. But to them, the sea was always an inconvenient extension of the land. They had learned to sail efficiently in the first place only because their enemies had ships and they had not. Consequently, a Roman sea battle always featured water-borne soldiers rather than fighting sailors. They managed their ships correctly because the servants of Caesar had to do everything in a businesslike manner, yet they lacked the instinctive skill of the sailor born and bred.

The Vikings

As the Roman army of occupation was to learn to its cost, north-east of newly conquered Britain was a race whose children handled boats as soon as they could walk, the Vikings. They were tiring of their native fiords and beginning to move steadily to-wards foreign shores. The Vikings

were a restless, hardy people whose most significant art form seems to be their ships. There is no archaeological evidence that the Scandinavians had sailing vessels before the seventh century, some time later than the Mediterranean peoples. It was not until the Vikings were overcome with a sudden overwhelming wanderlust that they ordered their boatbuilders to design a vessel capable of facing the high seas. They accordingly built a craft in the only shape they knew, that of the small boats that filled the fiords, but larger in size. Broad, with tall, curving stem and stern and unusually low freeboard, the Viking longship was one of the most flawlessly designed vessels ever built. With a huge, single square sail and as many as 32 oars, it was not only completely seaworthy but capable of entering rivers without danger of grounding.

Equipped with this superb vessel, the Vikings set about pillaging the neighbouring coasts. Within a century they were venturing farther out to sea, to the Faroes, to Iceland and beyond. Often, on some of the more inaccessible islands, they found Irish monks

had arrived before them. In their desire to spread the Gospel, these intrepid men of God had sailed out as eagerly as the Vikings themselves, only stopping when they had found some suitable rock or island on which to build a church or monastery, and so continue their work of conversion. There are tales of incredible voyages by these monks, which match even those of the Norsemen.

In A.D. 860, having already founded the dukedom in France that was one day to produce William the Conqueror, the Vikings sailed south to the Mediterranean and Italy. One band of warriors even reached Constantinople and took service under the Byzantine emperor.

On such voyages of 'exploration' once again there arises the question of who discovers and who is discovered. The Byzantine successors to the Roman Empire, at the height of a glorious culture, would have laughed at the idea of being 'discovered' by anyone, let alone a band of shaggy Norsemen in strange, long ships.

Leif the Lucky

As it turned out, nobody was in a position to laugh at the Vikings, for little more than 100 years later they were to sail their tall-prowed craft not only to Greenland but to North America itself. It was an incredible feat, and the historical record of it is incomplete. We know that the man who sailed there was Leif, known as

Lucky, son of Eric the Red, who was in turn the son of the outlaw, Thorvald. We know that they called the new country Vinland (or Wineland) the Good, because they found grapes there, and that they noted a lack of frost in winter. What we do not know is where exactly Leif the Lucky landed.

From what can be deduced of their voyage, Leif and his men might have been expected to reach some northerly point of the American eastern seaboard, and a popular guess is the area around Cape Cod. Nevertheless, the mild winter, grapes and a mention of long golden sands strongly suggests Florida. But whether it was Cape Cod or Florida, at the time the discovery created little attention.

While the Vikings were making their great journeys north and west, a new force had burst upon Mediterranean lands—that of the Arabs. Fired and united by the new religion of Islam, they overran the Byzantine empire, took control of the whole north coast of Africa, much of Persia and Spain, and even made a determined attempt at an invasion of France. It was an unexpected and shattering swing of power, but it heralded no new era of exploration, although the Arabs traded readily enough with India and China. What the scholars of the new empire did leave as a legacy to later seamen was a furtherance of the art of navigation, particularly by

Ivory chess pieces made for the East India Company to commemorate the Company's long history of trading with the sub-continent.

the stars, and a simple but practical device by which to direct ships—a rudder. Previously vessels had relied on a steering oar.

In later years the countries that had fallen to the Arabs freed themselves one by one, and in their independence cast about eagerly for new trade and power. The Moors had been driven from Portugal comparatively early and this small, not very wealthy country found itself quite suddenly in the forefront of the exploring nations of the world. This was due largely to Prince Henry the Navigator, who in the first half of the fifteenth century, made his country's sea power a force to be reckoned with. His patronage too helped to breed a new race of men

dedicated not so much to the discovery of new lands as to seeking out practical means of reaching them.

Passage to India

One of these men was Bartholomew Diaz, who, twenty-eight years after Henry's death, in 1488, rounded the Cape of Good Hope and found himself in the Indian Ocean. Another Portuguese was Vasco da Gama who, ten years later, dropped anchor off the city of Calicut in India after a voyage that had lasted eleven months. In due course he returned to Lisbon, carrying with him a letter from the local ruler addressed to the king of Portugal. It read: 'Vasco da Gama, a nobleman of your household, has visited my kingdom and given me great pleasure. In my land there is much cinnamon, cloves, ginger, pepper and many precious stones. What I seek from your country is gold, silver and coral'.

It was a handsome invitation to trade and one which the Portuguese were not slow to accept. For a century they were to hold a virtual monopoly of trade with India, although neither they nor the Dutch who became their rivals, were particularly interested in what happened in the interior of the massive country which they knew only by trading posts along its coastline. It was left to England's Elizabethan adventurers to change that.

Elizabethan Explorers

The name of Ralph Fitch does not appear often in the saga of the British in India, although there might well have been no Empire without him. He was one of that resolute breed of sea-going merchants living in Elizabethan England who roamed farther than

Arab travellers, from an old Persian manuscript.

most. In January 1583, he set off from his home shores in his ship, the *Tiger*, bound for Tripoli and Aleppo. From Aleppo he reached the Euphrates, crossed southern Mesopotamia to Basra, sailed down the Persian Gulf and finally reached the Portuguese colony of Goa in India. There he was arrested as a spy.

Fitch escaped from Goa and instead of seeking the easiest way home to England, turned inland and travelled through the heart of India to Agra, where he presented himself at the court of Akbar the Great. One imagines that Akbar, most liberal minded of the Mogul emperors, made him welcome, and the merchant continued his journey along the Jumna and Ganges in order to visit Benares.

Ralph Fitch must certainly have realised the huge potential of this country in terms of trade as he travelled on from Benares to Patna, and thence to Kuch, Chittagong and beyond. By then he must also have been gripped by the true spirit of exploration and discovery, because from Chittagong he went by sea to Burma, visited Rangoon, sailed up the Irrawaddy and even found his way into the Shan states of Siam. From

Animals locked in combat (above), an appliqué felt decoration on a saddle cloth from Central Asia (4th century A.D.). Persian miniature painting (left) of a feast given by the ruler Hulagu.

there his travels took him to Malacca, where he seems at last to have decided to return home. This he did by way of Bengal, round the Indian coast to Goa, up the Persian Gulf to Basra and back to England by way of the Mediterranean. It was a monumental journey that had taken eight years.

So far as England was concerned it was eight years well spent. Encouraged by Fitch's reports, in 1600 Elizabeth I granted a charter to 'The Governor and Company of Merchants of London Trading into the East Indies', and the long history of the East India Company had begun.

It was in 1615 that a fleet of four vessels set out with Sir Thomas Roe on board as ambassador from James I to the court of Akbar's son, the emperor Jahangir. Sir Thomas disapproved of much that he saw, and was greatly upset by his inability to convert the Moguls to Christianity. With unfailing courtesy they insisted that they preferred their own religion. 'We do not pretend,' they said, 'that our law is of universal application. God intended it only for us. We do not even say that yours is a false religion. It may be adapted to your wants and circumstances, God having, no doubt, appointed many different ways of going to Heaven.'

China and Mongolia

The vast land mass of China and Mongolia to the north of India was known for centuries to the western world principally as a source of silk. Some of the earliest travellers in those hitherto unknown lands lived in the middle of the thirteenth century. John de Carpini, a Franciscan friar,

Marco Polo leaving Venice, from a 14th-century Italian manuscript.

was sent by the pope as an envoy to the Great Khan in 1245 and reached Karakorum, the capital city of Mongolia. Eight years later, another Franciscan, William of Rubruck, also visited the Khan's court. But it was left to a Venetian not only to enter Cathay but to establish himself there officially.

About 1255 two merchants, Nicolo and Maffeo Polo had travelled from Venice to Constantinople in the course of business. From there they wandered north and eventually fell in with a party of Chinese who were returning to their own country after having completed a political mission on behalf of the emperor, Kublai Khan. The Polo brothers accompanied them and were well received at the Chinese court. Kublai Khan then sent them back to their own country, bearing messages for the pope. When Nicolo

Polo return to Cathay as the pope's representative, he took with him his seventeen-year-old son, Marco.

Marco Polo

The journey took four years and Marco, the 'young bachelor', as Kublai was to call him, was 21 years old when the Polos finally reached Shangtu in 1275. Marco Polo stayed many years at the court of Kublai Khan, learning four of the country's languages and entering the public service. It was in his official capacity that he travelled through the provinces of Shansi and Shensi, the wild country on the borders of Tibet and northern Burma. He loved travel for its own sake and, realising instinctively that the emperor shared his insatiable curiosity about people and places, he compiled vivid accounts of everything he saw.

Nothing could have strengthened his position more. Wealth and honour were heaped on the Venetian family who clearly had a natural affinity with the Chinese people they served. Indeed, so respected were the Polos that it was only with considerable difficulty that they managed to obtain permission to leave China. When they finally returned to Venice, they had been away for 24 years.

Marco Polo's record of his travels, written while a prisoner of war of the Genoese, is one of the great travel chronicles of all time. Perhaps more than any other single work, it convinced its readers of the true existence of Cathay, the Great Khan and all the splendours of the East.

Africa

The Greek proverb, often quoted by the Roman writer Pliny, 'There is always something new coming out of Africa', referred to the ancient belief that the country abounded in strange monsters. For all seamen, from the time of the ancient world to the medieval period, Africa was a vast land that could be circumnavigated only with difficulty. On the coast, townships could profitably be built up for the furtherance of trade, but no one ventured into the interior of the dark and unknown continent. From time to time native Africans emerged from the seemingly impenetrable forests to sell to Europeans spices, ivory, exotic animals and wretched creatures of their own kind, whose fate it was to be sold in their thousands as slaves.

For centuries human beings were Africa's principal export, a trade largely in the hands of the Arabs. As a country it lacked the storybook glamour of India. So far as anyone knew there were no magnificent courts to be visited, no old cultures to be studied, no rich supplies of jewels and gold. So what incentive was there to risk the hardships of the interior? Until 1768 there was none, but in that year a well-to-do Scottish gentleman named James Bruce decided that he would discover the source of the Nile.

The Amateur Explorer

In some ways it was a pointless quest, with only a certain academic interest. Yet it was exactly the challenge that appealed to the amateur explorer, and Bruce was adequately equipped for his task. He had travelled extensively in the Middle East, spoke Arabic fluently and had a sound idea of the perils he faced. Dressed as a Turk, Bruce spent two years in Abyssinia and in the Gojam highlands found what he at first thought to be the source of the Nile. This was, in fact, the origin of the Blue Nile. Bruce followed this river down to its confluence with the Nile proper.

A few years later a fellow Scot, Mungo Park, by profession a surgeon and by inclination an explorer, set off in 1795 to explore the Niger. During the journey he was imprisoned by a Moorish chief for four months, escaped and after a series of incredible adventures returned home in a state of physical collapse. In 1805 he headed a second expedition, consisting of himself, an army officer, 35 soldiers and two seamen: no one returned.

The Source of the Nile

But it was the Nile that held a special fascination for explorers, for Bruce's efforts had rekindled a 2,000-year-old controversy about the exact whereabouts of the source of Egypt's mighty river. It was a fitting enterprise for an adventurous man who was by nature an Elizabethan but who had the misfortune to live in Victorian times—Richard Burton.

Burton—he became Sir Richard just before he died—brightens the pages of history as only a true eccentric can. Officially, he was an officer of the Indian Army, but his hatred of any kind of discipline made the connection a loose one. He was possessed of iron strength, an absolutely insatiable curiosity about the manners and customs of the Islamic races and a reputed mastery of twenty-nine languages. He had already visited the forbidden city of Mecca and explored the middle of the Somali country on behalf of the British Government. Now, in 1856, he returned to Africa, commissioned by the Royal Geographical Society to discover the source of the Nile.

Accompanied by another army officer, Captain John Speke, a desperately ill Burton discovered Lake Tanganyika, which he was sure was the source of the river. Unable to move, he had to watch Speke go on alone to discover Lake Victoria. Speke returned convinced that it was this lake and not Tanganyika that was the true source of the great river.

Speke and Burton quarrelled over

Samuel Baker

Grandee's litter seen by Sir Richard Burton on his pilgrimage to Mecca.

the question and returned home. In a curious atmosphere of plot and counterplot, Speke gained the support of Sir Roderick Murchison, president of the Royal Geographical Society, who agreed to finance a further expedition to settle the question once and for all. So with Captain James Grant as a companion and 200 men, Speke returned to Africa in 1860. On reaching Lake Victoria he followed the western shore and arrived at the capital of Uganda, only to be detained there for three months by the local king. Speke eventually persuaded the king to supply him with guides, who took him to the very point where the Nile issued from the lake—the Ripon Falls.

Speke and Grant headed triumphantly for home, on the way meeting Samuel Baker who, with his Hungarian wife, Florence, had come in search of them.

Baker was another of the slightly larger than life characters who had made Africa their special province. He had farmed in Ceylon, supervised the construction of a railway between the Danube and the Black Sea and was an enthusiastic big game hunter. Having assured himself that Speke and Grant were in good health, Baker and his wife continued into the interior in search of a further lake, the supposed location of which Speke had given them. The lake was there, and turned out to be a contributory source of the Nile. Baker named it Lake Albert.

In many ways, history has sometimes been unfair to these men who were driven by as strong an urge to explore as any of the earlier travellers who had forced passages into remote corners of the globe. But the world was getting smaller and it no longer offered the almost limitless challenge that it once had. The petty rivalries, quarrels, and in some instances, the apparent triviality of the explorers' objectives in the nineteenth century, tend to be remembered, while the appalling hardships endured by these pioneers and the tenacity with which they overcame them, are forgotten.

It takes little time to read that Speke returned to Africa to confirm the source of the Nile, and it is perhaps easy enough to overlook the fact that it was a nightmare journey that lasted not weeks but two and a half years. Yet the rewards gained—or not gained—by the people concerned, confirm how curious was this era of exploration. Burton died embittered and largely forgotten as consul at Trieste; Speke accidentally shot himself when trying to kill a partridge; Samuel Baker, who had done no more than confirm that Lake Albert lay where

Livingstone's flat-bottomed steamer encounters an elephant on the Zambezi.

Speke had told him, gained a knight-hood.

The Sahara Desert

Far to the north of the great continent of Africa the secrets of the 4,800-kilometre (3,000-mile) wide Sahara desert held their own fascination, and men had been probing farther and farther into the vast waste of sand ever since the days of the Carthaginians and Phoenicians. Considering the difficulties involved in crossing such inhospitable terrain, a surprising amount of it had been mapped as early as the fourteenth and fifteenth centuries by Jewish cartographers. These men in the course of trade had gathered their information from the desert-dwelling tribes. During the 1800s numerous small expeditions gave further knowledge of the area. In 1822 the British travellers Oudney, Clapperton and Denham had worked their way from Tripoli to Lake Chad, and a year or two later Captain Alexander Laing had reached Timbuktu from Tripoli. The greatest explorer of the Sahara was probably the German, Heinrich Barth, who made his first exploratory trip across North Africa in 1845. Much of the northern Sahara was opened up in a series of expeditions by another German, Gerhard Rohlfs, in the 1860s and 1870s. But the very centre of the Sahara became the special province of the French army, who crossed and recrossed the sands as a military operation.

David Livingstone

For the rest of Africa no such rule applied. While the gentlemen adventurers had been disputing the source of the Nile, far to the south a Scots missionary had been spending his life in an attempt to accomplish something that would be of benefit, not just to the Royal Geographical Society, but to the men and women he had grown to love.

David Livingstone was by any standards a towering figure of a man. At a time when it was all too common for missionaries to judge their success merely on the number of their conversions, Livingstone had the ability to see further. He wanted to pioneer new ground, to know the people, and to leave those behind him who would slowly but surely see that conditions in the villages were improved. If by so doing he gathered men and women to his faith, that was also good.

Born in Lanarkshire in 1813, he was working in a cotton mill at the age of ten. Educating himself in his spare time to the point where he could qualify as a doctor, Livingstone was accustomed to a life of toil. He reached Africa in 1841, and until his death in 1873, travelled thousands of miles across the continent every year. During his journeys he discovered many things, perhaps the most important being the Victoria Falls which he first saw and named in 1855. He acquired a unique knowledge of the country and became obsessed with the mission that was to be the inspiration of his life—the suppression of the slave trade.

As many as 150,000 Africans were being exported each year, and on his travels Livingstone saw the horrors of slaving at close quarters. During his three great 'opening up' expeditions through south and east Africa over the course of 32 years, he sailed up uncharted rivers in his little steamboats *Pioneer* and *Lady Nyassa*. He was often carried, racked with fever, by his devoted servants through jungle and swamp, but Livingstone had always only one thought—that by learning about the country he could make it easy for settlers to start farms and build commercial enterprises. Once these were there he was sure the consequent demand for labour and more settled conditions could eventually put an end to the slave trade.

Livingstone died in a remote village on the Lulimala, worn out by work and tropical diseases. His death did more than just inspire Henry Morton Stanley, the American reporter and explorer who had been sent to find him. Stanley and Livingstone met dramatically at Ujiji, but the great missionary refused to return to England. So, revived by Stanley's company over a four-month period, he set off on his last journey with renewed strength.

The saint-like dedication of the great man's life brought a flood of missionaries and explorers to the country, and raised such a hatred of the slave trade throughout Europe that its decline is generally accepted as dating from Livingstone's death.

Even in modern times with all the aids of sophisticated transport, there are remote areas of the interior of Africa that are practically unknown and unexplored. These perhaps are the last areas of the Earth where some mystery may remain.

Exploration party in the Sahara Desert.

of North America and became the Indian tribes. Others made their way to Mexico where they founded the Aztec civilisation, or moved on towards the Isthmus of Panama where the Mayas developed. Far to the south on the west coast of South America, people settled in what was to be the home of the Incas. Of all these migrant peoples, the Eskimos were the last to arrive and travelled the shortest distance. North and south of the Bering Strait the people exhibit the same racial characteristics to this day.

This, then, was the state of the American people long before the

Eskimo carvings

The Americas

Had the first inhabitants of the Americas been native to the lands in which they lived, their presence there could be taken as part of the natural order of things. But neither North nor South America has as yet yielded any fossil remains of an ape-like, developing primate, or any equivalent of Java or Peking man. Nor, moreover, are there any fossil apes. In other words, man was not native to the New World, but at some early date made the long journey there from the Old.

This was not the achievement of one explorer but of many, and made, almost certainly, over a considerable period of time. Exactly when the migration took place is uncertain, but it seems likely that it occurred towards the end of the last Ice Age. It is generally believed that there was no crossing by any kind of boat—the newcomers arrived on foot from Asia by way of the Bering Strait and Alaska.

Perhaps we should not be too ready to dismiss totally the use of boats. Driven, as they undoubtedly were, by a shortage of food and with

the determination to seek it in some place other than their native land, these people had already man's basic skills for survival. They could clothe themselves, use tools and construct shelters, so if necessary they could probably have made some kind of craft. But we have no means of knowing if it was necessary. In those days the Bering Strait was most probably a land bridge, frozen solid or simply dry. Whether by boat or on foot, it was by this route that the first inhabitants of the Americas arrived.

It is generally agreed that these people came from Siberia, and that the racial differences that characterise the first Americans sprang, not so much from a difference in geographical origin, as from the type of man who was living there when each new wave set out. Their actions when they reached the new continent were not unlike those of the European emigrants who were to pour into New York during the last years of the nineteenth century, spreading out and making a life for themselves in the huge, promising land. Some plunged into the heart

Norsemen reached their shores. These original inhabitants were, in the manner of their time, waiting to be discovered. But it should not be forgotten that in the far distant past they themselves had been explorers.

Christopher Columbus

After the Siberian wanderers, Leif the Lucky came and went without making any lasting impression on the land. In the year 1492 Christopher Columbus 'discovered' the New World during the best known voyage of exploration in history.

The son of a weaver of Genoa, Columbus started his working life in his father's business and, according to his own words, went to sea at the age of fourteen. This may have been an exaggeration, because other records indicate that he was still working on land when in his twenties. Nevertheless he made several voyages when he was about thirty years old and had visited England, Iceland and the west coast of Africa.

Columbus's obsessive urge to sail west towards what he imagined would

114

be India seems to have sprung from his marriage to the daughter of one of Henry the Navigator's captains. The old seaman was dead, but Columbus spent months studying the logs and charts he had left. He corresponded with the great Florentine cosmographer, Paolo Toscanelli, listened to tales of the old Viking sagas and was hungry for news of any piece of flotsam that he considered might have come from the other side of the world.

The tenacity with which this dedicated man begged the money to buy ships is as remarkable as the voyage of discovery itself. He sought

American Indian mask of the False Face Society worn in a ritual to cast out evil spirits. (Below) a wagon train of settlers migrates to the American West in the 1850s.

support in his home town of Genoa, from the rulers of Spain, from Portugal, England and France. For seven long years he haunted the courts of Europe in a desperate quest for a patron. At last, through the good offices of a friend, Queen Isabella of Castile agreed to help him. Three ships, the *Santa Maria*, the *Pinta* and the *Niña* were eventually furnished. Stores and wages for the seamen cost Isabella just over £10,000.

The ships Columbus had been given were not of the best, and few of the 120 adventurers who accompanied him were volunteers. Many had been freed from prison on condition that they sailed, others were poverty-stricken and described as 'broken men'. A poor crew, but Columbus sailed them westwards for five weeks. Estimating the earth to be one-third of its actual size, the admiral was as perplexed as his men by the length of the voyage, and only kept his crew from mutiny by keeping two logs—an optimistic one to encourage the faint-hearted and a true record safely under lock and key.

At last there came the welcome signs of land birds, floating vegetation and carved pieces of wood. Finally came the moment of history, when a sailor, Rodrigo de Triana, saw white sands gleaming in the moonlight—now believed to be Watling's Island in the Bahamas—and the terrible voyage was over. Columbus was convinced that they were in India, but in actual fact, the explorers had reached the New World.

The name, the New World, was given not by Columbus but by

Amerigo Vespucci. A naval contractor turned voyager, he sailed down the coast of South America and realised what Columbus did not, that this was not India but a previously unimagined continent. Perhaps, then, it was appropriate that Amerigo should give America his name.

Merchant Adventurers

For a time it seemed as though the American continent was to be shared between the Spanish, the Italians and the Portuguese. The day of the Elizabethan adventurer was still to come, and when Henry VII of England sent a mariner to explore the land discovered by Columbus, he chose Giovanni, or John Cabot, a Genoese who had settled in England. Cabot headed west and discovered Newfoundland, which he reported as being the land of the Grand Khan. On a further voyage he sailed north to Greenland and then turned south along the coast of Labrador. His son, Sebastian, founder of the Company of Merchant Adventurers, followed an icy path to Hudson Bay, where he probed unsuccessfully for a northern passage to Russia.

Most of the explorers from Mediterranean lands were drawn to the southern hemisphere. By 1520 Ferdinand Magellan had sailed to the very tip of South America and beaten his way through the strait that today bears his name. His voyage was a constant fight against sickness, a mutinous crew and bad weather, until he reached the Philippines to die there at the hands of the natives.

Vasco de Balboa had crossed the Isthmus of Darien and, in 1513, became the first European to set eyes on the Pacific. But exploration was to change. The old captains were half-adventurers, half-dreamers, following their star wherever it might lead them. Not so the men who came after.

The Conquistadores

The European nations were swift to follow up the first hesitant landings on the American coast. Still with the vision of new trading passages to the east, the Spaniards in particular sent ship after ship to claim more territory in the region of Panama. Hernando Cortes and his small band of 500 men and 16 horses carried through the conquest of Mexico in two years of skilful and ruthless campaigning.

These hard-faced adventurers, the *conquistadores*, burned and slaughtered their way towards the centre of the fabulous Aztec Empire at Tenochtitlan.

The Aztec emperor was Montezuma II, the ruler-god of a rich, fierce and bloodthirsty people with a record of human sacrifice that has never been equalled before or since. Cortes, by intelligent diplomacy through the agency of a gifted native woman interpreter called Marina, succeeded in winning for himself sufficient Indian allies to overcome the numerical weakness of his forces. With extraordinary persistence he overcame every obstacle to gain control of Mexico, leaving Montezuma dead on the battlefield and the Aztec people plagued by the disease of smallpox introduced by his men from Spain.

In Peru the ancient civilisation of the Incas fared no better. The campaign waged by Cortes excites admiration for its skill and daring, despite the cruelty he inflicted on the Indians. It is less easy perhaps to admire Francisco Pizarro, soldier of fortune and a member of Balboa's party who first looked upon the Pacific. Pizarro, the conqueror of Peru, finally defeated the Inca king Atahualpa by calculated treachery, extorting the ransom of a room full of gold (a room which still stands today at Cajamarca in Peru) and then strangling his prisoner in cold blood. Pizarro became master of Peru, an achievement that matched that of Cortes in Mexico, for his force was equally small. The tenacity of the heavily armoured Spanish soldiers, who forced their way through apparently endless sub-tropical jungle and over high snowy passes, was almost unbelievable. But their feats were accomplished by appalling and wanton cruelty and a lust for gold.

The French in Canada

On the other side of the world, the French became restless as they watched the exploitation of the new continent by other nations. They considered themselves to be leaders of sixteenth-century Europe, yet clearly it was the Spaniards who were making the running in the New World. So when the Florentine navigator, Giovanni da Verrazano, suggested to the French king, Francis I, that he might be of service, he was made welcome. In due course he was despatched across the Atlantic on behalf of France. Verrazano kept faith with his new master. After making a landfall off North Carolina, he followed the coast up to the mouth of the Hudson River and along the coast of what would one day be New England before returning home. Where he had first set foot, many Frenchmen were to follow.

The speed with which the Americas were developed was truly remarkable.

Ferdinand Magellan

Juan de la Cosa's map of the New World, 1500. Europe and Africa are on the right and the then unknown shape of the Americas on the left.

A bare 25 years after Columbus's landing in the Bahamas the land north and south of Panama was crowded with Europeans. For some years the remains of Columbus's flagship the *Santa Maria*, which went aground on a reef off Haiti on Christmas Day 1492, served as a monument to an epic voyage. But before long expeditions from Europe to the New World became commonplace and the journey itself no longer remarkable.

Now it was the turn of North America to receive the attentions of the European explorers, soldiers and fortune hunters. Was it chance that sent the Spanish to the south and the French to the north? Probably not, for the Spaniards had sought gold above all else, and many of them still half believed they would eventually find gilded cities and some elixir of eternal youth in the strange new lands.

No actual record exists of Columbus's ship the *Santa Maria* but this drawing is based on the type of 15th-century vessel with which the great voyage of discovery was made in 1492.

Many portraits of Columbus exist, none of which can be said with any confidence to be a true representation, although the picture above is considered authentic and convincing.

The French, on the other hand, were more realistic. Exploration for them was concentrated on the practical search for something useful.

But it was with gold in mind that the Spaniard Fernando de Soto, a one-time officer of Pizarro's forces, struck inland from Florida with a force of 600 men. This was the start of what was to be one of the country's most memorable feats of exploration. With their minds full of stories of limitless riches somewhere ahead, de Soto's men marched through Florida, South Carolina, North Carolina, across the Blue Ridge Mountains to Tennessee, on through Georgia and Alabama. After three years those who were left reached the Mississippi, where de Soto died. Less than half the company finally reached their destination in Mexico. It would be a staggering journey to make on foot even today.

What it must have been like then to trudge through unknown country, wearing armour and beset by hostile Indians, defies the imagination. Needless to say, they found no gold.

A Long Walk

One of the early explorers of North America was a man who accomplished an incredible journey almost by accident. David Ingram was a British sailor who had arrived in the New World under John Hawkins, during the famous admiral's third voyage in the Caribbean in 1567. After a disastrous naval engagement with the Spanish, the British were left short of ships. Ingram was faced with the prospect of starving in a small ship that was carrying far too large a crew or of taking his chance of finding his way home by land. He chose the latter, and with about 20 companions struck

up north from the Gulf of Mexico. A year later, with two surviving friends, he reached St John in New Brunswick, having completed a walk of more than 4,800 kilometres (3,000 miles).

Ingram found a ship and returned to England, apparently thinking very little of his remarkable journey. It was more than ten years before he produced an account of his travels. Then he told his story to a commission that was collecting information regarding the New World. What the tough sailor had forgotten over the years he obviously made up, and his narrative included accounts of elephants and huge nuggets of gold. Probably he barely noticed the country as he tramped through it, intent only on getting home.

Jacques Cartier

Meanwhile the French had sent the

Spanish explorers in the Americas fought their way through hostile country.

or simply vanished. It was John Smith who held Jamestown together through the first testing winter, for being a master of survival himself, he taught others to survive too.

For many years Smith was considered to be an outrageous liar and even his contemporaries refused to believe a life story that included fighting the Turks in Hungary, being

Breton, Jacques Cartier, to explore the mighty St Lawrence River, and in spite of the almost unbelievable cold, between 1534 and 1541, he had reached the sites of the future Montreal and Quebec. Cartier had hoped to found a permanent settlement, but the Canadian winter defeated him. It was left to Samuel de Champlain, two generations later, to make Quebec the centre of France's vital fur empire, an enterprise he founded on cooperation and friendship with the Huron and Algonquin tribes.

Acadia, as the area between Quebec and Halifax came to be called, was an imaginative attempt at colonisation. The king of France even sent out parties of hardy peasant girls, the 'king's girls' they were called, as wives for the pioneers. To settle the land and populate it with French families was a worthy enough object and one to which Champlain devoted his life. Since this was the time of the long struggle for power between France and England, the French had to contend with ruthless attacks upon their settlements.

English Settlements

The English were late upon the American scene, in general showing little interest in spectacular feats of exploration. Sir Walter Raleigh, the father of the first English settlements in Virginia in 1584, had summed up the potential of the country quickly enough, and the early settlers set to work with ferocious industry to cut wood and raise crops of grain and tobacco. Yet it would have been surprising if, among the shiploads of impoverished English younger sons and out-of-work soldiers who joined the colonists, there was not at least one man with the flair of a Champlain, who combined restlessness with husbandry. There was such a man in Captain John Smith.

Jamestown, Virginia, was established in 1607, with a force of 120 men who might easily have gone the same way as the earlier colonists at Sagadahoc and Roanoke and dispersed

captured by them and made a Turkish slave. He was sold on an auction block at Constantinople before starting a fresh series of adventures in Russia. Evidence now suggests that the stories were all true, as was the well known incident when Smith was saved from death at the hands of the Indians by Princess Pocahontas and was subsequently enrolled in her tribe.

In New England, the *Mayflower* settlers, the first of whom had arrived in 1620, were laying out their quiet farms. Inland from New York, the English Quaker, William Penn, was organising his ideal state at the colony of Pennsylvania which he founded in

1681. It seemed orderly and perhaps rather dull after the adventurings of the early days of settlement, but the fact remained that once away from the tidy coastal areas, the huge, wild bulk of the continent remained virtually untouched. Prosperous though the new communities were, there was always the odd man on whom a settled life hung heavily, and who would one day pull on his jacket, pick up a long rifle and disappear over the beckoning hills to the west, perhaps for ever.

The Way to the West

The history of North America in the late eighteenth and early nineteenth centuries is full of tales of such men, many of whose names have passed into national folklore. At first their chief objective was to cross the north-to-south barrier of the Appalachians: men like Thomas Walker, who found the Cumberland Gap; or Daniel Boone, who had lived in the woods as a boy, and as a man blazed a trail through Kentucky that was to be followed by more than 300,000 settlers within 25 years; or James Robertson, who left the safety of North Carolina in 1779 to found a colony in the centre of Tennessee.

But the American continent had still to be crossed. In 1792, Alexander Mackenzie took a party from Canada's Fort Chipewyan across the Rocky Mountains till he reached the Pacific coast near Cape Menzies. In 1804, acutely aware that his newly independent country had an even greater need for the overland route, President Jefferson of the United States ordered two ex-army men, Meriwether Lewis and William Clark, to take a similar 'Corps of Discovery' from the Missouri to the mouth of the Columbia River in Washington State.

It proved to be an epic journey. With a party of 43 men, Lewis and Clark followed the Missouri to its source, crossed mountains and plains full of buffalo, built canoes, ate their horses to save themselves from starvation, and finally returned to St Louis a year and a half later with their mission triumphantly accomplished.

It was the West that was to be the ultimate goal, and just as there had been wanderers to blaze a trail across the Appalachians, so the new country threw up a new breed of pathfinders, the mountain men of the Rockies.

They were a special kind of wanderer. Lonely by choice, usually illiterate, more at home beside an Indian camp fire than among their own kind, they trapped, hunted and followed their instincts west—always west. Occasionally they would return to civilisation with a load of furs and tell tall stories in the saloons before slipping away again. Some of them became so obsessed with the life that they undoubtedly became a little mad. Others, like Jim Bridger and Kit Carson willingly passed on their knowledge to the army and to the hordes of would-be settlers, leading wagon trains along routes previously known only to the Indians and unconsciously pioneering the highways of the future.

The Pilgrim Fathers

Not all the explorers of North America travelled because of wanderlust or in the hope of finding rich land. Some at least journeyed into the unknown for the same reason as the Pilgrim Fathers—in search of a place where they could worship God as they chose. Of all the great American expeditions, few surpass the march of Brigham Young's Mormons in search of their new Zion. Starting from the Missouri River, companies of the faithful faced severe hardships in their long trek west before arriving in Utah in 1848 to found its present-day capital of Salt Lake City.

The vast lands of the Americas were there, and the people came. For perhaps a century and a half all of them were explorers of a kind. And when the huge waves of emigrants from Europe poured into the bleak reception areas of New York's Ellis Island at the beginning of the twentieth century, they carried on a tradition that America had made uniquely her own—that all men were pioneers in a golden land.

119

Oceania

While the successors of Magellan and Columbus crossed and recrossed the Atlantic Ocean in greater numbers, few mariners penetrated far into the vast Pacific Ocean. Although men believed there was a great land mass on the far side of the ocean on which Magellan had sailed, very little was done in the sixteenth and seventeenth centuries to discover it.

Perhaps the reason was that the Americas absorbed most of man's urge to explore, although it may have been simply that seamen were loath to pit themselves against the enormous Pacific Ocean. And yet men did find Australia despite themselves. The man who actually discovered it first is uncertain. It may have been le Testu of France, de Torres of Spain or any one of those captains who were blown off course by a storm and to their surprise found themselves in sight of land where none was shown on the charts.

In 1616, Dirk Hartog of Amsterdam landed on the shores of Australia and was probably the first white man to do so. He left a metal dinner plate with a message scratched on it to commemorate the fact—a plate that was still there when his fellow countryman, William de Vlamingh, arrived almost a century later.

of the accounts of his adventures. Dampier wrote astonishingly well, and his stories were to fire the imagination of generations of sailors, including, almost certainly, the young Englishman James Cook.

Captain Cook

Cook was the child of a poor family who made his way through his own intelligence and capacity for hard work. Born in Yorkshire in 1728, he ran away to sea, joined the navy as an ordinary seaman and worked his way up to captain—an extraordinary achievement in those days.

An acknowledged expert on mathematics and navigation, Cook was given command of HMS *Endeavour* in 1768 with orders to observe the transit of Venus in the Pacific, which was to take place the following year. He was also instructed to discover 'whether the unexplored part of the southern hemisphere be only an immense mass of water, or contain another continent'.

Cook studied the transit from Tahiti, then turned south and sailed about the Pacific in search of Australia. He cast anchor off New Zealand in October 1769 and spent six months surveying the coasts of the north and south islands. He then moved on to sight the

friendly, yet when James Cook studied the good-looking Polynesians, his unusually perceptive nature seemed to sense the ruin that the white man would eventually bring. Alone among his kind he questioned the moral rightness of what he was doing. 'In what other light can they first look upon us but as invaders of their country?' he noted sadly. It seemed a cruel twist of fate, that a man who had rare compassion for his time, should be destined to die at the hands of natives on the shores of one of his later discoveries, the Hawaiian Islands.

Although technically Australia had been discovered and claimed by the Dutch, under the convention of the time the claim had lapsed since it had not been substantiated. Britain took care to follow up Cook's claim on behalf of the Crown, and the first British colony was established in Botany Bay in 1788.

The Australian Interior

For a quarter of a century the settlers contented themselves with a narrow coastal strip of land. Then in 1813 three men, Blaxland, Lawson and Wentworth, crossed the Blue Mountains and struck inland to found the town of Bathurst. Once exploration

Aborigines gaze curiously at a party of explorers in the Australian interior.

The first Englishman to land on the new continent was a scholarly buccaneer, William Dampier. Dampier was a curious character who alternated between being a privateer on behalf of his country and sailing as a free roving pirate on his own account. In the course of two voyages he explored the north-west coast and came to the conclusion that it was not joined either to Asia, Africa or America. It seems likely that his most significant contribution to history was the writing

eastern coast of Australia on 19th April 1770 at a point now identified as Cape Everard. Later in the same month Cook went ashore farther north at Botany Bay and formally claimed the country on behalf of Britain.

When Cook visited it, Tahiti had already been discovered by Samuel Wallis in 1767. The latter had tried, unsuccessfully, to persuade people to call it King George's Island. The meeting between the British and Tahitians seems to have been generally

had started, the ultimate goal was clear—to cross the continent from south to north. So inhospitable was the interior that the task seemed virtually impossible, although by the middle of the nineteenth century the South Australian government was offering a prize of £10,000 for the first crossing. The most celebrated and deeply mourned contenders were to be Robert Burke and William Wills, who set out in 1860 leading an expedition equipped with both horses

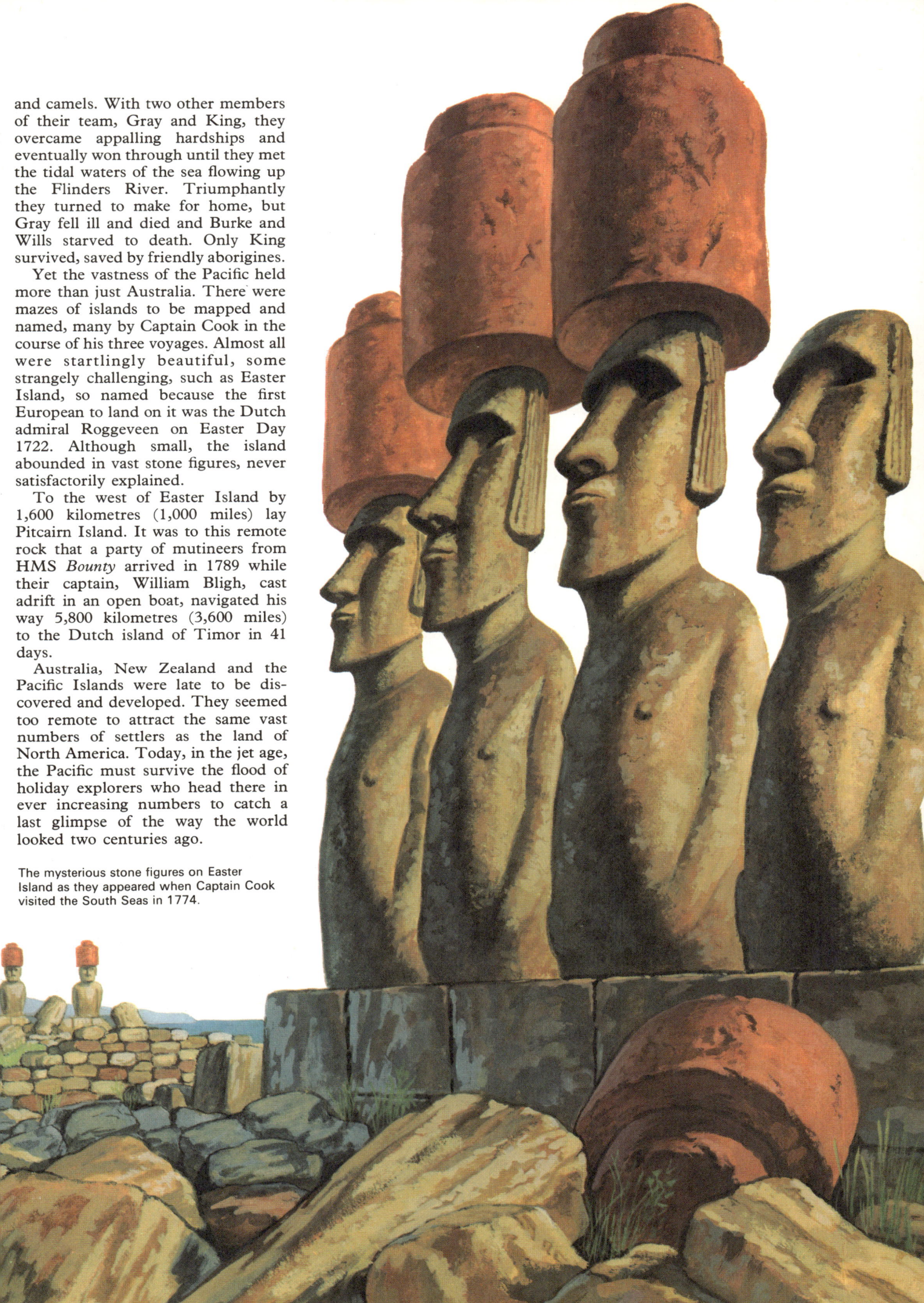

and camels. With two other members of their team, Gray and King, they overcame appalling hardships and eventually won through until they met the tidal waters of the sea flowing up the Flinders River. Triumphantly they turned to make for home, but Gray fell ill and died and Burke and Wills starved to death. Only King survived, saved by friendly aborigines.

Yet the vastness of the Pacific held more than just Australia. There were mazes of islands to be mapped and named, many by Captain Cook in the course of his three voyages. Almost all were startlingly beautiful, some strangely challenging, such as Easter Island, so named because the first European to land on it was the Dutch admiral Roggeveen on Easter Day 1722. Although small, the island abounded in vast stone figures, never satisfactorily explained.

To the west of Easter Island by 1,600 kilometres (1,000 miles) lay Pitcairn Island. It was to this remote rock that a party of mutineers from HMS *Bounty* arrived in 1789 while their captain, William Bligh, cast adrift in an open boat, navigated his way 5,800 kilometres (3,600 miles) to the Dutch island of Timor in 41 days.

Australia, New Zealand and the Pacific Islands were late to be discovered and developed. They seemed too remote to attract the same vast numbers of settlers as the land of North America. Today, in the jet age, the Pacific must survive the flood of holiday explorers who head there in ever increasing numbers to catch a last glimpse of the way the world looked two centuries ago.

The mysterious stone figures on Easter Island as they appeared when Captain Cook visited the South Seas in 1774.

The Polar Regions

During the 1839 Antarctic expedition two ships under the command of James Clark Ross anchor before the ice shelf.

The search for the Northwest Passage drew men to the merciless Arctic seas with a special kind of fascination. And indeed the prize appeared to be a rich one. In the days before the construction of the great canals, a quick route to the Pacific seemed the answer to an age-old dream. Encouraged by the English queen, Elizabeth I, Martin Frobisher tried and failed as early as 1576. Nine years later, John Davis set out with a charter for the 'search and discoverie of the Northwest Passage to China'—and also failed. As did Henry Hudson and William Barents—to name two more of the many who made the attempt. Robert Bylot and William Baffin very nearly did discover the route but, not realising how close they were to success, sailed for home.

In 1818 the British government sent two expeditions to the Arctic. One was under John Ross and William Edward Parry bound, if possible, for the Northwest Passage. The other, headed by David Buchan and John Franklin was to seek the North Pole. Buchan had trouble with his ship off Spitsbergen and had to turn back, with Franklin in attendance. Ross turned into Lancaster Sound and, had he but known it, stood on the threshold of success. He looked ahead and saw nothing but a great bank of cloud. Under the impression that it was a range of mountains barring his way he turned back—a decision that was to embitter him for the rest of his life.

The almost endless search was taken up in 1845 by John Franklin yet again, although he was nearing sixty at the time. With two ships, the *Erebus* and *Terror*, manned by 130 officers and men, he headed north. His ships were seen by whalers in Baffin Bay in July 1845. After that, they simply disappeared.

The government waited three years for news and then offered a £20,000 reward for the rescue of the missing men. It was a search that was to involve no less than 39 expeditions over a period of ten years before the story could be pieced together. Franklin and his crews had been trapped in the ice for two and a half years. Eventually they had set out on foot and died of cold and starvation, although not before they had proved that there was indeed a Northwest Passage. The route was finally sailed

The Norwegian Nansen planned to allow his vessel, the *Fram,* to be caught in the slowly moving ice and let it carry him to the North Pole—a plan that failed.

in 1906 by the Norwegian, Roald Amundsen, years after it had been accepted that such a passage was of no commercial use to anyone.

The North Pole

The ultimate goal, the North Pole itself, had even less practical value, but the urge to get there was just as strong. As early as 1853 an American, Elisha Kane had led an expedition that, although unsuccessful, produced a great deal of information about living in sub-zero conditions. Kane had also been prepared to spend much time with the Eskimos in order to learn all he could about their inherited skills in Arctic survival. His assistant, Hayes, followed him, as did American journalist, Charles Hall, who lived with the Eskimos for five years, finally to die of privation in Greenland in 1871.

Germany, Finland, Denmark, Britain—each produced explorers who tried heroically but unsuccessfully to beat the Arctic winter. Most found their ships trapped and even crushed by the huge ice floes, an apparently unbeatable problem. Then in 1893 the Norwegian, Nansen, set sail in a specially strengthened ship, the *Fram.* His plan was to allow his vessel to be caught in the slowly moving ice and let it carry him across the Pole. Taken off course, Nansen left the *Fram* in March 1895 and with a dog team and one companion set off to reach his objective on foot, only to be beaten back after an appalling journey lasting fifteen months.

The first man actually to reach the North Pole was an American, Admiral Robert E. Peary, who, like his countryman Kane, believed that success depended not on merely visiting the

Arctic, but on *living* there. He made eight Polar expeditions and became so accustomed to the life that he even allowed his wife to accompany him to the Arctic Circle.

Mounting his attack like a military operation, Peary set off with a team that included 28 sledges and 140 dogs. After sending back units at regular intervals when they had deposited stores along the route, Peary and a Negro, Matthew Henson, went on alone and finally stood at the Pole on 6th April 1909.

Antarctica

There were other frozen lands to the south, although Captain Cook had long ago observed that in his opinion no man would ever explore them, adding that if anyone did 'I shall not envy him the fame of his discovery, but I make bold to declare that the world will derive no benefit from it'.

The great navigator had assessed the situation with his usual accuracy, but the goal was there and over the years, men followed each other in their efforts to attain it. In 1839 the British Admiralty sponsored an expedition to the Antarctic under the command of James Clark Ross, who as a young man had gone to the Arctic with his uncle, Sir John Ross. Ross's account of his explorations was to supply much of the background information for those who followed him.

Ernest Shackleton reached a point 156 kilometres (97 miles) from the South Pole in 1909, then a farthest south record, but the Pole itself fell to Roald Amundsen, who made his camp on the Great Ice Barrier in January 1911. In October of that year he set off with dog sledges and reached the Pole on 14th December 1911, one month ahead of Captain Robert Scott, who was in charge of a rival British expedition. Scott's arrival at the Pole only to find the Norwegian flag already flying there, and the lonely death of his party while attempting the return journey, is one of the great tragic epics of exploration.

Scott, who hand-hauled his sledges partly because of his refusal to consider dogs expendable, remains with us as an almost mystic figure, whose character ennobled a quest for something essentially valueless—desirable only because it was the last truly unexplored land on Earth.

The New Continent

The Arctic population is growing and there are now air-strips and weather stations on the snows. Perhaps Antarctica, too, will not always be a wasteland. Already permanent bases have been set up and true international cooperation has been achieved in furthering scientific research. There are some hopes of exploiting mineral resources on the continent and already the remote wilderness of this inhospitable land is being tamed.

Exploration in Antarctica in modern times makes use of many forms of mechanical aid.

When Captain Scott reached the South Pole he found that Amundsen had got there first. Before setting off on their last fatal journey, Scott and his gallant party posed for a final photograph.

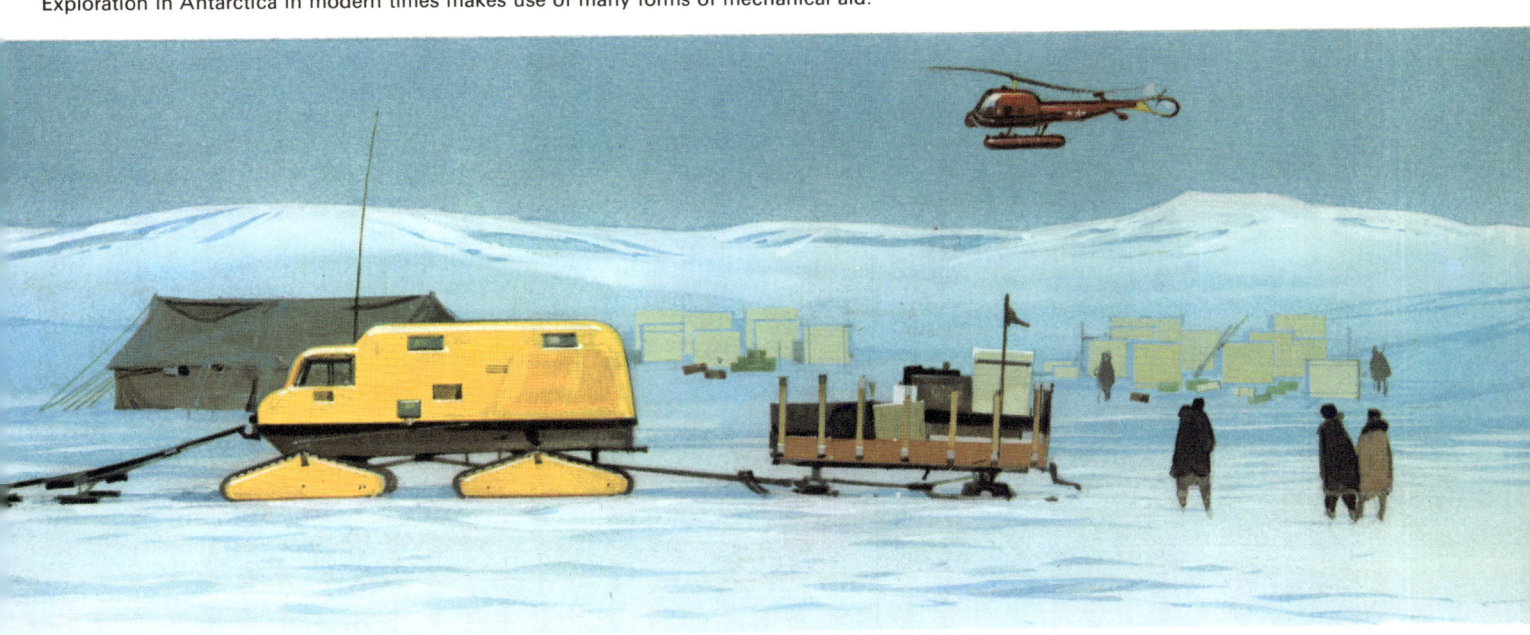

New Challenges

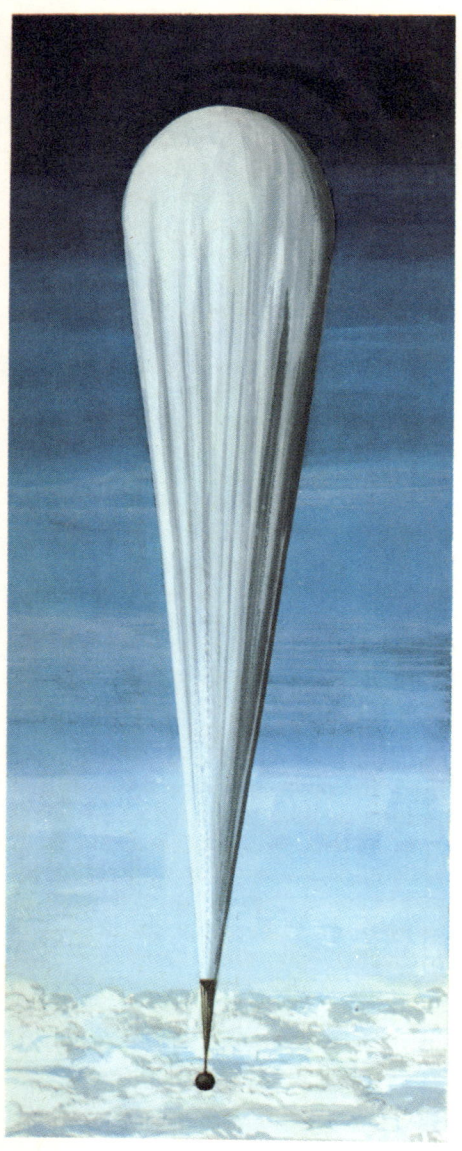

High altitude flights into the stratosphere.

With Amundsen at the South Pole, what was there left for the adventurous traveller to achieve? There were still corners of the globe, particularly in South America, which remained unexplored, but as a challenge such places seemed remote. As there were no new lands to be found, one of the ways men's eyes turned after the First World War was towards the great mountain peaks forming an east-west barrier across central Asia.

The more conveniently situated mountains in Europe had long since been climbed, but in the Himalayas, Nanga Parbat was still unconquered, as was Lhotse. No man had ever scaled Kinchinjanga, whose peak was supposed to be peopled with spirits and was reckoned by climbers to be the most dangerous mountain in the world. And certainly no one had beaten the queen of them all, the highest peak on earth, Mount Everest (8,847 metres, 29,028 feet).

The Himalayas

The moment for great achievements seems sometimes to be pre-ordained. Scientists can toil at a problem for years and then suddenly two men working independently on opposite sides of the world will produce an answer within months of each other. So it was with the mountains. On 29th May 1953, the New Zealander, Edmund Hillary and Sherpa Tensing stood on the summit of Everest, the highest men on Earth. Two months later Nanga Parbat was scaled in an amazing solo climb by the Austrian,

Hermann Buhl. A year later the second highest mountain, the peak known as K2 fell to two Italians, then Lhotse was conquered in May 1956 by a Swiss expedition. Even Kinchinjanga, climbed in May 1955, was not proof against the sudden thrust of the mountain men. In response, however, to a request from the neighbouring Sikkim government, its conquerors, George Band and Joe Brown, refrained from treading on the last few yards of windswept snow out of consideration for the spirits that dwelt there.

Could man go higher still? High altitude exploration has always been the province of balloons lifting specially designed capsules, and Auguste Piccard and his son Jacques led the way in pioneer flights into the stratosphere. In the United States manned balloons have now made flights of over 30,480 metres (100,000 feet), although compared with space flight, such heights are unremarkable.

Undersea Exploration

Man has now turned his attention with great enthusiasm to the last sizeable unexplored regions—not above the earth but beneath the sea. Undersea exploration has a twofold fascination. For the explorer it offers a true challenge, combining danger and difficulty with a practical consideration that has been lacking since the colonisation of Australia—the prospect of gaining new areas for the benefit of man.

To exist under water is not a new skill. In 1954 the French expert, Jacques Cousteau, had taken a diving team to the Persian Gulf to carry out a survey of the sea bed on behalf of an oil company. There they met a group of local pearl divers, men who were accustomed to going down 36 metres (120 feet) without even goggles to protect their eyes. The two parties stared at each other across the short distance that separated their boats. The world's most advanced divers faced the most primitive, with a 2,000-year difference in their methods.

As early as 1943 Cousteau had taken a major step forward in the design of diving equipment. He was a man totally absorbed by the potential of the sea. For him, it was as much man's natural heritage as the fields and hills of his native France, and he was determined to equip himself in such a way as to become a part of his adopted element as soon as possible. The equipment of wartime frogmen had stirred his imagination, but well aware

The ocean depths are largely unexplored regions.

that oxygen becomes toxic under pressure, he set about finding some means of breathing pressurised air safely.

When he had solved the problem satisfactorily, Cousteau sought to change the world's attitude towards diving, and with an instinctive flair for publicity he rapidly popularised his work. In 1963 he established a 'village under the sea' on a reef in the Red Sea. He used a star-shaped underwater house in which groups of divers could live for weeks at a time, leaving their home daily in order to photograph fish and collect specimens.

Cousteau's explorations were in comparatively shallow water, yet even the permanently dark sea bed beneath the surface was to be studied. The veteran underwater explorer, Auguste Piccard, developed a bathyscaphe named *Trieste* which carried its crew deep down into the north-west Pacific's Challenger Deep and returned safely. The bathyscaphe is in effect a vast tank filled with petrol for buoyancy and carrying an observation gondola beneath it. It is brought back to the surface by releasing huge quantities of metal pellets carried as ballast and held in place by electromagnets. A new version of the *Trieste* built for the United States Navy in Switzerland, established in 1960 a record ocean descent of over 10,660 metres (35,000 feet) in the same area of the Pacific.

Bathyscaphes such as the *Trieste* are essentially scientific instruments. A more significant vessel for underwater exploration came in 1955 when the

The nuclear submarine *Triton* was the first vessel to encircle the globe under the water without surfacing.

The great mountain peaks of the Himalayas have attracted climbers from every part of the world.

United States Navy launched the USS *Nautilus*, the first nuclear-powered submarine. Capable of cruising almost indefinitely under water at a speed of 20 knots, the *Nautilus* promised man something he had never achieved before—a life virtually independent of the atmosphere. In 1960 the USS *Triton*, a twin-reactor nuclear vessel became the first submarine to encircle the globe under the water without surfacing.

Marine Archaeology

On earth new generations of adventurers will always seek new challenges, but in many cases they find only new ways of doing things that have been done before. To climb an already familiar mountain by a new route, even if more difficult, is not genuine exploration. To search beneath the sea is, and a world-wide interest in subaqua clubs suggests that unprecedented numbers of people are equipping themselves with the necessary skills to enable them to go beneath the waves. Marine archaeology is a steadily expanding science, and wrecks are being explored that, in some cases, have been lost for 2,000 years. There is talk of an expedition to raise what is left of Columbus's *Santa Maria* and even to seek out the wreck of the *Titanic*. Yet in a time of expanding populations it may not be too fanciful to think that the last great adventure on earth will be the colonisation of the sea bed, and that man will one day return to the sea from which he first came millions of years ago.

The Universe and Space Trave

Astronomy, the study of the heavens, is the oldest and most widely practised of all the sciences. Few people, at some time or other, will not have been awed or puzzled by the tiny pin points of light we call stars. An experience involving either of these feelings can be considered elementary astronomy. For astronomy can be as simple as standing outside your back door looking at the Pole Star, or as complicated as tuning a giant radio telescope into the universe. Astronomy can be as cheap as the price of a pair of binoculars used to study the Moon, or as expensive as the enormous cost of building a satellite to investigate distant stars.

It is important to explain the differences between astronomy and astrology. Astronomy is the scientific study of the stars. It involves trying to find out more about stars; how they appear to have been formed, how they die, how big they are and how far away they are. It involves the study of our particular galaxy, that immense group of stars to which the Sun belongs, and the study of the countless numbers of other galaxies which seem to fill space, in all directions, as far as we can see.

Astrology, on the other hand, concerns superstitions about the stars. If considered as such it can be great fun, like telling fortunes from the pattern of tea leaves in a cup. The interest in astrology, like that in astronomy, goes back into the distant past. At one time it was believed that the stars and planets were made by various gods, like children building sand castles. With such a belief, it was natural to think that the gods could control the destiny of individuals on the Earth. Some people believe it even today. However, most people would agree that, in the same way as there is no scientific reason why a black cat running in front of you should bring good luck, so the apparent appearance of the sky when you are born cannot possibly control or predict your future.

Steps into Space
The age in which we live is the most exciting there has ever been in the history of astronomy. During our lifetime we have seen, with the Apollo landings on the Moon, the start of manned exploration of the solar system. This event far surpasses in both technological achievement and probably in historical significance any voyage of discovery on the Earth. Whatever else will be remembered in the twentieth century, one event seems

assured a place in the history books of the future—man's first faltering steps into space, after nearly a million years of development.

In our lifetime we have also begun to explore planets other than the Earth on which we live. Mercury, Venus, Mars and Jupiter have all been surveyed by long-distance spacecraft. Spectacular pictures of Mercury and Mars have been sent back to Earth, revealing secrets as exciting as those discovered by Galileo when he looked at the Moon through his first telescope. These pictures have brought some radical changes in our knowledge of these two planets. The new information on Mercury, in fact, is causing the current and almost universally believed theory of planetary evolution to be re-investigated.

Also up-dated is our knowledge and understanding of the planet Venus. Gone for ever is the cherished dream that beneath the thick layer of white cloud which envelops this planet there might be a world of steamy jungles, which men would one day explore and on which possibly they could live in relative comfort. Spacecraft landed on the surface have told us that it is a barren desert-like world, blisteringly hot and swept by fierce winds, which would make the Earth's most savage hurricane seem like a gentle summer breeze.

Also being looked at with new interest is the giant planet Jupiter. Almost big enough to be a star, the thick atmosphere surrounding this planet may be a breeding ground for the acids and primitive molecules of the type from which life on Earth is thought to have evolved.

A wonder of our age is the manner in which the use of satellites is advancing the science of astronomy. Every planet so far explored by satellites is now viewed in a new light and some former widely held beliefs have been shattered.

Radio Astronomy
Other great advances have been made through the relatively new art of radio astronomy. Although conventional optical telescopes enable us to peer immense distances into space, visible light waves provide only a limited picture of the universe around us. Radio telescopes not only enable us to probe much deeper into space, but provide information which cannot be obtained by any other means.

In addition to stars, planets, comets and meteors, there is a great variety

of other objects in space. Included among these are the mysterious stellar radio sources known as quasars, the most distant objects so far detected by man. One is apparently over 10,000 million light years away. A light year is the distance that light, speeding at 300,000 kilometres (186,000 miles) a second, travels in a year. In other words, the light and radio waves now reaching us, left these quasars 10,000 million years ago.

To be visible at such enormous distances it is estimated that a quasar, although only about as big as a million suns, must give off as much light as 50 galaxies, each containing 100 thousand million stars. Astronomers have not yet been able to think of any process that could produce such prodigious amounts of energy. Another puzzle is that some quasars seem to flicker, varying slightly in brilliance from month to month, or year to year.

Black Holes
A more recent astronomical discovery is what are called 'black holes'. These are the remains of large stars that have collapsed suddenly after they have run out of hydrogen fuel. The immense gravitational forces draw the material inwards until it is extraordinarily dense. The gravitational field of these unusual stellar objects is so great that no light or any other kind of radiation can escape from their surface. If a spaceship ever strayed close to a black hole it would instantly be drawn into it and vanish completely for ever.

Black holes thus cannot be located by ordinary means. Instead they are detected because of their effect on stars near them. The black hole sucks material away from its nearby companion. The violence of the action heats up the atoms being sucked from the visible star until they emit X-rays near the black hole, thus indirectly betraying its presence.

Astronomy is indeed a fascinating subject. It is not a static science, for it seems that as soon as astronomers solve one problem, two new ones appear.

With the spectacular Orion nebula as a background, this artist's impression shows a long distance Star-Ship of the future. Such a spaceship would be capable of carrying up to 400 persons, and would be designed to travel to the remote distances of our galaxy. Such journeys would take hundreds, or even thousands, of years and generation after generation would follow each other on board the ship, with no personal experience of the planet Earth from which they came.

The First Astronomers

History has not recorded the name of the first astronomer. But it must have been a very early man who was moved to look up and wonder about the Sun, the Moon and the tiny points of light that twinkled above him in a night sky.

As soon as man learned to live in groups or tribes, the heavenly bodies became of great practical importance. The Sun provided warmth and light during the day, and the Moon enabled hunting expeditions to be made at night.

During these early days the study of the stars was not the science it is today. It was a mixture involving a few facts, much superstition, and religion. However, the regular daily appearances of the Sun, the monthly phases of the Moon and the position of the Sun at different seasons, provided tribes with the means of regulating their lives. With the rise of civilisation some men began to devote their time entirely to the study of these heavenly motions. Before man had learned how to write, he had numbered the days, counted the months and determined the seasons and the years.

With the development of writing, records were kept of the motions of the heavenly bodies, with the result that lunar eclipses were being predicted long before men realised what caused them. So accurate were these early observations that the Chinese, for example, had a calendar of 365 days almost 5,000 years ago. In early Egypt the accurate prediction of the huge annual floods was literally a matter of life and death for the inhabitants living along the banks of the Nile. The lunar calendar was not accurate enough

God creates the heavens, a mosaic from Sicily.

and it was noticed that the floods came when the bright star Sirius started to be visible in the dawn sky. From observations of this star the Egyptians drew up a very accurate calendar of $365\frac{1}{4}$ days.

Greek Astronomers

Real progress in the science of astronomy, however, had to await the coming of the Greek civilisation. The first great Grecian astronomer was Thales of Miletus, who lived in the sixth century B.C. He believed that the universe was a great sphere and that the Earth was round. These ideas had no mathematical basis, but were derived from the belief that the circle and the sphere were perfect forms.

Three hundred years later Aristotle confirmed his belief that the Earth was not flat. He based this on the fact that he knew the positions of the stars changed if one went north or south, and, more important, he had observed the shape of the shadow of the Earth on the Moon during an eclipse.

Another great Greek astronomer

Zeus, the principal Greek god, was grandson of Uranus (Heaven) and Gaia (Earth).

was Hipparchus who, nearly 200 years before the birth of Christ, produced a catalogue showing the position of many stars, discovered the precession (the toy-top-like wobble) of the Earth's axis and invented trigonometry.

The most influential astronomer of the ancient world, however, was undoubtedly Ptolemy (*c.* A.D. 90–168), who was born in Egypt and worked in Alexandria. He knew that the Earth was a sphere and he had a great deal of information about the movement of the planets. He summarised his knowledge, and that of his predecessors, in a great book called the *Almagest*.

Ptolemy's great mistake was to put the Earth and not the Sun in the centre of the solar system. Around the Earth, stated Ptolemy, there orbited the Moon, the planets, the Sun and even the stars themselves. The Earth, he claimed, was the centre of the Universe. However, if one observes the planets, their movement is not as regular as it should be if they circled the Earth. To account for this, Ptolemy introduced a series of small secondary circles called epicycles into their basic orbit. The resultant path of the planets was thus very complicated indeed.

As time went by and more accurate observations were made, more and more epicycles had to be introduced to make Ptolemy's theory work. However, as a result of the collapse of the

Greek civilisation, and the subsequent dark ages when men for a time seemed to have forgotten how to learn, Ptolemy's ideas continued unchallenged for over 1,000 years.

Copernicus

Fresh thought on the subject did not seriously come until the birth in Poland of Nicolas Copernicus in 1473. Copernicus carefully observed the motions of the planets and soon concluded that these could not possibly be accounted for by the system of circles upon circles, as stated by Ptolemy.

If, however, the Sun was placed in the centre, with the Earth and planets revolving around it, then the motions could be accounted for satisfactorily. This, Copernicus argued, solved all the problems. Today, it might seem a simple matter to publish such an idea. But, 500 years ago, Ptolemy's idea was believed whole-heartedly by the Church, and to preach otherwise was heresy, punishable by death. Copernicus's theory was not published until 1543, the year he died.

Although Copernicus was right to put the Sun at the centre of the solar system, he was in error in assuming that the planets moved in perfectly circular orbits. In fact they move along ellipses. The difference generally is not very great, but it is sufficient to have to account for it.

The discovery that planets' orbits are ellipses was made by Johannes Kepler (1571–1630), a German assistant to Tycho Brahe (1546–1601) the great Danish astronomer. Brahe, a careful and conscientous observer, with a good observatory, did not believe the Copernicus system and devoted most of his life trying to devise a better system. He failed, because most of his theories restored the Earth to the centre of the solar system. When he died, his records were left to Kepler.

Kepler also tried to prove Copernicus wrong, but Brahe's excellent records gradually forced him to acknowledge that the Sun was the central body. Then, simply but brilliantly, he realised that the observed motions of Mars could be completely explained according to Brahe's records if he made its orbit slightly elliptical.

Galileo

A contemporary of Copernicus who experienced personally the terror and rigid beliefs of the Church authorities known as the Inquisition was Galileo (1564–1642). An Italian physicist, Galileo had used his early telescope to see things never before observed by Man. He saw that the Moon was indeed another world.

Readily visible were the four big satellites orbiting Jupiter. The arrangement was a solar system in miniature, and added to Galileo's conviction that the Sun and not the Earth was at the centre of the solar system. Final proof came when he saw the phases of Venus; these can only be explained satisfactorily if Venus is moving round the Sun. However, when Galileo tried to explain

The Mayan observatory at Chichen Itza from which astronomical observations were made.

Zodiac ceiling from an Egyptian temple at Dendera (100 B.C.). Ancient astronomers based their calendars on the varying positions of star groups throughout the year.

A medieval idea of heaven from a 16th-century woodcut.

that his finding tended to confirm Copernicus's theory, Church officials were far from pleased.

So firmly was the geocentric (Earth centred) theory fixed in people's minds, that even some fellow astronomers refused to believe the evidence of their own eyes, asserting that although Galileo's telescope worked well for objects on the Earth, it gave false pictures when pointed to the heavens. Other scientists refused even to look through the instrument.

Galileo was subjected to harassment by Church officials and ultimately was forced to sign a most humiliating 'confession'. In this he had to swear that he would 'abandon the false opinion which maintains that the Sun is the centre and immovable', and that because he had printed a book giving 'reasons with great force in support of the above views', was guilty of heresy.

He was sentenced to virtual life imprisonment, and died a broken man in 1642, going blind shortly beforehand. Persecution continued after his death, the Inquisition attempting to deny him burial, and disputing his right to make a will. Even the erection of a headstone on his tomb was forbidden. By so doing, the authorities hoped that he and his work would be forgotten and not passed on to future generations. It was, of course, an unfulfilled hope, for today no history of astronomy would be complete without reference to the exciting findings of Galileo.

Within a century of Galileo the telescope had grown into a powerful scientific weapon, and the truth of his observations could no longer be denied.

Newton

Gone too were the invisible spheres which in former times were assumed to support the planets and the stars. In their place Isaac Newton (1642–1727), born the year Galileo died, had substituted the force of gravity. Newton's genius enabled him to explain how this inherent force which until then had been responsible only for pulling things down to the surface of the Earth, could also keep the unfalling Moon up in its orbit.

After Newton, the science of astronomy entered a new phase. During the next 200 years, an army of dedicated, but relatively unknown astronomers painstakingly and accurately calculated the size, weight and orbits of the main bodies of the solar system.

Astronomers also began to consider more seriously the origins of the solar system. In 1755, the German philosopher Immanuel Kant, far-sightedly suggested that the system had developed from a huge cloud of gas. The particles in the cloud were pulled together by their gravitational attraction and, somehow, began to rotate in a common direction. As the cloud condensed more and more, it grew hotter and hotter, until the primitive Sun glowed. Kant argued that as the Sun continued to condense, its rate of spin increased, throwing off lumps of gaseous matter from which the planets in their turn condensed.

Thirty years later the French scientist, the Marquis de Laplace (1749–1827), also proposed a theory similar to that of Kant. However, as a mathematician, Laplace knew that the process of condensation could not by itself start a nebula rotating. Thus he suggested that the gas cloud was itself initially hot and rotating.

Over the succeeding years, the details of the Kant-Laplace theories have been refined, but the broad principles are still considered the most logical explanation of the origin of the solar system by the great astronomers of today.

In the 17th century telescopes got longer and longer in an effort to extend the focal length as far as possible.

The Instruments of Astronomy

Although the present day astronomer uses a great variety of equipment, the basic instrument for astronomical research is the telescope.

The enlarging properties of a convex lens, the heart of a telescope, were known long ago. Ancient documents often refer to burning glasses—an older term for magnifying glasses. Spectacles, which of course also enlarge, were in use as early as the thirteenth century. The invention of the telescope is sometimes attributed to Hans Lippershey, a seventeenth-century spectacle-maker in the little Dutch town of Middelburg. He is said to have delighted his friends with his magic glass which made distant objects look bigger and nearer.

But for the invention to become an instrument of astronomy, we must look to the great scientist Galileo. Realising that such an instrument could be used to study the heavens, Galileo fashioned a simple telescope consisting of two lenses; a convex object-glass and concave eyepiece. The object-glass or lens, collects the rays of light from a distant

they do not all focus at the same point. This phenomenon is known as chromatic aberration.

This drawback can be partially overcome by making the object-glass of very long focal length, so that the different colours are focussed as far beyond the lens as possible. Telescopes thus got longer and longer, leading eventually to the construction of huge 'aerial' telescopes. In these long telescopes the traditional tube was replaced by a structure which simply supported the main lens in front of the observer. One of these, built by Johannes Hevelius (1611–87), was 45 metres (150 feet) long, the height of

focus. In the 1730s an amateur astronomer discovered that the colour problem could be reduced by using compound lenses, that is, lenses made up of different types of glass cemented together. The two types of glass tend to cancel out the annoying fringe colour effects.

Another point of interest is that in the simple type of Galilean telescope described so far, with a convex object lens and a concave eyepiece, the image is seen the right way up. If, however, the eyepiece is made convex as well, as in the Keplerian telescopes, the object is seen inverted. This would be most awkward for viewing objects on the Earth, but is not a problem when studying the heavens. Because the Keplerian is a more satisfactory instrument, it is the more widely used by astronomers.

Reflecting Telescopes

However, all refractors are relatively unwieldy, and to overcome their inherent defects the great English scientist Isaac Newton developed a totally

Tycho Brahe's observatory at Uraniborg where he worked for 20 years.

object and directs them together at a point known as the focus. The resultant image at the focus is then enlarged by the eyepiece, which acts in exactly the same way as an ordinary magnifying glass.

Galileo's 'optik tube' was of course crude by present-day standards, but it effectively brought objects 30 times nearer compared with the range of the naked eye.

Refracting Telescopes

Soon bigger and better refracting telescopes, as this type is known, were made. But they suffered a basic disadvantage; the images were not only blurred but had colour fringes round them. This is because a simple lens also acts like a prism, bending the different colours (that is, wavelengths) of light by different amounts, so that

Copernicus   Brahe   Galileo   Newton

a twelve-storey building. It was used to map the Moon. Even bigger was an aerial telescope 64 metres (210 feet) long built by Christiaan Huygens (1629–93). This enabled Huygens to be the first man to see that the rings of Saturn were really rings, and not badly focussed moons—as Galileo thought they were.

These long aerial instruments were most unwieldy and difficult to keep in

new type of telescope which did not need an object-glass at all.

Known as a reflector, this type of telescope employs a deceptively simple-looking curved mirror, in place of the light-collecting object lens. On modern telescopes the mirror effect is obtained by covering a glass disc, accurately ground and finely polished, with a thin coating of aluminium. Thus light from a star does not penetrate the glass, but is instantly reflected off the mirror. In this manner, chromatic aberration does not take place, as all the wavelengths of light are bent equally by the curved mirror.

To catch the light rays before they escaped, Newton mounted a small second mirror, known as a 'flat', near the focal point to deflect the rays to the side of the tube, where they were brought into focus and the image enlarged by an eyepiece. It might seem that mounting a second mirror directly in the beam of incoming star-light would cast a shadow or obscure the image. It does not, but merely makes the picture slightly dimmer.

Refractor-type telescopes are easier to manage and maintain, while the reflector-type are cheaper, since it is much easier to make a mirror than a

alternative arrangement in some telescopes is to have a flat mirror which can either deflect the light sideways, as in Newton's telescope, or straight back to the mirror, where it passes through a large hole in the middle.

The 'eyepieces' of large telescopes are complex components, often embodying additional mirrors and lenses, slits, prisms, filters and cameras, so that the observer can study particular aspects of a star or galaxy.

One of the world's biggest reflecting telescopes is the 254-centimetre (100-inch) instrument on Mount Wilson, in California. When it was made in 1917 it was the biggest in the world. It was with this powerful telescope that the Californian astronomer, Edwin Hubble (1889–1953), proved that many of the cloud-like nebulae which had

a much larger sphere, 60 million light years in diameter, containing 200 more galaxies. Probing even deeper into space, where individual stars could not be seen, Hubble continued his 'voyage' of study to examine ultimately a sphere 2,000 million light years in diameter. No man had ever before enlarged the human horizon so rapidly in so short a time. Hubble's stupendous achievement is unlikely to be equalled or exceeded.

World's Biggest Telescope
The world's biggest telescope is the Hale instrument on Palomar Mountain in California. The huge 508-centimetre (200-inch) mirror took nearly eleven years to grind and polish. It is mounted in a framework 16·5 metres (55 feet) long weighing 125 tons. In spite of its awesome size, this is a delicate instrument of great precision. One hand can rotate it on special oil-pad bearings. The telescope's computer-governed mechanism can point it unerringly at a star millions of light years away. It can collect signals far too weak for the eye to see, hour after hour, night after night, until images form on film in sharp focus for astronomers to study.

Under construction in Russia is a reflector with a 604-centimetre (238-inch) mirror, but it is not known when this instrument will be ready for use.

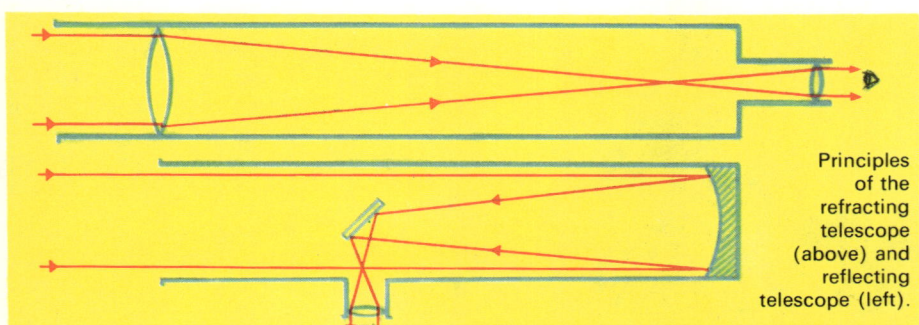

Principles of the refracting telescope (above) and reflecting telescope (left).

lens. For this reason, nearly all the world's big telescopes are reflectors.

In the very big reflector telescopes the astronomer and his camera equipment are often mounted inside the telescope itself, between the big mirror and the star under observation. An

intrigued astronomers for many years were, in fact, other great galaxies of stars, many thousands of light years beyond our own.

He used the telescope to examine a 'sphere' about six million light years in diameter containing about 20 galaxies. Then he extended his survey to

New Australian Telescope
One of the world's most powerful reflecting telescopes is the new 381-centimetre (150-inch) instrument on top of Siding Spring Mountain in Australia. Although not so big as the telescope on Mount Palomar, improved techniques have enabled a new process to be used for the mirror.

The world's biggest telescope, on Palomar Mountain in California.

For years astronomers have dreamed of using a temperature-proof mirror, that is, one whose shape would remain unaltered in spite of fluctuating temperatures. When the Mount Palomar telescope was under development in 1928, engineers spent two years trying to make a mirror of quartz. They failed, and had to use glass of the type manufactured for 5,000 years, a fusion

ton block of glass had to be carefully ground into a polished saucer-shaped, flawless mirror, a process that took three years.

The final silvering was done after the mirror had been shipped to Australia. This was done using just a thimbleful of liquid aluminium. Deposited on the surface as a vapour, it created an incredibly thin skin of one-

fifth of a micron, turning the entire surface into a brilliant mirror.

The Siding Spring's telescope is able to 'see' across distances nearly as vast as those over which the most sensitive radio telescopes can 'hear'. It has a unique capacity to penetrate deeper into the heart of the Milky Way to expose an area of our galaxy not previously available for study.

Most important of all, this telescope will enable the first detailed study to be made of the Clouds of Magellan, the most dramatic of all objects in the southern sky. These 'white birds' had been known for centuries, sailing serenely in the southern sky. Not until the 1920s was it realised that they were not just star clouds, but two separate galaxies in their own right. Only 180,000 light years away, they are closer to us than any others.

With the Siding Spring Mountain telescope their proximity means that astronomers will be able to see ten times as much detail in the clouds as their colleagues in the North can see in their nearest galaxies. In telescopic terms, this means that the Australian

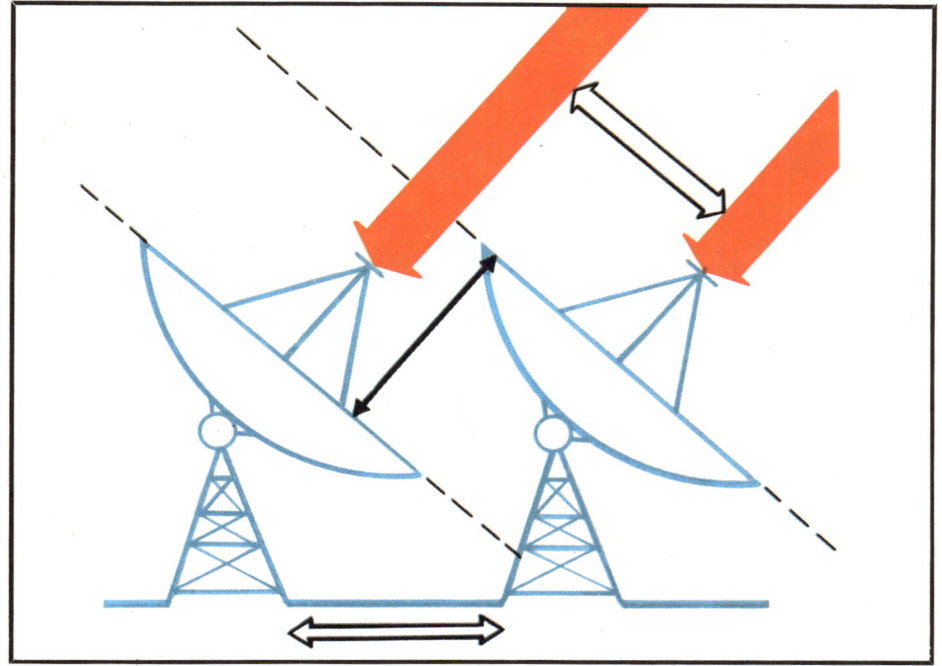

of sand with soda and other ingredients. The result is a mirror that is imperfect by the exacting standards of modern astronomy.

For the Siding Spring Mountain telescope, a glassworks in Toledo, Ohio, succeeded in making the glass in ceramic. Using a secret process, technicians fused micro-crystals of the glass ceramic to create a mirror that is almost perfectly stable. The breakthrough in the Toledo glassworks was, of course, only the beginning of a long and specialised process. The twenty-

A radio interferometer consists of two radio telescopes placed at a considerable distance apart. Signals from the two aerials can be used to determine accurately the position of a radio source in the sky. This is done by a series of calculations based upon the telescope's known positions relative to each other.

The projector used in a planetarium throws images of stars and planets into a dome which represents the sky.

One of the first bowl-shaped radio telescopes, at Jodrell Bank in England.

381-centimetre (150-inch) instrument is the equivalent of a 3,810-centimetre (1,500-inch) one in the northern hemisphere.

Schmidt Telescopes

The big reflector telescopes like the ones on Mount Palomar and Siding Spring Mountain enable astronomers to peer thousands of light years into space—and back in time. But, like a spot lamp, their beam is very narrow: it has to be to collect the incredibly weak light signals. These telescopes are thus ideal for photographing individual galaxies, but to obtain an overall map of the heavens would take centuries.

Thus, complementing the reflectors, are special wide-angle telescopes developed in 1930 by Bernhard Schmidt of Hamburg Observatory. Previously, attempts to produce such telescopes had failed owing to the excessive distortion of a wide-angle mirror. Schmidt overcame this problem by developing an exceptionally thin lens to counteract the distortion. The results were telescopes with a breadth of vision not achieved previously. They can view, without distortion, an area hundreds of times greater than the reflectors. These telescopes are often called cameras since they cannot normally be used for visual observation. By photographing large areas of sky, the relationship between various galaxies and stars can readily be seen.

In 1948 a 122-centimetre (48-inch) Schmidt telescope was installed on Mount Palomar, alongside the Hale reflector. This unique partnership makes the Palomar Observatory the finest in the world. It is these two great telescopes which have been largely responsible for our current impressions of the universe about us.

A telescope, even a big one, is of limited value in galactic (that is, of galaxies) observations, if used by the astronomer's naked eye. It is, for example, extremely difficult, if not impossible, to determine the slow movement of distant stars by visual observation alone. Thus, an integral part of all professional telescopes is a camera attached to the eyepiece. With these a portion of the sky can be photographed and recorded. The same portion can be photographed later, after an interval of days, weeks or years, and the two observations compared and any differences noted.

Also of great importance is the camera's ability to 'store up' light. Ultra-sensitive film can be exposed to

The 304-metre (1,000-foot) radio telescope at the Arecibo Ionospheric Observatory in Puerto Rico has made use of a natural bowl in the Earth which has been reshaped and lined with a steel mesh receiver.

the same portion of sky for long periods of time, perhaps for several nights. When this is done, stars and galaxies far too faint to be seen by the naked eye begin to register on the film. Thus, without increasing the power of a telescope, the photographic attachment enables us to see even further into space. Today, in fact, astronomers rarely 'look through' their telescopes; they spend their time taking photographs, and modern astronomical telescopes should, perhaps, be considered as cameras.

The Spectroscope

All we can see of even the nearest star, using the biggest telescope and longest photographic exposure, is a tiny pinpoint of light without dimension. How is it then that astronomers can determine not only the constituents of these remote objects, but also their temperature, age and speed?

They do this by deciphering the light received from the pinpoint with the aid of a spectroscope. Basically this is a simple instrument embodying a prism which splits up the star's light. It was in 1666 that Isaac Newton discovered that a beam of ordinary white light will break up into all the colours

of the spectrum when passed through a triangular prism of glass. It was also noticed that the spectrum was subdivided by a series of black lines. Two centuries were to pass before the true value of Newton's discovery and the significance of the black lines were fully understood.

Just over one hundred years ago it was discovered that different kinds of light sources produced different spectra with the black lines appearing in different positions. The spectrum of a light is governed by the density, chemical make-up and temperature of the light sources. Thus, a spectrum provides astronomers with a form of celestial 'fingerprint', revealing the composition and temperature of a star.

The importance of spectra to astronomy cannot be over-emphasised. On the interpretation of the colourful bands of colour is based all the modern theories of the stars, our galaxy and the very universe itself. As in the case of telescopes, spectra are rarely viewed visually. They are recorded photographically to produce what are known as spectrograms. In spite of their beauty, astronomers do not take their spectrograms in colour. A black and white photograph shows the position

of the 'fingerprinting' black lines equally well, and it is these lines which convey the secrets of the stars.

Radio Telescopes

The light collected by optical telescopes is but one of many forms of electromagnetic radiation emitted by stars and galaxies.

It was in 1931 that the American physicist Karl Jansky, while conducting research into the problems of radio communications, detected radio waves coming from outer space. Like light, these radio waves are forms of electro-magnetic radiation, the difference being that they have a wavelength many thousands of times longer than light waves. It is only within the last twenty years that the immense im-

portance of these radio waves has been fully appreciated. They have revealed new secrets of the universe and have enabled us to look deeper into space than ever before.

Like the light waves, the radio waves are extremely feeble when they reach the Earth. And like light, they have to be collected and magnified to give a worthwhile signal. Enormous radio telescopes are used for this purpose. Whereas with optical telescopes the mirror size is expressed in centimetres or inches, radio telescopes are measured in metres or feet.

One of the most famous is the 76-metre (250-foot) diameter instrument at Jodrell Bank in England. The huge bowl-shaped energy collector is mounted so that it can be both rotated and

tilted in order to point in any direction, or remain 'locked-on' a particular radio source under observation.

This type of radio telescope is difficult and expensive to build. Thus for some tasks astronomers use rows of what are known as dipole telescopes. These comprise large numbers of relatively simple rod-type antennae or aerials; all the antennae collect energy and feed their individual weak signals into a common amplifier. Disadvantages of such aerials are that they can 'look' only in the direction that the spinning Earth points them, and receive only a narrow band of wavelengths. However, the aerials are cheap and easily installed in their thousands to collect the energy of one particular wavelength of interest to astronomers.

The Solar System

The solar system is our local family of heavenly bodies. It is composed of one star—the Sun, nine planets of which the Earth is one, an assortment of moons, a ring of debris known as the asteroid belt, a large number of fast-moving, flimsy-tailed bodies called comets and many millions of tiny bodies known as meteors.

On the cosmic scale it is quite a compact family, for although Pluto, the outermost planet is some 5,800 million kilometres (3,600 million miles) away, the distance to the next nearest star is many thousands of times greater.

When mammoths roamed the Earth, men would not have known of the existence of the solar system as it is not readily detectable with the naked eye. At the dawn of history their world consisted of a small patch of land bounded by distant hills, or an apparently limitless stretch of water we now know as oceans. Seemingly close overhead was a curved sky regularly crossed by a benevolent Sun which gave warmth and light. The darkness of night was softened by the paler Moon, moving among innumerable twinkling points of light we call stars, and which faded with each dawn, not to reappear until night returned.

Our present picture of the solar system is the result of thousands of years of careful observation and thought.

The Planets

For example, many centuries must have passed before it was realised that although most of the other points of starlight seemed to be fixed relative to each other, five of them shifted and altered their positions from night to night. These points of light were known to Egyptian and Babylonian observers some 5,000 years ago. They were called planets, meaning 'wandering stars'. The Greeks and Romans gave them names by which they are known today. The quick-moving planet that moved near the Sun, small and difficult to see, was called Mercury after the swift-winged messenger of the gods. The brilliant 'evening' planet

Pluto
5,900,000,000 km.

Neptune
4,500,000,000 km.

Uranus
2,880,000,000 km.

Saturn
1,430,000,000 km.

Jupiter
777,000,000 km.

Mars
Earth
Venus
Mercury

228,000,000 km.
150,000,000 km.
108,000,000 km.
58,000,000 km.

Sun

The planets and their relative
sizes and distances from the Sun.

Planet	No. of Moons	Length of Year	Length of Day
Mercury	None	88 days	59 days
Venus	None	224 days	243 days
Earth	1	365 days	23h. 56m.
Mars	2	687 days	24h. 37m.
Jupiter	12	12 years	9h. 45m.
Saturn	10	29½ years	10h. 15m.
Uranus	5	84 years	10h. 45m.
Neptune	2	165 years	15h. 45m.
Pluto	None	248 years	6 days 9h.

was named Venus, after the goddess of love. Beyond Earth, the red-tinged planet was named Mars, after the god of war. Further away than Mars was the biggest planet of all. Obviously important, this was called Jupiter, king of the gods. Finally, the slow-moving planet that seemed to shine with a dull, yellowish light was named after the god Saturn, father of Jupiter and known as 'Old Man Time'.

We owe a debt to the people who were responsible for these romantic names. If the planets had been named by a contemporary committee they would probably be referred to, logically but unimaginatively, as Planet 1, Planet 2, and so on, out from the Sun.

The notion that there were only five planets, apart from the Earth, persisted for thousands of years. Then, in 1781 William Herschel (1738–1822), an amateur astronomer who earned his living as a musician, was studying the stars with a telescope he had made himself. He observed, in his own words, 'one star which appeared visibly larger than the rest'. At first he assumed the star was a comet, but it soon became clear that it was a new planet, much further out than Saturn. The discovery of the new planet, which was called Uranus, took the astronomical world completely by surprise and caused great excitement. Herschel was honoured, being made the King's Astronomer.

Soon after Uranus was discovered, observations established that it was not moving smoothly along its orbital trajectory. It did not follow its predicted path. Until 1822 it seemed to move too fast; after 1822, surprisingly, it slowed down. Obviously it was being affected by something and astronomers suspected this to be a body hitherto unknown. In 1845 a young Englishman, John Adams, calculated the weight and orbit of a body sufficient to perturb Uranus, and sent his results to the Astronomer Royal, who took no action. Thus, the actual discovery of the planet, now called Neptune, was made by a Frenchman, Urbain Le Verrier (1811–77) in 1846, using calculations similar to those of Adams. The discovery of the planet, nearly 4,500

million kilometres (2,800 million miles) from the Sun, within a degree of its predicted position, was a triumph both for Newton's laws of gravitation and for the two men involved.

Discovery of Pluto

For fifty years it was generally assumed that the discovery of Neptune had solved the problem of the unusual movements of Uranus. However, as the years passed, and its orbit was plotted even more accurately, it was seen to be making small, erratic movements, which could not be attributed to Neptune. Percival Lowell (1855–1916), an American astronomer, began to wonder if these movements were being caused by yet another planet.

Using calculations similar to those used by Adams and Le Verrier, he concluded that this body, if it existed, should have a mass six times that of the Earth, and orbit the Sun at a distance of 6,400 million kilometres (4,000 million miles) in a period of 282 years. Lowell then spent many years searching for it, but not until 1930, fourteen years after he had died, was it finally located, by Clyde Tombaugh at Lowell's Observatory. Known as Pluto, the planet is much smaller than Lowell predicted, but its actual distance from the Sun is 5,805 million kilometres (3,666 million miles) and its orbital period of 248 years are not too far out.

Two odd features of Pluto are its plane of orbit, which is tilted significantly compared with those of other planets, and its orbit, which is so eccentric that for part of the time it is actually inside that of Neptune. Pluto, in fact, may not be an original member of the solar system; it may be a captured asteroid.

Pluto also seems too small to cause the observed minor perturbations of Uranus, and this raises the possibility that there might exist yet another planet orbiting the Sun, even farther out. Such a body has not yet been detected. If a tenth planet does exist, however, it must be a very small world, almost invisible, incredibly remote and cold. Yet astronomers may find it one day.

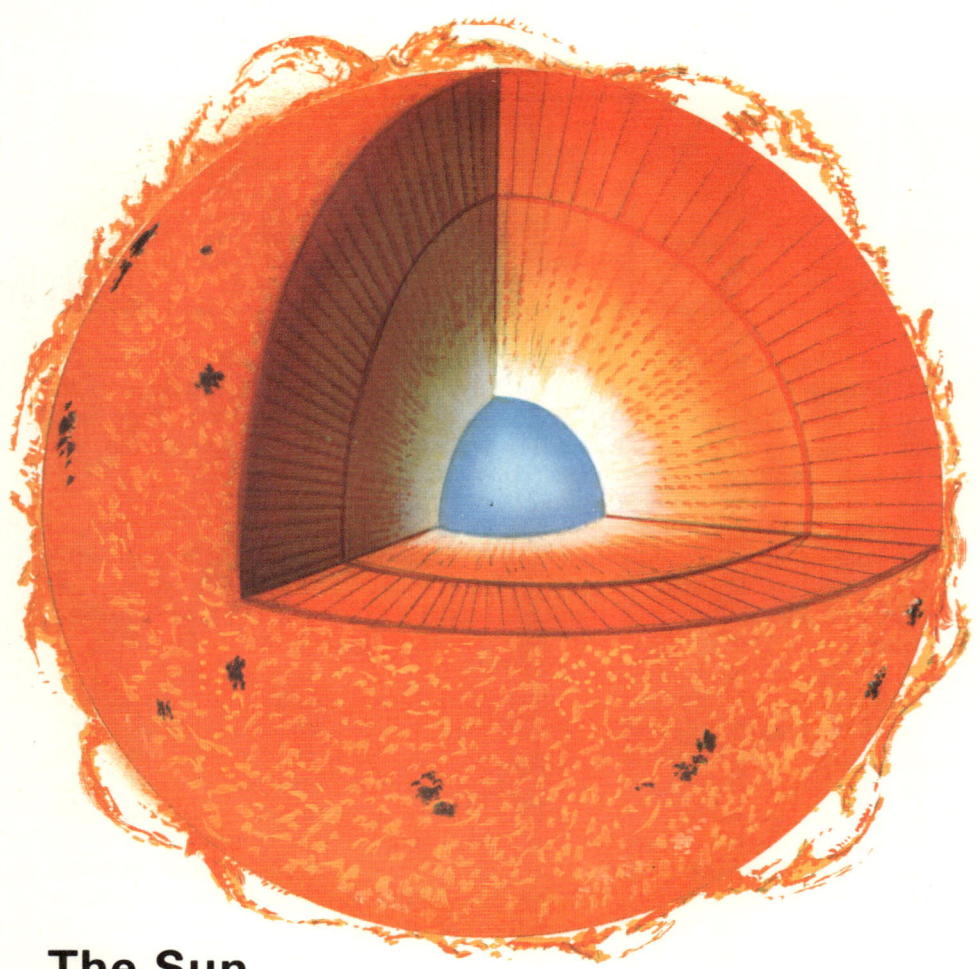

The Sun

Head of the solar system family, and controlling it far more firmly than any parent, is the star we call the Sun. It is fortunate that the Sun is an even-tempered parent—were its temperature to vary, as it does on many stars, even by a tiny fraction, we would quickly either freeze or burn to death.

Compared with the planets, the Sun is a very large body—its diameter of 1,390,000 kilometres (864,000 miles) compares with the Earth's 12,700 kilometres (7,900 miles). Its surface is very hot, about 6,000 degrees C., while near its centre the temperature is a blistering 20 million degrees C. It is a very ordinary star, just one of countless millions in our galaxy.

The vast bulk of the Sun could hold over a million Earths, and yet its mass is only about 330,000 times greater. The Sun is thus much less dense than the Earth. Its density, in fact, is about 1·4 times that of water, while that of the Earth is 5·5 times greater.

Unlike the planets, the Sun is a completely gaseous body; it has no rocky core or surface on which an asbestos spacecraft can ever land. At the centre the gas is highly compressed and very dense, while the outer regions are tenuous and of very low density. Being gaseous, the Sun does not

Cutaway section of the Sun (top) showing its core, sun-spots and solar prominences. (Below) a spectroheliogram of the Sun and a sun-spot close-up with the Earth to scale.

rotate in the same way as a solid body: different regions rotate at different speeds. At the equator the surface revolves once every 25 days, but near the poles once every 34 days. This unusual rotation is easily seen by watching the movement of the dark blotches, known as sunspots, on the surface. From the Earth these spots appear black and small, but they are neither. Some sunspots have diameters of 160,000 kilometres (100,000 miles) and could thus swallow many Earths. They appear black only because the rest of the surface is relatively bright. Sunspots are areas where the surface is slightly less hot—around 4,000 degrees C.—than the normal surrounding surface.

Small sunspots may last only a few hours, large ones several weeks. One of the longest-lasting appeared in 1943 and remained visible for 200 days. This was not the biggest sunspot, however, for this honour goes to a spot, one of a group, sighted in 1947. The group as a whole covered an area of 5,200 million square kilometres (2,000 million square miles).

Just what causes a sunspot is not known. We know that there are periods when the Sun is 'active' and many sunspots are visible, and other periods when it is 'quiet' and the disc is completely free. At the sunspot maximum there may be 500 or more a year; at sunspot minimum this figure drops to as low as 50 a year. The period between the two extremes is about eleven years. This solar cycle, as it is called, is not perfectly regular and the eleven-year period is only a rough average.

The Sun's Energy

It is well known that the Sun supplies the Earth with all the heat and light needed for life, and has been doing so for thousands of millions of years. How does the Sun generate this vast amount of energy?

If it was burning simply as coal burns, it would have been reduced to a pile of ash long ago. The process going on inside the Sun is one of nuclear fusion and involves the atoms of one element joining with those of another element. What happens is that atoms of hydrogen are fused together at temperatures of above 14 million degrees C. to form helium. When this happens, tremendous amounts of energy are released.

It is estimated that every second about 600 million tons of hydrogen are changed into helium in this manner. Each helium atom is slightly lighter

A series of pictures showing the positions of the Sun at intervals throughout the day and night in the Land of the Midnight Sun.

than the hydrogen atoms used to make it. This means that the Sun is losing mass all the time—the loss totalling about 4 million tons every *second*. This colossal rate of expenditure makes the consumption of oil and coal on the Earth seem very puny indeed. Fortunately for us, the Sun is so massive that it has a plentiful supply of hydrogen fuel left. The Sun is already thousands of millions of years old, but has used up only about 5 per cent of its hydrogen. So the amount of light and heat is not expected to alter significantly for several more thousands of millions of years.

Besides the visible light which we can see, the Sun emits other radiations over a whole range of wavelengths. These extend from the deadly, very short wavelength X-rays to long radio waves. The X-rays would kill all life on the Earth if they were able to penetrate the atmosphere.

The Sun also radiates streams of various particles in all directions, such as atoms, the central cores of helium atoms and other electrically charged particles. Many of these particles become trapped by the magnetic field of the Earth. They form the radiation belts surrounding the Earth and are responsible for the phenomena known as the *Aurora borealis* or Northern Lights and also for radio interference.

The stream of particles blown out from the Sun is known as the solar 'wind'. Its force, although incredibly diffused, is continuous and over long periods of time can affect the orbit of a satellite. When Mariner 10 was making its historic voyage to Mercury, its attitude in space was controlled by varying the angle of its solar-cell wings relative to the Sun, in much the same way that the sails of a yacht can be trimmed to help hold a particular course.

Death of the Sun

In spite of its bulk and the efficiency of its nuclear power-producing process, ultimately—in the far future—the Sun will use up all its hydrogen fuel and 'go out'. Go out, is not, however, quite the term to describe the end of the Sun.

As the hydrogen is used up, the sheer weight of ash in the Sun's core will cause the already prodigious temperature to rise and initiate new nuclear processes. Then hydrogen will start to be used in even vaster quantities than now.

The Sun will start swelling. Over a period of about 1,000 million years the temperature on Earth will rise to about 500 degrees C. The oceans will boil away, some of the surface will melt —and all life will disappear. Then the Sun will start to shrink and cool down. Over millions of years it will gradually dwindle in size, and lose its glow, until, eventually, it may be smaller than the Earth. It will be so dense that a matchbox full of matter will weigh thousands of tons. Then it will go out completely. The Sun will have died, and with it the solar system.

It is estimated that every second about 600 million tons of hydrogen are changed into helium in the Sun and tremendous amounts of energy are released.

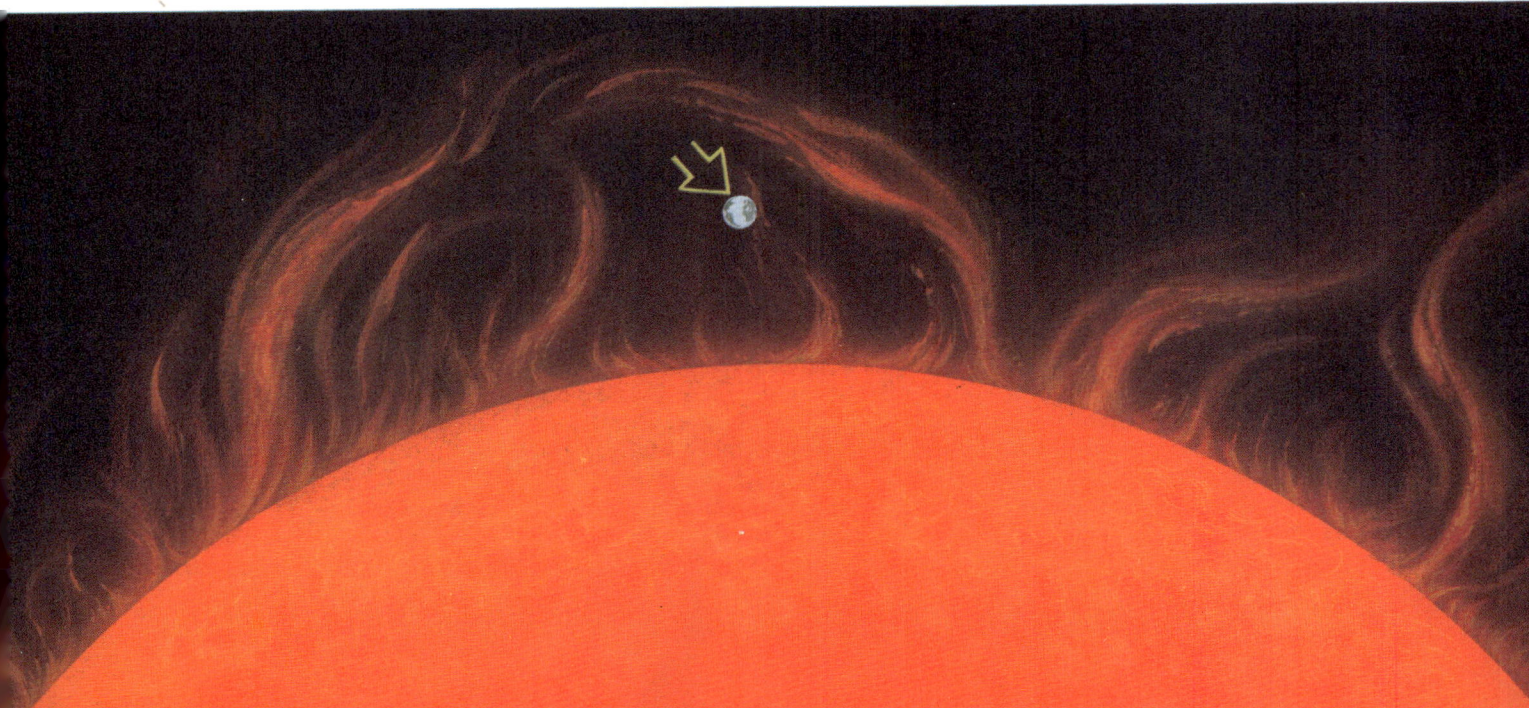

Planets and Their Satellites

Although we now know that the planets revolve round the Sun, and have a good idea of their size, weight and composition, there is one major question still left unanswered: 'Where did the planets come from?'

It is generally accepted that all the planets have a common parentage and are all of the same age. The reason for this assumption is the general orderliness of the solar system—the fact that the planets lie in approximately the same plane and that they all orbit the Sun in the same direction. This neatness makes it difficult to argue that the Sun captured, through its immense gravitational power, the planets one by one over a long period of time.

One theory is that the planets were formed when another star almost gas and dust. One reason for the wide support for this theory is that there are many such clouds in outer space, some of which seem to be evolving into stars now.

This supposed cloud of gas and dust is thought to have been extremely tenuous and widely distributed in space, but gravitational attractions within the cloud gradually caused the tiny particles of matter to drift together, into a number of ever-thickening clouds. Natural forces initiated movement which gradually assumed a spinning motion. The largest cloud, naturally, condensed at the centre, to form the basis of the Sun, its nuclear fire ignited by high temperatures caused by the immense internal gravitational forces. Around it smaller

Thus, as the Sun's gravitational attraction decreases with distance, we find that the planets move at different speeds.

Mercury, 57·8 million kilometres (36 million miles) from the Sun, moves at nearly 48 kilometres (30 miles) a second. At 149·6 million kilometres (93 million miles), the orbit of the Earth, the speed has dropped to 28·8 kilometres (18 miles) a second. Pluto, nearly 6,400 million kilometres (4,000 million miles) distant, crawls along at only 4·8 kilometres (3 miles) a second.

It was in the seventeenth century that the German astronomer Johannes Kepler drew up his three great discoveries regarding planetary motion. His first discovery was that planets do

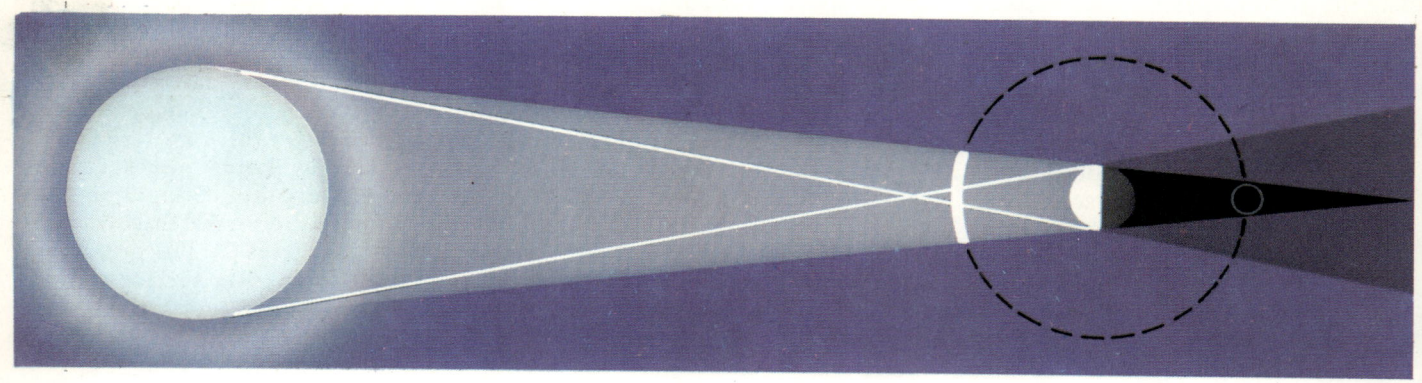

The diagram above illustrates both solar and lunar eclipses. When the Moon (far right) passes through the shadow of the Earth this cuts off the Sun's light and causes a lunar eclipse. The solar eclipse happens when the Moon passes between the Earth and the Sun.

collided with the Sun. According to this theory, the passing star caused gigantic gaseous tides on the Sun, resulting in the ejection of a massive stream of gas. This stream of gas then broke up into several clouds which condensed into the planets. A major stumbling block to this theory is the distances of the planets from the Sun, which are far too great for it to be likely.

A somewhat similar theory is that at one time the Sun was one member of a binary or pair of stars, revolving about each other. A passing star then sucked material out of one star, its twin then providing the gravitational forces necessary to account for the present distance of the planets from the Sun. The obvious snag to this theory is—where is the Sun's companion now?

Theory of Origin

The current, most widely supported theory of how the solar system evolved is that the complete system, the Sun and all the planets, developed from a single massive cloud of primordial (from the Latin words meaning first-born, or existing from the beginning)

clouds gradually condensed into the planets.

Although all the planets may thus have evolved from the same primordial cloud, they are by no means all similar. Four of the planets—Mercury, Venus, Earth and Mars—all orbit relatively closely to the Sun, and are small, solid bodies. Four other planets—Jupiter, Saturn, Uranus and Neptune—orbit at much greater distances from the Sun, and are huge bodies covered by immensely deep atmospheres. The outermost member of the solar system, Pluto, is a solid world, smaller than the Earth.

The Sun's Gravity

The planets move silently and endlessly in their orbits held rigidly on their respective paths by the gravitational attraction of the Sun. Their speed is such that centrifugal force, trying to make them fly off into space, exactly balances the Sun's gravity.

not move in perfectly circular orbits, but in ellipses. The second led to the knowledge that a planet moves fastest when nearest the Sun and slowest when farthest away.

Important as these two discoveries were, it was the third which assured Kepler of a permanent place in books on astronomy. This was the mathematical fact that the square of the time taken to complete an orbit depends upon the cube of the planet's distance from the Sun. This means that if the distance of one planet is known then the distance of the others can be calculated if their orbital period is known.

Mercury

Smallest of the planets and closest to the Sun is Mercury. Its small size—it is only slightly bigger than the Earth's Moon—and its nearness to the Sun, makes observations from the Earth difficult. Thus, although a great deal has been written about the planet, we actually know very little about it.

Faint markings have been observed and photographed on the surface. They are greyish in colour with some lighter markings verging on white. The

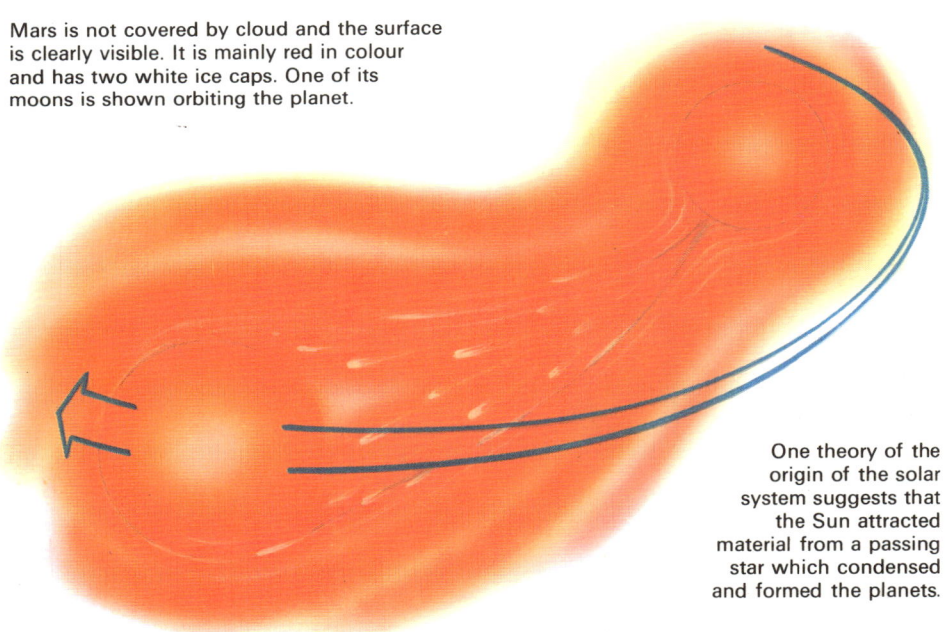

Mars is not covered by cloud and the surface is clearly visible. It is mainly red in colour and has two white ice caps. One of its moons is shown orbiting the planet.

One theory of the origin of the solar system suggests that the Sun attracted material from a passing star which condensed and formed the planets.

pattern and distribution of the markings seem to remain constant and are thus assumed to be permanent features.

Mercury has an eccentric or elongated orbit, moving as close as about 46 million kilometres (29 million miles) to the Sun and retreating to about 70 million kilometres (44 million miles). This elliptical orbit has contributed to the difficulties of observing Mercury as it is best studied at extreme range, because when it is closest to the Earth, it is silhouetted against the Sun.

A good indication of our lack of knowledge regarding this planet is the length of the Mercurian day. For nearly 100 years it was generally assumed that the planet rotated once on its axis during its period of revolution about the Sun, and therefore turned the same face towards the Sun, in the same way that one side of the Moon always faces the Earth. Then, in 1965, the great radio telescope at Arecibo on the Caribbean island of Puerto Rico measured the rotation of the planet by the shifts of wavelength in radar echoes from its surface. These showed that instead of rotating once every 88 days, as would be required to keep up with its movement round the Sun, it actually rotates once about every 59 days. This rate, and the planet's motion round the Sun gives Mercury a solar day equal to 176 Earth days, or two Mercury years!

Mercury's diameter is 4,876 kilometres (3,030 miles) and it has a density of 5·5 times that of water, the same as Earth. It is a heavy planet for its size. This is probably because it was formed near the centre of the primitive cloud of dust from which the planets are thought to have evolved— or the Sun's fierce radiation may have eroded away its outer, lighter, layers.

slightest chance of its being explored by Man for a long time.

Venus

Venus, the next planet outward from the Sun, is the one which shines so brilliantly in the evening sky. It has, like Mercury, presented a great challenge to multitudes of telescope-explorers. At times the planet, which is moon-less, comes within 40 million kilometres (25 million miles) of the Earth, much closer even than Mars. But when this happens Venus is almost unobservable as it then lies between the Earth and the Sun, so that its night side is turned towards us. When the day side is facing us, Venus is on the other side of the Sun, 257 million kilometres (160 million miles) away.

The main obstacle to telescopic observation, however, is the fact that the surface of Venus is completely hidden by a thick, turbulent atmosphere. Until recently we could not even determine the planet's period of rotation; estimates ranged from 1 to 200 days! All this did not prevent some astronomers from claiming that they could see great seas and continents. It has also not prevented astronomers from describing a wide variety of possible conditions on the surface, particularly when it was learned that the atmosphere was mainly carbon dioxide.

These theories included the suggestions that the entire surface is covered with water and inhabited by fish-like creatures, or was a world covered in oil, or a tropical world of steamy swamps, torrential rains and great forests, or a hot windy world of parched desert. We now know that the last guess was the correct one.

It was not until 1956 that the true picture began to emerge. Radio telescopes indicated surface temperatures in the 400 degree C. range—conditions ruling out water, oil, forests and life as we know it.

These early observations were later confirmed, first by the American Mariner 2 spacecraft, which flew by the planet in 1962, then by Mariner 5 of 1967 and in December 1970 by the Russian probe Venera 7, which made a soft-landing and transmitted information from the surface for nearly half-an-hour. These spacecraft confirmed that the surface temperature is 480 degrees C. and that the atmospheric pressure is about 100 times as great as that of our air at sea level.

What the actual surface is like is deduced from two sources. One, the

Initial data returned by the spacecraft also indicated the presence of a small moon circling the planet. Later studies, however, could not detect a moon and it is now thought not to exist.

Although Mercury may be slightly less harsh than was thought at one time, it is still a bitterly hostile world. Its day surface temperature of 370 degrees C. and the lack of an atmosphere to protect it from the searing radiation from the Sun, means that there is no chance that life as we know it exists there. Neither is there the

A more elaborate Newtonian reflector made by Sir William Herschel in 1781.

Our knowledge of Mercury increased dramatically in March 1974, when the planet was surveyed at close range by America's Mariner 10 spacecraft.

Launched from Cape Kennedy in November 1973, Mariner 10 first passed by Venus, in such a manner that this planet's gravity slowed the spacecraft down and it started to fall towards the orbit of Mercury. During the 'encounter' as the 'flyby' was called, Mariner 10 sent back hundreds of pictures revealing close-up details of the surface for the first time. These show that the planet is heavily cratered, like the Moon and Mars. Some of the pictures also revealed huge valleys in the scorched surface.

Jupiter is almost big enough to be a small star and could hold a thousand Earths.

at about 59 kilometres (37 miles), and a third layer between 29 and 48 kilometres (18 and 30 miles). Venus has no magnetic field, like the one protecting Earth which diverts the solar wind around our planet. The solar wind impinges directly on the Venusian atmosphere, generating fierce disturbances which are not yet fully understood.

Summing up, Venus is undoubtedly a disappointment. For long considered the Earth's twin, it was not unreasonable to hope that it would be a welcoming world which in time men could, perhaps, explore and populate. This is not the case. The planet has a thick, poisonous carbon dioxide atmosphere and its furnace-like surface is continually swept by fierce winds. Venus is thus of little practical value to us, although it remains of high scientific interest.

Earth

Orbiting the Sun at an average distance of 149 million kilometres (93 million miles) is the planet about which we know most, but as yet by no means all: this is, of course, the Earth.

Although astronomers take pains to point out that the Earth is merely an ordinary planet, it is already apparent that it is significantly different from the two planets Mercury and Venus, already described. It has, in fact, some very special features, which make it quite different from all the other planets.

A unique feature is the great oceans which cover most of the surface. On the other planets such seas would either boil away or be permanently frozen. The second important feature about the Earth is its atmosphere. All the other planets have no atmosphere

landings of the Russian Venera probes, which suggested a loosely packed material, and recent radar mapping exercises. The radar maps indicate a generally smooth and relatively flat surface, with some rough areas like the lunar highlands, and a number of large craters, one measuring 240 kilometres (150 miles) in diameter.

In 1962 radar measurements finally told us the length of the Venusian day —243 Earth days. The Venusian 'day' is thus longer than the Venusian year of 224 days, as the planet takes longer to rotate on its axis than to revolve around the Sun. Venus therefore appears to rotate backwards with respect to the Sun.

Further information was provided on Venus by the American spacecraft Mariner 10 on its way to Mercury. Passing the planet in February 1974, the spacecraft sent back 3,400 pictures.

These show the planet has a global cloud pattern, like the Earth, but much more violent. The Sun's heat on the equator creates gigantic convection currents which split the main atmospheric flow and send it swirling out to each pole. Wind speeds range from around 724 kilometres (450 miles) per hour to possibly the speed of sound— 1,216 kilometres (760 miles) per hour, at the poles!

The atmosphere seems to be divided into three distinct layers; a rather hazy layer 70 kilometres (44 miles) above the surface, a second more definite layer

Jupiter is thought to be a largely gaseous body, possibly with a solid core. The Great Red Spot may be a solid body floating in the moving atmosphere.

at all, like Pluto, or have one so thin it is hardly detectable, like Mercury and Mars, or are covered with vastly deeper and turbulent atmospheres of thick, poisonous, choking gases, like Venus.

A point to remember, however, is that the atmosphere on Earth was not always as it is today. In the Cambrian Period of some 500 million years ago, not very long geologically speaking, we would have choked upon the surface of the Earth. At that time the atmosphere consisted mainly of carbon dioxide, with very little free oxygen.

Gradually plant life evolved and began to spread across the face of the Earth. Then, by the wonderful process we call photosynthesis, the plants extracted the carbon dioxide and replaced it with oxygen. In time a balance was reached between animals, which breathe oxygen and expel carbon dioxide, and plants, which 'breathe' carbon dioxide and produce oxygen. Thus today the atmosphere remains practically constant in its composition.

We should not forget, however, that the Earth changed in the past—and could change again in the future. The natural balance is a delicate one which man has the power to upset, with disastrous consequences.

Moon

Circling the Earth is another celestial body about which we also know a great deal. The body is the Moon, the only 'new world' so far explored by man. America's Apollo programme started the exploration with the landing by Apollo 11 of Neil Armstrong and Edwin Aldrin in July 1969, and ended the brilliantly successful series in December 1972 with the Apollo 17 mission.

The Moon revolves around its axis once every 27 days. As it rotates about the Earth in the same time, it always keeps the same face turned towards us. The far side is thus permanently hidden from the Earth, and it was not until the Russian spacecraft Lunik III sent back pictures of the far side in 1959 that we knew for certain that it was heavily cratered like the visible face. Since then the rear side has been mapped in great detail, first by America's Lunar Orbiter satellites and then during the Apollo programme.

No unknown substances have been discovered on the Moon; it is essentially made of the same materials as the Earth. Although somewhat disappointing, it should not have been surprising in view of the widely held theory that the solar system evolved from the same cloud of gas. Whether later expeditions will discover materials of commercial value is not known, but it is unlikely ever to be worthwhile ferrying these back to Earth.

However, the Moon is an ideal place for scientific research, both for astronomers and geologists. The Moon lost its atmosphere many thousands of millions of years ago and so there has been very little erosion. The Moon's surface today is exactly as it was hundreds of millions of years ago when the Earth was populated by giant dinosaurs.

Mars

More than any other planet, Mars has fascinated astronomers. Although only about half the size of Earth, and orbiting the Sun at an average distance of 227 million kilometres (141 million miles), Mars is in many ways similar to Earth. The Martian day is 24 hours 37 minutes, not much different from our own. The tilt of its axis is almost the same as the Earth's so that Mars's seasons are basically similar.

Mars is not covered by cloud and the surface is clearly visible. It is predominantly reddish in colour, with large darker patches assumed by early observers to be seas. Of great interest is the presence of two great white polar caps. They are not thick sheets of ice, like those on Earth, but are probably patches of a thin frost.

The caps recede in summer when the adjacent areas darken towards the equator. It was tempting to attribute this darkening to the annual growth of plant life, perhaps even of cultivated crops.

In 1877 the Italian astronomer, Giovanni Schiaparelli, announced that he had seen a strange network of straight lines. He referred to these lines as *canali*, the Italian word for channel. An American astronomer, Percival Lowell, took up the story and claimed that the lines were, in fact, irrigation canals, dug by an intelligent race of Martians to transport water from melting polar ice caps. Lowell expanded the idea in a series of lectures, articles and books. The more he looked, the more canals he thought he saw. The lines, he explained, were not the actual water-courses, but the results of irrigation and cultivation on either side. Where the lines crossed there were great cities. At one stage, adherents of the belief were seriously suggesting that a message should be drawn in vast letters in the Sahara desert, for the Martians to see.

The development of better instruments showed that Lowell's sightings were but a dream, that the Martian atmosphere in particular is far too thin to support an Earth-type civilisation. But the idea that the seasonal changes in colour were somehow associated with plant growth continued until 1965, when the American spacecraft Mariner 4 sent back spectacular pictures of the planet showing that it was quite different from all previous ideas. There are no canals, or channels, or any straight features at all. There are no great areas of plant growth.

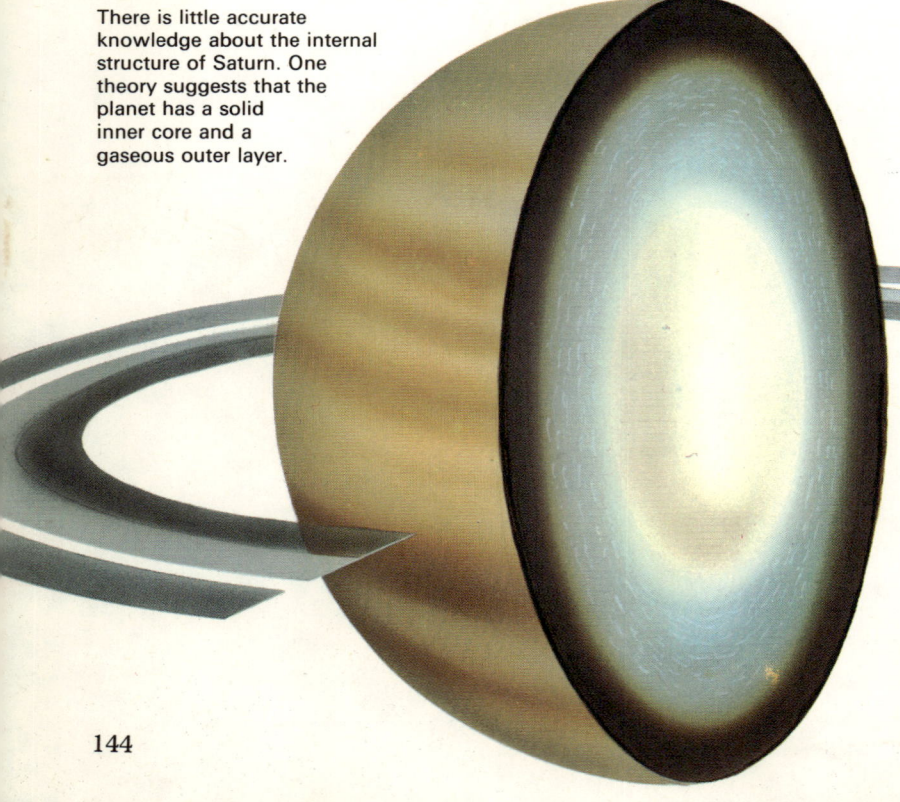

There is little accurate knowledge about the internal structure of Saturn. One theory suggests that the planet has a solid inner core and a gaseous outer layer.

The most interesting feature of Saturn is its rings, thought to be fragments of a disintegrated moon.

In this artist's reconstruction Saturn looms large, seen from the surface of one of its moons.

Instead it seems to be a dead world, covered with craters, like the Moon and Mercury. Mariner 4 also told us that the Martian atmosphere of carbon dioxide is incredibly thin—the pressure at the surface is equivalent to that in the Earth's atmosphere at a height of 30,000 metres (100,000 feet).

These findings were confirmed by Mariners 6 and 7 which surveyed Mars in 1969. In 1971 Mariner 9 went into orbit round the planet, and sent back another excellent series of pictures covering most of the surface. Although many of these showed craters, others showed enormous canyons with unusual tributaries, which could possibly have been formed by water several thousands of years ago.

The Giant Planets

Beyond Mars lie four planets—Jupiter, Saturn, Uranus and Neptune—which, although similar to each other, are quite unlike the four planets already described.

A major difference is their great size. Jupiter, for example, has a diameter of 142,700 kilometres (88,700 miles), sufficient to hold 1,000 Earths and almost big enough for a small star.

The second difference is their very great distance from the Sun, Jupiter 780 million kilometres (486 million miles), Saturn 1,434 million kilometres (892 million miles), Uranus 2,896 million kilometres (1,800 million miles) and Neptune 4,505 million kilometres (2,800 million miles). This means they are incredibly cold worlds—Jupiter is minus 150 degrees C. and Neptune minus 230 degrees C.

A third difference is that all four planets are covered by immensely dense, turbulent and poisonous atmospheres, thousands of kilometres deep. This, and the fact that some astronomers doubt if the planets have any solid cores, but only atmospheres which get denser and denser towards

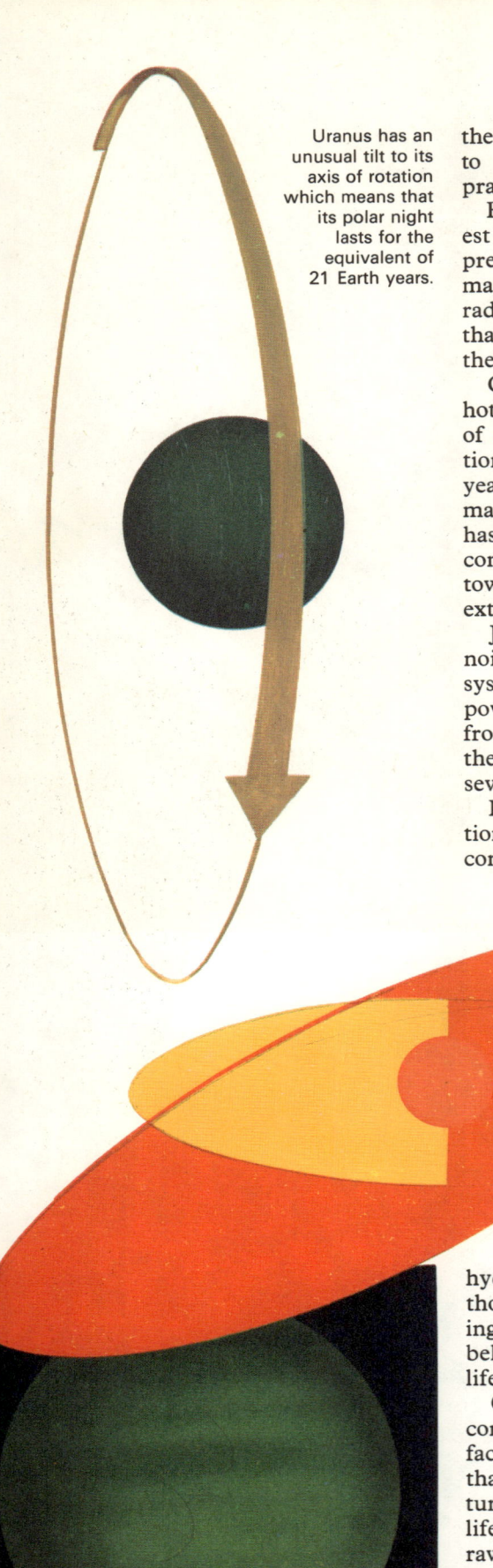

Uranus has an unusual tilt to its axis of rotation which means that its polar night lasts for the equivalent of 21 Earth years.

Pluto's eccentric orbit causes it to cross the path of that of Neptune.

Neptune

the middle, caused many observers to write them off as being of little practical interest.

Recently, however, renewed interest is being shown in Jupiter, which presents many scientific puzzles. A major one is that the giant planet radiates about three times more energy than it receives from the Sun. What is the source of this additional energy?

Current theories call for a relatively hot core, compared with earlier ideas of a supercold interior. One suggestion is that, despite the 5,000 million years that have passed since the formation of the other planets, Jupiter has not yet completed its gravitational condensation. This continued settling towards the centre could produce the extra heat energy.

Jupiter also transmits more radio noise than any object in the solar system except the Sun. The most powerful signals, believed to originate from huge lightning-like discharges in the atmosphere, have the power of several hydrogen bombs.

Perhaps the biggest current fascination for Jupiter is its atmosphere. Its constituents of ammonia, methane and hydrogen, along with the water also thought to be present, are the chemical ingredients of the primordial 'soup' believed to have produced the first life on Earth by chemical evolution.

On this evidence, Jupiter could contain the building blocks of life. In fact, some scientists have suggested that Jupiter may be like a huge factory turning out enormous quantities of life-supporting chemicals from these raw materials, using its own mysterious internal energy.

Jupiter has twelve moons, four of which, Io, Europa, Ganymede and Callisto, are the same size as, or bigger than, Earth's Moon. The outer seven moons are much smaller and more distant. Four of them are in retrograde orbits, contrary to the usual direction of planetary rotation, and may be asteroids captured by Jupiter's powerful gravity.

Beyond Jupiter lie Saturn, Uranus and Neptune, with respective diameters of 120,000, 48,000 and 44,000 kilometres (75,000, 30,000 and 28,000 miles).

The most interesting feature of Saturn is its famous rings. These extend to a diameter of no less than 272,000 kilometres (170,000 miles) and yet are only about 16 kilometres

The outermost member of the solar system, Pluto, is a solid planet with little or no atmosphere.

(10 miles) thick. They are so thin, in fact, that when turned edge on they are invisible to all but the biggest and most powerful telescopes. The nature of the rings is a mystery, but it is thought they may be the fragments of a disintegrated moon.

Pluto

The outermost member of the solar system is Pluto. Like the other planets, Pluto presents its share of puzzles. Its small diameter of about 5,700 kilometres (3,600 miles) and its immense average distance of 5,850 million kilometres (3,666 million miles) from the Sun, makes it very difficult to observe. One major puzzle is its density. For the planet to have its calculated effects on the orbits of giants such as Uranus, it must be much heavier than iron, which seems unlikely. How, then, does it affect Uranus?

Pluto is a solid planet, and has little or no atmosphere; if it had one, it would now lie frozen on its bitterly cold surface. Pluto is in a highly elliptical orbit, tilted considerably to the plane of all the other planets. The orbit is such that at times, in fact for the next few decades, it will actually be inside the orbit of Neptune.

The Stars

On a cloudless night many hundreds of stars can be seen twinkling in the sky. This number can be increased to thousands by the use of binoculars and to millions by the use of a telescope. It is not easy to realise that each of these points of light is, in fact, a huge body like our Sun.

In spite of the tremendous size of the stars, they are so far away that all we can see is a pinpoint of light. That is all we can see using even the biggest telescope. The reason why we can see only a point of light is due to the vast distances that separate us from even the nearest stars.

In fact, apart from the Sun, all other stars are so far away that a special unit of measurement is used. To express the distances in the units of kilometres or miles would require so many noughts that the number would be difficult to describe.

The Light Year

The unit of measurement generally used to describe the distance to other stars is the Light Year. In space, light travels at a speed of 300,000 kilometres (186,000 miles) a second,

and a light year is the distance it travels in one year. In ordinary terms one light year is about 9·6 million million kilometres (6 million million miles). Even using this unit of measurement, the nearest star is over 4 light years away. Others are hundreds of light years away, and some thousands of millions of light years away.

Stars are divided into groups of magnitudes of apparent brilliancy. Stars of a certain brightness are known as 1st magnitude, those slightly less bright 2nd magnitude, and so on. The faintest stars that are normally visible without a telescope are graded as 6th magnitude. Large telescopes can detect stars as faint as 20th magnitude.

This is a useful scale, but it is important to remember it only grades stars according to their *apparent* brightness, and this may be very different from their real brightness. For example, Sirius has an apparent magnitude brightness one and a half times as great as Rigel which, in fact, is 700 times brighter. Rigel only appears dimmer because it is much farther away. If we represent Sirius by a torch a short distance away,

Rigel is a 100-watt bulb about 400 metres (1,300 feet) away.

Another point to remember about stars is that the familiar twinkling is due to disturbances in the Earth's atmosphere; it is not caused by any sudden changes in brightness in the stars themselves.

Star Spectra

As mentioned in the chapter on *The Instruments of Astronomy*, one of the essential tools is the spectroscope, used to split the light received from a star into its constituent colours to provide what is known as a spectrum. Nearly everything we know about stars has been learned from analysing their spectra. In addition to the use of degrees of magnitude to indicate the apparent brightness of stars, astronomers have divided the stars into eleven groups, according to their spectra.

It would have made the study of stars simpler if in the beginning the groups had been numbered 1, 2, 3 and so on, starting with the hottest stars and ending with the coolest. Instead, it was decided to use letters and these, unfortunately have got out of order and the sequence is now: W.O.B.A.F. G.K.M.R.N.S., with W the hottest and S the coolest. Each group is further divided into ten sub-groups numbered 0 to 9.

The hottest stars, Groups W and O, have surface temperatures of more than 35,000 degrees C., and the coolest, Group S, only 2,300 degrees. The Sun, an average star, is of spectral class G2, and thus comes roughly in the middle of the sequence. In general, W, O and B stars are bluish; A, white, F and G, yellow; K, orange; and the remainder orange-red.

A basic requirement of astronomy is to know the distance of stars from the Earth. This is not an easy task and for many hundreds of years astronomers had no idea at all of their immense distances from us. Then, in 1838, Friedrich Bessel, director of a German observatory, partially solved the problem by using what is now called the method of parallax.

Parallax

A few words on parallax may be useful here. A simple experiment will help to explain it. Hold a pencil in one outstretched hand, close your left eye, and line the pencil up with an object, such as a clock, on the other side of the room. Then, without moving, close your right eye and open the left one. The pencil will appear to have moved slightly, because you are looking at it from a slightly different direction. By measuring the amount by which the pencil appears to have moved, and by knowing the distance between your eyes, the distance of the pencil from your face can be calculated. The degree of shift of the clock is a measure of parallax.

To measure the distance of stars, a long base line is required. Even the distance across the Earth is not big enough and astronomers make use of the yearly movement of the Earth round the Sun. The angle to a particular star is measured when the Earth is on one side of the Sun, and then again six months later when the Earth has moved round to the other side.

This provides a baseline of 300 million kilometres (186 million miles), which seems a lot, but in fact is not, so far away are the stars. Using this method, the angle subtended to the nearest star is that of a triangle with a base the equivalent of the width of a pin head and a height of 800 metres

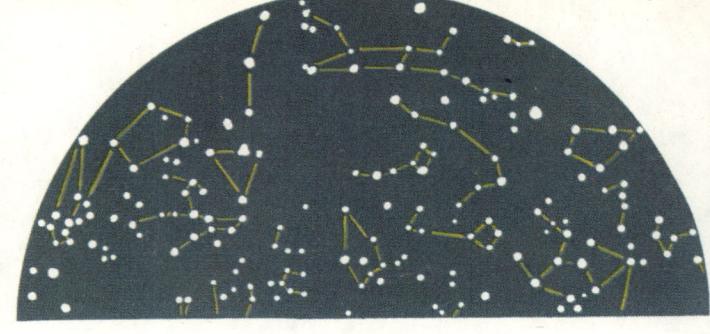

Northern sky in winter (December).

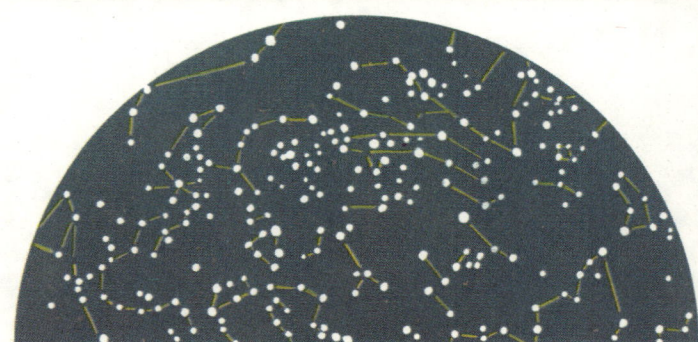

Southern sky in winter (December).

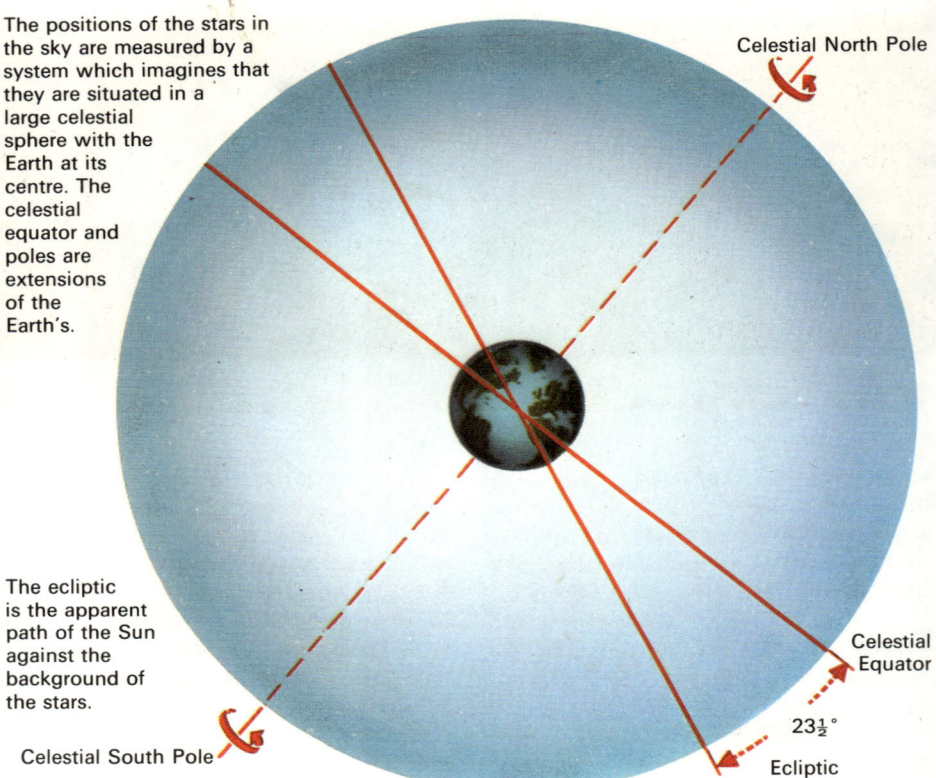

The positions of the stars in the sky are measured by a system which imagines that they are situated in a large celestial sphere with the Earth at its centre. The celestial equator and poles are extensions of the Earth's.

The ecliptic is the apparent path of the Sun against the background of the stars.

Celestial North Pole

Celestial Equator

23½°

Ecliptic

Celestial South Pole

(half a mile). Thus this method requires very precise measurements for even the nearest stars, and cannot be used at all for remote stars.

For stars more than about 400 light years away another method is used. This involves estimating the real luminosity of a star and then comparing this with its apparent magnitude. The real luminosity is determined by studying the star's spectrum. A spectrum, remember, gives us a good idea of the surface temperature of a star. And, knowing the spectral group and the temperature, it is possible to estimate the actual luminosity of the star.

Imagine this star has the same brightness as a nearer star the distance of which has been calculated using the parallax method. Because its light has travelled a shorter distance, it appears more intense. The distance of the first star can then be calculated, since it is known by how much the extra faintness results from the extra distance travelled by its light.

Remoteness of Stars

The remoteness of the more distant stars staggers the imagination. The most distant yet detected in an optical telescope are in a galaxy in the constellation of Bootes. A study of its

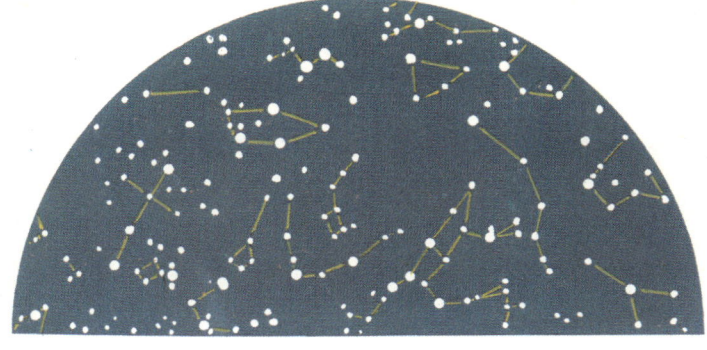

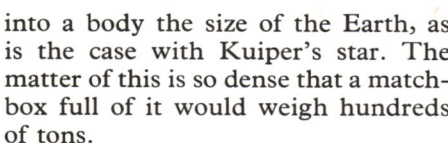
Northern sky in summer (August).

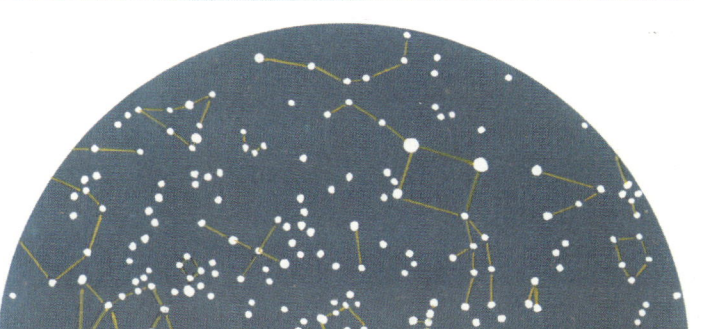

Southern sky in summer (August).

into a body the size of the Earth, as is the case with Kuiper's star. The matter of this is so dense that a matchbox full of it would weigh hundreds of tons.

Variable Stars

In addition to size, mass, colour and brilliance, stars vary in yet another manner—stability. Not all stars are as constant in their light output as the Sun. Some stars vary enormously, some vary regularly and others irregularly.

One of the best known variable, or pulsating stars as they are known, is Mira in the constellation Cetus. The unusual behaviour of this star was first noted hundreds of years ago.

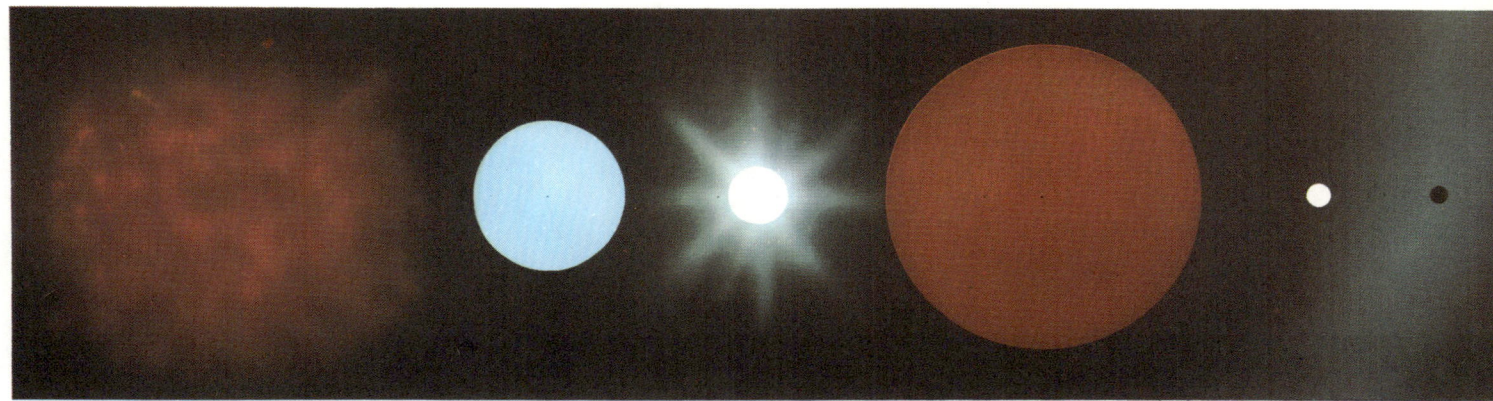

spectrum indicates that it is about 5,000 million light years away—that is 48,000 million million, million kilometres (30,000 million, million, million miles). At present this marks the limit of the observable universe.

A point of interest about starlight is the fact that when we look at a star, we are really looking back in time. When we look at the Sun, we are not seeing it actually as it is now, but as it was eight minutes ago when its light left it. When we look at Polaris, the Pole Star, we are seeing it as it was 250 years ago. It may have 'gone out' or exploded 200 years ago—but we will not know of this catastrophic event for another 50 years.

In addition to having different surface temperatures and brightnesses, and being located at widely varying distances from the Sun, stars also vary greatly in size. Stars much bigger than the Sun are considered giants and small ones are called dwarfs.

The biggest stars are red giants, some of which are truly huge. One such star is Betelgeuse. This has a diameter of over 320 million kilometres (200 million miles), so that were it to replace the Sun, the Earth

The life cycle of a star (from left to right): gas cloud; contracting into a sphere; steady or stable star; red giant; white dwarf; extremely dense neutron star.

would be orbiting inside it. Betelgeuse is by no means the biggest star. Another red giant, Epsilon Aurigae in the constellation Charioteer, has a diameter of 2,900 million kilometres (1,800 million miles), big enough to envelop all the planets circling the Sun as far out as Saturn.

At the other end of the scale there are white dwarf stars considerably smaller than the Earth.

In spite of the tremendous variation in the size of stars, their actual weight or mass does not seem to vary nearly as much. If this is so, then their densities must vary tremendously. Betelgeuse, some 250 times as big as the Sun, has an average density of less than 1/100,000 that of the Sun, or less than one-millionth that of water. If somebody gave you a box full of 'Betelgeuse' you would accuse them of giving you an empty box.

On the other hand, the white dwarf stars have their matter compressed to incredible densities. Imagine a body the size of Betelgeuse compressed

Mira, a giant red star, when dimmest has a brightness of magnitude 9. Over a period of about 47 weeks, the star increases in brilliance by a factor of 300, to magnitude 3.

Not all variable stars vary as slowly as this or by as much. Delta Cephei ranges from only magnitude 3.75 to 4.5, over a period of 5 days, 8 hours, 47 minutes 27 seconds. It is as regular as an accurate clock. Delta Cephei is a very bright star and when at maximum it shines 660 times as brilliantly as the Sun.

Generally speaking, the brighter a variable star is on the average, the longer it takes to pulsate. Stars that vary over a period of 30 days are usually about 4,000 times as bright as the Sun.

Of great interest to astronomers are the variable stars known as Cepheids, so named after the first of their type to be observed. These have relatively short periods, rising quickly to maximum brilliance and then fading slowly. Their importance lies in the definite relationship between their periods and their absolute brightness. Once the period is known, their true brightness can be calculated. This can then be

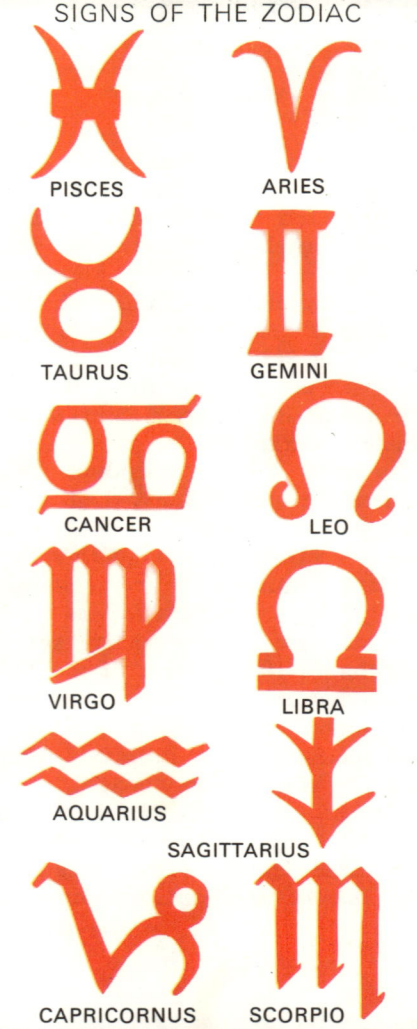

compared with their apparent brightness and their distance computed as described earlier.

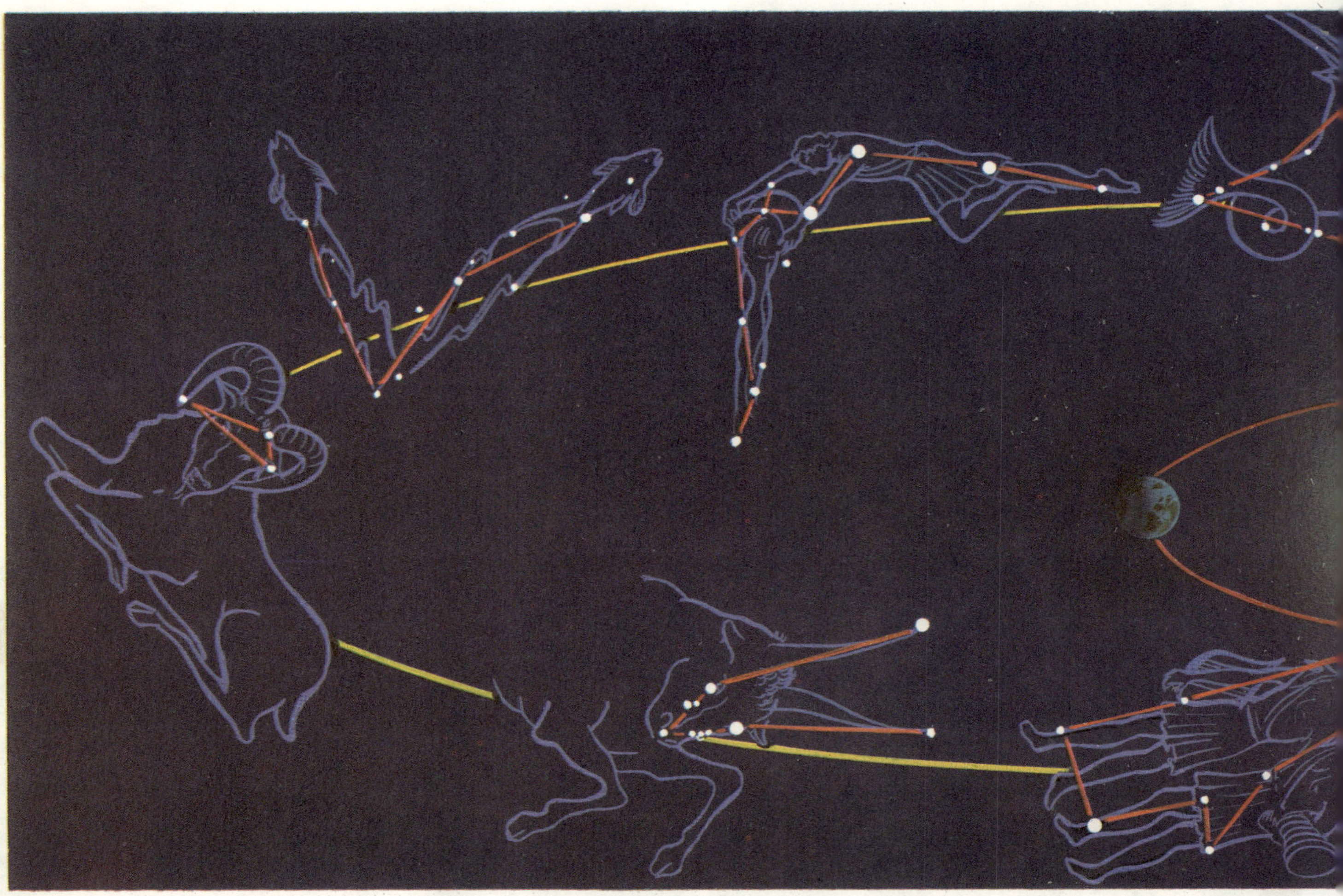

The reason why some stars vary or pulsate in this manner is not known. They seem to expand and contract like a balloon being alternately blown up and then deflated.

Double Stars

We do know, however, why some stars appear to vary in brightness. These are what are called double stars, or binary stars, that is, two stars close together. Some of these pairs of stars are merely optical doubles, the two stars actually being very far apart but lying in the same line of sight.

Most of them, however, are true double stars, revolving around each other, or rather around their common centre of gravity. Some of these double stars are widely separated so that it is easy to plot their motions and orbits. Others are so close that powerful telescopes are required to separate the two components. There are a few double stars which cannot be seen as twins at all, but appear to be a single star varying regularly in brightness. These are known as eclipsing binaries, and the variation in brightness is due

SIGNS OF THE ZODIAC

PISCES

ARIES

TAURUS

GEMINI

CANCER

LEO

VIRGO

LIBRA

AQUARIUS

SAGITTARIUS

CAPRICORNUS

SCORPIO

Ancient astronomers divided the Zodiacal belt into twelve constellations: Aries (the Ram), Taurus (the Bull), Gemini (the Twins), Cancer (the Crab), Leo (the Lion), Virgo (the Virgin), Libra (the Scales), Scorpio (the Scorpion), Sagittarius (the Archer), Capricornus (the Goat), Aquarius (the Water-bearer) and Pisces (the Fishes).

to the two stars revolving in front of each other.

In binary systems one star may be much bigger, or hotter than its associate. Such a system is Algol, perhaps the best known eclipsing binary. In Algol, in the constellation of Perseus, the two stars are 11.2 million kilometres (7 million miles) apart. One star has a diameter of 4 million kilometres ($2\frac{1}{2}$ million miles) and is very hot, while its companion is much bigger, but cooler and less dense. The period of rotation is five days. Some binary stars are so close that they almost touch, their huge gaseous bodies grotesquely distorted into the shape of eggs.

Double stars are quite common—in fact one third of all the stars appear to be doubles, while over one third are triples or even close clusters of stars. Only a quarter of the stars we can see seem to be on their own. Some systems

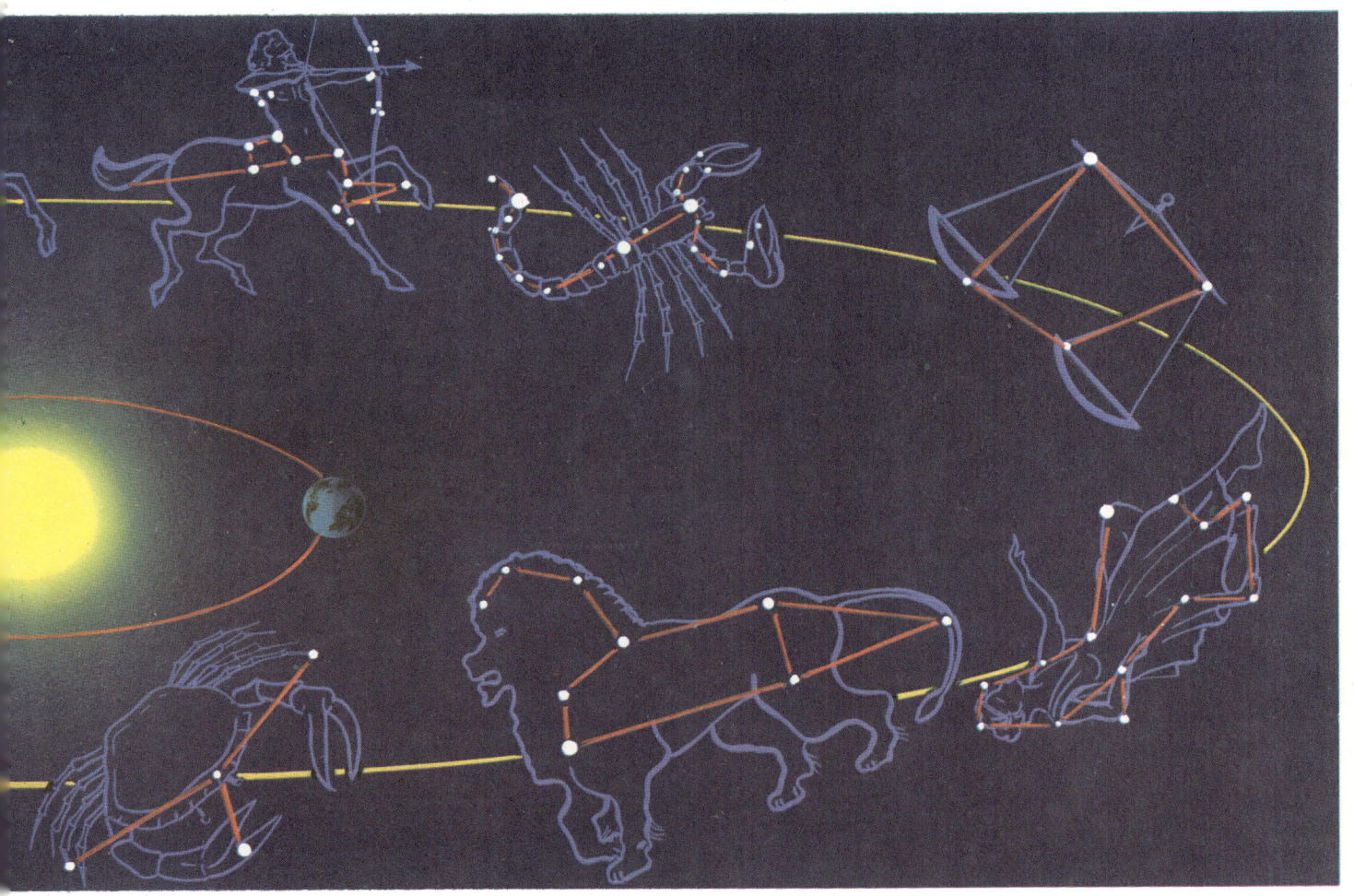

rotate in a few days, while others take thousands of years.

Life and Death of a Star

It is generally assumed that stars began their life as a cloud of interstellar gas and dust. The gas is practically all hydrogen, the most abundant element in the universe, and probably has an initial diameter of something like 8 to 9 million million kilometres (5 to 6 million million miles).

Gravitational forces between the atoms cause them to move together and gradually over a period of millions of years, the huge cloud, known as a protostar, starts to contract. As the cloud contracts it attracts additional atoms at an increasing rate. In speeding towards the centre of the protostar the atoms become hotter and hotter, and move even faster and start to collide with other atoms.

Not all the gas condenses into the star. In at least one case—the Sun—some of the gas condensed into a number of planets. It is most unlikely that the Sun is unique in this respect, and so it is probable that many other stars have planets.

To return to our protostar. The cloud of gas has now perhaps shrunk to a ball 1·6 million kilometres (1 million miles) in diameter. The temperature of the core continues to rise steadily and when it passes the million-degree mark, thermonuclear reactions commence in which hydrogen is converted into helium to produce prodigious quantities of energy.

The new star shines, emitting a brilliant blue-white light. Vast quantities of hydrogen fuel are used up in the thermonuclear processes, but so massive are the stars that the process continues for several thousand million years, for most of its life, in fact, with little major change in the star.

But obviously the process cannot continue indefinitely. In time the sheer weight of 'ash' in the centre of the star initiates new nuclear processes. Thus, as the star gets older it gets hotter, the temperature of the core, in time, rising to 100 million degrees. The part of the star where the hydrogen is actually converted into helium is confined to a relatively thin layer around the core. The core increases in size as the hydrogen-burning layer moves outwards, and the star as a whole slowly expands into what is called a red giant.

Events then move quickly on the cosmic scale. The thermonuclear processes become more intense and build up a concentration of heavier elements, and the star gets hotter and hotter and expands rapidly.

During this period a star can become very unstable and explode to become what is known as a supernova. Or it can suddenly collapse inwards, to become what is known as a 'black hole' star. Most stars, however, avoid this fate. As red giants they start to lose a lot of their outer layers of gas into space. Having burnt up most of its hydrogen fuel, the star starts to shrink. Little by little, as its nuclear fires die down, the star continues to shrink until it is as small as the Earth and becomes a dense white dwarf.

For further thousands of millions of years the star continues to cool, growing fainter and fainter. Finally its nuclear fire goes out, and the star becomes black and as cold as the space around it.

How do astronomers know this? Simply by looking among the millions of stars in our galaxy we can see hundreds in the various stages of evolution just described. Our Sun is now about 5,000 million years old and is in the middle of its life.

Our Galaxy

The Sun and its planets are part of a huge group of stars known as a galaxy. The group contains about 100 thousand million individual stars. This vast collection of stars has the shape of a huge disc measuring about 100,000 light years in diameter.

The disc is shaped like a gigantic Catherine-wheel, with a dense bunch of stars in the centre and streams of less closely packed stars in the whirling arms. The Sun is located in one of these arms, about 30,000 light years from the centre. The entire galaxy is rotating in space, taking about 225 million years to complete one whole revolution. Thus, as you read this, you are actually taking part in a voyage round the galaxy!

The Milky Way

On a dark night a luminous band of light can be seen running across the sky. It looks 'milky' and is, in fact, known as the Milky Way—the semi-official name of our galaxy. This band of light, if observed even through a pair of binoculars, can be seen to comprise myriads of stars packed closely together. When you look up at the Milky Way you are looking along the disc; in other directions you are looking across the 'thinness' of the galaxy and thus see fewer stars.

In addition to the stars, the Milky Way contains a vast quantity of thinly spread gas and interstellar dust. Although this gas and dust is extremely rarefied when seen edge on for great distances, it does absorb and distort the light of very distant objects. This happens when we look towards the centre of the galaxy, so that we cannot actually see right to the centre using optical telescopes.

The dust has other effects which interfere with scientific study. In absorbing starlight the dust scatters some of the light away from the Earth; this seems to make distant stars appear fainter than they really ought to be. In the past, this has caused errors in the calculation of distances. The dust also tends to make stars appear redder than they really are. This is because the dust scatters short-wave light, such as blue, more than it scatters long-wave light, such as red. The result is that the spectra of very distant stars have the red part boosted artificially, making the delicate analysis procedures much more difficult.

Stars in the galaxy are in all stages of evolution, and of a wide variety of size and brightness. Some are many times more powerful than the Sun,

The vast collection of stars making up our galaxy form a disc shaped like a giant Catherine wheel. The galaxy is seen (below) edge on. The arrows indicate the approximate position of our solar system in one arm of the spiral.

some are so big that they could contain our solar system out to the orbit of Mars; others are smaller than the Earth. Some are millions of times less dense than the air we breathe and thus on Earth would be considered a high vacuum, while others are so heavy that a spoonful of their matter would weigh many tons. Some stars are fiercely hot, some glimmer only faintly. A few stars have probably 'gone out' and are dark and cold. We cannot see such stars as their gravitational pull is so great that it prevents any light—if there is any— from escaping from the surface.

Star Groups

The stars are not distributed evenly throughout the galaxy. Many of them form groups or clusters containing any number of stars, from as few as ten to many thousands. A loose association of stars is known as an open cluster. The best known example of this type is the *Pleiades* which is clearly visible to the naked eye not far from the giant red star in the constellation Taurus. This cluster is also known as The Seven Sisters. To the early Greeks the sisters were originally seven very pretty girls who were chased by the hunter Orion and fled across the sky. Jupiter, hearing their cries of alarm, helped them with a godly act—he changed them into stars. Actually, most people can see seven stars in the cluster with their naked eyes, although those with keen sight can see up to eighteen. Through a telescope about a hundred can be seen. The stars of the *Pleiades* are orbiting within a faint cloud of luminescence. This is actually a cloud of incredibly rarefied gas, but neverthe-less shining by reflecting the light of the stars within the cluster. Astron-omers have charted over 300 open clusters of stars which contain any-thing from a few to several hundred stars.

A second type of star group is the globular cluster. This is almost a miniature galaxy in its own right and contains up to 100 thousand stars

much older than the stars in the spiral-ling arms. Astronomers call the younger stars Population 1 and the older stars Population 2. The fact that there seems to be these two distant 'populations' is very important, as they provide several clues about the way the galaxy came into being.

Astronomers consider that, just as each individual star seems to have condensed out of a local cloud of dust

the tiny particles of gas, stars started to condense out of denser pockets of the gas. More stars formed near the centre of the cloud where the gas was densest.

If these stars were the first to evolve in the galaxy, then it would be expected that these stars would be the oldest. This is, in fact, the case. Most of the stars in the hub of the galaxy belong to Population 2.

 Globe-shaped elliptical

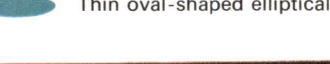 Oval-shaped elliptical   Thin oval-shaped elliptical

packed—cosmically speaking—very close together. Globular clusters are often located well away from the main disc of stars of the galaxy.

Halo and Disc
The term galaxy, in fact, does not only comprise the Catherine-wheel of rotating stars. It also encompasses a halo, a relatively sparsely populated sphere of stars, with a diameter about equal to that of the main disc.

Within this halo there are several thousand million individual stars trav-elling along lonely orbits that take them into and out of the main disc at all angles. Astronomers have located a few passing through the disc near the Sun. They can be detected by their high speed. It is not that they are actually moving round the hub of the galaxy any faster than the other stars, but they seem to be because their comet-like orbits take them right through the disc at highly oblique angles, at speeds of up to 320 kilometres (200 miles) a second.

Although the myriad of stars making up our galaxy are in various stages of evolution, there is a marked difference between the stars of the disc and those of the halo. In general, the stars of the halo and the centre of the disc are

 Tightly wound spiral

Astronomers have divided galaxies into a number of elliptical and spiral shapes. These two main groups contain varying degrees of roundness or ovalness and, in the case of the spirals, degrees of looseness or tightness in the spiral arm. Each of the different galaxies is given an identifying symbol. The differences in shape of the galaxies has to do with the speeds at which they rotate.

and gas, so the galaxy itself was formed from a gigantic spherical cloud of primordial hydrogen. The gas was not evenly distributed throughout space, and as it started to contract through the mutual gravitational attraction of

 Loosely wound barred spiral

Nebulae
The Milky Way, the main disc of stars comprising our galaxy, contains a number of misty light patches and many dark patches. These patches are known as nebulae, from the Latin for clouds. Some of these patches are, in fact, other galaxies and these are des-cribed later on. Many of the patches, however, are genuine galaxial clouds of gas and dust—the breeding matter from which stars condense.

153

The gas of which the nebulae are composed is mainly hydrogen—the most abundant matter in the universe. The clouds of gas shine for one of two reasons. Some nebulae shine because they absorb energy from the stars nearby and re-emit this as light that we can see. Other nebulae shine by the light of nearby stars being reflected from dust particles in the cloud.

One spectacular nebula, shining by emitted energy, is the Great Nebula, in the constellation Orion. On a cold, clear night, this can just be seen as a misty patch of light in the 'sword' of the constellation. Through a telescope, the cloud can be seen to be glowing brightly from the many very hot stars in its centre. The Great Nebula is 26 light years across and about 1,600 light years away from the Sun.

Dark nebulae are simply clouds of dust which obscure the light of stars behind them, and many can be seen with the naked eye. One of the better known. It could be due to the star's thermonuclear 'fire' settling down in the same way that a flare-up often accompanies the settling down of a piece of coal in a fire. Another stellar nebula is the Veil Nebula in the constellation Cygnus the Swan. Having the appearance of a diaphanous veil waving in a wind, this is thought to be the outer layers of an unstable star which were ejected into space some 50 thousand years ago. Today the star's fragments have formed into a huge cloud 480 thousand million kilometres (300 thousand million miles) across, moving through space at 480,000 k.p.h. (300,000 m.p.h.)

Supernovae

Some stars, nearing the end of their lives, explode with a force of countless megatons. Such explosions are known as supernovae. Astronomers have not yet seen one in our galaxy, as they seem to occur only once every few hundred years in the average galaxy. However, by looking at the distant galaxies far beyond ours, astronomers can see several every year. A supernova is the cosmic event of all cosmic events; the grand finale of cosmic firework shows. The brightest of them emit about as much light as the galaxy itself—try and imagine one single star, however big, equalling the brilliance of thousands of millions.

The last recorded supernova in the Milky Way exploded in A.D. 1604, the one before that occurring in A.D. 1572. Oriental astronomers recorded the latter event very clearly, indicating where it was seen. In that particular area of sky today is the Crab Nebula. Even now, after nearly 400 years, the remains of the explosion are still expanding at a speed of 4 million k.p.h. (2½ million m.p.h.), creating strong radio signals as they do so. At the centre of the cloud is the remains of the parent star, faint blue in colour, indicating a star moving towards white dwarfdom and oblivion.

known is the Horse's Head nebula in the constellation Orion, so called because of its uncanny resemblance to the head of a knight in chess. Another dark nebula, appropriately called the Coal Sack, is located close to the Southern Cross.

Most nebulae seem to be remnants of the primordial cloud of gas and dust from which our galaxy condensed, but some seem to have been blown into space from stars. One such nebula is the Dumb Bell in Vulpecula. This is a huge sphere of gas ejected from a nearby small hot blue star. What causes these stellar upheavals is not

Very large stars may end their lives in a stellar explosion called a supernova. Ordinary novae are caused by the sudden flare-ups of relatively small stars which subside fairly quickly to their original brightness. But supernovae emit as much light as a single galaxy in a great cosmic upheaval.

The steady-state theory maintains that the universe as a whole has always been the same. According to this theory individual stars and galaxies evolve and die to be replaced continually by new ones being born into spaces created by the expanding galaxies.

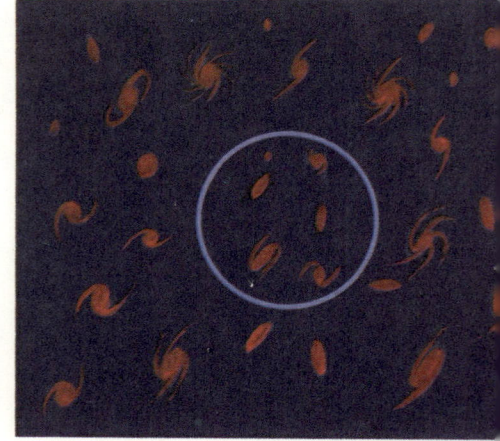

The Universe

Most of the stars that we can see in the night sky are at an immense distance from our Sun. The word 'most' does not mean that some stars are close to us—but that others are even farther away. In fact, they are not even in our own galaxy at all. Enormous as it is, they are outside it, in other great galactic collections of stars.

These other galaxies occur in a wide variety of shapes, sizes and colours. Some transmit powerful radio waves, others emit hardly any radio waves at all. Some of the other galaxies have the shape of a gigantic ellipse, others are called barred spirals, many of them having great spiralling arms, like our own. Most galaxies are smaller than the Milky Way, but some are much bigger. But they are all similar in one respect: they are all enormous clouds of gas each one containing anything from 100 million to 100 thousand million stars.

Other Galaxies

It was in the eighteenth century that astronomers first began wondering seriously if some of the patches of cloud and dust, known as nebulae, which they could see in the sky, might indeed be other island galaxies. These might be so far away that individual stars could not be detected. Whatever they were, they were a nuisance to astronomers as they were easily confused with approaching comets.

Towards the end of the last century, more and more astronomers were becoming convinced that most of the nebulae they could see were, in fact, other galaxies, but were unable to prove it. It was not until the advent of the new 254-centimetre (100-inch) reflector-telescope on Mount Wilson, then the world's biggest, that it became possible to measure the dis-

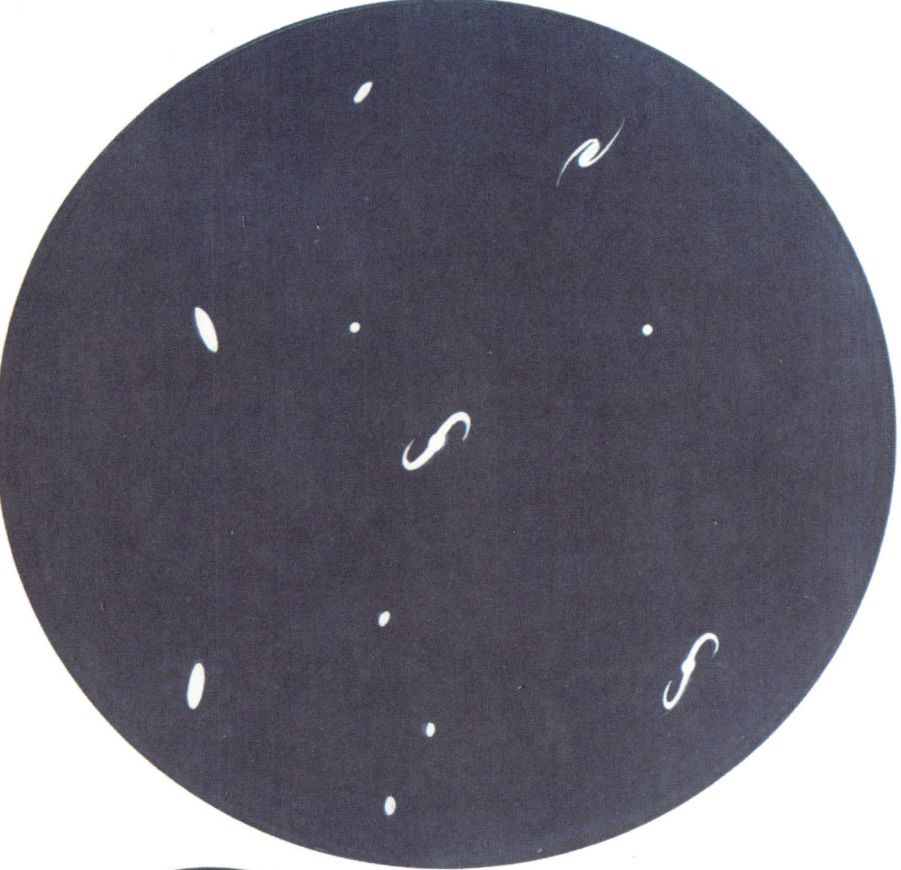

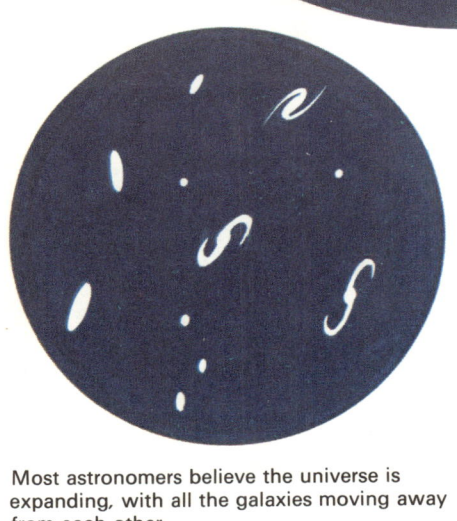

Most astronomers believe the universe is expanding, with all the galaxies moving away from each other.

tance to one of these objects and show with a high degree of probability that it was indeed far beyond our galaxy.

The object whose distance was measured was the Great Nebula in Andromeda, which on most cold, clear nights is visible to the naked eye as a faint Moon-sized patch of brightness in the sky.

The Californian astronomer Edwin Hubble made the discovery in 1925, using the new telescope. To help measure the distance to Andromeda, Hubble made use of the peculiar properties of the cepheid pulsating stars. These are the important variable stars whose brightness varies regularly, and for which the time between periods of maximum brightness depends upon the true brightness of the star.

Andromeda is so far away that, for all practical purposes, its individual stars are all the same distance from the Earth, in the same way as all the passengers in a liner steaming over the horizon can be considered the same distance from the shore, even though the passengers are actually spaced out along the ship's decks. Thus, any difference in apparent brightness detected between cepheid stars in the

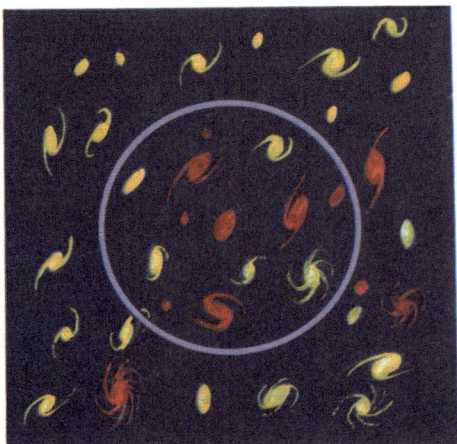

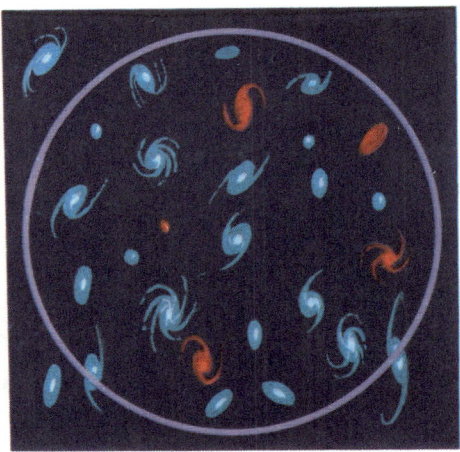

nebula indicates a difference in their real brightness, and not merely a difference in their distance.

By measuring the period of pulsation of a cepheid star, astronomers can immediately determine its real brightness. Then, by comparing this luminosity with the brightness of a cepheid whose position has been determined mathematically, the distance to the first cepheid can be calculated.

Hubble compared cepheid stars in the nebula under observation with a nearer one in our own galaxy whose distance had been calculated by trigonometry. The comparison showed that the cepheid stars in the nebula were, in fact, much further away than any stars in our galaxy. They were over 2 million miles more distant than our nearest star and over a thousand times more distant than the faintest star you can see with your naked eye. This proved without doubt that the 'cloud' was indeed another galaxy.

Andromeda

When Hubble measured the galaxy of Andromeda, he calculated its distance as 750,000 light years away, from which it seemed that Andromeda was smaller than our galaxy. In 1952, however, it was discovered that the variable scale Hubble used regarding the cepheid stars was incorrect. Cepheids of Population 1 (new) stars were proved to be brighter than those of Population 2 (old) stars, and Hubble in his experiment had assumed that the cepheids he had measured were Population 2 stars. Consequently, the distance of the Andromeda galaxy was revised to over 2 million light years. With the correction, astronomers realised that the galaxy was, in fact, bigger than our own.

Andromeda is very similar to our galaxy. Basically, the bulk of the stars are in a broad disc comprising a central hub and spiral arms, with a 'halo' of stars surrounding the hub spherically. Our galaxy and that of Andromeda are not alone in space, but are members of a cluster of galaxies. Known as the Local Group, the cluster includes about seventeen systems joined together by the common bond of gravity.

The Milky Way is at one end of this gigantic formation and Andromeda at the other. Other galaxies in the Group are the Small Magellanic Cloud and Large Magellanic Cloud; these are so much smaller that they may almost be considered as satellites of the two main galaxies. The remaining

The Earth with its satellite Moon (top) rotate around the Sun and are part of the solar system which, in its turn, is but a tiny part of our galaxy. The bottom picture shows that the galaxy itself is only one of 27 local groups. Even at this scale the local galaxies are simply a drop in the vastness of the universe.

galaxies are even smaller and have not been given individual names, but have merely been allotted numbers in the new General Catalogue, the official list of stars and galaxies kept by astronomers.

Incredibly remote as they are, and sparsely scattered in an immense void, this Local Group of galaxies is united by the mysterious force we call gravitation, the whole group slowly wheeling about a common centre of gravity somewhere between our galaxy and Andromeda.

Beyond our group of galaxies we can see many more galaxies and these too seem to be arranged in groups. As far as the universe as a whole is concerned,

our Local Group is quite a tiny one. In general, the outer galaxies seem to combine into enormous groups of about 500. In their huge wanderings two galaxies occasionally collide. However, such a cosmic collision does not have the catastrophic effect of a pile-up on a motorway, because the galaxies pass through one another. And, so great is the distance between the individual stars, that the chance of collision is slight—about the same as that of two midges hitting each other while flying around in a football stadium.

On the other hand, the gas and dust intermingled with the stars does create a reaction; the dust heats up slightly and emits radio waves. Astronomers can see several galaxies in the process of colliding and they are emitting radio signals. However, 'radio galaxies' are too numerous to be explained entirely by collisions. Discovering the answer to this is just one of the many problems which astronomers are attempting to solve.

Galaxies by the Million
Galaxies are visible, in all directions, as far as our telescopes can see. Together they make up what is known as the universe.

The astronomer Fred Hoyle gave a graphic description of the content and extent of the universe: 'Imagine the average galaxy to be reduced to the size of a bee. Our galaxy, which is a good deal bigger than the average, would be roughly represented in shape and size by a small coin. The average spacing of the galaxies would be three metres (ten feet), and the range of

Radio telescopes that use two or more aerials at once are called interferometers. Many of these are very large with fixed aerials hundreds of metres long.

galaxies can be seen with the big 508-centimetre (200-inch) telescope on Mount Palomar. Many of them are over 5,000 million light years away. As the age of the Earth is estimated at about 4,500 million years, it means that we are seeing these immensely distant bodies as they were 500 million years before the Earth was formed. One wonders what these galaxies look like now.

Are There Other Planets?
We now know that the Sun, and its family of planets, is but one member of a huge group of stars known as a galaxy, and that our own galaxy is

solar system—that the Sun and planets all evolved from a gigantic cloud of dust—is correct, then it seems safe to assume that many other such systems have evolved.

Unfortunately, we cannot prove this, because even the biggest planet we can imagine is much too small for it to be visible in telescopes. Also, we must not forget that, in spite of its vast bulk, all we can see of a star itself is a tiny, featureless, pinpoint of light. Astronomers are convinced that, no matter how cleverly or big we build

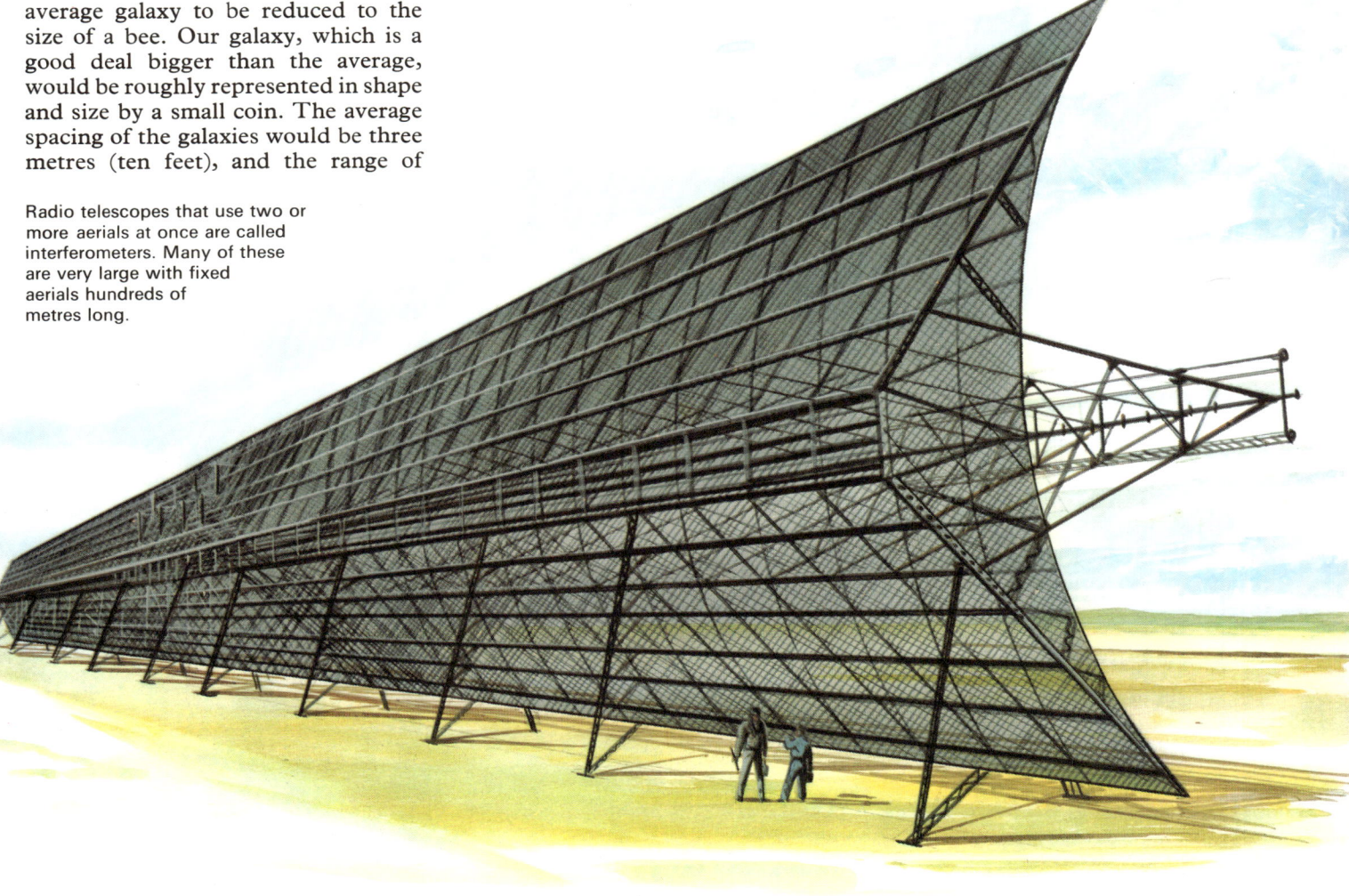

vision is about sixteen kilometres (ten miles). So sit back and imagine a swarm of bees spaced at about three metres (ten feet) apart and stretching away from you in all directions for sixteen kilometres (ten miles). Now for each bee substitute the vast bulk of a galaxy and you have an idea of the universe that has been revealed by the large American telescopes.'

All together, well over 1,000 million

only one of millions of similar islands of stars. Collectively, these vast bodies contain great numbers of stars— millions upon millions upon countless millions.

A fascinating and important question is: have any others of these stars got families of planets surrounding them? Unfortunately, there is as yet no certain answer to this vital question. If the theory about the evolution of the

future telescopes, they will never be able to reveal tiny bodies like a planet, shining only by the light reflected from its adjacent star.

That other planets do exist, however, there is little doubt. For those who find this difficult to believe, surely the opposite—that there are no other planets—is even more difficult to comprehend. It seems unlikely that the solid bodies travelling round the

Sun are the only such bodies in the entire universe. And, if other stars have planets, some of these surely must be orbiting at a habitable distance, that is, not so close that the surface frizzles, or so distant that everything would be frozen solid. On planets within this habitable zone, water could remain as water, gas could be held as an atmosphere, and radiation from the Sun could be received in warming amounts.

In the same way that it is possible to accept the likelihood of the existence of other planets, so it is but another step to accept the probability that on many of these life has evolved. If so, some of this life may be similar, if not identical to, that which has evolved on Earth.

It is, of course, difficult to estimate the number of stars that may have planets, and on which of these life may have evolved. Some astronomers consider that almost one star in every thousand could have a planetary system, which means that there must be many millions of planets in our galaxy alone. Estimating how many of these could support life is an even more daunting task. In this case astronomers have calculated that there should be about one site for life for every cube of space measuring 1,500 light years. On this basis, there are several million potential Earths in the Milky Way alone.

The Expanding Universe

Information gleaned from telescopes and spectroscopes has indicated many wonders of the universe. It has told us of hot stars and cold stars; of giant stars and dwarf stars; of old stars and young stars. It indicates a universe populated by millions of galaxies, each containing hundreds of millions of stars.

The information gathered from spectroscopes also indicates another strange fact about the galaxies. As explained in the chapter *The Instruments of Astronomy*, a spectroscope spreads out light according to its wavelength to provide a multi-coloured band called a spectrum.

There are two important breaks in a spectrum, each one indicating that a particular wavelength of light is missing—it has been absorbed by the cooler gas surrounding the galaxy. The position of these breaks varies from galaxy to galaxy, the breaks moving towards the 'red' end of the spectra of the fainter galaxies. This 'red shift', as it is known, is thought to be due to the

Doppler effect—that is, the increase in wavelength that occurs when the source of a light is moving away.

Many other explanations have been suggested to explain the reason for this red shift, for example, that light somehow gets 'tired' when travelling immense distances, that intergalactic dust affects it in some way, or that it is due to gravitational forces. Of all the suggestions made so far, however, the only one that agrees with established knowledge and that can be checked in laboratories is that all the galaxies are moving away from the Earth.

Thus, most astronomers believe that the Universe is expanding, with all the galaxies moving away from each other, like spots of ink on a balloon being blown up. As the balloon expands, the surface stretches, and all the spots move farther apart from each other.

Examination of the red shift of different galaxies shows that the more distant a galaxy is, the faster it seems to be moving away from us. Thus, a huge cluster of several thousand galaxies in the constellation Virgo, estimated to be about 50 million light years distant, is moving away from our galaxy at 1,200 kilometres (750 miles) a second. Another group, in the Great Bear, 650 million light years away, is receding at 14,900 kilometres (9,300 miles) per second. A cluster estimated to be 940 million light years away, is moving at 21,400 kilometres (13,400 miles) a second. In Hydra, a group of faint galaxies 2,700 million light years away, is receding at the stupendous speed of 60,000 kilometres (38,000 miles) per second—about one fifth the speed of light. Galaxies at the limit of vision in the Mount Palomar telescope are, if the 'red shift' in their spectra is correct, travelling at two-thirds the speed of light. Those at the limits of radio telescopes seem to be travelling at nine-tenths the speed of light.

There may be galaxies actually moving away from us at a speed faster than light—but we shall never be able to detect or see them, as their rays will never reach us.

Big Bang

Perhaps the most awesome questions facing astronomers are: How did the

Colours and temperatures of typical stars, an indication of the difference in the magnitude of stars and (below) the comparative sizes of four stars, the two smaller ones being the Sun (top) and Cygni (below).

25,000°C.
Spica

11,000°C.
Sirius

6,000°C.
Sun

4,000°C.
Arcturus

3,000°C.
Betelgeuse

Arcturus

Betelgeuse

Universe begin—and when? Has it existed for ever, or did it begin at a particular time in the remote past? If it did have a beginning, what was there before it began? Currently, there are two main theories which seek to answer these basic questions. They are known popularly as the Steady-State and the Big Bang theories.

The Steady-State theory maintains that the universe as a whole has always been the same—and always will be. According to this theory, individual stars and galaxies evolve and die, to be replaced continually by new ones being born in the space created between the expanding galaxies. Thus the general arrangement of galaxies remains the same—for ever and ever.

The Big Bang theory, on the other hand, suggests that the universe was formed about 20,000 million years ago when a primeval atom, containing all the material of the universe, exploded

(Top right) One of the strangest of modern theories about the universe concerns extremely dense black holes, which may absorb material from a nearby star by an immense gravitational pull until it 'disappears', since no light can escape from it. (Bottom right) A densely packed globular cluster of stars.

with unimaginable fury, sending its matter out in all directions. Some of this material was thrown out more quickly and its remains are now the distant galaxies, still travelling faster than some of the closer galaxies.

Which of these two theories is correct? If it is that of the Steady-State, then the distribution of galaxies should be about the same over long periods. In theory we can check this because when we look at a distant galaxy, we are, in effect, looking back into the past; we are not seeing it now, but as it was when its light started on its long journey to us millions of years ago.

On the other hand, if the Big Bang theory is correct, the more distant galaxies should be more widely spaced out, like shrapnel from an exploding shell.

At the moment optical telescopes cannot quite reach out far enough, that is, do not allow us to look back in time sufficiently for us to decide. The evidence that has been collected tends to indicate that the galaxies are not evenly distributed; the nearer ones seem to be more closely packed than those farther away. The Big Bang theory has thus been partially confirmed.

The Constellations

The stars of the night sky appear to be arranged in a number of distinctive groups or patterns. These groupings are known as constellations and there are 88 of them. Ancient astronomers gave the more prominent patterns the names of gods, animals and everyday objects. Although the forms of a few groups are apparent, a good deal of imagination is needed to make most of them fit in with the shapes appropriate to their popular names.

Although the constellations appear to comprise stars fixed to a black celestial sphere, it is important to remember that this is not so. Stars which appear to be side by side, like two objects on a painting, are usually one behind the other, many hundreds of millions of kilometres apart.

Because of the rotation of the Earth, the complete celestial sphere appears to rotate once a day, making the constellations move across the sky. In addition, as the Earth travels round the Sun, different constellations become visible in the night sky. The constellations rise four minutes earlier each day until, after a year, they return to their original positions. As the Earth is a sphere it is not possible to see all the constellations from one point on the Earth's surface.

Signposts in the Sky

It is fascinating and often helpful to learn the positions and names of some of the constellations. The night sky is so full of stars that at first glance this appears a daunting task. If, however, you learn to recognise one or two at a time it is surprisingly easy.

In the northern hemisphere the first constellation to learn is undoubtedly the Great Bear, also known as the Plough or, in America, as the Big Dipper. Astronomers usually use the term Ursa Major, which is Latin for Great Bear.

The constellation is recognised by its seven bright stars which appear to resemble a huge plough in the sky. The two end stars of the blade, Merak and Dubhe, are noteworthy because they signpost Polaris, the Pole Star. Although only the 49th brightest star in the sky, Polaris is important to us because the Earth's axis of rotation points almost straight at it. Because of this, Polaris appears to remain still, while everything else revolves round it once in 24 hours.

Polaris is actually a very bright star, over 600 times as bright as the Sun; it only appears dim because of its great distance from us—250 light years.

Orion

When you have learned to locate the Great Bear and the Pole Star, the next constellation to learn is Orion, the mighty hunter, a splendid sight in the sky during the winter months. The stars of this constellation are brighter than those of the Plough. A good deal of imagination is required to convert the star pattern into a hunter, but the three stars Mintaka, Alnilam and Alnitak make up his belt. Below the belt is a faint patch of mist—the hunter's sword. Through a telescope the sword is a wonderful sight, a long cloud of shimmering gas housing thousands of twinkling stars.

As a sign-post Orion is even more useful than the Great Bear. For example, the line of stars forming the belt point up to Aldebaran, and down to Sirius. Aldebaran is a giant red star of the first magnitude in the constellation Taurus, and is often referred to as the 'eye of the bull'. Sirius, in the constellation Canis Major, the Great Dog, is the brightest of all the stars, and very prominent during winter evenings, low down in the sky. It is popularly known as the Dog Star. In addition to these two prominent stars, Orion can be used to help you find many other constellations and individual stars.

Mythology provides us with some fascinating stories regarding the constellations. One of the most famous concerns Cassiopeia, the wife of King Cepheus, who boasted that she was more beautiful then even the glamorous Nereid sea-nymphs. Now, although Cassiopeia was undoubtedly very pretty, the Nereids were nieces of the sea-god Neptune, who did not take kindly to the comparison. Losing his temper, Neptune sent storms and floods over Cepheus's kingdom, issuing an ultimatum that he would only spare the people if the King and Queen would chain their daughter, Andromeda, to a rock on the coast to be eaten by a sea-monster. The King did so, but his daughter was saved in the nick of time. The rescuer was Perseus, who had borrowed Mercury's winged sandals in order to help him kill the terrible Gorgon Medusa, who had the power of turning men into stone with her glance. Perseus had completed his mission, and was on his way home when he spotted Andromeda. Quickly

Interstellar 'dust' in our galaxy can be seen in the sky as a dark nebula such as the Horse's Head Nebula.

this belt, about eighteen degrees wide and stretching right round the heavens, that is known as the Zodiac. The Moon and planets all move within this band of sky.

Ancient astronomers divided up the Zodiacal belt into twelve constellations. The fanciful names given to these star patterns are: Aries (the Ram), Taurus (the Bull), Gemini (the Twins), Cancer (the Crab), Leo (the Lion), Virgo (the Virgin), Libra (the Scales), Scorpio (the Scorpion), Sagittarius (the Archer), Capricorn (the Goat), Aquarius (the Water-bearer) and Pisces (the Fishes).

Although the Earth is actually revolving round the Sun, it is the Sun which appears to move over us. To the ancients, the passage of the Sun round the Zodiac was important, as it enabled them to estimate the seasons and so plan the sowing of crops. Thus, study of the Zodiac was sensible and important.

Mixed with this useful study was the strong belief that the motions of the Sun, Moon and planets influenced the behaviour of people on Earth. In particular, the arrangement of the planets under which people were born,

The spiral galaxy of Andromeda, which has two smaller satellite galaxies, is the nearest to our own galaxy, to which it is similar in many respects.

The Ring Nebula in Lyra is a typical planetary nebula and was formed from the explosion of a star.

he lifted up Medusa's severed head in front of the monster, which was instantly changed into a rock.

These mythological scenes are there in the sky for us to see today—providing we have the imagination. Cepheus is there, Queen Cassiopeia is sitting in the royal chair, Perseus is brandishing the Gorgon's head. Andromeda waits, thankfully, beside him. The sea-monster, Cetus, is also there, a small constellation near the horizon.

The Zodiac

Most people have heard the term zodiac, but few seem to know exactly what it means. To help to understand it, a few comments on the solar system may help. This system comprises the Sun and its nine orbiting planets. All the planets except for Pluto lie in approximately the same plane. If reduced in scale, the orbits of the planets would all fit inside a dinner plate. This means that the planets keep to a certain belt in the sky. It is

was thought to be a prime factor in determining the nature of this influence. A few hours' difference in the time of birth is, of course, sufficient to alter significantly the apparent arrangement.

Today this folklore, known as astrology, is still believed by many people and the casting of horoscopes is a flourishing business.

In astrology, the position of the planets 'in' a particular constellation is supposed to be important, as Saturn 'in' Aquarius has a different effect from the one it would exert in Sagittarius and so on. But of course a planet is never 'in' a particular constellation. The planets are millions of times nearer to us than the constellations, and even the stars of each constellation are hundreds of millions of kilometres behind each other.

The apparent path of the Sun among the stars is known as the Ecliptic, and the Earth's equator extended to the sky is known as the Celestial Equator. Owing to the tilt of the Earth's axis, the two circles cross. The point at which they first cross is

The Great Nebula in Orion (above) is just visible to the naked eye as a faint, hazy patch in the Sword of Orion. It is a huge glowing mass of gas and it would take 26 light years to travel across it. The Crab Nebula (right) is the remnant of a supernova recorded by Chinese astronomers in 1054. The Trifid Nebula (below) is a shimmering cloud of gas and like all galactic nebulae is the birthplace of the stars.

important to astrologers. When the cult began, this point lay in the constellation of Aries and this was taken as the First Zodiacal Sign.

However, although the ecliptic remains constant, the celestial equator does not, due to the fact that the Earth is wobbling like a toy top. Since Aries was established as the First Zodiacal Sign, the point of crossover has moved backwards into the neighbouring constellation of Pisces. Consequently, the Zodiacal signs are thus out of step with the constellations.

Another idiosyncrasy is that in the Zodiacal belt of sky there is actually a thirteenth constellation, Ophiuchus, the Serpent bearer. This is, however, not considered as one of the Zodiacal constellations, because if it were, there would be more constellations than months in a year, which would be awkward for astrologers.

Comets, Meteors and Meteorites

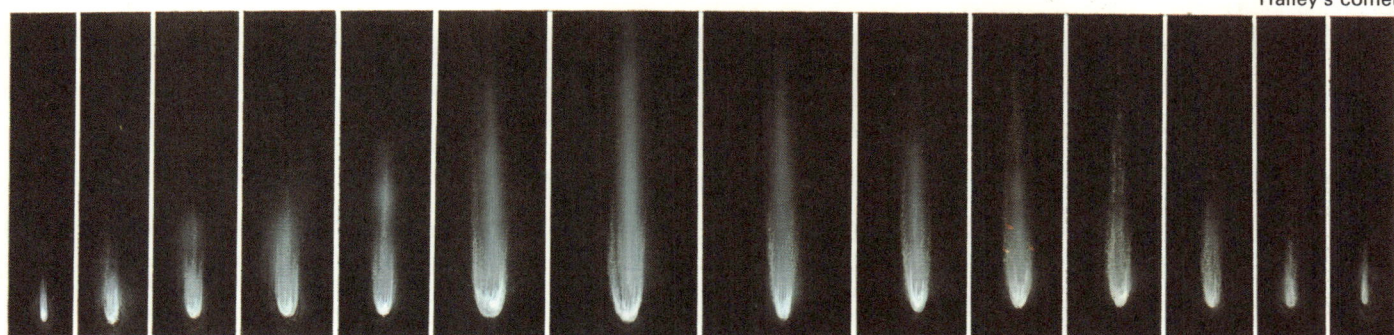

In addition to the Sun, planets, moons and asteroids, the solar system includes a vast number of tiny bodies known as comets and meteors.

In ancient times it was believed that the approach of a comet, or of a 'hairy star' as they were known, was a sign of impending disaster. Even today, when a comet appears, many people tend to remember particular earthquakes, fires or floods, conveniently forgetting that such events occur frequently, even when there are no comets in sight. It is fortunate that they do not really bring bad luck, as it is estimated that there are about 100 thousand million of them roaming about the Sun.

When passing close to the Sun, a comet is often a splendid sight, its distinctive tail extending away from it for distances of several million kilometres, and visible in the day time.

It is therefore surprising to learn that comets seem to consist of a ball of frozen gases and tiny particles of grit, only a few kilometres in diameter. Deep in space, then, a comet is a very insignificant object. As it approaches the Sun, however, the heat vaporises the outer layers to form a much bigger fuzzy 'head', and then pushes some of the vapour away to form the long tail. Because the tail is formed by the pressure of the Sun's radiation, it always points straight away from the Sun. Thus a receding comet seems to be going backwards, as the tail is in 'front' of it.

Each time a comet passes close to the Sun, it forms a new tail, and thus gradually becomes smaller and smaller. Comets are thus continuously being lost due to this slow erosion. Some comets have been seen to break up into two or more parts.

One famous comet that broke up was Beila's. This broke into two parts as it approached the Sun in 1846. The pieces drifted apart and appeared as two comets as they approached the Sun in 1852. On this approach they broke up and vanished. Twenty years

later, Europe was treated to a spectacular display of shooting stars—the remains of Beila's comet.

This fate also seems to have befallen the comet Kohoutek. Great excitement was aroused in 1973 when the Czech astronomer Kohoutek spotted the new comet when it was about 770 million kilometres (480 million miles) from the Earth. To be visible so far away meant that the comet was a big one, and it seemed as if Earth was going to witness one of the great comets of history. Calculations indicated that it would be fifty times as brilliant as Halley's famous comet, and that its tail would be over 160 million kilometres (100 million miles) long. Unfortunately, as it neared the Sun, the solar radiation caused the head to vaporise and to shrink rapidly. Although the comet was of interest to

astronomers, and was closely examined by the crew manning the American space station Skylab, it was barely visible to the naked eye on Earth.

Comets travel in extremely extended elliptical orbits, one end being near the Sun and the other hundreds of millions of kilometres away, far beyond the orbit of Pluto, the outermost planet of the solar system. The time taken to complete one orbit varies enormously, ranging from a few years to several million.

Sometimes a comet never completes an orbit. This is because it is so small and light that it is readily deflected by the gravitational attraction of giant planets like Jupiter and Saturn. As it approaches the Sun, its orbit is distorted so that it flies off into space again, never to return.

Halley's Comet

The most famous comet, the one named after the astronomer Edmond Halley (1656–1742), has a period of 76 years. It was last seen in 1910 and should be with us again in 1986.

Halley's comet is so bright that its appearances have been recorded since 240 B.C. Halley was the first astronomer to state that comets are members of the solar system, travelling in long orbits, firmly under control of the Sun. He closely studied the appearance and orbit of the comet of 1682, noting that they were similar to those of records of the comets seen in 1531 and 1607. Could they be the same comet? He thought so, and predicted that it would return in 1759. As the time approached, astronomers all over the world waited eagerly. It duly appeared, although Halley did not live to see it. In 1910 it was a wonderful sight, its tail being over 80 million kilometres (50 million miles) long.

The Earth has been struck by a comet in recent times. In June 1908 a gigantic explosion erupted in the middle of a vast forest in Siberia. Trees were blown over for distances up to 48 kilometres (30 miles) from the

Solar radiation causes a comet's tail to point away from the Sun at all points in its orbit.

blast. Windows were broken up to 160 kilometres (100 miles) away. A startled engine driver on the Trans-Siberian Railway 640 kilometres (400 miles) away, braked fiercely to a halt as the track heaved in front of him as if disturbed by an earthquake. Pressure waves from the explosion affected barometers in England.

The cause of the explosion remained a mystery for over fifty years. The most popular theory was that the Earth had been hit by a large meteorite, but although many searches were made, no crater was found, nor were any meteoric fragments. This caused some people to suggest that the blast was a nuclear explosion caused by the crashing of a spaceship from another star.

The mystery was solved in 1960 when the Soviet Academy of Sciences conducted a thorough survey. The explosion, the Academy reported, was caused by a comet, probably several kilometres in diameter and weighing about a million tons. This is very small and light—about a millionth of the weight of most comets. Earth was lucky.

Meteors

Meteors are responsible for the 'shooting stars' which are often seen in the night sky. They are, however, nothing to do with stars. They are simply tiny pieces of rock speeding through space, and being burnt up by friction when they hurtle into the Earth's atmosphere at speeds of up to 72 kilometres (45 miles) a second.

The vast majority of meteors are no bigger than a single grain of sand. This is fortunate, because it has been estimated that about 100 thousand million of them strike the atmosphere each day. Although individually light, the accumulated total of this vast number of meteors has been estimated to amount to over two million tons a year, falling to the surface as a fine dust. It is strange to think that the flowers in your garden are growing in a mixture of 'star dust'.

Where do meteors come from? Some seem to be debris resulting from the grinding together of asteroids as they orbit endlessly round the Sun. Most of them, however, seem to be the remains of disintegrated comets.

Meteors appear to travel in groups or clouds, and when the Earth passes through such an accumulation, the number of 'shooting stars' increases dramatically.

Some meteors are slightly larger and these cause spectacular fire balls when

Exploding meteor.

they strike the atmosphere. A small number, known as bolides, explode fiercely upon entry.

Meteorites

Every year about 1,500 meteors are so big that they do not burn up in the atmosphere, but survive to strike the surface of the Earth. These are known as meteorites. Often the meteorite breaks up before reaching the ground, scattering its fragments far and wide. Meteorites are thus relatively rare, and as over three-quarters of the Earth's surface is water, only a few strike dry land.

Meteorites are of particular interest to astronomers and are tracked by radio telescopes to give information about light and radio waves.

Really large meteorites are estimated to strike the Earth about once every 10,000 years. When they do, they sink deep into the crust and then explode with the force of an atom bomb. This creates a huge mound known as an astrobleme, that is a 'star-scar'. Many astroblemes have been drilled and found to be full of meteoric rubble. However, there is usually little or no trace of the meteorite itself, as these usually vaporise on impact.

There is little doubt that, but for the protective screen of the atmosphere and the levelling force of erosion, the Earth would be as pock-marked as Mercury and Mars.

In South Africa, there is a meteorite weighing 60 tons, and one in Greenland weighing 36 tons. The most famous meteoric crater is one in Arizona, in the United States. This is over a kilometre in diameter and 180 metres (600 feet) deep. The meteorite responsible, which landed in prehistoric times, is estimated to have weighed about 50,000 tons. In spite of numerous bore holes no trace of the meteorite has been found, and it is assumed to have exploded on impact.

The biggest known meteorite is estimated to have been about 160 kilometres (100 miles) in diameter and to

Some of the larger meteorites weigh many tons.

have weighed many millions of tons. The explosion on impact was enormous, and shook the entire body of the Moon where it landed. The vast hole it left is known as the Imbrium Crater. Evidence of this momentous event is a circular ring of mountains, some of them over 20,000 feet high. The outer rings are more than 1,600 kilometres (1,000 miles) in diameter. Immediately after the explosion the crater was probably 160 kilometres (100 miles) deep, but with the passage of time, the sides have crumbled inwards while other material has risen from below.

Meteorites are of particular interest to astronomers. All astronomical knowledge comes to us in the form of light waves and radio waves. By studying

The meteoric crater at Arizona in the United States is over a kilometre in diameter.

these waves astronomers deduce what has existed millions of kilometres away and what has happened in the remote past. But all their evidence is based on light and radio waves. Supposing interstellar gravitational forces do affect these waves in a manner not yet understood, the universe could be very different from the one thought to exist now.

Meteorites, the debris of outer space, however, can be physically studied in a laboratory. It has been found that they can be divided into three main classes: the stones, known as aerolites, the irons, known as siderites, and a mixture of both, known as siderolites.

The majority of meteorites are aerolites, and they are not very different from the rocks making up the crust of the Earth. Iron meteorites, the siderites, live up to their name, being almost solid iron with some nickel. Only a few meteorites are siderolites, that is, a mixture of both stone and iron. Significantly, no unknown substance has ever been found in a meteorite.

It is, perhaps, natural to wonder if meteorites contain any evidence of life, and from that point wonder if the original germs of living matter were brought to the Earth inside a meteorite.

Every now and again an announcement is made that the remains of a fossil has been found in a meteorite, but so far, further study has shown that the fossils are not organic at all, but ordinary crystals. It has also been claimed that evidence of microbes has been found in meteorites.

Tektites

Tektite is the name given to unusual lozenge-like pebbles which have arrived on Earth from space. However, unlike normal meteorites, these do not appear to have come from outer space. Only found in certain areas of the world, mainly in Australasia, there is strong evidence that these tektites came from the Moon. It appears that a meteorite the size of a small mountain hit the Moon about 700,000 years ago. The resultant explosion caused the 96 kilometre-wide (60-mile), 14 kilometre-deep (nine-mile) crater called Tycho, and shot an immense plume of rock and debris into space—straight towards the Earth.

It is strange to think that NASA sent astronauts to the Moon to collect Moon rock, when some scientists think that there is 100 million *tons* of it on the Earth already.

Man in Space

'I saw for the first time the Earth's spherical shape. You can see its curvature when looking at the horizon. The view of the horizon is strange and very beautiful. You can see the impressive transition from the bright surface of the Earth to the completely black sky in which you can see the stars. The range of transition is a thin one, like a film or narrow belt girdling the globe. It is a soft light-blue colour, and the entire transition from blue to black is smooth and beautiful.'

Thus cosmonaut Yuri Gagarin reported his first-hand observations from space, after his historic orbit in the spacecraft Vostok 1 on 12th April 1961. It is difficult to believe that this first flight into space was made less than four years after the first artificial satellite of all, Sputnik 1, was launched.

The twentieth century may be remembered for many things, such as its disastrous wars, its energy crisis, or the development of nuclear power. But in the history books of the far future it will undoubtedly be recorded primarily as the century when mankind took its first faltering steps into space.

Gagarin was soon followed by other brave men. In August, 1961, the Russian cosmonaut Titov became the first man to spend a whole day in space. In February 1962, John Glenn became the first American to orbit the Earth when he made three exciting circuits in the Mercury spacecraft *Friendship 7*. The figure 7 was included in the name in honour of the original United States team of seven pioneering astronauts.

A notable feature of the American flight was the completely open manner in which it was conducted. Technical details of the complicated countdown procedure before lift-off were relayed by television and radio to technicians, newsmen and ordinary people all over the world. Russian launchings on the other hand were notable for their extreme secrecy.

This open approach has been a feature of all the American manned spacecraft missions, enabling people not only to share in the excitement— and the moments of danger—of these pioneering voyages of exploration into space, but also to assess the degree of success achieved, and the value of the scientific experiments performed.

Other cosmonauts and astronauts followed Gagarin, Titov and Glenn.

In August 1962 the cosmonaut Popovich was launched into orbit in Vostok 4 while his colleague Nikolayev was also in space in Vostok 3. In June 1963 the Russian girl Valentina Tereschkova proved that women could undertake the rigorous training required for flights into space as well as men. While orbiting in Vostok 6 she passed close by another cosmonaut, Bykovsky, who had been launched into orbit in Vostok 5 two days previously. In October 1964 the first multicrew spaceship, Russia's Voskhod 1, was launched carrying a crew of three.

In these early days each flight into space made headline news in most of the newspapers of the world. A notable exception was China, where the people remained ignorant even of the American manned landings on the Moon, until years after those historic explorations of a new world.

A Walk in Space

One event in this era of space news that made even larger headlines occurred in March 1965. In that month, while in orbit in the spacecraft Voskhod II, cosmonaut Leonov opened the hatch and stepped out into the vacuum and cold of outer space. Then, for a few historic minutes, while tethered

The lonely Martian landscape with the Viking Lander shown taking soil samples.

to the spacecraft by a slender lifeline, he 'walked' in space while speeding round the Earth at 29,000 kilometres (18,000 miles) an hour. He was not, however, conscious of the tremendous speed. On the contrary, the Earth, largely covered by clouds, seemed to drift by quite lazily. This event, while demonstrating the bravery of the cosmonaut, was also important technically as it demonstrated that man, suitably protected, could work in space in much the same way as divers can work on the seabed. At that time, however, few men would have believed that within eight years, successive teams of astronauts would be working feverishly in space to repair a space station as big as a house.

Meanwhile, American astronauts had progressed from the tiny, cramped, one-man Mercury capsules to the much bigger two-man Gemini spacecraft. During the Gemini programme ten missions were made, each taking the art of astronautics one step further.

During the Gemini 4 flight, in June 1965, Edward White emulated Leonov's exploit and made a walk in space. While out for his 'walk' in space, White experimented with a 'self-manoeuvring unit'. This directed tiny spurts of gas when a trigger was pressed, the reaction propelling the astronaut gently along. The degree of control was quite good, and provided confidence for the development of more advanced units in the future that would assist the construction and assembling of large structures in space.

In December 1965 Gemini 6, crewed by astronauts Walter Schirra and Thomas Stafford, successfully rendezvoused in space with Gemini 7 which, piloted by Frank Borman and James Lovell, had been launched into orbit eleven days previously.

Successful docking experiments were conducted with Gemini 10, launched in July 1966 and Gemini 11, launched in September 1966. In these tests, the two-man spacecraft docked with special Agena targets launched into space for this purpose.

Space Casualties

The manned exploration of space has not been carried out without some casualties. Mercifully these have perhaps been far fewer than might have been expected, in view of the serious hazards involved.

The first casualty was Komarov. After testing the first of the new Russian Soyuz manned spacecraft, Komarov began the re-entry through the atmosphere. This tricky manoeuvre was carried out without any trouble until almost the last moment. Having safely slowed down from the high orbital speed and only a few miles above the surface of the Earth, the landing parachutes did not open properly and Komarov plummetted like a stone to his death.

There were other Russian casualties during the testing of their Salyut space station. Launched into orbit in April 1971, the space station was approached by Soyuz 10 which docked with it for a short time. Soyuz 11, launched on 6th June, docked with the station on 7th June, after which the crew of three, Dobrovolski, Volkov and Patseyev, entered the station. On board, the cosmonauts conducted a series of experiments. Then, after twenty-four days in space, a record at that time, the crew left Salyut and climbed back into Soyuz 11 to get home. Unfortunately, a hatch seal failed to work properly and the air leaked out rapidly, so that the cosmonauts were dead when the heat-scarred spacecraft was recovered after making an automatic landing in the middle of the Russian steppes at Kazakhstan.

Lucian in A.D. 200 described a journey in a sailing vessel which was caught up in a whirlwind and carried him to the Moon.

This solution is, of course, not feasible, as the initial shock would kill any passengers and wreck all instruments, and air friction would burn up the projectile within seconds of its leaving the barrel. Apart from this point, the inadequacy of which Verne was fully aware, the story is based on scientific principles.

Konstantin Tsiolkovsky

Perhaps the greatest dreamer of all was a Russian schoolmaster named Konstantin Tsiolkovsky. Born in 1857, Tsiolkovsky became deeply interested in the problems of space travel at an early age. He soon realised that rockets provided the means of escaping from the Earth, thus becoming one of the first men to do so. By 1898 he had formulated the fundamental mathematical laws of rocket motion, upon which the design of all space vehicles is based. In 1903, the year that the Wright Brothers made their historic first flight in a powered aircraft, he published the results of his main research on rocket fuels and rocket motor efficiency and thus laid the foundations of astronautics.

At a time when some learned scientists were debating whether men

Early Experiments

The powerful engines used to launch satellites into space, probes to the planets, and men to the Moon, are the result of hundreds of years of research and development.

Rockets were used in China over 700 years ago, when the defenders of the city of Pieping astounded invading Mongols in A.D. 1232 with a barrage of these fiery weapons. Since then,

East during the Arab-Israeli war of 1973.

All the early military rockets were of the solid propellant firework type. A more powerful rocket was needed, however, to get men into space.

Before the experiments and rockets, however, there came the dreamers. One dreamer who has deservedly survived the passage of time is Jules Verne, who published his book *From the Earth to the Moon* in 1865. Verne

In the 1920s another pioneer, Fritz von Opel, used the rocket to propel both his cars and aircraft with astounding success. He pointed the way to the rocket-powered aircraft that were seen during the latter part of the Second World War.

rockets have played an increasingly important part in war. During the siege of Copenhagen in 1807 25,000 Congreve missiles were fired. Rockets played a major part in the defeat of the United States forces in Vietnam in the 1960s, and dramatically altered the balance of power in the Middle

was an engineer, and his story is a semi-scientific description of a voyage to the Moon. The major task was, of course, to attain the very high speed needed to escape from the Earth. To achieve this, Verne describes the construction of a gigantic gun, sunk like a missile silo, vertically in the ground.

could fly—notwithstanding the Wright Brothers' achievement—Tsiolkovsky was writing about satellites, solar energy, space suits, the use of plants to provide food and oxygen on extended space voyages, and on the suitability of liquid hydrogen and liquid oxygen as propellants. His breadth of vision extended from the problems and prospects of the colonisation of the solar system to the problem of having baths in conditions of zero gravity. Tsiolkovsky died in 1935, a national hero in his homeland, but relatively unknown to the world outside.

Robert Goddard

Another early dreamer, who became one of the first great experimenters, was Robert Goddard, a young American physics professor. Born in Worcester, Massachusetts in 1882, Goddard's interest in the heavens became a passion when, as a boy of seventeen, he climbed a cherry tree to trim some dead branches. While up the tree Goddard thought how wonderful it would be to invent a

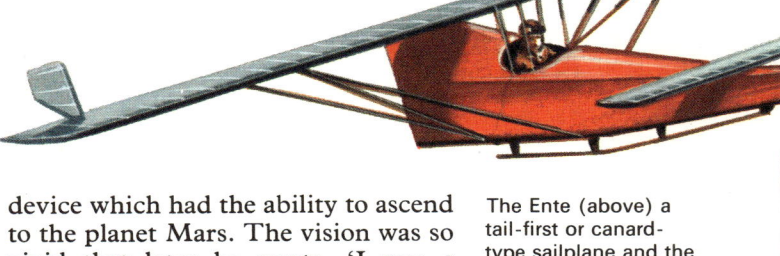

device which had the ability to ascend to the planet Mars. The vision was so vivid that later he wrote, 'I was a different boy when I descended from the tree.'

Later that year Goddard made several wooden models in which lead weights were to furnish lift by moving back and forth in vertical arcs, or by striking against metal pieces as they whirled around horizontal axes.

These experiments naturally produced negative results— but served the purpose of convincing Goddard that there might, after all, be something about Newton's Laws of Motion!

Gradually he realised that, if a way to navigate in space were to be discovered or invented, it would be the result of a knowledge of physics and mathematics. Graduating from high school, Goddard began making a neat set of notes on a wide variety of related subjects, ranging from the mass of explosive required to raise a given weight great heights to oxygen rockets; and from the use of solar energy for electrostatic repulsion to plans to send a camera round distant planets.

In 1916, with the aid of a $5,000 grant from the Smithsonian Institute, Goddard began to turn his dreams into reality, and began making small test rockets.

In 1919 the Smithsonian Institute published a slim pamphlet by Goddard entitled *A Method of Reaching Extreme*

The Ente (above) a tail-first or canard-type sailplane and the first successful rocket-powered aircraft.

Robert Goddard during the early 1920s pioneered the liquid-fuelled rocket we know today. Even when scorn was poured on him, he, together with a handful of assistants, continued his researches to perfect and establish the true stable rocket vehicle. The picture shows his 1926 rocket.

Altitudes, describing what today would be called an instrumented meteorological sounding rocket. It is unlikely that such a technical treatise would have attracted much attention. But at the end of it Goddard stated that the principle of rocket propulsion could be used to land a charge of magnesium on the Moon bright enough to be visible to telescopes on the Earth.

This attracted the interest of several newspapers and Goddard was ridiculed. The influential *New York Times* solemnly declared that Goddard was 'lacking the knowledge daily ladled out in high schools.'

Undeterred, Goddard continued his experiments. Men had, of course, been making rockets for many hundreds of years. But during this time the principles remained substantially unchanged. Gunpowder was packed into a hollow tube and when ignited the hot gases exhausted through a nozzle. Goddard significantly improved the performance of this 'fire-work' type of rocket by developing special nozzles.

These experiments, however, soon led to the conclusion that liquid fuels such as propane and oxygen would be more suitable, as theoretically they were capable of producing much more thrust. Also the thrust could be controlled or shut off at will; a solid rocket, on the other hand, once ignited burned until exhausted.

By 1923 Goddard had constructed a small rocket in which the liquid oxygen and petrol were fed by pumps. The rocket was successfully test fired on a proving stand, but was not launched in free flight. After further experiments a second rocket was constructed. This employed a nitrogen pressure feed system for the propellants.

In 1926 Goddard completed his latest rocket. It was a spidery contraption, with the combustion chamber mounted over and in front of the fuel tanks which were protected by a conical shield, bearing little resemblance to a modern rocket. However, when on 16th March 1926 it covered 56 metres (184 feet) in $2\frac{1}{2}$ seconds, it made history as the first liquid propellant rocket in the world to fly.

Goddard went on to make many other rockets, using methods and materials—a child's wrist watch, a length of piano wire, a car sparking plug—that would astound present-day engineers. His last rocket, built in 1940, embodied all the features of a modern rocket—and was almost identical, except in size, to the rocket known as the V–2 which the Germans were to produce three years later. One rocket expert later declared, 'Every liquid-fuel rocket that flies is a Goddard rocket.'

Hermann Oberth

Another early dreamer is Hermann Oberth, who in 1929 published a book entitled *The Way to Space Travel.* This is undoubtedly one of the great books on the subject. It described in remarkable detail all the fundamental

The Rheintochter (Daughter of the Rhine), a two-stage solid propellent anti-aircraft missile with a range of 40 kilometres (25 miles) developed by German rocket engineers during the Second World War.

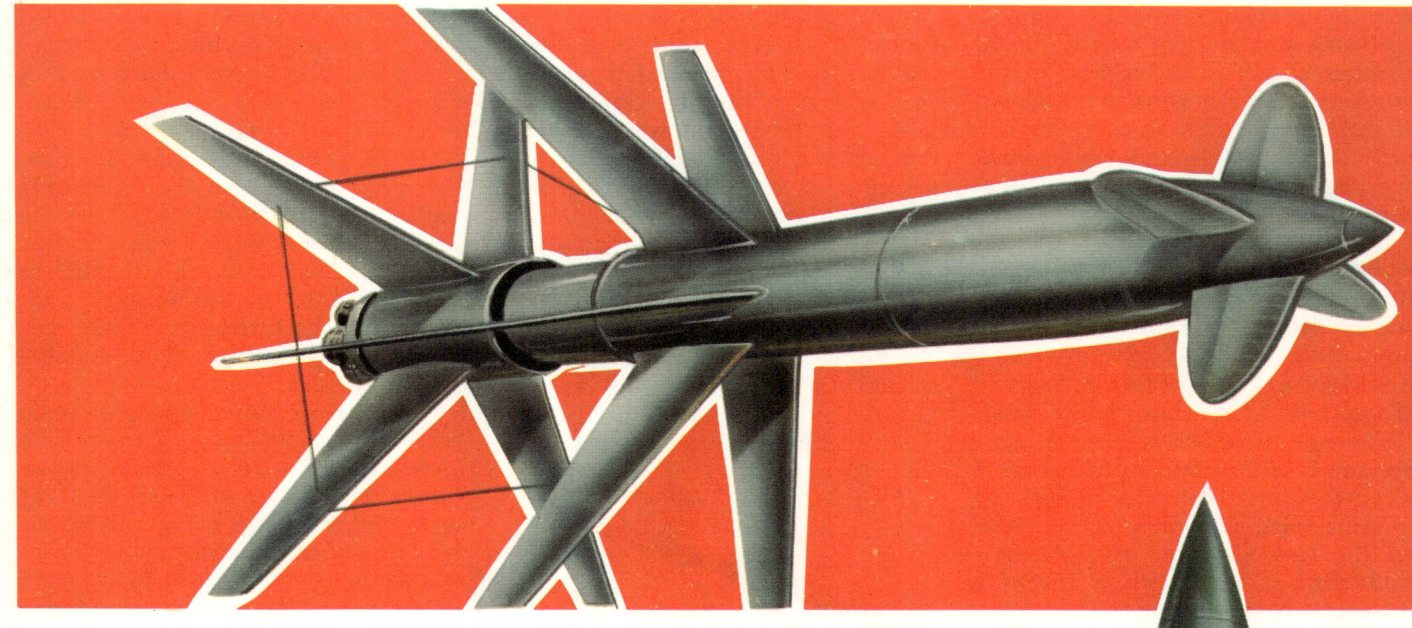

The V-2 rocket, the first ballistic heavy rocket to be used during wartime, had a tremendous influence on future rocket engineering.

problems of space flight, covering not only the mathematical aspects, but the engineering side of the subject as well. All this at a time when the biggest rocket ever built weighed only a few kilos.

The book attracted great interest, particularly in Germany. It resulted in many more theoretical studies and, of more importance, much practical experimentation. Rocket societies sprang up everywhere. Two of the most important and enduring were the *Society for Space Travel* formed in Germany in 1927 and the *British Interplanetary Society* in Britain.

Members of the *British Interplanetary Society* soon discovered that the difficulties in overcoming the legal problems regarding the manufacture and testing of explosive devices were even more daunting than the technicalities. Their German counterparts met with less official resistance and were much more successful. Students and young engineers with little money but much enthusiasm started to design and build rockets.

By 1930 membership of the German Society had reached about 1,000. Using a stretch of land at Reinickendorf, a suburb of Berlin, a number of liquid propellant Mirak and Repulsor rockets were made and fired with varying degrees of success.

Some of these early experiments were not without their moments of excitement. One Repulsor took off, hit the roof of the firing shelter and roared up at an angle of 70 degrees. After climbing for a few seconds, it

began to loop, spilled its motor cooling water, and then came down in a power dive. Due to the loss of the cooling water, the combustion chamber burned through, and with the resultant side thrust, the Repulsor careered around like a Catherine-wheel. Fortunately for the watching members of the Society, the fuel quickly ran out and the rocket crashed harmlessly.

Wernher von Braun
This period was one of political unrest in Germany and in 1933 Hitler came to power. After a demonstration of a Repulsor rocket, German officials realised that rockets that could carry instruments could also carry warheads. Accordingly, a secret research establishment was set up on the remote island of Peenemunde.

At about this time the German Space Travel Society collapsed suddenly, its demise ending all large-scale private research work in Europe.

Development, however, continued apace at Peenemunde. In charge was an enthusiastic former member of the German Society, a young student named Wernher von Braun. This work led first, during the Second World War, to the development of the large 25,000 kilogram (56,000 pound) thrust V–2 bombardment rocket, and then in the following years of peace, to the development of the massive multi-million-pound thrust Saturn launch vehicles which boosted America's Apollo spacecraft to the Moon.

Satellites at Work

Since Russia launched Sputnik 1 on 4th October 1957, the manner in which artificial satellites have been put to work has been remarkable. A month later Sputnik 2 was launched, carrying the dog Laika, thereby laying an early stepping stone towards mankind's historic giant leap on the Moon in July, 1969.

In January 1958 America launched her Explorer 1. This was the first of a long series of scientific satellites designed to explore the near space environment around the Earth.

For example, Explorer 51 launched in December 1973 is being used for a global study of Earth's outer atmosphere. It is surveying the area between 110 to 190 kilometres (70 to 120 miles) altitude where important energy transfer, atomic and molecular processes and chemical reactions occur that are critical to the heat balance of the atmosphere.

Several Explorer satellites have been launched as a special series of spacecraft intended to investigate in detail a particular aspect of the Earth's space environment. For example, ten Explorer satellites, the last one being Explorer 50, launched in October 1973, were known as IMPs, or Interplanetary Monitoring Platforms. They are studying and monitoring the plasmas, magnetic fields and energetic particle populations of interplanetary space, and have provided the first accurate measurements of the interplanetary magnetic field, the magnetosphere boundary, and the shockwave associated with the interaction of the geomagnetic field and solar wind. During the American Apollo manned landings on the Moon and the Skylab programme, IMP spacecraft provided warning of possible solar flare radiation events to the astronauts.

Six OGO (Orbiting Geophysical Observatory) spacecraft were launched between 1964 and 1969, three into polar orbits and three into highly elliptical orbits with apogees (that part of the orbit furthest from the Earth) of around 160,000 kilometres (100,000 miles).

The Earth's Environment

Resembling giant insects, because of their numerous antennae and booms, these spacecraft studied the relationship between the Sun and the nature of the Earth's environment during a period of increased solar activity. Because a detailed scientific picture of the Earth's environment continually changes, information from several satellites was required to help scientists to distinguish changes due to time from changes due to position. OGO satellites have provided new knowledge concerning the magnetospheric boundary, the transition region, the bow shockwave, the magnetosphere tail, the aureol regions, and the upper atmosphere.

The most important feature of the OGO series was the high rate at which information was transmitted, providing scientists with a 'moving picture' of the Earth's environment. Previous results from smaller satellites sent back the equivalent of 'snapshot' views.

Specially designed to investigate and study the Sun, is a series of OSO (Orbiting Solar Observatory) spacecraft. The Sun is the source of most energy for life on Earth. Only by viewing the Sun from above the Earth's energy-absorbing atmosphere can scientists get a truly sharp view of this nearby star and learn more about its influence on Earth.

Knowledge gained from the OSOs is aiding scientists in their search for an unlimited and pollution-free power source on Earth. The extremely hot plasma existing in the solar atmospheric phenomena seems to be the source of the generation of nuclear fusion energy. In research to develop a pollution-free power source, the primary problem encountered in laboratory studies of controlled nuclear fusion is the producing and controlling of an extremely hot plasma. The sun can achieve this and scientists hope to learn how.

Variations in the Sun's output of energy can drastically change the Earth's ionosphere and cause geomagnetic storms. These upper atmos-

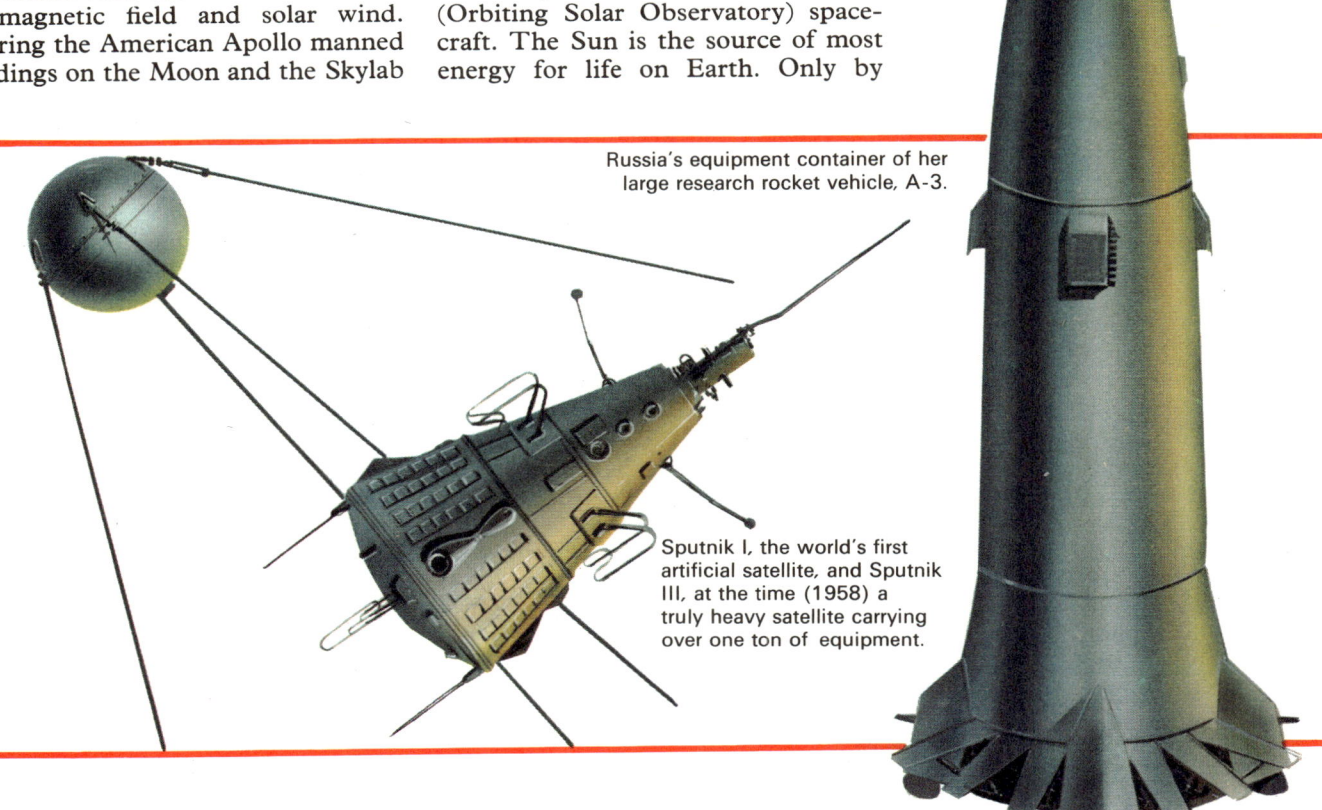

Russia's equipment container of her large research rocket vehicle, A-3.

Sputnik I, the world's first artificial satellite, and Sputnik III, at the time (1958) a truly heavy satellite carrying over one ton of equipment.

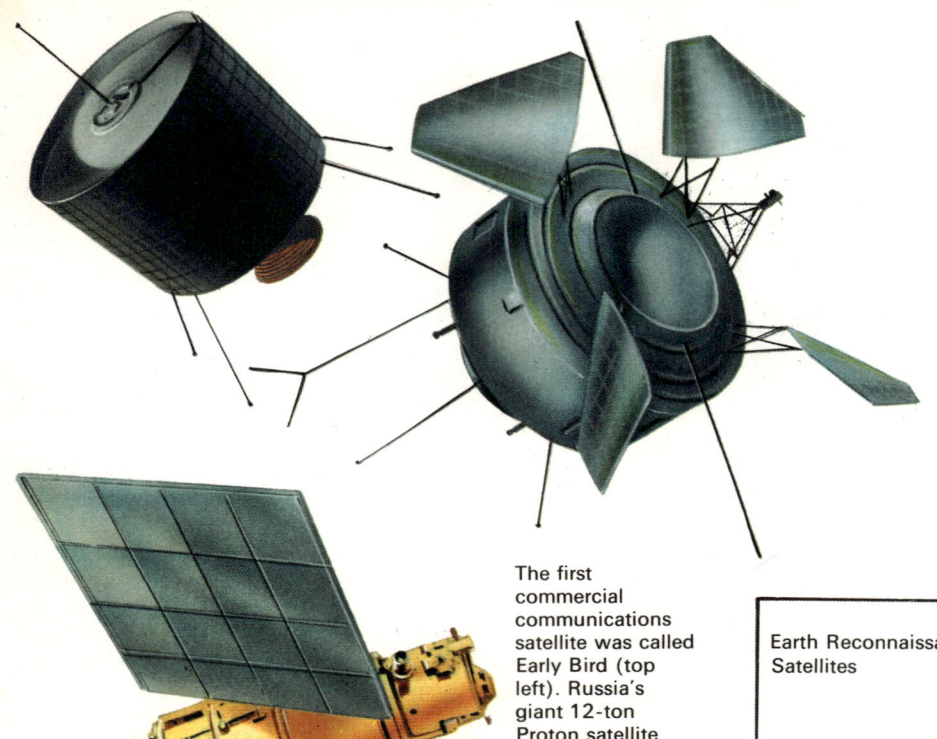

The first commercial communications satellite was called Early Bird (top left). Russia's giant 12-ton Proton satellite (top right). Russian Cosmos meteorological satellite (left).

mitted to ground bases. Their orbit takes them within range of every point on the Earth twice in each period of 24 hours.

Although one can feel sad that some satellite technology should be devoted to such devices, it is undoubtedly necessary in view of the present immature state of world social development. In the same way that policemen work to prevent crime, reconnaissance satellites are working to help preserve world peace. There can surely be no more important work in this age of nuclear armed missles.

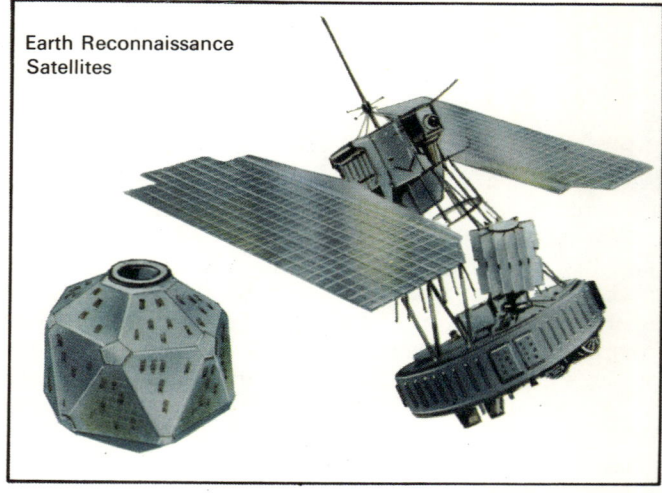

Earth Reconnaissance Satellites

pheric changes can wipe out shortwave radio communications for periods up to many hours. Solar energy impinging upon the Earth's lower atmosphere and surface also cause the wind pressure circulation patterns which move the complicated weather systems around the globe.

In addition to its importance to and influence on Earth and human life, the Sun provides man with his only opportunity to study a star at close range. It is 50 billion kilometres (30 billion miles) closer to Earth than the next nearest star.

Scientists are able to observe the solar disc and study single features such as solar flares and sunspots. It is considered that an understanding of solar physics is indispensable to the understanding of the physics of Earth. Solar flare observations have so far, in fact, taught scientists more about plasma physics that can be applied on Earth than about the mysteries of what constitutes a solar flare.

Cosmos Satellites

Russia too has a large programme of scientific satellites. Launched under the name of Cosmos, of which there are now over 600, these investigate the upper layers of the atmosphere and outer space, including detailed studies on subjects such as the concentration of charged particles in the

ionosphere for the purpose of investigating the propagation of radio waves; or the energy composition of the Earth's radiation belts for further evaluating the radiation danger in prolonged space flights; and on the distribution and formation of cloud patterns in the Earth's atmosphere, to improve weather forecasting. In addition Cosmos satellites are used to evaluate and refine many details of spacecraft construction.

The name Cosmos is also given to a large number of spy reconnaissance and other types of military spacecraft launched secretly by the Soviet Union. The reconnaissance satellites stay in orbit for about a week and then, presumably having exposed all their film, re-enter the atmosphere and are recovered. America too launches reconnaissance satellites to help keep an eye on what is going on in the vast inner land areas of Russia. Nicknamed *Big Bird*, these weigh over 12 tons, and carry cameras with telescopic lenses that are thought to be capable of photographing an object on the surface of the Earth as small as a motor car. It is believed that on these big satellites the photographs are processed in orbit and then trans-

Weather Satellites

The benefits from scientific satellites are not always either immediate or apparent. The work of several types of satellite, however, is already contributing to enhancing our everyday living. Foremost among these are the weather satellites.

Every day millions of decisions are made regarding the weather. Most of these are simple decisions such as when to hang out the washing or when to go out without a raincoat. Some are of much greater importance and include such decisions as whether to reap a crop today or tomorrow, or to make a major power cut. A few are vital, such as the necessity for a ship to return to port because of an approaching storm, or that people should be evacuated from a particular area in the path of a typhoon.

The need for accurate weather forecasts is thus of great importance. For a typical 24-hour European forecast, accurate observations are needed throughout most of the northern hemisphere, and in particular the area extending from Iceland to the Mediterranean, and from America to Central Europe. The longer-range

The Mercury Freedom 7 spacecraft in which, during May 1961, Commander Alan Shepard became the first American astronaut.

the forecast, the bigger the area that has to be surveyed. Thus, it is not surprising that one of the first purposes for which satellites were set to work was weather forecasting.

The first experimental weather satellite was Tiros 1. Launched by America in April 1960, this embodied two TV cameras, one with a wide-angle lens taking pictures covering a 1,300-kilometre (800-mile) square, and the other having a narrow angle lens covering a 130-kilometre (80-mile) square area in greater detail.

The first pictures gave meteorologists an overall view of the weather they had not previously seen and transformed the art of meteorology. Cloud systems were seen to be much more highly organised than previously supposed. One particular formation could be directly linked with another system thousands of kilometres away. One series of pictures showed a gigantic cyclonic formation 3,200 kilometres (2,000 miles) across, a phenomenon never before observed. When the batteries of Tiros 1 failed after 78 days, over 22,000 photographs had been sent back.

Tiros 1 was followed by nine other Tiros and nine ESSA weather satellites. These proved their value to meteorologists, and in turn have been followed by Improved Tiros Operational Satellites (ITOS).

Mapping the Earth

These second generation satellites represent a significant improvement over their predecessors in that they are capable of mapping the Earth's cloud cover at night as well as by day. A complete picture of the world is thus possible in twelve hours rather than once a day.

Picture equipment includes two advanced vidicon cameras, with tape storage, and two automatic picture transmission (APT) cameras. Data from the APT cameras are picked up by over 500 relatively simple APT ground receiving stations located in fifty countries. ITOS satellites are launched by NASA but, once in orbit, they are handed over to the United States National Oceanic and Atmosphere Administration and are then known as NOAA spacecraft.

At times these weather satellites prove their value dramatically. In August 1969, an ESSA satellite spotted the fierce Hurricane Camille heading from the United States Gulf Coast. Immediately the areas likely to be affected were evacuated, and afterwards the authorities estimated that 50,000 people would have perished if the warnings had not been received.

It is not really possible to put a monetary value on human life but compensation of up to £100,000 has been paid for people killed in motor car or aircraft accidents. If this value is put on the lives saved from the Hurricane Camille the total is £5,000 million—many, many times the cost of the weather satellites.

A world map showing the flight path of Yuri Gagarin. The lift-off was from Baikonur and after his single orbit Gagarin landed in a field close to the Russian village of Saratov.

World Meteorological Service

Russia too has developed a series of meteorological satellites. Given the name Meteor, these provide information about the state of the atmosphere both on the 'day' and 'night' sides of the Earth. Information received from Meteors is supplied to the Soviet hydro-meteorological service and to the World Meteorological Organisation. Cloud cover picture charts are transmitted to Washington, Geneva, Tokyo, Sydney and other foreign weather stations.

Another major step forward in the advance of weather forecasting was marked by the launching in May 1974 of SMS–1, the world's first synchronous meteorological satellite.

From its lofty perch 35,000 kilometres (22,000 miles) above the equator just off the coast of Brazil, this satellite can scan about 45% of the globe, compared with the 3% of a normal weather satellite in a 320-kilometre (200-mile) orbit.

The basic payload is a telescope called the Visible Spin-Scan Radiometer providing both infra-red and high resolution visible photography. Full disc pictures are being transmitted every thirty minutes. In addition to its main task of weather surveillance, the spacecraft is acting as the orbital compartment of the Geostationary Operational Environmental Satellite system planned by NASA, NOAA and the United States Department of Commerce. In this role, the satellite will receive data from up to 10,000 data-collection platforms spread around the United States on land, in rivers and lakes and aboard ships and buoys at sea.

The platforms are small environmental sensing stations that collect information and transmit it through the satellite, first to the Command and Data Acquisition Station and then on to NOAA's Data Processing Facility. Most are small, unmanned platforms, although those on ships are, of course, manned. Information collected is meteorological, hydrological, oceanographic, seismic and tsunami. For example, fixed platforms in remote land areas will send information on earthquakes, wind direction and velocity, rainfalls and humidity. River platforms will measure currents, water levels and temperatures. Platforms at sea will measure tides, water temperatures and air temperatures and give tsunami warnings.

The United States and Soviet linking experiment using components of the standard boosters of both nations, but carrying laboratories suitably modified so as to enable them to fit together in orbit and allow crews to move through to each unit.

Below: The first rendezvous in space on 15th December 1965, when Frank Borman and James Lovell orbited the Earth together with Walter Schirra and Thomas Stafford in a similar Gemini spacecraft, proving that when the two craft were within less than a metre of each other, the joining of two spaceships was possible.

A New Ice Age?

There is some evidence that the average temperature of the world has dropped slightly. If this is true it could mean that the Earth is heading towards another ice age at what is, geologically speaking, an alarming

A composite picture showing various types of Molabs (mobile laboratories) operating on the Moon's surface.

rate. If this is so, the effect would be catastrophic. Long before thick sheets of ice spread south to cover much land that currently is heavily populated, the world's harvests would drop dramatically, causing starvation on a scale not before experienced in the long history of the world. It may be, however, that the cooling is only temporary.

To obtain more information, so that the trend can be assessed more accurately, seventy nations co-operated in 1974 in a massive study of world-wide weather as part of a big international scientific study into influences on the Earth's climate. This was known as the Global Atmospheric Research Programme (GARP).

Spearheading GARP was SMS–1 and its twin SMS–2, located over the Pacific, which are working in conjunction with three other synchronous satellites and one or two near-Earth satellites in polar-orbits.

Towards the end of the 1970s, the European Space Research Organisation (ESRO), Japan and the Soviet Union are expected to join the United States in providing additional meteorological satellites in synchronous orbit. The spacecraft will be about 70° apart, spaced evenly around the world. The U.S. satellite will cover the western hemisphere; ESRO's satellite will observe Europe, the Near East and Africa; the U.S.S.R. spacecraft will cover the Soviet Union and other parts of Asia and India; the Japanese craft will complete the coverage by looking after the Far East and the Western Pacific Ocean.

These five satellites will be working to provide information that could be of vital importance to our children, if not to ourselves.

Communications Satellites

Another field in which satellites are being used extensively is that of communications. In fact, an entire industry has grown out of research for and the development of communications satellites. Progress in this field has dramatically reduced the cost of a single telephone channel across the Atlantic.

The first experimental communications satellite was launched in December 1958. Known as Score Atlas, it carried a tiny tape recorder, and while in orbit broadcast a Christmas message from President Eisenhower. Most famous of the early communications satellites, however, was Telstar, which was used for a series of exciting test television programmes across the Atlantic in July 1962.

Telstar had one big drawback. Because television signals travel in straight lines, it could only be used while it was in view simultaneously to the transmitting and receiving stations on both side of the Atlantic. When it was 'below' the horizon it could not be used.

The higher the orbit, the longer a satellite remains visible, and the Russians place their Molniya communications satellites in highly elliptical orbits that takes their high point 40,000 kilometres (24,800 miles) above the Earth. In this way they can transmit messages for eight hours during each orbit.

Most communications satellites today, however, are in synchronous or stationary orbits, 35,888 kilometres (22,300 miles) up. At this altitude they take a day to complete an orbit and thus, keeping pace with the rotation of the Earth, appear to remain motionless in the sky above a particular spot, so can be used continuously.

The first commercial communications satellite, that is, the first one intended for everyday business telephone calls, newspaper reports and television programmes was launched in April 1965. Known as Early Bird, this could handle 240 telephone conversations at once.

Intelsat

Development since then has been rapid. Today, Intelsat spacecraft, in synchronous orbits, provide a global service and are able to carry 6,000 two-way telephone calls or transmit twelve colour television broadcasts simultaneously. The spacecraft are operated by the International Telecommunications Satellite Consortium (Intelsat).

Pointing the way to even more advanced communications satellites are those being launched in NASA's Applications Technology Satellite (ATS) programme. The programme involves launching satellites which provide both commercial service and scientific information.

ATS–1, launched in December 1966 into a synchronous orbit, was manoeuvred into position over the Pacific Ocean. In addition to scientific experiments, this satellite was used to relay a number of special television events, such as Canada's EXPO 67, to demonstrate its capabilities. During an Alaskan flood in 1967, the satellite was used to relay emergency communications between Alaska and Government agencies below the border, saving many lives and millions of dollars. The satellite is currently being used for primary and secondary educational broadcasting to Alaska and the Pacific Ocean.

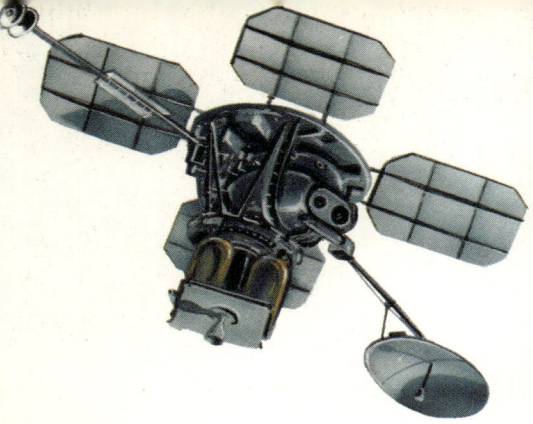

The Lunar Orbiter spacecraft together with four others surveyed and photographed over 99% of the Moon's surface in preparation for the manned landings.

The launch vehicle for ATS–2 unfortunately malfunctioned, but ATS–3 was successfully launched into a synchronous orbit in November 1967, and subsequently stationed over the Atlantic Ocean.

This satellite was used for the first ground-to-spacecraft-to-aircraft communications link over the Atlantic. This historic event took place in November 1967 during a Pan American flight from New York to London. The communications engineer aboard the aircraft was able to speak to both airline officials in New York and NASA officials in the Goddard Space Flight Centre. Other calls were made to officials in London, Hamburg and Buenos Aires. ATS–3 is, however, perhaps best remembered for sending back the first really clear colour photographs of the complete earth. The satellite has also been used in a series of maritime experiments involving both the location of ships and ship-to-shore communications, demonstrating that such spacecraft can assist major improvements in the management of shipping fleets.

ATS–4, like ATS–2, unfortunately malfunctioned, but ATS–5 was successfully launched in August 1969, and has since been used for an extensive series of scientific experiments.

Earth Viewing Module

ATS–6 was launched in May 1974, a complex, versatile and powerful communications satellite. Weighing 1,400 kilograms (3,090 pounds) the spacecraft consists basically of a box of electronic gadgetry, known officially as the Earth Viewing Module, and a large reflector antenna 9 metres (30 feet) in diameter. The antenna, together with a powerful onboard communications transponder, enable the spacecraft to relay high quality communications to simple land, sea and air receivers located over a wide geographical area.

Serving the international community as a special broadcasting station in space, ATS–5 was initially located in a synchronous orbit over the Galapagos islands. From this station, which covers the whole of the continental United States, the satellite was used, along with ATS–1 and ATS–3, to conduct a Health Education experiment pioneering high quality educational and health services to millions of Americans in remote areas of the Rocky Mountains, the Appalachian states, Washington and Alaska, whose mountainous nature make difficult TV reception from ground-based transmitters.

The satellite was then repositioned over Lake Victoria in Kenya, East Africa, and used by the Indian Government to conduct a Satellite Instructional Television Experiment involving the broadcasting of programmes dealing with agriculture, family planning, hygiene and occupational training. While in this position the satellite was also used to track and relay data from the docked U.S. Apollo and U.S.S.R. Soyuz spacecraft.

In addition to this work, the satellite is equipped to perform twenty other experiments, including the evaluation of a high-resolution radiometer for meteorological work.

ERTS

One of the hardest working spacecraft is the Earth Resources Technology Satellite, ERTS–1. Launched in July 1972, this important satellite represents a major step towards the creation of a 'doomsday' book of the Earth's natural resources and its surface environment. This information will enable the world's authorities to manage the Earth's resources more efficiently and also greatly aid understanding of the changes taking place in the environment.

Although the world is a large globe, with massive areas of land and ocean, its resources are finite, like those of a ship in space or at sea. The environment and resources of the Earth's atmosphere, its continents, its coastal shelves and its oceans, seas and lakes have rightly become of great concern to people everywhere.

Agriculturalists, foresters and range managers deal primarily with renewable natural resources, including agricultural crops, timber, forage and livestock. If such resources are wisely managed they can provide mankind with a sustained yield of food and fibre not merely for a few generations to come, but perhaps, as some experts have hopefully claimed, 'in perpetuity'.

We know that the teeming millions of human beings have made a significant impact on the globe, but it is not easy to measure this impact, or to differentiate between man-caused and natural effects. To do this, a large amount of data must be sensed, often remotely, and gathered from the various regions of the world. Only satellites give promise of doing this; to do it from ground level would be impractically expensive, if not impossible.

What is remote sensing? Very simply, it is the measuring of an object from a distance. For example, a camera is a remote sensor in that it measures reflected light without touching the object being photographed.

The ERTS spacecraft carries two such remote sensors. One comprises a battery of three video cameras, each being sensitive to a selected colour and telling something different about the Earth. Another device, known as a multispectral scanner, picks up reflected electromagnetic waves which supply data on surface features which cannot be seen by the naked eye.

These two sensors provide an astonishing range of information, such as where to search for minerals. They detect shoals of fish. They show where water pollution has reached dangerous levels. They indicate where new land should be brought into cultivation and new roads built.

Owing to an electrical fault, the video cameras had to be switched off after only a few weeks in orbit.

This mishap, however, did not prevent the satellite from returning over 34,000 pictures in its first year of operation, covering North America ten times and most of the rest of the world at least once.

These are being studied by teams of scientists in thirty-seven countries. Many have already provided information of interest and use to experts in agriculture, forestry, geology, geography, hydrology, pollution control, oceanography, meteorology and ecology. One series of pictures has located a hitherto unknown region of rich copper ore deposits, worth many hundreds of millions of pounds— many times the cost of the ERTS satellite. Agricultural benefits over the next twenty years could well exceed £20,000 million—more than twice the entire cost of the American lunar landing programme.

The Ranger spacecraft, responsible for sending the first close-up pictures of the Moon's surface.

The Moon Landings

For thousands of years men on Earth have looked up at the Moon in the sky. For several hundred years they dreamed of journeying to this strange world. But for those hundreds of years they were able to dream only.

Then, in the middle of the twentieth century, the dream began to turn into reality. A mission to the Moon started in earnest in May 1961, when President John F. Kennedy declared that America should place a man on the Moon and return him safely to Earth 'before this decade is out'. Kennedy went on to emphasise that the project would be 'difficult and expensive to accomplish'.

This was one of the great understatements of history. At that time only one American had approached even the threshold of space—the astronaut Alan Shepard who on 5th May 1961, in a fifteen-minute suborbital flight, had reached an altitude of 160 kilometres (100 miles). Earlier, on 12th April 1961, one Soviet cosmonaut, Yuri Gagarin, had completed a single orbit of the Earth.

At the time of Kennedy's speech, America had plans for a Moon exploration programme, but this involved flights round the Moon only. There were no ideas for a Moon landing craft and there was no booster big enough to launch one if there had been.

Lunar Orbit Rendezvous

Thus, the first task was to prepare detailed plans for a manned lunar landing mission. There are several ways of achieving this, and the method selected by the National Aeronautics and Space Administration (NASA) is known as Lunar Orbit Rendezvous. In this the Moon spacecraft is launched initially into a parking orbit near the Earth. It then moves out of orbit and coasts to the Moon and goes into orbit round it. From the spacecraft a small excursion vehicle descends onto the surface of the Moon. The bulk of the mother craft containing the fuel, propulsion system and guidance equipment for the return journey, and the landing vehicle for re-entry through the Earth's atmosphere, remains in lunar orbit.

The basic advantage of the LOR scheme is that the total weight of fuel and equipment that has to be boosted to escape velocity is minimised. This reflects down through the entire system making it lighter, simpler and cheaper.

Of historical interest is the fact that eight years earlier, two members of the *British Interplanetary Society,* Anthony Kunesch and Kenneth Gatland, also concluded that LOR was the best overall method for man's first landing on the Moon. A detailed description appears in their book *Space Travel,* published in 1953.

With the method of landing on the Moon settled, America embarked on the greatest engineering task ever undertaken in the history of the world, to turn the plans into a spacecraft and a launching rocket.

While this Apollo work, as the project was named, was under way, six one-man Mercury flights between 1961 and 1963 proved that man could survive in space. These were followed in 1965 and 1966 by ten two-man Gemini orbiting flights, which proved that it was possible to stay in space for up to two weeks, to move outside the spacecraft and do useful tasks on these 'space walks'.

Three unmanned flights testing the Saturn 1B rocket and Apollo command and service modules were also conducted. This great adventure was marred by only one fatal accident, unhappily occurring on the ground in most unexpected circumstances. Three

The mighty Saturn Apollo rocket (left) which carried the first men to land on the Moon. This great rocket stands as high as St Paul's Cathedral in London, and accelerates to over 38,000 kilometres (24,000 miles) per hour when the ship is on target for the Moon. On the right to the same scale is a Russian Vostok launch vehicle.

astronauts, Virgil Grissom, Edward White and Roger Chaffee died in a fire while testing their craft on the launch pad. Their deaths delayed the programme but resulted in improvements in the spacecraft which made it safer and more reliable.

Unmanned flights were made to test the Saturn V Moon launching rocket and the Lunar Module. Manned flights began with Apollo 7 when astronauts Walter Schirra, Donn Eisele and Walter Cunningham orbited the Earth in an Apollo Command Module for ten days in October 1968.

Mission to the Moon

In December 1968 came the first mission to the Moon, not to land on it, but to go round it. On this historic Apollo 8 mission, the first men to go out to the Moon were astronauts Frank Borman, James Lovell and William Anders. Their mission completed ten orbits of the Moon on Christmas Eve and Christmas Day. For the first time men looked down at the Moon from a height of only 100 kilometres (60 miles), giving a hint of the wonders that would be experienced during the months to come.

An appropriate surprise on this highly successful mission was the broadcast on Christmas Eve of a reading from the Book of Genesis, the passage in the Bible describing the Creation of the World.

Major Anders began with the words: 'In the beginning, God created the heaven and the earth . . .'

Then, from 370,000 kilometres (230,000 miles) out in space, the voice of Captain Lovell continued: 'And God called the light Day and the darkness He called Night . . .'

Colonel Borman completed the reading with the verses: 'And God said, Let the waters under the heaven be gathered together unto one place, and let the dry land appear also . . .' Colonel Borman ended this moving reading with: 'And from the crew of Apollo 8, we close with good night, good luck, a merry Christmas, and God bless all of you—all of you on the good Earth'.

Two more manned Apollo-Saturn V flights were made—Apollo 9, launched on 3rd March 1969 with astronauts James McDivitt, David Scott and Russel Schweickart which tested the full Apollo spacecraft and the planned rendezvous and docking techniques in Earth orbit, and Apollo 10, launched on 18th May 1969 with Thomas Stafford, John Young and Eugene Cernan,

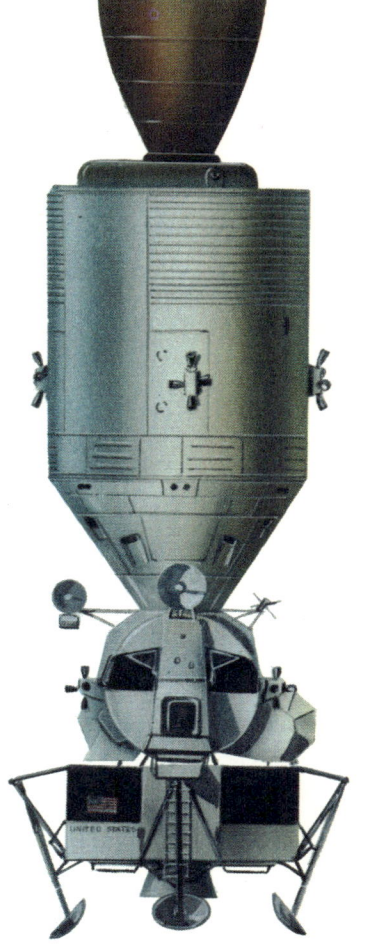

The components of the Apollo Mission before separation. The Lunar Module (bottom), a two-stage vehicle designed to convey two astronauts to the Moon's surface and provide living accommodation for them plus the facility to lift them off and rendezvous with the Command and Surface Module which orbits the Moon. The Service Module (top), responsible for the life support systems and the safe return of the re-entry vehicle or Command Module. The Command Module (centre), the heart of the Apollo mission, designed to carry the three astronauts in their final re-entry into the Earth's atmosphere, capable of floating when landing in the sea, and containing its own parachute system.

which repeated the tests in orbit round the Moon as a full dress rehearsal for the Moon landing mission itself.

Apollo 11

This was Apollo 11. The objective of the mission was stated simply: 'Perform a manned lunar landing and return'. Nearly 400,000 Americans in private industry and in government agencies had worked towards this moment. The cost was high: $392 million for the Mercury flights; $1,280 million for Gemini and a staggering $21,349 million for Apollo up to Apollo 11.

Watched by countless millions all over the world, the Saturn V, with its precious cargo of equipment and men, astronauts Neil Armstrong, Edwin Aldrin and Michael Collins, perched on its nose, lifted off on schedule at 1432 BST on 16th July 1969, providing the privileged press men and VIPs at the launching site with a spectacle they will ever remember.

The two-and-a-half day, quarter-million mile journey to the Moon was uneventful. Soon the Command Module, named *Columbia*, was circling the Moon. While doing so, excellent colour TV pictures of the lunar surface were transmitted. These showed clearly, from a height of about 128 kilometres (80 miles), the chosen landing area, known as Site 2, in the Sea of Tranquility adjacent to the crater Moltke and a prominent road-like rill nicknamed US Highway One.

On Sunday, 20th July, Armstrong and Aldrin entered the Lunar Module *Eagle*, and Collins was left alone in

The nerve centre of the Lunar Module.

179

Columbia. A few minutes later Armstrong announced 'The Eagle has wings', as he began the two hour descent to the surface. During the later stages of the descent a number of alarm signals sounded in the *Eagle*, but Mission Control instructed the two astronauts to ignore the bells and flashing lights. Just before touchdown Armstrong noticed that *Eagle* was heading towards a boulder-littered crater and taking over manual control, he guided the craft to safety.

The words, 'Houston, Tranquility base here. The *Eagle* has landed', will never be forgotten by those who heard them. At 2118 BST on Sunday, 20th July 1969, man had landed on the Moon. As his foot first touched the lunar surface, Armstrong commented 'That's one small step for a man, one giant leap for mankind'.

Armstrong and Aldrin were on the Moon for 21 hours and 36 minutes. They lifted off at 1854 BST on 21st July. After joining Command Module pilot Collins in the Moon-orbiting *Columbia*, the Apollo 11 crewmen set out for their home planet. Splashdown occurred safely at 1751 BST on 24th July, on time and on target.

The national goal established by President Kennedy had been reached. Once more, before the end of the decade, men explored the Moon.

Further Exploration

The second visit was by Apollo 12, launched on 14th November 1969, which landed Charles Conrad and Alan Bean in the Ocean of Storms. As planned, the Lunar Module *Intrepid* made a pinpoint touchdown near the Surveyor III craft which had landed on the Moon in April 1967. Although the mission was primarily intended to check out the spacecraft, two moon-

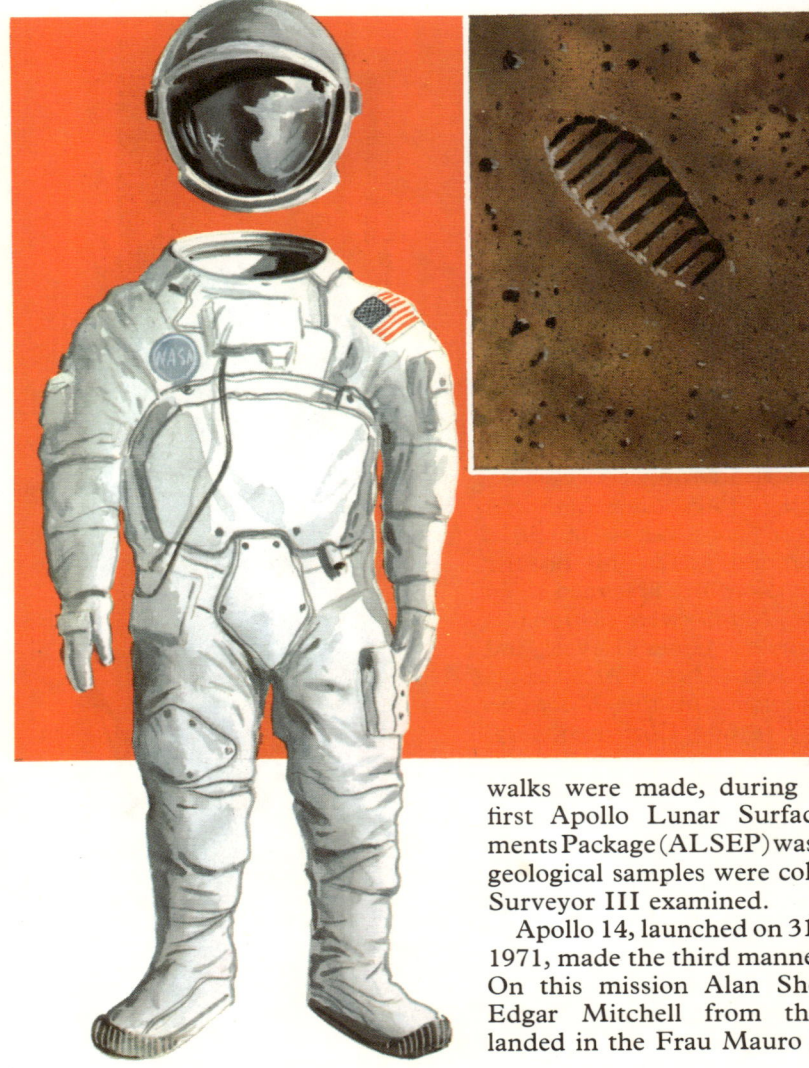

The spacesuit, a complete living environment.

walks were made, during which the first Apollo Lunar Surface Experiments Package (ALSEP) was deployed, geological samples were collected and Surveyor III examined.

Apollo 14, launched on 31st January 1971, made the third manned landing. On this mission Alan Shepard and Edgar Mitchell from the *Antares* landed in the Frau Mauro highlands.

The ill-fated Apollo 13 mission. A catastrophic explosion happened in the service module over 320,000 kilometres (200,000 miles) away from Earth. The rescue mission lasted 3½ days. Happily all ended well and the skill of thousands of technicians returned the three astronauts safely to Earth.

In two moon-walks, they deployed an ALSEP and in addition collected 43 kilograms (96 pounds) of lunar rocks and soil, including two boulders of about 4·5 kilograms (10 pounds) each, the largest obtained to date.

The Frau Mauro region was to have been explored by Apollo 13, launched on 11th April 1970, crewed by James Lovell, Fred Haise and John Swigert. Unfortunately, while coasting to the Moon, an oxygen tank in the Service Module exploded, causing a power failure of the command and service modules' electrical systems, and prevented the crew from making the planned landing on the Moon.

In conditions of extreme danger, the crew used the Lunar Module (*Aquarius*) as the command post and living quarters for the remainder of the flight to the Moon and then during the free-return trajectory back to Earth. Expertly advised by technicians in Mission Control, the engine on the lunar descent module was used

lunar surface for 18 hours during their stay of 66 hours, 55 minutes on the Moon. They collected 77 kilograms (170 pounds) of lunar samples, deployed geophysical instruments and described geological features. Command Module pilot Alfred Worden conducted extensive scientific experiments while orbiting the Moon in the *Endeavour*, which included the operation of two cameras and gamma and X-ray sensors mounted in the Service Module. While in orbit round the Moon, Worden ejected a sub-satellite and during the return to Earth left the Command Module to retrieve the camera film.

Apollo 16, the fifth lunar landing mission, was launched on 16th April 1972. During this mission, John Young and Charles Duke, landing in the Lunar Module *Orion*, set records for the longest stay on the moon (71 hours 12 minutes), and for the longest exploration of the surface in the Descartes highlands. Three periods of

was launched on 7th December 1972. Lift-off was at night, providing spectators at the launching pad with a sight not previously experienced and never likely to be forgotten. The Mission was commanded by Eugene Cernan, a veteran of Gemini 9 and Apollo 10, Command Module pilot Ron Evans and Lunar Module pilot Harrison Schmitt, the first geologist to visit and work on the Moon.

This last mission set many records, including the longest stay on the surface, nearly 75 hours, the longest single period on the surface, 7 hours 37 minutes and the longest total exploration time on the Moon, 22 hours 5 minutes.

Landing in the Lunar Module *Challenger* at Taurus Littrow, Eugene Cernan and Harrison Schmitt covered 35 kilometres (22 miles) in the Lunar Roving Vehicle and collected over 115 kilograms (250 pounds) of lunar samples. Ron Evans spent the longest time in lunar orbit, 147 hours 48

to make corrections to the flight path and guide the three astronauts to a safe splashdown in the Command Module *Odyssey* in the Pacific 142 hours 54 minutes after lift off.

The fourth manned lunar landing by Apollo 15, in July 1971, opened a new era in manned scientific exploration by utilising a Lunar Roving Vehicle (LRV) for the first time. Landing in the Hadley Apennine site, David Scott and James Irwin left the Lunar Module *Falcon* to explore the

exploration on successive days, totalled 20 hours 14 minutes. The lunar explorers returned with about 95 kilograms (210 pounds) of Moon rocks and soil samples to Earth. While this was being collected, astronaut Thomas Mattingly spent 3 days, 9 hours, 39 minutes orbiting the Moon in the Command Module *Casper*.

Night Lift-Off

The sixth and final Moon mission in the Apollo Programme, Apollo 17,

minutes.

The Command Module *America* landed safely in the Pacific on 17th December 1972—69 years to the day after Wilbur and Orville Wright made the first powered aeroplane flight.

This mission, perhaps the most technically perfect of the series, ended the Apollo lunar project. During it a total of twenty-seven men went round the Moon and twelve walked upon its surface, and all returned safely.

The ascent stage of the Lunar Module as it curves away from the Moon's surface.

Stations in Space

Long before artificial satellites became practical the idea of space stations attracted great interest.

Astronautical pioneers such as Kund Lasswitz, Tsiolkovsky, Oberth and von Pirquet all referred to the potential value of manned stations orbiting the Earth.

Later, military protagonists declared that space stations were vital as a means of obtaining political control of the Earth. This line of thought was admirably summed up in a celebrated Space Flight issue of the American magazine, *Colliers*, which appeared in 1952: 'In the hands of the West, a space station, permanently established beyond the atmosphere, would be the greatest hope for peace the world has ever known. No nation could undertake preparations for war without the certain knowledge that it was being observed by the ever-watching eyes aboard the "sentinel in space". It would be the end of Iron Curtains wherever they might be.'

The potential military value of space stations was developed further in many books, such as *Guided Missiles : Rockets and Torpedoes*, by Frank Ross : 'No one on Earth would be safe from attack by bombardment with missile weapons which could be launched from such a space station.'

This is one purpose for which, fortunately, space stations are not likely to be used. The path of a body in orbit is accurately predictable, and a space station would be a 'sitting duck' target should its actions become unfriendly. Russia, in fact, already possesses manoeuvrable satellites capable of intercepting and destroying such space stations. These 'space-interceptors' have already destroyed several target satellites, launched by Russia for this purpose, during development trials.

Space Laboratories

When the space age arrived, however, it soon became apparent that, despite the excellent results obtained by unmanned satellites, manned space stations, or rather space laboratories, would have an important future. Early pioneering manned flights proved the value of observations by astronauts and also the value of their unique ability to deal with the unexpected.

The first manned space stations were, however, considerably different from the large structures initially envisaged by early enthusiasts. Although a few writers foresaw that for reasons of economy and time-saving, the first space stations would probably utilise existing spacecraft and rockets as much as possible, most described massive prefabricated structures.

One of the best known was proposed in 1952 by Dr von Braun, designer of the V-2 missile and the Saturn booster rocket. This space station, shaped like a wheel 75 metres (250 feet) in diameter, consisted of twenty sections of flexible nylon-and-plastic fabric. Each section was a self-contained unit, and when connected, provided a series of compartments each of which could be used for specialist purposes. The sections were to be carried into space in the collapsed state, and after being joined and sealed against leaks, were to be inflated. Internal structure, floors and other supporting sections, would then be added to provide the living quarters, laboratories and control rooms, together with all the equipment to enable the station to operate.

Power for heating, lighting, and the various experiments and laboratory equipment, was to be obtained from the Sun. For this purpose, the station embodied a semi-circular polished trough round the rim, which focussed the Sun's rays onto a pipe containing mercury. When heated, the mercury emerged as hot vapour to drive a turbo-generator. Its task done, the hot vapour would then be cooled by passing through pipes at the back of the trough.

Entry to the space station was by air locks located in the hub. Once inside, the men moved out along hollow 'spoke' members to the living quarters round the rim.

The circular shape, which was first proposed by the Austrian Captain Potocnik in 1928, was dictated by the desire to provide the station's crew with a sensation of weight which would otherwise be absent while in orbit. The entire station was to have been made to spin slowly to produce an artificial effect.

Quite different was the space station proposed in 1947 by H. Ross and R. Smith, members of the *British Interplanetary Society*. Their project for a station comprised a huge bowl-shaped mirror 60 metres (200 feet) in diameter, which focussed the Sun's rays on a central stalk-like electricity power generating system. Living quarters and laboratories were arranged in two rings behind the mirror. To provide artificial gravity, the whole

station was designed to rotate, taking seven seconds for one revolution. This speed was selected to give an effect equal to normal Earth weight in the outer ring of compartments. The inner ring, nearer the centre, would produce a centrifugal force equal to half normal gravity.

Manned Space Station

The first steps towards a true manned

In the not so distant future, these giant space stations will take the place of Skylab, now in orbit around our Earth.

space station were taken by Russia, with the automatic rendezvous and docking between Cosmos 186 and 188 in 1967. Both of these satellites were equipped with special approach systems and docking units. The two spacecraft remained linked for $3\frac{1}{2}$ hours and were then released. After separation the satellites were manoeuvred, by commands from the ground, into different orbits, from which they were subsequently safely recovered. The experiment was repeated, with Cosmos 212 and 213, in 1968. On this occasion, Cosmos 212 carried a TV camera which transmitted pictures of the docking manoeuvre.

The satellites were similar to the manned Soyuz spacecraft which continued Russia's development of space stations. Soyuz 3, launched in October 1968 and piloted by Colonel Beregovy rendezvoused with a similar unmanned spacecraft.

This experiment was the prelude to what has been called the world's first experimental space station. This was established for 4 hours 35 minutes on 16th January 1969, when two manned spacecraft, Soyuz 4 and 5, were successfully docked in Earth orbit. Each craft had a spherical orbital compartment for scientific experiments, in addition to the re-entry module.

alone in Soyuz 5, re-entered the atmosphere and landed safely the following day.

Salyut 1 and 2

Russia then launched her first, specially designed space station. Known as Salyut 1, this was launched on 19th April 1971. Described officially as an 'orbital scientific station' this was clearly intended to advance further space station design, operations and techniques, as well as for conducting scientific research and experiments in space.

Salyut was an impressive piece of space engineering although it was not so elaborate and versatile as was initially surmised. The station consisted basically of a series of cylindrical sections of differing sizes. At the 'front' end, the smallest, about 1·8 metres (6 feet) in diameter, formed the docking unit. Behind this the second compartment 3 metres (10 feet) in diameter, was attached to the third

Georgi Dobrovoski, Vladislav Volkov and Victor Patsayev, was launched and docked with Salyut. The crew entered the station through the passage compartment to begin a programme of research. On 30th June, after a record 24 days in space, the cosmonauts left the relative spaciousness of Salyut and transferred to their Soyuz 11 spacecraft for the return home.

The retro-rocket functioned correctly, but just before re-entry, possibly when the orbital compartment module was jettisoned, a leak developed. The air was exhausted rapidly and the three cosmonauts were asphyxiated. The Soyuz craft with its grim cargo continued to descend under the control of its automatic equipment. The landing parachutes were deployed and retrorockets cushioned the impact with the ground. Ground crews, opening the entry hatch, discovered the three dead cosmonauts sitting calmly on their couches, as if asleep.

Salyut 2, launched in April 1973, was the first test of an improved design, and later broke up in orbit. Other test

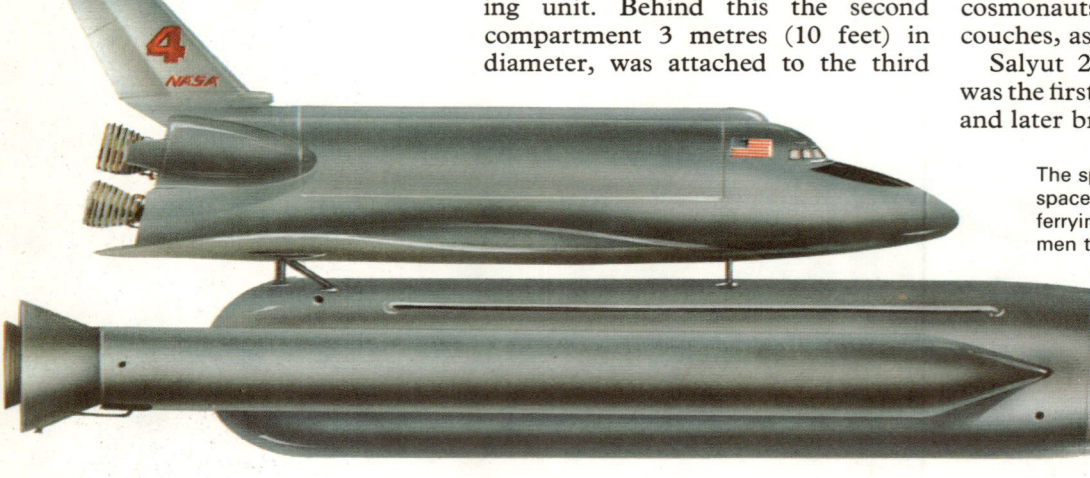

The space shuttle will help to build the space stations of the future by ferrying large loads of equipment and men to the construction zone.

Soyuz 4, piloted by cosmonaut V. Shatalov, was launched on 14th January, followed by Soyuz 5 the next day, crewed by B. Volynov, Y. Khrunov and A. Yeliseyev.

For two days, prior to docking, the crew of Soyuz 5 conducted scientific experiments. After docking the Soyuz 5 cosmonauts Khrunov and Yeliseyev donned spacesuits, the orbital compartments of both craft were sealed and depressurised and the two men emerged through a hatch into outer space. Outside, their work included the installation of a cine-camera and TV equipment. The men also performed various movements simulating more complicated assembly procedures.

After one hour the two men entered Soyuz 4 to join Shatalov, their passage being assisted by hand-rails mounted on the outside of the craft. Soyuz 4 then undocked and returned to Earth on 17th January, after a flight lasting just over 71 hours. Volynov, now

section 4 metres (13 feet) in diameter. A 2-metre (6-foot) tube at the rear completed the structure.

The first section, basically a passage compartment, contained equipment for astrophysical experiments and some control panels. A hatch led to the main work compartment, the 3 metres (10 feet) diameter section, which extended into the third and biggest section, the aft part of which was occupied by propellant tanks. The small tube at the rear housed the engine and nozzle of the onboard propulsion system.

While in orbit Salyut was approached by Soyuz 10, launched on 22nd April, and carrying cosmonauts Vladimir Shalatov, Alexei Yeliseyev and Nikolai Rukavishnikov, which docked with it for 5½ hours before undocking and landing. The shortness of this mission led to speculation that something had gone wrong with either the craft or a cosmonaut.

On 6th June, Soyuz 11, crewed by

Salyuts failed in May and July 1973. Salyut 3, launched in June 1974, was however rendezvoused with by Soyuz 13, which successfully docked with the station. The improved Salyuts have three solar arrays, which are rotatable through 180°, compared with the four fixed arrays on the original stations.

Skylab 1 and 2

Impressive as Salyut is, however, it was far surpassed by Skylab, launched by the U.S. in May 1973. This space station uses much of the 'hardware' developed for the Apollo/Moon spacecraft. Basically, it consists of the massive 14·6 metre (48 feet) long, 6·4 metre (21 feet) diameter S-IVB stage of the Saturn launch rocket, to which is attached specially developed equipment, the crew being ferried up in a modified Apollo Command-Service Module. The S-IVB was to be launched as an empty shell, and then equipped and fitted out while in orbit.

However, in July 1969, a fundamental change was made and the decision taken to launch the station fully equipped.

Designated Skylab 1, the station was launched on 14th May 1973 and although the initial lift-off was successful, when the spacecraft reached the period of maximum aerodynamic pressure, one section of the meteoroid shield extended prematurely. It was instantly torn off and in doing so caused one of the main solar panel arrays to break off also.

Subsequently in orbit the large telescope deployed satisfactorily, its four long solar arrays extending completely. However, the remaining main solar panel on the body of the station failed to extend fully. The result was that the station was immediately restricted to half power operation, using only power supplied from the main panels of the telescope.

A more serious situation developed on the day following the launch when, due to the loss of the meteoroid shield, the station began to overheat, the internal temperature reaching 48°C.

On the ground, rapid steps were taken to diagnose the problems and to prepare repair schemes. Thus the first crew comprising Charles Conrad, Dr Joseph Kerwin and Paul Weitz, did not take off in the Apollo Command Module, designated Skylab 2, until 25th May.

Arriving at the crippled station, Conrad surveyed the damage. Weitz donned a spacesuit and attempted to free the jammed solar panel but was unsuccessful. The spacecraft then docked with the station, and the workshop boarded.

Three different emergency sun screens were on board Skylab 2 and the one shaped like an oversized sunshade was eventually erected. The screen was immediately effective, the temperature dropping to about 27°C. Later the astronauts managed to free the jammed solar panel.

In spite of the reduced power supplies, much useful work was accomplished, the telescope in particular recording some significant solar activity. Most important of all, the prime objective of the mission—to determine man's ability to live and work in space for extended periods—was dramatically demonstrated during the record-breaking 28-day mission.

Eighty-four Days in Orbit

This ability was further demonstrated by the second crew, comprising Alan Bean, Dr Owen Garriott and Jack Lousma, which took off in Skylab 3 on 28th July 1973.

The main objectives of this mission were to reactivate the space station, obtain medical data on the crew and perform further in-orbit experiments. Despite a succession of problems and equipment failures, the crew settled down to working 12 to 16 hours a day, so that they accomplished much more scientific work than was originally planned. For example, the mission plan called for 26 of the important earth-orientated earth-resources passes; the crew actually accomplished 39. Jack Lousma also erected an improved sun shield to replace the one put up by the crew of Skylab 2. After 56 days in orbit the crew returned safely.

The Skylab space station programme ended with the mission of the third and last crew—Gerald Carr, Dr Edward Gibson and William Pogue—which was launched in Skylab 4 on 16th November 1973.

Major tasks of this mission included further earth-resources experiments, during which information of value to research in agriculture, forestry, ecology, geology, geography, meteorology, hydrology, hydrography and oceanography was obtained.

Numerous experiments were also conducted in the on-board electric furnace, helping to lay the foundation of a brand new branch of zero-gravity metallurgy technology.

Other in-orbit experiments included the flight testing of the Astronaut Manoeuvring Unit. Resembling a jet-propelled armchair, such devices could be useful during the erection of future large manned space stations. After a record-breaking stay of 84 days in orbit, the Skylab 4 crew returned safely on 8th February 1974.

Eventually man will use the Moon as a base, and shown here is the possible appearance of a typical base set up on the Lunar surface.

Index